Prices in Financial Markets

Prices in Financial Markets

MICHAEL U. DOTHAN
University of Minnesota

New York   Oxford
OXFORD UNIVERSITY PRESS
1990

Oxford University Press

Oxford   New York   Toronto
Delhi   Bombay   Calcutta   Madras   Karachi
Petaling Jaya   Singapore   Hong Kong   Tokyo
Nairobi   Dar es Salaam   Cape Town
Melbourne   Auckland

and associated companies in

Berlin   Ibadan

Published by Oxford University Press, Inc.,
200 Madison Avenue, New York, New York 10016

Oxford is a registered trademark of Oxford University Press

Library of Congress Cataloging-in-Publication Data

Dothan, Michael U.
Prices in financial markets / Michael U. Dothan.
p.   cm.
Includes bibliographical references and index.
ISBN 0-19-505312-5
1. Finance – Mathematical models. I. Title
HG174.D68 1990
332′.01′5192 – dc20
89-23020   CIP

9 8 7 6 5 4 3 2 1

Printed in the United States of America
on acid-free paper

To the Memory of my Father

Preface

The objective of this book is to offer a unified treatment of selected topics in the theory of financial markets and to serve as an introduction to the mathematics of this theory. The book focuses on the problem of identifying the cash flows that are attainable through either discrete or continuous trading in securities, and the associated problem of pricing these attainable cash flows. Theoretically, the first problem is the more important of the two. Once the attainable cash flows have been identified, the idea behind pricing them is straightforward.

In addition, the book contains many results for incomplete markets and some fundamental results on the relationship between risk and return. It does not deal, however, with the existence of equilibria in financial markets and only touches upon methods of optimal portfolio selection. Although this choice of topics is incomplete, it permits a special focus and integration in the treatment of the selected topics. Furthermore, the mathematics developed in this book is central to many other results in the theory of financial markets, and prepares the reader to pursue these topics further.

The book may be divided into three parts. Chapters 1 to 6 contain the discrete theory, chapters 7 to 9 describe the Black-Scholes model, and chapters 10 to 12 deal with the general theory. One of the distinctive features of this book is the unified treatment of the discrete theory and the general theory. In this treatment, the development of the discrete theory is tailored to the later introduction of the general theory and emphasizes the similarity of results between the two frameworks. Many aspects of the general theory are identified early within the framework of the discrete theory, and are explained there with intuitive simplicity, without the conceptual weight of continuous time mathematics. Subsequently, the unfolding of the general theory exploits the intuition developed in conjunction with the discrete theory, and the many analogies between the continuous time and the discrete time results.

Throughout the book, the economics and the mathematics are developed simultaneously. The discrete theory uses only elementary probability theory and linear algebra. The continuous theory uses many results from the general theory of stochastic processes. The book starts with a simple theory of financial markets and elementary mathematics, and describes the simultaneous evolution of the financial theory and the required mathematics. This method of exposition shows how the mathematical concepts of advanced financial theory are based on transparent and graphic ideas that appear naturally in the simple theory. The only mathematical prerequisites for reading this book are calculus, linear algebra, and elementary probability.

The central mathematical concept of the theory of financial markets is the stochastic integral. The stochastic integral is basic to the theory because it describes the gain from trading in securities. Stochastic integrals are different from ordinary integrals and, therefore, require a theory of their own, called stochastic calculus. A large part of the mathematical development in this book leads to the notion of a stochastic integral, its properties, and its role in the theory of financial markets.

The financial theory in this book is a basis for some very successful practical applications to a large and growing segment of financial markets: the markets for commodity, interest rate, and stock index futures, and the markets for commodity, interest rate, stock, and stock index options. The continuing development of the theory guarantees a steady growth of other successful practical applications.

A detailed outline of the book is as follows. Chapter 1 describes a discrete one-period model, the notions of a budget set and an equilibrium, the connection between completeness and Pareto efficiency, a characterization of budget sets in both complete and incomplete markets, and a characterization of complete markets.

Chapter 2 introduces risk-adjusted probabilities, or state prices in the one-period model, under the name of an equilibrium price measure. The chapter then describes a characterization of complete markets in terms of equilibrium price measures, and delivers a representation of prices as discounted expected values with respect to any equilibrium price measure. Chapter 2 also identifies a special portfolio of securities that represents the single risk factor in the discrete one-period model.

Chapter 3 introduces a discrete multiperiod model. It starts with the definition of information structures and the interpretation of measurability as informational consistency. This chapter also offers a characterization of complete price systems in the discrete multiperiod model, and the description of certain special trading strategies, called self-financing trading strategies.

Chapter 4 defines risk-adjusted probabilities, or equilibrium price measures, in the discrete multiperiod model and offers a characterization of complete price systems in terms of equilibrium price measures. This chapter also delivers the martingale property of discounted prices with respect to equilibrium price measures, and describes a representation of the price functional as discounted expected value with respect to any equilibrium price measure. The chapter ends with a characterization of budget sets for both complete and incomplete price systems.

The subject of Chapter 5 is a discrete analog of continuous time stochastic calculus. The concepts in this chapter include quadratic covariation processes, stochastic integrals, stochastic exponentials, likelihood ratio processes, and the representation of martingales as sums of stochastic integrals. The techniques of Chapter 5 are used in Chapter 6 to deliver further results in the discrete multiperiod model. In addition, discrete stochastic calculus is an intuitive and instructive introduction to the mathematics of the continuous multiperiod models in Chapters 9 to 12.

Chapter 6 offers a further characterization of the discrete multiperiod model. The results in this chapter include the representation of equilibrium price measures as stochastic exponentials, and the application of such representations to the derivation of option pricing formulas. Drawing on the results in Chapter 5, this chapter offers a characterization of attainable cash flows in terms of a representation of certain martingales as sums of stochastic integrals with respect to discounted prices, and a characterization of complete price systems in terms of a representation of all martingales as sums of stochastic integrals with respect to discounted prices. The final result in Chapter 6 is the characterization of the likelihood ratio process as the single risk factor in the discrete multiperiod model.

Chapter 7 introduces general information structures and the Wiener stochastic process. The Wiener process is central to the Black-Scholes option pricing model. All the ideas in this chapter are suitable modifications of the corresponding concepts in Chapter 5. Chapter 7 emphasizes the properties of the Wiener process that are important in the definition of an integral with respect to the Wiener process.

Chapter 8 describes an integral with respect to the Wiener process. Such an integral, called an Itô integral, is a special case of the general stochastic integral in Chapter 11. Paralleling the role of stochastic integrals in the discrete multiperiod model, Itô integrals are used to represent the gain process in the Black-Scholes model. The important results in Chapter 8 include Itô's formula for the change of variables in an Itô integral, and a theorem on the representation of certain martingales as Itô integrals, which matches a similar result in discrete stochastic calculus.

Chapter 9 describes the Black-Scholes model and emphasizes the analogies with the discrete multiperiod model. Paralleling the representation of equilibrium price measures in the discrete multiperiod model as stochastic exponentials, the equilibrium price measure in the Black-Scholes model has a similar representation. Other analogies include the characterization of attainable cash flows in terms of a representation of certain martingales as Itô integrals, and the characterization of completeness of Black-Scholes prices in terms of the equilibrium price measure and in terms of the representation of certain martingales as Itô integrals.

In preparation for the general definition of a stochastic integral, Chapter 10 describes the stochastic processes that serve as integrators and integrands in stochastic integrals. The processes in this chapter include local martingales, semimartingales, and predictable processes. This chapter also includes general definitions of predictable and optional quadratic covariation processes.

Chapter 11 describes the general stochastic integral. The definition of the integral is done in five steps. The first step is a direct extension of the Itô integral in Chapter 7. The fifth step extends the definition to a large set of predictable integrands and semimartingale integrators. The high level of generality in the definition of a stochastic integral affords a similar level of generality of prices and trading strategies for which the stochastic integral is the gain from trade.

The basic properties of the general stochastic integral parallel the basic properties of the discrete stochastic integral. In particular, the general stochastic integral preserves local martingales and is associative with respect to the optional quadratic covariation process. Chapter 11 also describes the general version of Itô's formula, stochastic exponentials, Girsanov's theorem, and linear spaces of stochastic integrals.

The subject of Chapter 12 is the general multiperiod model. Following the definition of equilibrium price measures and trading strategies, this chapter describes restrictions on trading strategies that are sufficient for the absence of arbitrage. Following these preliminaries, Chapter 12 offers a characterization of complete price systems that resembles the results in the discrete theory of Chapter 6.

Next, Chapter 12 proves and uses a version of Girsanov's theorem to characterize the likelihood ratio process as the single risk factor in the general multiperiod model, and to deliver a representation of the equilibrium price measure for a complete price system. This representation result permits the calculation of equilibrium prices of derivative securities in the general framework of this chapter. The remainder of Chapter 12 extends the preceding results to include intermediate consumption in the general model. A comparison of the theory in Chapter 12 with the discrete theory in Chapter 6 shows the many similarities between the discrete theory and the general theory.

Throughout the book, proofs are provided for all the theorems that have explicit economic content, and for selected mathematical results. Studying the selected mathematical proofs helps the reader to acquire a working knowledge of the financial theory.

The notes at the end of each chapter acknowledge only the first significant statement of results that appear in the text of the chapter. The theorems that are not mentioned in the notes are either well known, or, to the best of my knowledge, new. I have not tried to put together a complete bibliography of the topics treated in this book.

This book is directed at academic specialists and Ph.D. students in economics, finance, accounting, management science, mathematics, and statistics who are interested in a theoretical treatment of the structure and operation of financial markets or who want to learn the methods of stochastic calculus for possible application in their fields of interest. The book may also benefit advanced students in M.B.A. programs in finance, and finance professionals whose careers are in research and trading of futures and options, and who want to learn how to modify existing models or how to build their own pricing and trading models.

The first nine chapters of the book can be used for an intensive single quarter course that covers the discrete and the simple continuous models. The whole book can be used as an intensive single semester course that also covers the advanced continuous theory. Alternatively, the book may be used as a basis for a relaxed two quarter, or, with supplements, two semester sequence of introductory and advanced theory.

I would like to thank the former Dean Preston Townley of the Carlson School of Management at the University of Minnesota for his encouragement and support. I am also grateful for financial support from the McKnight Foundation through the Carlson School of Management, and from Piper, Jaffray, and Hopwood, Inc. through the Department of Finance and Insurance at the School and its Institute of Financial Studies. In addition, I would like to acknowledge with thanks comments on various parts of this book from the following people: Kevin Ahtou, John Bohannon, Chun Chang, Ellie Harris, Paul Fackler, Ravi Jagannathan, John Kareken, Juan Ketterer, Isabel Ladd, Srinivasan Maheswaran, Frank Marinaro, Tom Nohel, Cheri Ostroff, Michael Sher, and Michael Stutzer. Finally, I thank the editors at Oxford University Press for their patience, helpful suggestions, and editorial improvements.

Minneapolis, Minnesota   Michael U. Dothan
April 1989

Contents

Prices in Financial Markets

Chapter 1

Introduction to Models of Financial Markets

1.1   Models of Financial Markets

Traders in a financial market exchange securities for money. As they trade, the traders watch monitors and teletypes that carry price information and general economic and political news. In addition to trading, traders receive income from work and other sources, and they spend part of their income on the consumption of various goods. Traders' uncertainty about their future combined income makes them uncertain about their future consumption. Traders, however, have definite preferences regarding their various possible present and future patterns of consumption.

The theory of financial markets reflects this reality. A theoretical model of a financial market involves uncertainty, consumption goods, and securities. It also involves traders, their information, incomes, and consumption preferences. The building blocks of such a model are:

- **Time** - includes both the time period of the model and the dates on which traders trade and consume.

- **Uncertainty** - is described as a listing of all the basic events or states that could occur during the time period of the model and their probabilities.

- **Exchange goods** - which traders receive, exchange, and consume, including money.

- **Securities** - contracts for a future delivery of exchange goods, contingent on the prevailing state.

3

- **Traders** - also called consumers, investors, or agents, and the information available to them on trading and consumption dates.

- **Endowments** - of consumption goods that the traders receive from sources other than trading.

- **Consumption possibilities** - of traders during the time period of the model.

- **Preferences** - of traders over their consumption possibilities during the time period of the model.

When all these items are specified, the model determines the demands for securities by traders, their consumptions, and the prices of securities on trading dates.

The simplest model of this kind is the discrete one-period model. This model involves a finite time interval, which stretches from an initial date to a terminal date. There is only a finite number of states on the terminal date. Securities can be exchanged for goods only on the initial and terminal dates. The initial date is the only trading date, and the securities market closes after the initial date.

The discrete multiperiod model is a step up from the one-period model in both realism and complexity. There is still only a finite number of states, but information arrives and securities can be traded on a finite number of dates inside the time period of the model. The main difference in results between the one-period model and the multiperiod model is that intermediate trading expands the set of consumptions that can be attained with the existing securities.

Given the large number of states, the frequent and irregular arrival of information, and the large number of trading dates in an actual financial market, the greatest degree of realism is achieved with the continuous multiperiod model. Such a model has an infinite number of states, and both the arrival of information and trading in securities are continuous. Not surprisingly, the continuous multiperiod model is much more complicated than the discrete multiperiod model. Although the discrete model requires only concepts from linear algebra and elementary probability, the continuous model uses ideas from the theory of continuous stochastic processes, with special emphasis on integration with respect to stochastic processes. The reward for this complexity is the understanding of how a consumption set of infinite dimension can be attained by trading in a finite number of securities.

This book provides an introduction to the theory of financial markets. Starting with the discrete one-period model and continuing with the discrete multiperiod model, the text describes the building blocks of the models, defines the concept of an equilibrium, and characterizes and prices consumptions that can be attained through trading. The transition to the continuous model then motivates the introduction of additional mathematical concepts and theorems leading to stochastic integrals and their properties. Using these, the continuous model emerges as a natural extension of the discrete model.

1.2   A Discrete One-Period Model

Elements of the Model

The elements of the discrete one-period model are:

- Initial date 0, terminal date T, trading at time 0 only, consumption at time 0 and time T only.

- States belong to a finite sample space Ω with K elements

$$\Omega = \{\omega_1, \ldots, \omega_K\}$$

  Each state $\omega \in \Omega$ occurs with a positive probability $P(\omega)$.

- There is only one perishable consumption good. This model ignores problems associated with the allocation of consumption among various goods, and disregards the possibly special role of money. The perishable consumption good cannot be stored, and therefore, the only way that individual traders can transfer consumption between the initial and terminal dates is by trading in securities. Society cannot transfer consumption over time.

- There is a finite number N of endogenous securities, and there are no exogenous securities. This means that all the securities are created by the traders, and that there are no entities outside the model, such as firms or governments, that supply securities. Trading in securities occurs only at time 0. Before the beginning of trade at time 0, traders decide what securities to supply. Within the model, traders determine only the quantities of securities traded. Furthermore, the securities in the model are infinitely divisible, meaning that any quantity can be demanded or supplied. Finally, there are no taxes or trading costs in this model.

  The securities are completely characterized by their payouts in terms of the consumption good at time T, and these payouts depend on the prevailing state. Thus, for each $1 \le n \le N$, security n is formally defined as a random variable d_n on the sample space Ω. It is convenient to arrange security payouts in a matrix D, in such a way that each row represents a state and each column represents a security

$$D = \begin{pmatrix} d_1(\omega_1) & \ldots & d_N(\omega_1) \\ \ldots\ldots & \ldots & \ldots\ldots \\ d_1(\omega_K) & \ldots & d_N(\omega_K) \end{pmatrix}$$

- There is a finite number I of traders. At time 0 traders know only the set of possible states Ω, and at time T they know the prevailing state $\omega \in \Omega$. All traders are price takers in that they determine their demands and supplies of securities without paying attention to the impact that their actions have on the ultimate market prices of securities.

- At time 0 trader i receives an endowment $e^i(0)$ of the consumption good, and at time T he or she receives the endowment $e^i(T, \omega)$ contingent on the prevailing state ω. The pair $e^i = \{e^i(0), e^i(T)\}$ is called the endowment process of trader i.

- Each trader consumes at times 0 and T. The uncertain terminal endowments and payouts of securities introduce uncertainty into consumption at time T. The consumption process of trader i is the pair $c^i = \{c^i(0), c^i(T)\}$, where the first element of the pair is consumption at time 0 and the second element is the random consumption at time T. Therefore, all traders have the same consumption set $X = \mathcal{R} \times \mathcal{R}^\Omega$, where $\mathcal{R}$ denotes the set of real numbers, and $\mathcal{R}^\Omega$ stands for the set of random variables on the sample space Ω, that is, $X = \mathcal{R}^{K+1}$.

- On the consumption set X traders have complete (weak) preference orderings that are continuous, increasing, and convex. The meaning of these terms is as follows.

A preference ordering is *complete* if and only if it satisfies the following condition:

For any two consumption processes $c', c'' \in X$, either c' is preferred to c'', or c'' is preferred to c'.

A preference ordering is *continuous* if and only if it satisfies the following condition:

For any consumption process $c \in X$, both the set of the consumption processes that are preferred to c, and the set of the consumption processes to which c is preferred, are closed.

A preference ordering is *increasing* if and only if it satisfies the following two conditions:

1. For any two consumption processes $c', c'' \in X$, if $c' \geq c''$,, then c' is preferred to c''.

2. For any two consumption processes $c', c'' \in X$, if $c' \geq c''$ and $c' \neq c''$,, then c' is strictly preferred to c''.

A preference ordering is *convex* if and only if it satisfies the following condition:

For any three consumption processes $c', c'', c''' \in X$ such that $c' \neq c''$, c' is preferred to c''' and c'' is preferred to c''', and for any real number $0 < \alpha < 1$, it is true that $\alpha \cdot c' + (1 - \alpha) \cdot c''$ is preferred to c'''.

Budget Sets

At time 0 given security prices in terms of the consumption good, $p_1, \ldots, p_N$, each trader i faces constraints on consumption imposed by his or her endowment process $e^i = \{e^i(0), e^i(T)\}$. This is formalized in the concept of a budget set.

Definition 1.1 For an endowment process e^i and security prices

$$p = (p_1, \ldots, p_N)$$

the budget set $B(e^i, p)$ of trader i is the subset of the consumption set X such that

$$c \in B(e^i, p)$$

if and only if there are numbers $\theta_1, \ldots, \theta_N$ such that

$$c(0) = e^i(0) - \sum_{n=1}^{N} \theta_n p_n$$

$$c(T) = e^i(T) + \sum_{n=1}^{N} \theta_n d_n$$

The vector $\theta = (\theta_1, \ldots, \theta_N)$ is called a trading strategy, and the consumption process $\{c(0), c(T)\}$ is said to be generated by the endowment process e^i and the trading strategy θ.

This definition says that the budget set of trader i consists of all the consumption processes that trader i can attain by acquiring at time 0 and holding until time T a portfolio of $\theta_1, \ldots, \theta_N$ units of the securities $1, \ldots, N$.

Example 1.1 There are $K = 2$ states and $N = 4$ securities. The terminal payouts of the securities are

$$d_1(\omega_1) = 100, \ d_2(\omega_1) = 40, \ d_3(\omega_1) = 60, \ d_4(\omega_1) = 120$$
$$d_1(\omega_2) = 100, \ d_2(\omega_2) = \ 0, \ d_3(\omega_2) = 40, \ d_4(\omega_2) = \ 80$$

and their prices are

$$p_1 = 50, \quad p_2 = 4, \quad p_3 = 22, \quad \text{and} \quad p_4 = 44$$

A trader has the endowment process

$$e(0) = 9, \ e(T, \omega_1) = 10, \ e(T, \omega_2) = 20$$

The consumption set is the three dimensional real space $X = \mathcal{R}^3$. A consumption process $\{c(0), c(T, \omega_1), c(T, \omega_2)\}$ belongs to this trader's budget set if and only if the system of linear equations

$$
\begin{array}{rrrrrrrrrr}
-50\,\theta_1 & - & 4\,\theta_2 & - & 22\,\theta_3 & - & 44\,\theta_4 & = & c(0) & - & 9 \\
100\,\theta_1 & + & 40\,\theta_2 & + & 60\,\theta_3 & + & 120\,\theta_4 & = & c(T, \omega_1) & - & 10 \\
100\,\theta_1 & & & + & 40\,\theta_3 & + & 80\,\theta_4 & = & c(T, \omega_2) & - & 20
\end{array}
$$

has a solution $\theta_1, \theta_2, \theta_3, \theta_4$. The left sides of equations two and three are linearly independent. Multiply the second equation by $-\dfrac{1}{10}$ and the third equation by $-\dfrac{4}{10}$ and add. This produces the first equation. Therefore, the system has a solution if and only if the right sides satisfy

$$c(0) - 9 = -\frac{1}{10}[c(T, \omega_1) - 10] - \frac{4}{10}[c(T, \omega_2) - 20]$$

or

$$c(0) + \frac{1}{10}c(T, \omega_1) + \frac{4}{10}c(T, \omega_2) = 18$$

The budget set is a plane in $\mathcal{R}^3$, see Figure 1.1.

Equilibrium

Looking at their budget sets for various prices, traders determine those trading strategies that optimize their preferences. Trading does not take place until prices are such that the market clears, that is, the aggregate demand for each security is zero, $\sum_{i=1}^{I} \theta_n^i = 0$, for each $1 \le n \le N$.

The market clearing condition says that for each trader i who demands some security n, $\theta_n^i > 0$, there is another trader j who creates security n, $\theta_n^j < 0$, and sells it to trader i. This heuristic description motivates the following formal definition of equilibrium.

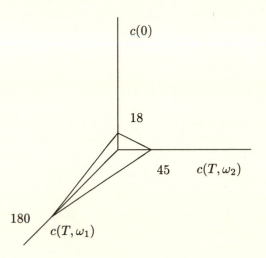

Figure 1.1: The budget set in Example 1.1.

Definition 1.2 Equilibrium at time 0 consists of prices p_n, $1 \le n \le N$, and trading strategies θ_n^i, $1 \le n \le N$, $1 \le i \le I$, such that for each $1 \le i \le I$ the consumption process generated by the given endowment process e^i and the trading strategy $\theta_1^i, \ldots, \theta_N^i$ optimizes the preference ordering of trader i over $B(e^i, p)$ and the market clears, that is, $\sum_{i=1}^{I} \theta_n^i = 0$ for all $1 \le n \le N$.

The consumption processes $c^i = \{c^i(0), c^i(T)\}$ associated with the equilibrium trading strategies form the equilibrium allocation of consumption $\{c^i\}$.

1.3   Pareto Efficiency

Pareto efficiency is a weak normative criterion for the social desirability of an allocation of consumption. Consider the following two definitions.

Definition 1.3 An allocation $\{c^i\}$, where $c^i = \{c^i(0), c^i(T)\}$, is feasible if and only if each c^i belongs to the consumption set and

$$\sum_{i=1}^{I} c^i(0) = \sum_{i=1}^{I} e^i(0)$$

$$\sum_{i=1}^{I} c^i(T) = \sum_{i=1}^{I} e^i(T)$$

The definition of feasibility is simply that at each time aggregate consumption equals aggregate endowment. Terminal aggregate consumption cannot exceed terminal aggregate endowment because the consumption good is perishable. On the other hand, aggregate consumptions that are less than aggregate endowment are wasteful and need not be considered when traders have increasing preferences.

Definition 1.4 A feasible allocation $\{c^i\}$ is Pareto efficient if and only if there is no other feasible allocation $\{b^i\}$ such that each trader i strictly prefers b^i to c^i.

Definition 1.4 says that an allocation is Pareto efficient when it is impossible to reallocate consumption in a way that will make every trader better off, without going out of the consumption set or violating the requirement that aggregate consumption does not exceed aggregate endowment.

An equilibrium allocation of consumption is feasible because of the condition that the market clears. Is the equilibrium allocation Pareto efficient? This question is answered in Theorems 1.1 and 1.2. First, a definition.

Definition 1.5 A consumption process $c = \{c(0), c(T)\}$ is attainable at prices $p = (p_1, \ldots, p_N)$ if and only if there is an endowment process $e = \{e(0), e(T)\}$ such that $e(T) = 0$ and $c \in B(e, p)$. The set of attainable consumption processes is denoted M.

The preceding definition states that a consumption process is attainable if and only if it is possible to give a trader with zero terminal endowment an initial endowment such that the given consumption process belongs to his or her budget set. This concept of an attainable consumption process captures the property of prices that allows a given terminal consumption to be attained by trading rather than by a fortunate coincidence with the terminal endowment. The attainability of a consumption process $c = \{c(0), c(T)\}$ depends only on the terminal consumption part, $c(T)$, of c and does not depend at all on the initial part $c(0)$. In fact, in the one-period model the definition of an attainable consumption process is really a definition of an attainable terminal consumption. Stated differently, a consumption process $c = \{c(0), c(T)\}$ is attainable if and only if there exists a trading strategy θ such that

$$c(T) = \sum_{n=1}^{N} \theta_n d_n$$

The reason for the seemingly unnecessary complication that comes from discussing an attainable consumption process rather than an attainable terminal consumption is the desire to use definitions that can be replicated with a minimum of change when the model is extended to a multiperiod setting. In this chapter, we use the terms attainable consumption process and attainable terminal consumption interchangeably.

Theorem 1.1 *If every consumption process is attainable, then every equilibrium allocation of consumption is Pareto efficient.*

Proof. The proof is by contradiction. Suppose that the equilibrium allocation $\{c^i\}$ is not Pareto efficient. Then, by definition, there exists a feasible allocation $\{b^i\}$ such that each trader i strictly prefers b^i to c^i. By hypothesis, each consumption process $a^i = b^i - e^i$ is attainable, and therefore there are trading strategies θ_n^i and numbers α^i such that for each i

$$a^i(0) \;=\; \alpha^i - \sum_{n=1}^{N} \theta_n^i p_n \tag{1.1}$$

$$a^i(T) \;=\; \sum_{n=1}^{N} \theta_n^i d_n \tag{1.2}$$

The proof proceeds in two stages. First, notice that

$$\sum_{n=1}^{N} \left(\sum_{i=1}^{I} \theta_n^i \right) p_n = 0$$

Indeed, summing Equation 1.2 over i and using the fact that $\{b^i\}$ is a feasible allocation implies that

$$\sum_{n=1}^{N} \left(\sum_{i=1}^{I} \theta_n^i \right) d_n = 0$$

This in turn implies that

$$\sum_{n=1}^{N} \left(\sum_{i=1}^{I} \theta_n^i \right) p_n = 0$$

for otherwise either the trading strategy $\sum_{i=1}^{I} \theta_n^i$, $1 \le n \le N$, or the trading strategy $-\sum_{i=1}^{I} \theta_n^i$, $1 \le n \le N$, has a negative cost and trader i can add it to his or her equilibrium trading strategy creating a new consumption that is larger than c^i at time 0 and the same as c^i at time T. Because his or her preferences are increasing, trader i strictly prefers the new consumption to

c^i. But this contradicts the assumption that c is an equilibrium allocation of consumption.

Second, notice that the consumption process $\{b^i(0) - \alpha^i, b^i(T)\}$ belongs to the budget set $B(e^i, p)$. If for some i the number $\alpha^i \leq 0$, then trader i prefers the consumption process $\{b^i(0) - \alpha^i, b^i(T)\}$ to the consumption process b^i, and therefore strictly prefers it to the consumption process c^i, thus contradicting the optimality of c^i. Therefore, $\alpha^i > 0$ for all i. This also leads to a contradiction, for summing the equations

$$a^i(0) = \alpha^i - \sum_{n=1}^{N} \theta^i_n p_n$$

over i and using the fact that $\displaystyle\sum_{n=1}^{N} \left(\sum_{i=1}^{I} \theta^i_n \right) p_n = 0$ implies that

$$\sum_{i=1}^{I} b^i(0) > \sum_{i=1}^{I} e^i(0)$$

which contradicts the assumption that b is a feasible allocation of consumption. ∎

The preceding theorem is not very satisfactory because it imposes conditions on the endogenous trading strategies rather than on some exogenous elements of the model. Fortunately, it is possible to impose a condition on the exogenous elements of this model that will guarantee the Pareto efficiency of an equilibrium.

It is convenient to state this condition in terms of the rank of the matrix D of terminal payoffs. The rank of a matrix is the largest number of linearly independent rows or columns. In the matrix D each row is a vector of payoffs of all the securities in a single state and each column is a vector of payoffs of a single security in the various states. The theorem requires that the number of independent rows and columns be equal to the number of states.

In the proof of this theorem, and even more so in the sequel, it is convenient to interpret trading strategies and price systems as N-dimensional column vectors, and random variables on Ω as K-dimensional column vectors. Transposes of matrices and vectors are denoted with a prime.

Theorem 1.2 *If* rank$(D) = K$, *then every consumption process is attainable and consequently every equilibrium allocation of consumption is Pareto efficient.*

Proof. A consumption process $c = \{c(0), c(T)\}$ is attainable if and only if the system of linear equations

$$D\theta = c(T)$$

has a solution θ, or equivalently, if and only if the vector $c(T)$ is a linear combination of the columns of D. But as D has K independent columns and $c(T)$ is a K-dimensional vector, $c(T)$ is a linear combination of the columns of D. ∎

The preceding theorem states that if there are sufficiently many linearly independent securities, then every consumption process is attainable. On the other hand, when there are not enough linearly independent securities, $\text{rank}(D) < K$, then a given consumption process may be either attainable or not attainable through trading. The attainability of consumption processes has a characterization by the Kronecker-Capelli theorem from linear algebra. Consider the augmented matrix $D^+ = [D, c(T)]$ obtained from the matrix D by adding to it the vector $c(T)$ as the $(N + 1)$th column. Then this theorem says that a necessary and sufficient condition for the system of linear equations

$$D\theta = c(T)$$

to have a solution is that $\text{rank}(D^+) = \text{rank}(D)$. Thus, when the vector $c(T)$ is linearly independent of the linearly independent columns of D the corresponding consumption process $c = \{c(0), c(T)\}$ is not attainable. Conversely, if the vector $c(T)$ is in the span of the linearly independent columns of D, then the consumption process c is attainable.

Example 1.2 There are $K = 3$ states and $N = 4$ securities with the terminal payouts

$$d_1(\omega_1) = 1, \ d_2(\omega_1) = 2, \ d_3(\omega_1) = 3, \ d_4(\omega_1) = 6$$
$$d_1(\omega_2) = 2, \ d_2(\omega_2) = 0, \ d_3(\omega_2) = 2, \ d_4(\omega_2) = 4$$
$$d_1(\omega_3) = 4, \ d_2(\omega_3) = 1, \ d_3(\omega_3) = 5, \ d_4(\omega_3) = 10$$

A consumption process with the terminal consumption

$$c(T, \omega_1) = 2, \ c(T, \omega_2) = 4, \ c(T, \omega_3) = 8$$

is attainable, whereas a consumption process with the terminal consumption

$$c(T, \omega_1) = 2, \ c(T, \omega_2) = 1, \ c(T, \omega_3) = 2$$

is not attainable. To verify this consider the matrix of terminal payouts

$$D = \begin{pmatrix} 1 & 2 & 3 & 6 \\ 2 & 0 & 2 & 4 \\ 4 & 1 & 5 & 10 \end{pmatrix}$$

In this matrix the third column is the sum of the first two columns, the fourth column is twice the third column, and the first two columns are linearly independent. Consequently $\text{rank}(D) = 2$. For the first terminal consumption the vector $c(T)$ is

$$c(T) = \begin{pmatrix} 2 \\ 4 \\ 8 \end{pmatrix}$$

so that the augmented matrix is

$$D^+ = \begin{pmatrix} 1 & 2 & 3 & 6 & 2 \\ 2 & 0 & 2 & 4 & 4 \\ 4 & 1 & 5 & 10 & 8 \end{pmatrix}$$

The added fifth column of the augmented matrix is twice the first column, therefore, $\text{rank}(D^+) = 2$, and the consumption process in question is attainable. For the second terminal consumption, however, the augmented matrix is

$$D^+ = \begin{pmatrix} 1 & 2 & 3 & 6 & 2 \\ 2 & 0 & 2 & 4 & 1 \\ 4 & 1 & 5 & 10 & 2 \end{pmatrix}$$

and after discarding columns 3 and 4 the resulting matrix has a nonzero determinant. Therefore $\text{rank}(D^+) = 3$, and the second consumption process is not attainable.

1.4   Attainable Set and Budget Sets

This section offers an additional characterization of the attainable set and the budget sets in the discrete one-period model.

Definition 1.6 The image, $\text{im}(H)$, of a linear operator

$$H : \mathcal{R}^u \to \mathcal{R}^v$$

is a subset of $\mathcal{R}^v$ such that $y \in \text{im}(H)$ if and only if there is an $x \in \mathcal{R}^u$ that satisfies $y = H(x)$.

We interpret the $K \times N$ payout matrix D as a linear operator

$$D : \mathcal{R}^N \to \mathcal{R}^K$$

defined by $D(\theta) = D\theta$. This leads to the following characterization of the attainable set.

Theorem 1.3

$$M = \mathcal{R} \times \operatorname{im}(D)$$

Theorem 1.3 implies a second, more convenient, characterization of the attainable set. First a definition.

Definition 1.7 The kernel, $\ker(H)$, of a linear operator

$$H : \mathcal{R}^u \to \mathcal{R}^v$$

is a subset of $\mathcal{R}^u$ such that $x \in \ker(H)$ if and only if $H(x) = 0$.

The kernel of a linear operator H is a linear space, also called the null space of H. We have the following theorem.

Theorem 1.4 *For any linear operator H from $\mathcal{R}^u$ to $\mathcal{R}^v$ there exists a linear operator G from $\mathcal{R}^v$ to $\mathcal{R}^{v-\operatorname{rank}(H)}$*

$$\mathcal{R}^u \xrightarrow{H} \mathcal{R}^v \xrightarrow{G} \mathcal{R}^{v-\operatorname{rank}(H)}$$

such that $\operatorname{im}(H) = \ker(G)$.

The next characterization of the attainable set follows from Theorem 1.4.

Corollary 1.1 *There is a linear operator*

$$F : \mathcal{R}^K \to \mathcal{R}^{K-\operatorname{rank}(D)}$$

such that

$$M = \mathcal{R} \times \ker(F)$$

Corollary 1.1 states that the space of attainable terminal consumptions is characterized by $K-\operatorname{rank}(D)$ linear equations. The next example clarifies this corollary.

Example 1.3 Consider a market with $K = 4$, $N = 3$, and a payout matrix

$$D = \begin{pmatrix} 1 & 3 & 9 \\ 1 & 1 & 5 \\ 1 & 5 & 13 \\ 1 & 7 & 17 \end{pmatrix}$$

The first two rows of D, $(1,3,9)$ and $(1,1,5)$, are linearly independent and

$$
\begin{aligned}
2 \times (1,3,9) - 1 \times (1,1,5) &= (1,5,13) \\
3 \times (1,3,9) - 2 \times (1,1,5) &= (1,7,17)
\end{aligned}
$$

Therefore, rank$(D) = 2$ and the attainable set M is determined by the terminal consumptions $c(T)$ that satisfy $c(T) = D\theta$. The structure of the matrix D implies that a vector $c(T)$ is attainable if and only if it satisfies

$$
\begin{aligned}
2c(T,\omega_1) - c(T,\omega_2) &= c(T,\omega_3) \\
3c(T,\omega_1) - 2c(T,\omega_2) &= c(T,\omega_4)
\end{aligned}
$$

and, therefore, the linear operator F has the matrix representation

$$F = \begin{pmatrix} 2 & -1 & -1 & 0 \\ 3 & -2 & 0 & -1 \end{pmatrix}$$

The characterization of budget sets rests on the following result.

Theorem 1.5 *For any endowment process e, price system p, and consumption process c, we have $c \in B(e,p)$ if and only if the net trade $c - e$ is attainable at zero initial cost, or equivalently, if and only if $c - e \in B(0,p)$.*

Proof. For any consumption process c we have $c \in B(e,p)$ if and only if there are numbers $\theta_1, \ldots, \theta_N$ that satisfy

$$
\begin{aligned}
c(0) &= e(0) - \sum_{n=1}^{N} \theta_n p_n \\
c(T) &= e(T) + \sum_{n=1}^{N} \theta_n d_n
\end{aligned}
$$

Transposing the endowment process to left side of these equations we get

$$c(0) - e(0) = -\sum_{n=1}^{N} \theta_n p_n$$

$$c(T) - e(T) = \sum_{n=1}^{N} \theta_n d_n$$

The preceding equations say that the net trade $c - e$ is attainable at the initial cost

$$c(0) - e(0) + \sum_{n=1}^{N} \theta_n p_n = 0$$

This completes the proof. ∎

Notice that $B(0, p)$ is a linear subspace of the attainable set M. We offer a further characterization of budget sets in Chapter 2, after the introduction of the price functional.

1.5 Arbitrage Strategies

An arbitrage trading strategy is a good deal. A trader using an arbitrage strategy gets a sure return without any investment. The precise definition is as follows.

Definition 1.8 An arbitrage trading strategy is a trading strategy that gives a trader with a zero endowment a nonnegative, nonzero, consumption process.

This definition includes two possibilities. An arbitrage trading strategy is a trading strategy $\theta_1, \ldots, \theta_N$ such that either:

1. The initial value $\sum_{n=1}^{N} \theta_n p_n \leq 0$.

2. The terminal payout $\sum_{n=1}^{N} \theta_n d_n(\omega) \geq 0$ for all $\omega \in \Omega$.

3. The terminal payout $\sum_{n=1}^{N} \theta_n d_n(\omega) > 0$ for some $\omega \in \Omega$.

   or:

1. The initial value $\sum_{n=1}^{N} \theta_n p_n < 0$.

2. The terminal payout $\sum_{n=1}^{N} \theta_n d_n(\omega) \geq 0$ for all $\omega \in \Omega$.

Example 1.4 There are $K = 3$ states and $N = 3$ securities with the payouts

$$d_1(\omega_1) = 6, \ d_2(\omega_1) = 11, \ d_3(\omega_1) = 3$$
$$d_1(\omega_2) = 5, \ d_2(\omega_2) = 11, \ d_3(\omega_2) = 3$$
$$d_1(\omega_3) = 12, \ d_2(\omega_3) = 9, \ d_3(\omega_3) = 3$$

and prices

$$p_1 = 8, \quad p_2 = 10, \quad \text{and} \quad p_3 = 3$$

Consider the trading strategy

$$\theta_1 = 1, \ \theta_2 = \frac{7}{2}, \ \theta_3 = -\frac{87}{6}$$

The initial cost of this strategy is

$$1 \times 8 + \frac{7}{2} \times 10 - \frac{87}{6} \times 3 = -\frac{1}{2}$$

and its terminal payout is 1 in state ω_1, and 0 in states ω_2 and ω_3. This trading strategy produces one half unit of the consumption good at time 0, and one unit of the consumption good at time T, state ω_1 . It requires no spending of the consumption good at any time. Therefore, it is an arbitrage strategy.

Unfortunately, arbitrage strategies do not exist in equilibrium. The prices in the preceding example cannot be equilibrium prices.

Theorem 1.6 *Arbitrage trading strategies do not exist in equilibrium.*

Proof. The proof relies on the assumption that consumption preferences of traders are increasing. For each i, let $\theta_1^i, \ldots, \theta_N^i$ be a trading strategy that generates the equilibrium consumption of trader i. If there exists an arbitrage trading strategy $\theta_1, \ldots, \theta_N$ at the given equilibrium prices, then the trading strategy $\theta_1^i + \theta_1, \ldots, \theta_N^i + \theta_N$ generates at equilibrium prices a consumption that is never less than the original equilibrium consumption, and exceeds the latter either at time 0 or in some state at time T. This new consumption is in the budget set and, with increasing preferences, trader i strictly prefers this new consumption to the original equilibrium consumption. This contradicts the fact that at equilibrium prices there is no consumption that a trader strictly prefers to his or her equilibrium consumption. ∎

1.6   Completeness

The discussion in Section 1.3 shows how the condition $\text{rank}(D) = K$ implies that any equilibrium allocation of consumption is Pareto efficient. Here we treat another implication of this property of the matrix of terminal payouts. Imagine adding to the market an extra security, numbered $N+1$, with the terminal payout d_{N+1}. Next, consider an equilibrium in this expanded market of $N+1$ securities. As usual, denote by $p_1, \ldots, p_{N+1}$ equilibrium prices, and denote by D_N the matrix of terminal payouts of the securities $1, \ldots, N$. Assume that $\text{rank}(D_N) = K$ and consider the system of linear equations

$$D_N \theta = d_{N+1}$$

Because these equations are linearly independent, the system has a solution

$$\theta = \begin{pmatrix} \theta_1 \\ \cdot \cdot \\ \theta_N \end{pmatrix}$$

The trading strategy $\theta_1, \ldots, \theta_{N+1}$, where $\theta_{N+1} = 0$, attains the consumption process $\{0, d_{N+1}\}$ and therefore it synthesizes — or duplicates — security $N+1$ from securities $1, \ldots, N$. In every state $\omega \in \Omega$ the terminal payout of this trading strategy is the same as the terminal payout of security $N+1$.

Does the initial price of security $N+1$ equal the initial cost of this trading strategy, $p_{N+1} = \sum_{n=1}^{N} \theta_n p_n$? The answer is affirmative because otherwise one of the two trading strategies: $\theta_1, \ldots, \theta_N, -1$, or $-\theta_1, \ldots, -\theta_N, 1$ is an arbitrage strategy, and as such is inconsistent with equilibrium.

Example 1.5 There are $K = 2$ states and $N = 3$ securities with the following terminal payouts

$$d_1(\omega_1) = 1.1, \; d_1(\omega_2) = 1.1$$

$$d_2(\omega_1) = 6, \; d_2(\omega_2) = 21$$

$$d_3(\omega) = \max[0, d_2(\omega) - 10]$$

Security 3 is a call option on security 2 with an exercise price of 10. When the terminal payout of security 2 is less than 10, security 3 has a zero payout, and when the terminal payout of security 2 is more than 10, security 3 pays what security 2 pays less 10. Specifically

$$d_3(\omega_1) = 0, \; d_3(\omega_2) = 11$$

If the equilibrium prices of securities 1 and 2 are $p_1 = 1$ and $p_2 = 9$, then what is the equilibrium price of the call option? The payout matrix of securities 1 and 2

$$D_2 = \begin{pmatrix} 1.1 & 6 \\ 1.1 & 21 \end{pmatrix}$$

has rank 2, so we know that the call option can be duplicated by trading in securities 1 and 2. The specific duplicating strategy is

$$\theta_1 = -4, \quad \theta_2 = \frac{11}{15} \quad (\text{and} \quad \theta_3 = 0)$$

and the equilibrium price of the call option is

$$p_3 = -4 \times 1 + \frac{11}{15} \times 9 = 2.6$$

We have shown that when the number of linearly independent securities is large enough, then any other security can be synthesized from these linearly independent securities. This situation is captured in the following definition.

Definition 1.9 A market is complete if and only if every consumption process is attainable.

If $p_1, \ldots, p_N$ are equilibrium prices, and if a subset S of the securities $1, \ldots, N$ forms a complete market, then the equilibrium prices of the remaining securities are linear combinations of prices of the securities in the subset S. The proof of this assertion is just a restatement of the argument at the beginning of this section. Consider a security not in S with the terminal payout d, and let $c(T)$ be a terminal consumption such that $c(T) = d$. Then there is a trading strategy in the securities in S that attains this terminal consumption, that is, duplicates the security in question. Because equilibrium does not permit arbitrage strategies, the initial price of the security in question equals the initial cost of the duplicating strategy.

Using the notion of a complete market, Theorems 1.1 and 1.2 can be restated as follows.

Theorem 1.7 *If the market is complete, then every equilibrium allocation of consumption is Pareto efficient.*

Theorem 1.8 *The market is complete if and only if* $\mathrm{rank}(D) = K$.

Problems

1. There are $K = 3$ states and $N = 3$ securities with the payouts

$$d_1(\omega_1) = 60, \ d_2(\omega_1) = 110, \ d_3(\omega_1) = 30$$
$$d_1(\omega_2) = 50, \ d_2(\omega_2) = 120, \ d_3(\omega_2) = 30$$
$$d_1(\omega_3) = 53, \ d_2(\omega_3) = 127, \ d_3(\omega_3) = 30$$

   The prices of these securities are

$$p_1 = 28, \quad p_2 = 59, \quad \text{and} \quad p_3 = 15$$

   A trader has the endowment process

$$e(0) = 400, \ e(T, \omega_1) = 500, \ e(T, \omega_2) = 1270, \ e(T, \omega_3) = 300$$

   Find the budget set of this trader.

2. Prove that if a complete price system permits an arbitrage strategy, then the budget sets of all traders coincide with the consumption set.

3. There are $K = 3$ states and $N = 3$ securities with the payouts

$$d_1(\omega_1) = 24, \ d_2(\omega_1) = 44, \ d_3(\omega_1) = 12$$
$$d_1(\omega_2) = 20, \ d_2(\omega_2) = 44, \ d_3(\omega_2) = 12$$
$$d_1(\omega_3) = 48, \ d_2(\omega_3) = 36, \ d_3(\omega_3) = 12$$

   The prices of these securities are

$$p_1 = 35, \quad p_2 = 40, \quad \text{and} \quad p_3 = 12$$

   (a) Find the set of all the attainable consumption processes.
   (b) Is the consumption process

$$c(0) = 10, \ c(T, \omega_1) = 6, \ c(T, \omega_2) = 5, \ c(T, \omega_3) = 12$$

   attainable? Find the initial endowment and the trading strategy that attain it.
   (c) Is the consumption process

$$c(0) = 0, \ c(T, \omega_1) = 9, \ c(T, \omega_2) = 1, \ c(T, \omega_3) = 17$$

   attainable? Find the initial endowment and the trading strategy that attain it.
   (d) Does the given price system permit arbitrage strategies?

4. Show that Definition 1.4 is equivalent to the requirement that there be no feasible reallocation of consumption that is strictly preferred by all traders.

Notes

The concepts and results in this chapter are an interpretation, for the case of uncertainty, of the general equilibrium theory for a pure exchange economy. The concept of a general equilibrium is due to [73]. There are several early proofs of the existence of a general equilibrium, among them [2]. The interpretation of the general theory as a model of uncertainty appears first in [4].

The early proofs of the existence of an equilibrium apply only to a complete market. Using additional restrictions on endowments and security payouts [9] and [74] establish the existence of an equilibrium in an incomplete market.

The modern version of Theorem 1.1 is due to [3] and [18]. The possibility that an equilibrium allocation may be Pareto inefficient is demonstrated in [43].

Chapter 2

One-Period Equilibrium Price Measures

2.1 Equilibrium Price Measures

In this chapter we assume that one of the securities in the market is a bond whose initial price is positive and whose terminal payout is positive and does not depend on the state. Given a price system, we define a new concept called an equilibrium price measure, which is derived from the given price system and constitutes a risk-adjusted probability measure on the state space Ω. It turns out that equilibrium price measures exist if and only if the given price system does not permit arbitrage strategies. Alternatively, equilibrium price measures exist if and only if the given price system is an equilibrium price system for some population of traders with continuous, increasing, and convex preferences.

If equilibrium price measures exist, then the initial cost of any attainable terminal consumption is the expected value of that terminal consumption relative to any equilibrium price measure, discounted at the bond rate of interest. When an equilibrium price measure exists, it is unique if and only if the market is complete. Equilibrium price measures are important in both discrete and continuous models.

If the bond is security number j, then we define $r = \dfrac{d_j}{p_j} - 1$ and interpret r as the rate of interest on the bond. Notice that, by assumption, $r > -1$. Also, when convenient, we consider prices p and trading strategies θ as vectors in $\mathcal{R}^N$, and denote transposed matrices and vectors with a prime, so that D' is the transpose of the payout matrix D.

Definition 2.1 If for a given price system p the system of linear equations

23

$$D'Q = (1 + r)p$$

has a positive solution $Q(\omega_1) > 0, \ldots, Q(\omega_K) > 0$, then this Q is called an equilibrium price measure for the price system p.

An equilibrium price measure is a probability measure on the sample space Ω. Because security j is a bond, the jth equation in the preceding system is

$$\sum_{k=1}^{K} Q(\omega_k) = 1$$

That, together with the requirement $Q(\omega) > 0$, establishes Q as a probability measure on Ω. The justification of the name equilibrium price measure comes from two observations. First, the relationship between Q and equilibrium follows from the fact that an equilibrium price measure Q exists if and only if the given price system p is an equilibrium price system for some population of traders with continuous, increasing, and convex preferences. Second, Q is a price measure because the initial cost of any attainable terminal consumption is the expected value of that terminal consumption relative to any equilibrium price measure discounted at the bond rate of interest. These facts are established in Theorem 2.1, Corollary 2.1, and Theorem 2.3.

Theorem 2.1 *An equilibrium price measure Q exists if and only if the given price system p does not permit arbitrage strategies.*

Proof. Suppose that the system of linear equations

$$D'Q = (1 + r)p$$

has a positive solution Q. Then for any trading strategy θ, such that the elements of the vector $\theta'D'$ are nonnegative, the initial cost $\theta'p$ is also nonnegative, and if, in addition, some element of $\theta'D'$ is positive, then $\theta'p$ is also positive. Indeed, premultiply the preceding system of linear equations by θ' to obtain

$$\theta'D'Q = (1 + r)\theta'p$$

and use the fact that all the elements of the vector Q are positive. This establishes the direct part of the theorem.

Conversely, suppose that the price system p does not permit arbitrage strategies. Consider the budget set $B(0, p)$ of a trader with a zero endowment process and the set H of all the consumption processes

$$c = \{c(0), c(T)\}$$

attainable or not, such that:

1. The consumption process c is nonnegative, that is, $c(0) \geq 0$, $c(T) \geq 0$.

2. The consumption process c satisfies $c(0) + \sum_{k=1}^{K} c(T, \omega_k) \geq 1$.

The budget set $B(0, p)$ is a linear subspace of X, the set H is a nonempty, convex, and closed subset of X and the sets $B(0, p)$ and H are disjoint, for otherwise there exist arbitrage strategies. Therefore, there exists a linear functional $f : X \to \mathcal{R}$ such that $f(c) = 0$ for all $c \in B(0, p)$ and $f(c) > 0$ for all $c \in H$.

Let $\alpha_0, \alpha_1, \ldots, \alpha_K$ be the orthonormal basis in X

$$\alpha_0 = (1, 0, \ldots, 0)$$

$$\alpha_1 = (0, 1, \ldots, 0)$$

$$\ldots \ldots \ldots \ldots \ldots$$

$$\alpha_K = (0, 0, \ldots, 1)$$

Then any consumption process $c = \{c(0), c(T)\}$, considered as a vector in $\mathcal{R}^{K+1}$, has the representation

$$c = c(0)\alpha_0 + \sum_{k=1}^{K} c(T, \omega_k)\alpha_k$$

and because f is a linear functional

$$f(c) = c(0)f(\alpha_0) + \sum_{k=1}^{K} c(T, \omega_k)f(\alpha_k)$$

Because for all $0 \leq k \leq K$ the consumption processes α_k are in H, it follows that $f(\alpha_k) > 0$ for all $0 \leq k \leq K$. To complete the proof notice that for every $1 \leq n \leq N$ the consumption process $\{-p_n, d_n\} \in B(0, p)$ and therefore

$$-p_n f(\alpha_0) + \sum_{k=1}^{K} f(\alpha_k)d_n(\omega_k) = 0$$

Defining

$$Q(\omega_k) = (1+r)\frac{f(\alpha_k)}{f(\alpha_0)}$$

yields

$$D'Q = (1+r)p$$

This completes the proof. ∎

Example 2.1 There are $K = 3$ states and $N = 4$ securities. The terminal payouts of the securities are

$$D = \begin{pmatrix} 100 & 40 & 60 & 120 \\ 100 & 0 & 40 & 80 \\ 100 & 20 & 100 & 200 \end{pmatrix}$$

and their prices are

$$p_1 = 50, \ p_2 = 7, \ p_3 = 31, \ p_4 = 62$$

Here $1 + r = \dfrac{100}{50} = 2$ and the system of equations for Q is

$$\begin{pmatrix} 100 & 100 & 100 \\ 40 & 0 & 20 \\ 60 & 40 & 100 \\ 120 & 80 & 200 \end{pmatrix} \begin{pmatrix} Q(\omega_1) \\ Q(\omega_2) \\ Q(\omega_3) \end{pmatrix} = \begin{pmatrix} 100 \\ 14 \\ 62 \\ 124 \end{pmatrix}$$

This system has the solution

$$Q(\omega_1) = \frac{1}{5}, \ Q(\omega_2) = \frac{1}{2}, \ Q(\omega_3) = \frac{3}{10}$$

and therefore, the given price system does not permit arbitrage strategies.

Example 2.2 In the market of Example 1.3 the system of equations for Q is

$$\begin{pmatrix} 6 & 5 & 12 \\ 11 & 11 & 9 \\ 3 & 3 & 3 \end{pmatrix} \begin{pmatrix} Q(\omega_1) \\ Q(\omega_2) \\ Q(\omega_3) \end{pmatrix} = \begin{pmatrix} 8 \\ 10 \\ 3 \end{pmatrix}$$

Notice that here the bond is security 3 and that $1 + r = 1$, that is, the rate of interest is 0. The solution of the preceding system is

$$Q(\omega_1) = -\frac{1}{2}, \ Q(\omega_2) = 1, \ Q(\omega_3) = \frac{1}{2}$$

so that an equilibrium price measure does not exist. As shown in Example 1.3, these prices permit arbitrage strategies.

Corollary 2.1 *An equilibrium price measure Q exists if and only if the given price system p is an equilibrium price system for some population of traders with continuous, increasing, and convex preferences.*

Proof. An equilibrium price system for such a population of traders does not permit arbitrage opportunities and the existence of Q follows from Theorem 2.1.

Conversely, suppose that Q exists for the given p. On the consumption set $X = \mathcal{R}^{K+1}$ consider traders $1 \le i \le I$ with arbitrary endowment processes $e^i \in X$ and preferences given by the following rule. Trader i prefers a consumption process c to a consumption process b if and only if

$$c(0) + \frac{\sum_{k=1}^{K} Q(\omega_k) c(T, \omega_k)}{1+r} \ge b(0) + \frac{\sum_{k=1}^{K} Q(\omega_k) b(T, \omega_k)}{1+r}$$

For these traders, the price system p and the allocation $c^i = e^i$ are an equilibrium. Indeed, the endowment process e^i belongs to the budget set $B(e^i, p)$. Suppose that a consumption process $c^i = \{c^i(0), c^i(T)\}$ belongs to the budget set $B(e^i, p)$. Then there exists a trading strategy θ^i such that

$$c^i(0) = e^i(0) - \sum_{n=1}^{N} \theta_n p_n \quad \text{and} \quad c^i(T) = e^i(T) + \sum_{n=1}^{N} \theta_n d_n$$

Therefore, the expression

$$c^i(0) + \frac{\sum_{k=1}^{K} Q(\omega_k) c^i(T, \omega_k)}{1+r}$$

is equal to

$$c^i(0) + \frac{\sum_{k=1}^{K} Q(\omega_k) e^i(T, \omega_k)}{1+r} + \frac{\sum_{n=1}^{N} \theta_n \sum_{k=1}^{K} Q(\omega_k) d_n(\omega_k)}{1+r}$$

which is equal to

$$c^i(0) + \frac{\sum_{k=1}^{K} Q(\omega_k) e^i(T, \omega_k)}{1+r} + \sum_{n=1}^{N} \theta_n p_n = e^i(0) + \frac{\sum_{k=1}^{K} Q(\omega_k) e^i(T, \omega_k)}{1+r}$$

That is, trader i is indifferent between c^i and e^i. Consequently, given prices p, the endowment process optimizes each trader's preferences over his or her budget set. There is no trade in this equilibrium. The remainder of the proof is left as an exercise for the reader. ∎

When the system of equations $D'Q = (1+r)p$ has a solution, then this solution is unique if and only if rank$(D) = K$. This establishes the next theorem.

Theorem 2.2 *If an equilibrium price measure exists, then it is unique if and only if the market is complete.*

Example 2.3 There are $K = 3$ states and $N = 3$ securities with the terminal payouts

$$D = \begin{pmatrix} 1 & 3 & 9 \\ 1 & 1 & 5 \\ 1 & 5 & 13 \end{pmatrix}$$

and prices

$$p_1 = 1, \; p_2 = 2, \; p_3 = 7$$

The system of equations for Q is

$$\begin{pmatrix} 1 & 1 & 1 \\ 3 & 1 & 5 \\ 9 & 5 & 13 \end{pmatrix} \begin{pmatrix} Q(\omega_1) \\ Q(\omega_2) \\ Q(\omega_3) \end{pmatrix} = \begin{pmatrix} 1 \\ 2 \\ 7 \end{pmatrix}$$

In this system, equations one and two are linearly independent, and equation three is a linear combination of the first two with weights 3 and 2, respectively. Therefore, rank$(D') = 2$, the market is incomplete, and the preceding system of equations has an infinite number of positive solutions

$$Q(\omega_1) = 1/2 - 2Q(\omega_3)$$
$$Q(\omega_2) = 1/2 + Q(\omega_3)$$
$$0 < Q(\omega_3) < 1/4$$

Because an equilibrium price measure exists, the given prices do not permit arbitrage strategies. In this incomplete market, not all consumption processes are attainable. If the terminal consumption $c(T)$ is part of an attainable consumption process, then there is a trading strategy θ such that

$$D\theta = \begin{pmatrix} c(T, \omega_1) \\ c(T, \omega_2) \\ c(T, \omega_3) \end{pmatrix}$$

For such a trading strategy to exist, the linear relationship that exists among the rows of D must also exist among the elements of the vector on the right hand side of the preceding system. An examination of D reveals that the third row is a linear combination of the first two rows with the weights 2 and -1, respectively. Therefore, the set of attainable consumption processes is the three-dimensional subspace of $X = \mathcal{R}^4$ given by the equation $2c(T, \omega_1) - c(T, \omega_2) = c(T, \omega_3)$.

It is easy to verify that all the equilibrium price measures in this example produce the same expectation for any given terminal consumption that is part of an attainable consumption process. However, consider the call option $d_4 = \max(0, d_2 - 2)$. The terminal payout of this option is

$$d_4(\omega_1) = 1, \;\; d_4(\omega_2) = 0, \;\; d_4(\omega_3) = 3$$

The option is not attainable because $2 \times 1 - 0 \neq 3$ and it is easy to check that different equilibrium price measures produce for d_4 different expectations.

2.2   The Price Functional

The next concept of this chapter is the price functional. For any price system p that does not permit arbitrage strategies, the price functional assigns to each attainable consumption process c the initial cost of c, that is, the initial endowment $e(0)$ such that $c \in B(e, p)$, where $e = \{e(0), 0\}$. As before, denote by M the set of all the attainable consumption processes. The formal definition is as follows.

Definition 2.2 Let p be a price system that does not permit arbitrage strategies. The price functional $\phi : M \to \mathcal{R}$ is such that for every $c \in M$

$$\phi(c) = c(0) + \sum_{n=1}^{N} \theta_n p_n$$

for any trading strategy θ such that

$$c(T) = \sum_{n=1}^{N} \theta_n d_n$$

When the given price system p does not permit arbitrage strategies, then the initial cost of any two trading strategies that attain the same consumption process is the same. Therefore, this definition does not depend on the particular trading strategy chosen to attain any given consumption process. Also, notice that M is a linear subspace of the consumption set X and that ϕ is a linear functional on M.

The price functional ϕ has a nice representation in terms of the equilibrium price measure Q.

Theorem 2.3 *If the price system p does not permit arbitrage strategies, then for every c $\in$ M and every equilibrium price measure Q*

$$\phi(c) = c(0) + \frac{E_Q[c(T)]}{1+r}$$

In particular, for any security $1 \leq n \leq N$

$$p_n = \frac{E_Q(d_n)}{1+r}$$

Proof. Let Q be an equilibrium price measure and c an attainable consumption process. Then

$$D'Q = (1+r)p$$

and there exists a trading strategy θ such that $\theta'D'$ is the terminal consumption part of c. It follows that

$$\phi(c) = c(0) + \theta'p = c(0) + \frac{\theta'D'Q}{1+r} = c(0) + \frac{E_Q[c(T)]}{1+r}$$

The second part of the theorem follows from the fact that for every n the terminal consumption d_n is attainable, and its initial cost is p_n. ∎

In addition to providing an easy way to compute the price functional, Theorem 2.3 also delivers the interpretation of $Q(\omega)$ first, as a risk-adjusted probability and, second, in a complete market, as the future value of consuming nothing at the initial date and consuming exactly one unit at the terminal date in state ω. Furthermore, using the representation of the price functional in Theorem 2.3, we can characterize the budget sets of traders in terms of $K - \text{rank}(D) + 1$ linear equations.

Theorem 2.4 *Suppose that the price system does not permit arbitrage strategies. Then there exists a linear operator*

$$F : \mathcal{R}^K \rightarrow \mathcal{R}^{K-\text{rank}(D)}$$

such that for any consumption process c we have c $\in$ B(e, p) if and only if F(c − e) = 0 and ϕ(c − e) = 0.

Proof. The proof follows immediately from Theorem 1.5 and the definition of the price functional. ∎

Notice that the equations $F(c - e) = 0$ and $\phi(c - e) = 0$ are linear constraints on the consumption process c. In equilibrium, traders optimize their preferences subject to these linear constraints. Let F have the matrix representation $F = (F_{jk})$, where $1 \le j \le K - \text{rank}(D)$ and $1 \le k \le K$. Furthermore, denote the representation of the price functional in Theorem 2.3

$$\phi(c) = c(0) + \sum_{k=1}^{K} \phi_k c(T, \omega_k)$$

Then the explicit budget constraints are

$$\sum_{k=1}^{K} F_{jk}[c(T, \omega_k) - e(T, \omega_k)] = 0$$

for $1 \le j \le K - \text{rank}(D)$ and

$$c(0) + e(0) + \sum_{k=1}^{K} \phi_k[c(T, \omega_k) - e(T, \omega_k)] = 0$$

Example 2.4 In Example 1.3 add the initial prices

$$p_1 = 1, \quad p_2 = 4\frac{5}{6}, \quad \text{and} \quad p_3 = 12\frac{2}{3}$$

There are no arbitrage strategies, but because $K = 4$ and $\text{rank}(D) = 2$ this market is incomplete and the equilibrium price measure is not unique. It is easy to verify that the set of equilibrium price measures Q is given by

$$Q(\omega_1) = \frac{23}{12} - 2Q(\omega_3) - 3Q(\omega_4)$$

$$Q(\omega_2) = -\frac{11}{12} + Q(\omega_3) + 2Q(\omega_4)$$

$$Q(\omega_2) > 0, \quad Q(\omega_3) > 0, \quad \text{and} \quad \frac{11}{12} < 2Q(\omega_3) + 3Q(\omega_4) < \frac{23}{12}$$

We obtain the following representation of the price functional

$$\phi(c) = c(0) + \sum_{k=1}^{4} Q(\omega_k)c(T, \omega_k)$$

$$= c(0) + \left[\frac{23}{12} - 2Q(\omega_3) - 3Q(\omega_4)\right] c(T, \omega_1)$$

$$+ \left[-\frac{11}{12} + Q(\omega_3) + 2Q(\omega_4) \right] c(T, \omega_2)$$

$$+ Q(\omega_3)c(T, \omega_3) + Q(\omega_4)c(T, \omega_4)$$

$$= c(0) + \frac{23}{12}c(T, \omega_1) - \frac{11}{12}c(T, \omega_2)$$

The last equality follows from the fact that $c \in M$. For any endowment process e, using the abbreviated notation $c(0) = c_0$, $c(T, \omega_k) = c_k$, $e(0) = e_0$, and $e(T, \omega_k) = e_k$ for $1 \leq k \leq 4$, the budget set $B(e, p)$ is described by the equations

$$
\begin{array}{rrrcrrr}
2c_1 & - \ c_2 & - \ c_3 & = & 2e_1 & - \ e_2 & - \ e_3 \\
3c_1 & - \ 2c_2 & - \ c_4 = & & 3e_1 & - \ 2e_2 & - \ e_4 \\
c_0 + \frac{23}{12}c_1 & - \frac{11}{12}c_2 & & = & e_0 + \frac{23}{12}e_1 & - \frac{11}{12}e_2 &
\end{array}
$$

In equilibrium, traders optimize their preferences subject to these budget constraints.

The price functional is positive, and there is a one-to-one correspondence between positive extensions of the price functional from M to X and equilibrium price measures. Formally, the definition of a positive functional is as follows.

Definition 2.3 Let M be a linear subspace of the linear space $X = \mathcal{R}^{K+1}$, and $\pi : M \to \mathcal{R}$ be a linear functional on M. The functional π is called positive if and only if for all $c \in M$, if $c \geq 0$, then $\pi(c) \geq 0$, and if $c \geq 0$ and $c \neq 0$, then $\pi(c) > 0$.

The observation that the price functional ϕ is positive follows immediately from the definition of an arbitrage strategy, and the fact that arbitrage strategies do not exist in equilibrium.

Let $M \subset N \subset X$ and consider a linear functional

$$\psi : N \to \mathcal{R}$$

such that for every $c \in M$ we have $\psi(c) = \phi(c)$. Then the linear functional ψ is called an extension of the linear functional ϕ.

Denote by $\chi_{\{\omega\}}(\xi)$ the elementary terminal consumption

$$\chi_{\{\omega\}}(\xi) = \left\{ \begin{array}{ll} 1 & \text{if } \xi = \omega \\ 0 & \text{otherwise} \end{array} \right.$$

Stated in words, the elementary terminal consumption $\chi_{\{\omega\}}(\xi)$ represents one unit of consumption in state ω and no consumption in all the other states. Then the correspondence between positive extensions of the price functional and equilibrium price measures is as follows.

Theorem 2.5 *The formulas:*

1. $\psi(c) = c(0) + \dfrac{E_Q[c(T)]}{1+r}$

2. $Q(\omega) = (1+r)\psi\left(\chi_{\{\omega\}}\right)$

establish a one-to-one correspondence between equilibrium price measures Q and positive extensions $\psi : X \to \mathcal{R}$ of the price functional ϕ.

Proof. Theorem 2.3 implies that a functional ψ defined by (1) is an extension of the price functional ϕ. This ψ is positive because the expected value of a nonnegative terminal consumption is nonnegative and if, in addition, $c(T, \omega) > 0$ for some ω, then the expected value is positive.

Conversely, each $Q(\omega)$ defined by (2) is positive because ψ is a positive functional. Second, Q is a probability measure on Ω because

$$\sum_{k=1}^{K} Q(\omega_k) = (1+r)\psi(\chi_{\{\Omega\}}) = (1+r)\frac{1}{1+r} = 1$$

Third, for any n

$$\sum_{k=1}^{K} Q(\omega_k)d_n(\omega_k) = (1+r)\psi(d_n) = (1+r)p_n$$

Finally, if Q_1 and Q_2 are two equilibrium price measures and ψ_1 and ψ_2 are the corresponding extensions of the price functional, then $\psi_1 = \psi_2$ implies

$$Q_1(\omega) = (1+r)\psi_1\left(\chi_{\{\omega\}}\right) = (1+r)\psi_2\left(\chi_{\{\omega\}}\right) = Q_2(\omega)$$

This completes the proof. ∎

Example 2.5 This is a continuation of Example 2.4. The price functional has a representation

$$\phi(c) = c(0) + \frac{23}{12}c(T, \omega_1) - \frac{11}{12}c(T, \omega_2)$$

and although the coefficient of $c(T, \omega_2)$ is negative, the price functional is positive on the linear space M. The functional

$$\phi'(c) = c(0) + \frac{23}{12}c(T, \omega_1) - \frac{11}{12}c(T, \omega_2)$$

is not, however, positive on the consumption set X.

Without the explicit use of the linear equations that define M, the price functional ϕ has a representation with positive coefficients. For instance, the choice

$$Q(\omega_1) = \frac{1}{4}, \quad Q(\omega_2) = \frac{1}{6}, \quad Q(\omega_3) = \frac{1}{12}, \quad \text{and} \quad Q(\omega_4) = \frac{1}{2}$$

results in the representation

$$\phi(c) = c(0) + \frac{1}{4}c(T, \omega_1) + \frac{1}{6}c(T, \omega_2) + \frac{1}{12}c(T, \omega_3) + \frac{1}{2}c(T, \omega_4)$$

As mentioned previously, this equation also represents a positive extension of the price functional to the consumption set X. The general form of a positive extension ψ of ϕ is

$$\psi(c) = c(0) + \frac{1}{4}c(T, \omega_1) + \frac{1}{6}c(T, \omega_2) + \frac{1}{12}c(T, \omega_3) + \frac{1}{2}c(T, \omega_4)$$

$$+\lambda_1[2c(T, \omega_1) - c(T, \omega_2) - c(T, \omega_3)]$$

$$+\lambda_2[3c(T, \omega_1) - 2c(T, \omega_2) - c(T, \omega_4)]$$

$$= c(0) + \left(\frac{1}{4} + 2\lambda_1 + 3\lambda_2\right)c(T, \omega_1) + \left(\frac{1}{6} - \lambda_1 - 2\lambda_2\right)c(T, \omega_2)$$

$$+ \left(\frac{1}{12} - \lambda_1\right)c(T, \omega_3) + \left(\frac{1}{2} - \lambda_2\right)c(T, \omega_4)$$

where the numbers λ_1 and λ_2 are such that

$$\frac{1}{4} + 2\lambda_1 + 3\lambda_2 > 0, \quad \frac{1}{6} - \lambda_1 - 2\lambda_2 > 0, \quad \frac{1}{12} - \lambda_1 > 0, \quad \text{and} \quad \frac{1}{2} - \lambda_2 > 0$$

The set of parameters λ_1 and λ_2 that satisfy these inequalities is the convex polyhedron Λ_Q

$$\lambda_1 < \frac{1}{12}, \quad \lambda_2 < \frac{1}{2}, \quad \text{and} \quad -\frac{1}{4} < 2\lambda_1 + 3\lambda_2 < \frac{3}{4}$$

Of course, a different choice of the initial equilibrium price measure Q would result in a different convex polyhedron Λ_Q. Regardless of the choice of

Q, however, the set Λ_Q represents all the positive extensions of the price functional. Because every equilibrium price measure Q is strictly positive, every polyhedron Λ_Q contains a convex neighborhood of 0. The latter property means that if $\psi(c-e) = 0$ for every positive extension ψ of the price functional ϕ, then $c \in B(e, p)$. Indeed, choose the three positive extensions of the price functional that correspond to the points $(0, 0)$, $(\lambda_1, 0)$, and $(0, \lambda_2$ in Λ_Q, with $\lambda_1 \neq 0$ and $\lambda_2 \neq 0$. Then the net trade $c - e$ is attainable at zero initial cost, and by Theorem 1.5, $c \in B(e, p)$.

Example 2.5 can be generalized. The positive extensions of the price functional ϕ have the following representation. Denote $m = K - \text{rank}(D)$ and assume that $m \geq 1$, otherwise the only positive extension of ϕ is ϕ itself. Then every positive extension ψ of the price functional ϕ has the representation

$$\psi(c) = c(0) + \sum_{k=1}^{K} \left(\phi_k + \sum_{j=1}^{m} \lambda_j F_{jk} \right) c(T, \omega_k)$$

where the numbers $\lambda_1, \ldots, \lambda_m$ are such that

$$\phi_k + \sum_{j=1}^{m} \lambda_j F_{jk} > 0$$

for all $1 \leq k \leq K$. We have the following theorem.

Theorem 2.6 *If the price system does not permit arbitrage strategies, then $c \in B(e, p)$ if and only if $\psi(c - e) = 0$ for all the positive extensions ψ of the price functional ϕ.*

The representation of the price functional in terms of an equilibrium price measure simplifies the calculation of equilibrium prices of various attainable securities.

Example 2.6 Returning to the market in Example 2.1, imagine adding to it securities 5 and 6 as follows. Security 5 is a call option on security 4 with the exercise price 100, and security 6 is a convertible bond that pays at the terminal time T the larger of the bond, d_1, and security 4, d_4, that is

$$d_5 = \max(0, d_4 - 100)$$
$$d_6 = \max(d_1, d_4)$$

Explicitly

$$d_5(\omega_1) = 20, \ d_5(\omega_2) = 0, \ d_5(\omega_3) = 100$$
$$d_6(\omega_1) = 120, \ d_6(\omega_2) = 100, \ d_6(\omega_3) = 200$$

Because the original market in securities 1, 2, 3, and 4 is complete, securities 5 and 6 are attainable, the equilibrium price measure from Example 2.1, given by $Q(\omega_1) = \frac{1}{5}, Q(\omega_2) = \frac{1}{2}, Q(\omega_3) = \frac{3}{10}$, is unique and the equilibrium prices of securities 5 and 6 are

$$p_5 = \frac{\frac{1}{5} \times 20 + \frac{1}{2} \times 0 + \frac{3}{10} \times 100}{2} = 17$$

$$p_6 = \frac{\frac{1}{5} \times 120 + \frac{1}{2} \times 100 + \frac{3}{10} \times 200}{2} = 67$$

Reviewing the results of this section suggests that any equilibrium price measure Q is a risk-adjusting mechanism in the multiperiod model. For the actual probability measure P, the representation of prices as discounted expected terminal payouts would hold in a market populated by risk-neutral traders. The risk-adjusting property of Q makes this representation true with respect to Q even when traders are not risk-neutral.

2.3   Risk and Return

We show now that if the price system p does not permit arbitrage strategies, and Q is an equilibrium price measure, then the likelihood ratio $z = \frac{Q}{P}$ is the single risk factor in the discrete one-period model. Specifically, we demonstrate that the risk premium of each security is proportional to the covariance between the likelihood ratio and the rate of return of that security.

To give a precise statement of this result, we define the following decomposition of the rate of return of security $1 \leq n \leq N$

$$\mu_n = \frac{E_P(d_n)}{p_n} - 1$$

$$x_n = \frac{d_n - E_P(d_n)}{p_n}$$

The sum $\mu_n + x_n$ is the rate of return of security n. We call μ_n the predictable part of the rate of return $\mu_n + x_n$, and x_n the innovation part of $\mu_n + x_n$. It follows immediately from the preceding definition that the terminal payout of each security has the representation

$$d_n = p_n(1 + \mu_n + x_n)$$

and this representation implies that

$$\frac{d_n}{1+r} - p_n = (\mu_n - r + x_n)\frac{p_n}{1+r} \tag{2.1}$$

Next, for any equilibrium price measure Q

$$E_Q\left[\frac{P}{Q}\left(\frac{d_n}{1+r} - p_n\right)\right] = E_P\left(\frac{d_n}{1+r} - p_n\right)$$

and because

$$E_Q\left(\frac{d_n}{1+r} - p_n\right) = 0$$

we also have

$$E_Q\left[\left(\frac{P}{Q} - 1\right)\left(\frac{d_n}{1+r} - p_n\right)\right] = E_P\left(\frac{d_n}{1+r} - p_n\right)$$

Notice that for any random variable u we have $E_Q(u) = E_P(uz)$. Therefore, in the preceding equation we can convert the expectation with respect to the probability measure Q to an expectation with respect to the probability measure P to get

$$E_P\left[\left(1 - \frac{Q}{P}\right)\left(\frac{d_n}{1+r} - p_n\right)\right] = E_P\left(\frac{d_n}{1+r} - p_n\right)$$

or

$$E_P\left(\frac{d_n}{1+r} - p_n\right) = -E_P\left[(z - 1)\left(\frac{d_n}{1+r} - p_n\right)\right] \tag{2.2}$$

Now, substitute Equation 2.1 into Equation 2.2 to obtain

$$\mu_n - r = -E_P[(z - 1)x_n]$$

and because $E_P(z) = 1$ and $E_P(x_n) = 0$, we have the following result.

Theorem 2.7 *If the price system p does not permit arbitrage strategies, then for any equilibrium price measure Q and any security $1 \leq n \leq N$*

$$\mu_n - r = -\text{covar}_P(x_n, z)$$

Theorem 2.7 establishes a simple relationship between the predictable and the innovation components of the rate of return of security $1 \leq n \leq N$. Alternatively, the preceding is a relationship between the risk premium of any security and the covariance between the innovation of return of that security and the likelihood ratio.

Next, suppose that $c(T) = \sum_{n=1}^{N} \theta_n d_n$ is an attainable terminal consumption. Then $c(T)$ has the representation

$$c(T) = \left(\sum_{n=1}^{N} \theta_n p_n \right) (1 + \mu + x)$$

where μ is the predictable component and x is the innovation component of the rate of return of the trading strategy θ. The relationship between the predictable and the innovation components of the rate of return of the trading strategy θ is the same as for any individual security

$$\mu - r = -\mathrm{covar}_P(x, z) \qquad\qquad (2.3)$$

If there is a trading strategy ζ such that $z = \sum_{n=1}^{N} \zeta_n d_n$, then we also have the representation

$$z = \left(\sum_{n=1}^{N} \zeta_n p_n \right) (1 + \nu + y)$$

where ν and y are, respectively, the predictable and the innovation parts of the rate of return of the trading strategy ζ. Substituting this representation of z into Equation 2.3 we get

$$\mu - r = - \left(\sum_{n=1}^{N} \zeta_n p_n \right) \mathrm{covar}_P(x, y)$$

and, in particular

$$\nu - r = - \left(\sum_{n=1}^{N} \zeta_n p_n \right) \mathrm{var}_P(y)$$

This implies the following theorem.

Theorem 2.8 *Suppose that the price system p does not permit arbitrage strategies, the market is complete, Q is the equilibrium price measure, θ is any trading strategy, ζ is a trading strategy that attains the likelihood ratio*

z, μ and ν are the predictable parts of the rates of return of the trading strategies θ and ζ, and x and y are the innovation parts of the rates of return of the trading strategies θ and ζ. Then

$$\mu - r = \frac{\operatorname{covar}_P(x, y)}{\operatorname{var}_P(y)}(\nu - r)$$

We call the ratio

$$\beta(x, y) = \frac{\operatorname{covar}_P(x, y)}{\operatorname{var}_P(y)} = \frac{\operatorname{covar}_P(\mu + x, \nu + y)}{\operatorname{var}_P(\nu + y)}$$

the beta of the trading strategy θ with respect to the trading strategy ζ. Theorem 2.8 says that if the likelihood ratio is attainable, then the risk premium of any trading strategy θ is proportional to the risk premium of the trading strategy ζ, and that the coefficient of proportionality is the beta of the trading strategy θ with respect to the trading strategy ζ.

A suitable modification of Theorem 2.8 can be extended to an incomplete market that does not permit arbitrage strategies. In that modification the likelihood ratio z is replaced by a terminal consumption $z^*(T)$ that may be different from the likelihood ratio $\frac{Q}{P}$ for every equilibrium price measure Q. This modified extension of Theorem 2.8 can be proved either directly or as a consequence of the representation theorem of F. Riesz. We describe the latter proof, using this opportunity to introduce Riesz's theorem for future reference. We begin with a definition.

Definition 2.4 A scalar product in $\mathcal{R}^m$ is a function $(\cdot, \cdot) : \mathcal{R}^m \times \mathcal{R}^m \to \mathcal{R}$ such that:

1. For any $\alpha^1, \alpha^2 \in \mathcal{R}$ and $c^1, c^2, c^3 \in \mathcal{R}^m$

$$(\alpha^1 c^1 + \alpha^2 c^2, c^3) = \alpha^1(c^1, c^3) + \alpha^2(c^2, c^3)$$

2. For any $c^1, c^2 \in \mathcal{R}^m$ we have $(c^1, c^2) = (c^2, c^1)$.

3. For any $c \in \mathcal{R}^m$ we have $(c, c) \geq 0$.

4. For any $c \in \mathcal{R}^m$ we have $(c, c) = 0$ if and only if $c = 0$.

Two vectors in $\mathcal{R}^m$ are called orthogonal if and only if their scalar product is zero.

Theorem 2.9 (F. Riesz) *If M is a linear subspace of $\mathcal{R}^m$ and f is a linear functional on M, then there is a unique element $z \in M$ such that for every $c \in M$ we have $f(c) = (c, z)$.*

Proof. Denote by N a linear subspace of M such that $c \in N$ if and only if $f(c) = 0$. Consider two cases:

- There is no $b \in M$, $b \neq 0$, such that b is orthogonal to every element of N. Now, every $c \in M$ can be written $c = a + b$, where $a \in N$ and b is orthogonal to N. Because there is no such $b \neq 0$, then $b = 0$ and $c = a$, that is, $M = N$ and $z = 0$. In this case the theorem is trivial.

- There is a $b \in M$, $b \neq 0$, such that b is orthogonal to every element of N. Because b does not belong to N we have $f(b) \neq 0$. Denote $\tilde{b} = \dfrac{b}{f(b)}$ and for any $c \in M$ write

$$c = [c - f(c)\tilde{b}] + f(c)\tilde{b}$$

The element $c - f(c)\tilde{b}$ belongs to N because $f[c - f(c)\tilde{b}] = 0$, and therefore, $c - f(c)\tilde{b}$ is orthogonal to both b and $\tilde{b}$. Finally, denote $z = \dfrac{\tilde{b}}{(\tilde{b}, \tilde{b})}$ so that $c - f(c)\tilde{b}$ is also orthogonal to z. It follows that $(c, z) = (c - f(c)\tilde{b}, z) + f(c)(\tilde{b}, z)$, where the first scalar product on the right hand side vanishes because $c - f(c)\tilde{b}$ is orthogonal to z, and the second scalar product on the right hand side equals 1 because of the way that z is defined. The result is $(c, z) = f(c)$. The element z is unique, because if $(c, z') = (c, z'')$ for every c, then for $c = z' - z''$ we have $(z' - z'', z' - z'') = 0$, and consequently $z' = z''$. ∎

In the consumption set $X = \mathcal{R}^{K+1}$ define the scalar product

$$(c^1, c^2) = c^1(0)c^2(0) + \sum_{k=1}^{K} \frac{P(\omega_k)}{1+r} c^1(T, \omega_k)c^2(T, \omega_k)$$

and let M be the attainable set. From the Riesz representation theorem, there is a consumption process $z^* = \{z^*(0), z^*(T)\} \in M$ such that the price functional ϕ has the representation

$$\phi(c) = c(0)z^*(0) + \sum_{k=1}^{K} \frac{P(\omega_k)}{1+r} c(T, \omega_k)z^*(T, \omega_k)$$

In particular, $E_P[z^*(T)] = 1$, and for any $1 \leq n \leq N$

$$p_n = \frac{E_P[z^*(T)d_n]}{1+r}$$

Therefore

$$E_P \left(\frac{d_n}{1+r} - p_n \right) = -E_P \left\{ [z^*(T) - 1] \frac{d_n}{1+r} \right\} \quad (2.4)$$

$$= -E_P \left\{ [z^*(T) - 1] \left(\frac{d_n}{1+r} - p_n \right) \right\} \quad (2.5)$$

which is analogous to Equation 2.2. Thus, we have the following result.

Theorem 2.10 *Suppose that the price system p does not permit arbitrage strategies, Q is the equilibrium price measure, θ is any trading strategy, ζ is a trading strategy that attains the terminal consumption $z^*(T)$, μ and ν are the predictable parts of the rates of return of the trading strategies θ and ζ, and x and y are the innovation parts of the rates of return of the trading strategies θ and ζ. Then*

$$\mu - r = \frac{\text{covar}_P(x, y)}{\text{var}_P(y)} (\nu - r)$$

The condition

$$p_n = \frac{E_P [z^*(T) d_n]}{1+r}$$

indicates that the random variable $u(\omega) = P(\omega) z^*(T, \omega)$, interpreted as a K-dimensional vector, satisfies the linear system of equations

$$D'u = (1+r)p$$

Therefore, the terminal consumption $z^*(T)$ is a likelihood ratio for some equilibrium price measure Q if and only if this terminal consumption is positive. Also, it is obvious that when the market is complete, then $z^*(T) = z$. We now prove that the trading strategy ζ has certain minimal properties.

Theorem 2.11 *Suppose that the price system p does not permit arbitrage strategies, Q is the equilibrium price measure, θ is any trading strategy, ζ is a trading strategy that attains the terminal consumption $z^*(T)$, μ and ν are the predictable parts of the rates of return of the trading strategies θ and ζ, and x and y are the innovation parts of the rates of return of the trading strategies θ and ζ. Then we have:*

1. *If $\mu = \nu$, then $\text{var}_P(y) \geq \text{var}_P(x)$.*

2. *Suppose that $\mu \geq -1$ and $\nu \geq -1$, then $\text{var}_P(y) = \text{var}_P(x)$ implies that $\mu \geq \nu$.*

Proof. Equation 2.5 implies that

$$\mu_n - r = -E_P\left\{[z^*(T) - 1]x_n\right\}$$

and because $E_P(x_n) = 0$, we have

$$E_P[(\mu + x)z^*(T)] = r$$

Then this equation implies that

$$E_P[(\mu + x)(1 + \nu + y)] = E_P[(\nu + y)(1 + \nu + y)] \qquad (2.6)$$

and therefore, if $\mu = \nu$, then

$$E_P[(\mu + x)(\nu + y)] = E_P[(\nu + y)^2]$$

and

$$
\begin{aligned}
\text{var}_P(x) - \text{var}_P(y) &= E_P\left[(\mu + x)^2\right] - E_P\left[(\nu + y)^2\right] \\
&= E_P\left\{[(\mu + x) - (\nu + y)]^2\right\} \\
&\geq 0
\end{aligned}
$$

This completes the proof of item 1. To prove item 2, first notice that Equation 2.6 entails that

$$E_P\left\{[(\mu + x) - (\nu + y)]^2\right\}$$

is equal to

$$E_P\left[(\mu + x)^2\right] - E_P\left[(\nu + y)^2\right] + 2(\mu - \nu) \geq 0$$

Second, if $\text{var}_P(y) = \text{var}_P(x)$, then the preceding equation implies

$$\mu^2 - \nu^2 + 2(\mu - \nu) = (\mu - \nu)(\mu + \nu + 2) \geq 0$$

This ends the proof. ∎

Example 2.7 Find the special terminal consumption $z^*(T)$ for the market in Example 2.3. This $z^*(T)$ is attainable and therefore satisfies

$$2z^*(T, \omega_1) - z^*(T, \omega_2) = z^*(T, \omega_3)$$

Also, because the rate of interest is $r = 0$, for every attainable $c(T)$ and every equilibrium price measure Q the expression

$$Q(\omega_1)c(T,\omega_1) + Q(\omega_2)c(T,\omega_2) + Q(\omega_3)c(T,\omega_3)$$

is equal to

$$P(\omega_1)z^*(T,\omega_1)c(T,\omega_1) + P(\omega_2)z^*(T,\omega_2)c(T,\omega_2)$$
$$+P(\omega_3)z^*(T,\omega_3)c(T,\omega_3)$$

Substituting

$$c(T,\omega_3) = 2c(T,\omega_1) - c(T,\omega_2)$$

$$Q(\omega_1) + 2Q(\omega_3) = 1/2$$

$$Q(\omega_2) -\ Q(\omega_3) = 1/2$$

and equating the coefficients of $c(T,\omega_1)$ and $c(T,\omega_2)$ on both sides of the resulting equation yields

$$[P(\omega_1) + 4P(\omega_3)]z^*(T,\omega_1) - 2P(\omega_3)z^*(T,\omega_2) = 1/2$$

$$-2P(\omega_3)z^*(T,\omega_1) + [P(\omega_2) + P(\omega_3)]z^*(T,\omega_2) = 1/2$$

Solving this system for $z^*(T,\omega_1)$ and $z^*(T,\omega_2)$ produces

$$z^*(T,\omega_1) = \frac{P(\omega_2) + 3P(\omega_3)}{2[P(\omega_1)P(\omega_2) + P(\omega_1)P(\omega_3) + 4P(\omega_2)P(\omega_3)]}$$

$$z^*(T,\omega_2) = \frac{P(\omega_1) + 6P(\omega_3)}{2[P(\omega_1)P(\omega_2) + P(\omega_1)P(\omega_3) + 4P(\omega_2)P(\omega_3)]}$$

and finally

$$z^*(T,\omega_3) = \frac{2P(\omega_2) - P(\omega_1)}{2[P(\omega_1)P(\omega_2) + P(\omega_1)P(\omega_3) + 4P(\omega_2)P(\omega_3)]}$$

The terminal consumption $z^*(T)$ is not always the likelihood ratio $\dfrac{Q}{P}$ of an equilibrium price measure Q and the probability measure P. Recall that the necessary and sufficient condition for $z^*(T)$ to be such a ratio is $z^*(T) > 0$, or equivalently

$$2P(\omega_2) > P(\omega_1)$$

Theorems 2.8 and 2.10 deliver still another representation of the price functional ϕ. Denote

$$\lambda = \frac{\nu - r}{\operatorname{var}_P(y)}$$

and

$$\sigma_{\theta\zeta} = \operatorname{covar}_P(x, y)$$

The parameter λ is called the ζ-price of risk, $\sigma_{\theta\zeta}$ is called the ζ-risk of trading strategy θ, and the mean rate of return of the strategy θ has the representation

$$\mu = r + \lambda \sigma_{\theta\zeta}$$

In terms of these parameters the price functional has the representation

$$\phi(c) = c(0) + \frac{E_P[c(T)]}{1 + \mu} = \frac{E_P[c(T)]}{1 + r + \lambda \sigma_{\theta\zeta}}$$

where the trading strategy θ attains $c(T)$. This establishes $r + \lambda \sigma_{\theta\zeta}$ as the risk-adjusted discount rate for the trading strategy θ.

Problems

1. There are $K = 3$ states and $N = 3$ securities with payouts

$$D = \begin{pmatrix} 24 & 44 & 12 \\ 20 & 44 & 12 \\ 48 & 36 & 12 \end{pmatrix}$$

and prices

$$p_1 = 35, \ p_2 = 40, \ p_3 = 12$$

(a) Do equilibrium price measures exist? Find them all.

(b) Does the given price system permit arbitrage strategies?

(c) Is this market complete? Find the set M of all the attainable consumption processes.

(d) Find the equilibrium prices of the following securities:

     i. A call option on security 1 with the exercise price of 25.

     ii. A put option on security 2 with the exercise price of 40.

iii. A security whose terminal payout in each state is the maximum payout of securities 1 through 3 in that state, less the average payout of securities 1 through 3 in that state.

2. There are $K = 3$ states and $N = 3$ securities with payouts

$$D = \begin{pmatrix} 600 & 1100 & 300 \\ 500 & 1200 & 300 \\ 530 & 1270 & 300 \end{pmatrix}$$

and prices

$$p_1 = 276, \ p_2 = 594, \ p_3 = 150$$

(a) Is this market complete? Find the set M of all the attainable consumption processes.

(b) Is the consumption process

$$c(0) = 0, \ c(T, \omega_1) = 6, \ c(T, \omega_2) = 5, \ c(T, \omega_3) = 12$$

attainable? Find the initial endowment and the trading strategy that attain it.

(c) Is the consumption process

$$c(0) = 100,000, \ c(T, \omega_1) = 12, \ c(T, \omega_2) = 2, \ c(T, \omega_3) = 5$$

attainable? Find the initial endowment and the trading strategy that attain it.

(d) Does the given price system permit arbitrage strategies?

(e) Do equilibrium price measures exist? Find them all.

(f) Find the equilibrium prices of the following securities:

i. A call option on security 1 with the exercise price of 550.

ii. A put option on security 2 with the exercise price of 1150.

iii. A security whose terminal payout in each state is the maximum payout of securities 1 through 3 in that state.

3. There are $K = 2$ states and $N = 3$ securities with payouts

$$D = \begin{pmatrix} 20 & 44 & 12 \\ 48 & 36 & 12 \end{pmatrix}$$

and prices

$$p_1 = 24, \ p_2 = 40, \ p_3 = 12$$

(a) Is this market complete? Find the set M of all the attainable consumption processes.

(b) Is the consumption process

$$c(0) = 10, \ c(T, w_1) = 6, \ c(T, w_2) = 5$$

attainable? Find the initial endowment and the trading strategy that attain it.

(c) Is the consumption process

$$c(0) = 0, \ c(T, w_1) = 9, \ c(T, w_2) = 1$$

attainable? Find the initial endowment and the trading strategy that attain it.

(d) Does the given price system permit arbitrage strategies?

(e) Do equilibrium price measures exist? Find them all.

(f) Find the equilibrium prices of the following securities:

   i. A call option on security 1 with the exercise price of 25.

   ii. A put option on security 2 with the exercise price of 40.

4. Complete the proof of Corollary 2.1.

5. In Example 2.3, show that any attainable terminal consumption has the same expectation under all the equilibrium price measures, but the security $d_4 = \max(0, d_2 - 2)$ has different expectations under different equilibrium price measures.

6. Prove Corollary 2.6.

7. Suppose that preferences of traders can be represented by separable utility functions

$$u^i[c^i(0), c^i(T)] = c^i(0) + b^i v^i[c^i(T)]$$

such that trader i prefers $b = \{b(0), b(T)\}$ to $c = \{c(0), c(T)\}$ if and only if

$$E_P[u^i(b)] \geq E_P[u^i(c)]$$

where

$$v^i(x) = \begin{cases} A^i x^2 + B^i x & \text{for } x \leq \xi^i \\ (2A^i \xi + B^i)(x - \xi^i) + A^i(\xi^i)^2 + B^i \xi^i & \text{for } x \geq \xi^i \end{cases}$$

and, for each i, $2A^i \xi^i + B^i > 0$. Suppose further that the market is complete, and that the parameters A^i, B^i, ξ^i, b^i are such that the equilibrium allocation of consumption $c - \{c^i\}$, $c^i - \{c^i(0), c^i(T)\}$ satisfies $c^i(T) \leq \xi^i$ for all i.

(a) Show that the equilibrium terminal consumption of each trader is perfectly correlated with the likelihood ratio $z = \dfrac{Q}{P}$.

(b) Show that the equilibrium price measure Q is such that z is perfectly correlated with the terminal aggregate endowment

$$\sum_{i=1}^{I} e^i(T)$$

Notes

In the context of a complete market, equilibrium price measure is a modern term for the vector of the future value of prices of elementary terminal consumptions. For a statement of the basic separation theorem used in the proof of Theorem 2.1 see for example [5]. The equivalence of equilibrium price measures and positive extensions of the price functional in Theorem 2.4 is an adaptation to the discrete model of a corresponding theorem in [39].

The modified security market line in Theorems 2.7, 2.8, and 2.10 resembles, but does not coincide with, the traditional Capital Asset Pricing Model of [71] and [56]. The two market lines coincide when the likelihood ratio is perfectly correlated with aggregate terminal consumption. For the one-period model the modified security market line has been obtained also by [32]. In this book, however, we present the modified security market line for the discrete one-period model, the discrete multiperiod model (Section 6.6), and the general continuous multiperiod model (Section 12.6). Potential inconsistencies between the absence of arbitrage, completeness, and the traditional Capital Asset Pricing Model are studied in [34].

Chapter 3

A Discrete Multiperiod Model

3.1   Elements of the Model

The discrete multiperiod model in this chapter is a step up from the one-period model in both realism and complexity. This multiperiod model has a finite number of states and securities that can be traded on a finite number of intermediate dates between the initial and the terminal times.

There are two reasons to bring in intermediate trading opportunities to a model of a financial market. The first reason is the need of traders for intermediate consumption. This is not a very good reason because intermediate consumption can be accomplished without intermediate trading by introducing either nonperishable consumption goods or securities with intermediate payouts. A better reason for the introduction of intermediate trading opportunities is the intermediate arrival of new information.

The main difference in results between the one-period model and the multiperiod model is the dimension of the set of attainable consumption processes. Intermediate trading may attain all consumption processes that are consistent with the manner in which new information arrives with fewer linearly independent securities than would be required without intermediate trading.

The specific elements of the discrete multiperiod model are as follows:

- Initial date 0, terminal date T, intermediate dates $1, \ldots, T-1$, trading on dates $0, \ldots, T-1$.

- States belong to a finite sample space Ω with K elements

$$\Omega = \{\omega_1, \ldots, \omega_K\}$$

48

Each state $\omega \in \Omega$ occurs with a positive probability $P(\omega_k)$.

- There is only one, perishable, consumption good.

- There is a finite number N of endogenous securities, and there are no exogenous securities. The securities are infinitely divisible, and there are no taxes or other costs associated with trading. The securities make only random terminal payouts d_n. The payouts are arranged in a matrix D, which is the same as in the one-period model.

- There is a finite number I of traders. At time 0 the traders know only the set of possible states Ω, and at time T they know the prevailing state ω. On intermediate dates the traders have knowledge that is between these two extremes. This resolution of uncertainty over time is common to all the traders and is described by a given information structure. The precise meaning of this statement is the subject of Sections 3.2 and 3.3.

- Each trader receives an endowment of the consumption good at times $0, 1, \ldots, T$. The endowment process of trader i is

$$e^i = \{e^i(0), e^i(1), \ldots, e^i(T)\}$$

where $e^i(0)$ is a number and each $e^i(t)$ is a random variable. The endowment process of each trader is required to be consistent with the given information structure.

- Each trader consumes at times $0, 1, \ldots, T$. The consumption process of trader i is $c^i = \{c^i(0), c^i(1), \ldots, c^i(T)\}$, where $c^i(0)$ is a number and each $c^i(t)$ is a random variable. Furthermore, traders' consumption processes are required to be consistent with the given information structure. This condition and the description of the consumption set X are discussed in detail in Section 3.3.

- On the consumption set X the traders have complete preference orderings that are continuous, increasing, and convex.

It is clear that any further discussion of this model requires the introduction of the formal concept of an information structure and the appropriate consistency conditions between this information structure and endowments, consumption processes, prices, and trading strategies.

3.2   Information Structures

Imagine an experiment consisting of a toss of two coins: a nickel and a dime. Instead of observing the outcome directly you receive only the count of the coins that came heads up in the toss. What kind of information do you have about the outcome of this experiment?

Obviously, you have only partial information. If the outcome happens to be two heads or two tails (zero heads), then from the head count you know that both coins landed either heads up or tails up. However, when the nickel comes up heads and the dime comes up tails or the nickel comes up tails and the dime heads, then from the head count (one) you know only that the outcome is one of these two, but you do not know which one.

Formally, the toss of two coins is a sample space with four outcomes or states: $\Omega = \{hh, ht, th, tt\}$. The information in the head count can then be represented by the following arrangement of the sample points

$$\mathbf{f} = \{\{hh\}, \{ht, th\}, \{tt\}\}$$

Defined like this $\mathbf{f}$ is a set of events, that is, a set of subsets of the sample space Ω. The information that $\mathbf{f}$ represents is this: you know only the event in $\mathbf{f}$ that contains the prevailing state. Thus, if the outcome of the toss (the prevailing state) is either hh or tt, then you know it because these two form subsets of $\mathbf{f}$ all by themselves. However, when the outcome is either ht or th, then you know it is one of these two, but you do not know which one because they both are in the same subset of $\mathbf{f}$.

In general, this example leads to the notion of a partition of the sample space Ω as a formal representation of information.

Definition 3.1 A set $\mathbf{f} = \{f_1, \ldots, f_u\}$ of subsets of a sample space Ω is called a partition of Ω if and only if:

1. For every $i \neq j$ we have $f_i \cap f_j = \emptyset$.

2. The union $f_1 \cup \ldots \cup f_u = \Omega$.

Two states in the same subset of $\mathbf{f}$ are called indistinguishable. If the prevailing state is ω, then $\mathbf{f}(\omega)$ denotes the set of the partition $\mathbf{f}$ that contains the state ω.

Thus, a partition is a collection of disjoint events that together exhaust the sample space. A partition represents information through the specification of what is known: only the partition set $\mathbf{f}(\omega)$ that contains the prevailing state ω is known.

Example 3.1 The following examples are on the sample space

$$\Omega = \{\omega_1, \ldots, \omega_K\}$$

1. The null partition $\mathbf{f} = \{\{\omega_1, \ldots, \omega_K\}\}$ represents no information beyond the identity of the sample space.

2. The discrete partition $\mathbf{f} = \{\{\omega_1\}, \ldots, \{\omega_K\}\}$ represents full information, each state is a distinct event in this partition.

3. The partition

$$\mathbf{f} = \{\{\omega_1\}, \{\omega_2, \omega_3, \omega_4\}, \{\omega_5, \omega_6\}, \{\omega_7, \ldots, \omega_K\}\}$$

represents the following information. If the prevailing state is ω_1, then each trader knows it. If the prevailing state is ω_2, ω_3, or ω_4, then each trader knows that it is one of these three, but does not know which one. Similarly, if the prevailing state is ω_5 or ω_6, then traders know it is one of these two but not which one, and if the prevailing state is ω_7 or higher, then again traders know that, but do not know the specific state.

Splitting some sets of a partition produces another, finer, partition. Because some sets of the finer partition are smaller, and none are larger, the finer partition represents more information than the original partition.

Example 3.2

$$\begin{aligned}
\Omega &= \{\omega_1, \ldots, \omega_6\} \\
\mathbf{f} &= \{\{\omega_1\}, \{\omega_2, \omega_3, \omega_4\}, \{\omega_5, \omega_6\}\} \\
\mathbf{g} &= \{\{\omega_1\}, \{\omega_2, \omega_3\}, \{\omega_4\}, \{\omega_5\}, \{\omega_6\}\}
\end{aligned}$$

The partition $\mathbf{g}$ is finer than $\mathbf{f}$ and represents more information than $\mathbf{f}$.

This leads to the following formal definition.

Definition 3.2 A partition $\mathbf{g} = \{g_1, \ldots, g_v\}$ is finer than the partition $\mathbf{f} = \{f_1, \ldots, f_u\}$ if and only if every set of $\mathbf{g}$ is a subset of some set of $\mathbf{f}$, that is, for every $1 \le j \le v$ there is an $1 \le i \le u$ such that $g_j \subset f_i$. A partition $\mathbf{f}$ is coarser than a partition $\mathbf{g}$ if and only if $\mathbf{g}$ is finer than $\mathbf{f}$.

The ground is now ready for the concept of an information structure. In the context of the discrete multiperiod model an information structure describes the information that traders have on each trading date.

Definition 3.3 An information structure $\{\mathbf{f}_t\}$ is a sequence of partitions $\mathbf{f}_0, \ldots, \mathbf{f}_T$ such that:

1. At the initial time $\mathbf{f}_0 = \{\{\omega_1, \ldots, \omega_K\}\}$.

2. At the terminal time $\mathbf{f}_T = \{\{\omega_1\}, \ldots, \{\omega_K\}\}$.

3. For each $0 \le t \le T - 1$ the partition $\mathbf{f}_{t+1}$ is finer than the partition $\mathbf{f}_t$.

This definition standardizes the initial and terminal information and requires that traders do not forget their past information, that is, as time passes their knowledge does not decrease.

Intuitively, informational consistency between a given information structure and any endowment or consumption process requires that the latter do not represent more information than is known to traders. To formulate this precisely requires the concept of information represented by a random variable like endowment or consumption. This takes two definitions.

Definition 3.4 A random variable x is measurable on a partition $\mathbf{f}$ if and only if it is constant on each set of $\mathbf{f}$.

Example 3.3 $\Omega = \{\omega_1, \ldots, \omega_5\}$, $\mathbf{f} = \{\{\omega_1, \omega_2\}, \{\omega_3, \omega_5\}, \{\omega_4\}\}$

$$x(\omega_1) = 1, \ x(\omega_2) = 1, \ x(\omega_3) = 2, \ x(\omega_4) = 3, \ x(\omega_5) = 2$$
$$y(\omega_1) = 1, \ y(\omega_2) = 2, \ y(\omega_3) = 2, \ y(\omega_4) = 3, \ y(\omega_5) = 2$$

The random variable x is measurable on $\mathbf{f}$, and the random variable y is not measurable on $\mathbf{f}$. The reason for the latter is that y is not constant on the set $\{\omega_1, \omega_2\}$ of $\mathbf{f}$.

Definition 3.5 For a random variable x, the coarsest partition on which x is measurable is called the partition generated by x and is denoted $\mathbf{f}^x$.

Example 3.4 For the sample space and the random variable x from Example 3.3, x is measurable on the partitions

$$\{\{\omega_1\}, \ldots, \{\omega_5\}\} \ \text{and} \ \{\{\omega_1, \omega_2\}, \{\omega_3, \omega_5\}, \{\omega_4\}\}$$

and is not measurable on the partitions

$$\{\{\omega_1, \ldots, \omega_5\}\} \ \text{and} \ \{\{\omega_1, \omega_2, \omega_3, \omega_5\}, \{\omega_4\}\}$$

In fact, the partition $\{\{\omega_1, \omega_2\}, \{\omega_3, \omega_5\}, \{\omega_4\}\}$ is the coarsest partition on which x is measurable, that is

$$\mathbf{f}^x = \{\{\omega_1, \omega_2\}, \{\omega_3, \omega_5\}, \{\omega_4\}\}$$

Definition 3.5 immediately implies the following corollary.

Corollary 3.1 *A random variable x is measurable on a partition $\mathbf{f}$ if and only if $\mathbf{f}$ is finer than $\mathbf{f}^x$.*

Like a partition, a random variable represents information. The realization of a random variable may reveal something about the prevailing state. At one extreme, observing a random variable that has a different value in each state reveals the prevailing state. At the other extreme, observing a random variable that has the same value in all states does not reveal anything about the prevailing state.

In intermediate situations, observing a random variable that is not constant but has the same value in several, but not all, different states narrows down the set of potentially prevailing states, but leaves some states indistinguishable. The observer of such a random variable can distinguish among states in which the random variable has different values, but cannot distinguish among states in which the random variable has the same value. This is just like the ability to distinguish among states that are in different partition sets, and the simultaneous inability to distinguish among states that are in the same partition set.

There is a simple relationship between the information represented by a partition and the information represented by a random variable. A random variable x represents exactly the same information as the partition $\mathbf{f}^x$ that x generates. This observation serves as the formal definition of the information represented by a random variable.

Definition 3.6 The information represented by a random variable x is the information represented by the partition $\mathbf{f}^x$.

With this preparation completed, the next step is to consider the precise statement of informational consistency.

3.3 Informational Consistency

Section 3.1 left open some elements of the model. Equipped with the notions of Section 3.2, we can complete these items as follows:

- All traders have the same information given by an information structure $\{\mathbf{f}_t\}$.

- At time t trader i receives an endowment $e^i(t)$ that is measurable on $\mathbf{f}_t$, that is, $\mathbf{f}_t$ is finer than $\mathbf{f}^{e^i(t)}$.

- The consumption process of trader i is

$$c^i = \{c^i(0), c^i(1), \ldots, c^i(T)\}$$

where each $c^i(t)$ is measurable on $\mathbf{f}_t$. Using the notation $\mathcal{R}^{(\Omega, \mathbf{f}_t)}$ for the set of $\mathbf{f}_t$-measurable random variables, the consumption set X is

$$X = \prod_{t=0}^{T} \mathcal{R}^{(\Omega, \mathbf{f}_t)}$$

The preceding items are the requirements for informational consistency of endowments and consumptions. If the random variable $e^i(t)$ is not measurable on $\mathbf{f}_t$, then the endowment contains more information than trader i supposedly has, which cannot happen when trader i observes his or her endowment. Notice that because $e^i(0)$ is measurable on the null partition $\mathbf{f}_0$, it is constant on Ω, that is, nonrandom. Similar requirements of informational consistency apply to consumption processes c^i.

To avoid the constant repetition of the measurability conditions that guarantee informational consistency, the subsequent discussion uses the concept of an adapted sequence of random variables. In addition, it is convenient to introduce at this stage the concept of a predictable sequence of random variables. In the discrete model, the difference between an adapted sequence and a predictable sequence is only a matter of notation. The distinction between the two, however, will acquire substance and importance in the continuous model. The definitions are as follows.

Definition 3.7 A sequence of random variables $x(0), \ldots, x(T)$ is adapted to the information structure $\{\mathbf{f}_t\}$ if and only if each $x(t)$ is measurable on $\mathbf{f}_t$. An adapted sequence of random variables is also called an adapted process. When convenient, an adapted process is also denoted by $\{x(t, f_{tj})\}$, where f_{tj} is a set of the partition $\mathbf{f}_t$ and $x(t, f_{tj})$ is the common value of $x(t, \omega)$ for $\omega \in f_{tj}$. This latter notation emphasizes the fact that each $x(t)$ is constant on each partition set f_{tj}.

In terms of this concept, the requirement of informational consistency for endowments and consumptions is that the endowment process and the consumption process of each trader be adapted to the given information structure.

Definition 3.8 A sequence of random variables $x(1), \ldots, x(T)$ is predictable on the information structure $\{\mathbf{f}_t\}$ if and only if each $x(t)$ is measurable on $\mathbf{f}_{t-1}$. A predictable sequence of random variables is also called a predictable process.

The sequence $x(1), \ldots, x(T)$ is predictable if and only if the sequence $y(t) = x(t+1)$ for $0 \leq t \leq T-1$ is adapted. The concept of a predictable sequence of random variables is not really necessary in the discrete model, but once introduced it helps to streamline the exposition, and it will help smooth the subsequent transition to the continuous model.

Budget Sets

On each date $0 \leq t \leq T - 1$, given security prices $p_1(t), \ldots, p_N(t)$, each trader i faces constraints on consumption imposed by his or her endowment process $e^i = \{e^i(0), \ldots, e^i(T)\}$. This is again formalized in the concept of a budget set.

Definition 3.9 Given an endowment process e^i and prices $p = \{p_n(t)\}$, the budget set $B(e^i, p)$ is the subset of the consumption set X such that $c^i \in B(e^i, p)$ if and only if there is a predictable sequence of random variables $\theta_n^i(t)$, $1 \leq t \leq T$, such that for all $0 \leq t \leq T$

$$c^i(t) = e^i(t) + \sum_{n=1}^{N} [\theta_n^i(t) - \theta_n^i(t+1)]p_n(t) \tag{3.1}$$

where, by convention, $\theta_n^i(0) = \theta_n^i(T+1) = 0$ and $p_n(T) = d_n$. The sequence of random variables $\theta_n^i(t)$ is called a trading strategy.

As before, this definition says that the budget set of trader i consists of all those consumption processes that trader i can attain by acquiring at time $t - 1$ and holding until time t a portfolio of $\theta_n^i(t)$ units of security n, $1 \leq n \leq N$. The requirement that $\theta_n^i(t)$ be predictable, that is, each $\theta_n^i(t)$ be measurable on $\mathbf{f}_{t-1}$, is a condition of informational consistency saying that trader i knows at time $t - 1$ how many units of each security n he or she acquires at time $t - 1$.

Equilibrium

Looking at their budget sets for various prices, traders determine those trading strategies that optimize their preferences. Trading does not take place until prices are such that the market clears, that is, the aggregate demand for each security is zero

$$\sum_{i=1}^{I} \theta_n^i(t, \omega) = 0 \quad \text{for each} \quad \omega \in \Omega, \ 1 \leq n \leq N, \text{ and } 1 \leq t \leq T$$

This heuristic description motivates the following formal definition of a multiperiod equilibrium.

Definition 3.10 Given endowment processes e^i, a multi-period equilibrium consists of adapted prices $p_n(t)$ for all $1 \leq n \leq N$ and $0 \leq t < T$ and predictable trading strategies $\theta_n^i(t)$ for all $1 \leq i \leq I$, $1 \leq n \leq N$, and $1 \leq t \leq T$, such that the consumption process generated by e^i and θ_n^i optimizes the preferences of trader i over $B(e^i, p)$ and the market clears

$$\sum_{i=1}^{I} \theta_n^i(t,\omega) = 0 \quad \text{for each} \ \omega \in \Omega, \ 1 \le n \le N, \ \text{and} \ 1 \le t \le T$$

The adapted consumption processes $c^i = \{c^i(t)\}$ associated with the equilibrium trading strategies form the equilibrium allocation of consumption $c = \{c^i\}$.

3.4   Pareto Efficiency

Up to a point, the treatment of Pareto efficiency of equilibrium in the discrete multiperiod model follows closely the development in Section 1.3 that deals with the discrete one-period model. The departure from the analogy occurs with the count of the linearly independent securities. In the multiperiod model a condition weaker than $\text{rank}(D) = K$ may be sufficient for Pareto efficiency and other desirable properties of the equilibrium. This weaker condition may guarantee a Pareto efficient equilibrium even when the number of linearly independent securities, $\text{rank}(D)$, is substantially smaller than the number of states K.

The following three definitions and a theorem closely follow the treatment in Section 1.3.

Definition 3.11 We say that an allocation of consumption $c = \{c^i\}$, where $c^i = \{c^i(t)\}$, is feasible, if and only if each consumption process $c^i \in X$, and for all $0 \le t \le T$

$$\sum_{i=1}^{I} c^i(t) = \sum_{i=1}^{I} e^i(t)$$

Definition 3.12 A feasible allocation $c = \{c^i\}$ is Pareto efficient if and only if there is no feasible allocation $b = \{b^i\}$ such that each trader i strictly prefers b^i to c^i.

Definition 3.13 An adapted consumption process, $c = \{c(0),\ldots,c(T)\}$, is attainable at prices p if and only if there is an endowment process e such that $e(1) = e(2) = \ldots = e(T) = 0$ and $c \in B(e,p)$. The set of consumption processes that are attainable at given prices p is denoted $M(p)$.

This definition of attainable consumption processes extends the notion of attainability in the one-period model. As before, the attainability of a consumption process does not depend on its initial element $c(0)$. A consumption process is attainable if and only if it can be attained with a predictable trading strategy by a trader with zero intermediate and final endowments.

Theorem 3.1 *If every adapted consumption process is attainable, then every equilibrium allocation of consumption is Pareto efficient.*

The proof here is analogous to the proof in the discrete one-period model. Assumptions that guarantee that all adapted consumption processes are attainable, assuring completeness, are the subject of Section 3.5.

3.5   Completeness

The definition of completeness in the multiperiod model differs in one respect from the corresponding definition in the one-period model. Without intermediate trading, attainability is defined in terms of terminal consumptions only, and therefore, depends only on the terminal payouts of the securities and does not depend on prices. Stated differently, in the one-period model either all price systems guarantee the attainability of all consumptions, or for every price system there is a nonattainable consumption. By contrast, in the multiperiod model, attainability is defined in terms of consumptions on all dates except 0. Because of this involvement of intermediate consumptions, some price systems may guarantee that every consumption process is attainable, whereas other price systems may not have this property. It follows that the definition of completeness in the multiperiod model should be for a specific price system rather than for the market.

Definition 3.14 A multiperiod price system p is complete if and only if, at these prices, every adapted consumption process is attainable, that is, $M(p) = X$.

In an obvious way, Theorem 3.1 on Pareto efficiency can be restated as follows.

Theorem 3.2 *If an equilibrium price system is complete, then its associated allocation of consumption is Pareto efficient.*

Less obvious at this stage is a useful characterization of a complete price system. Consider first a preliminary definition and an example.

Definition 3.15 The splitting function ν of an information structure $\{f_t\}$ is defined for all $0 \leq t \leq T - 1$ and $\omega \in \Omega$ and assigns to each (t, ω) the number of sets of the partition f_{t+1} that are subsets of $f_t(\omega)$.

For any date $0 \leq t \leq T - 1$ and any state $\omega \in \Omega$, the partition f_t has a set $f_t(\omega)$ that contains ω. Because the partition f_{t+1} is finer than f_t, the set $f_{t+1}(\omega)$ in f_{t+1} that contains ω is a subset of $f_t(\omega)$. Now, either $f_{t+1}(\omega) = f_t(\omega)$, or f_{t+1} has other sets that are subsets of $f_t(\omega)$. The total number of these sets, including $f_{t+1}(\omega)$, is $\nu(t, \omega)$. Stated differently, f_{t+1}

descends from $\mathbf{f}_t$ by splitting some sets in $\mathbf{f}_t$. The splitting function $\nu(t, \omega)$ is the number of sets into which $\mathbf{f}_t(\omega)$ is split.

Definition 3.16 The splitting index ν of an information structure is the maximum value of the splitting function of that information structure

$$\nu = \max\left\{ \nu(t, \omega) \;\middle|\; 0 \leq t \leq T - 1 \text{ and } \omega \in \Omega \right\}$$

Even though a splitting function and a splitting index are different objects, it is convenient to denote them both by the same letter ν. The specific meaning of the letter ν will always be clear from the context in which it is used.

Example 3.5 $\Omega = \{\omega_1, \ldots, \omega_6\}$, $T = 3$

$$\mathbf{f}_1 = \{\{\omega_1, \omega_2\}, \{\omega_3, \omega_4, \omega_5, \omega_6\}\}, \quad \mathbf{f}_2 = \{\{\omega_1, \omega_2\}, \{\omega_3, \omega_4\}, \{\omega_5, \omega_6\}\}$$

and, as usual

$$\mathbf{f}_0 = \{\{\omega_1, \omega_2, \omega_3, \omega_4, \omega_5, \omega_6\}\}, \quad \mathbf{f}_3 = \{\{\omega_1\}, \{\omega_2\}, \{\omega_3\}, \{\omega_4\}, \{\omega_5\}, \{\omega_6\}\}$$

Then

$$\nu(0, \omega_k) = 2 \text{ for all } 1 \leq k \leq 6$$
$$\nu(1, \omega_k) = 1 \text{ for } 1 \leq k \leq 2, \quad \nu(1, \omega_k) = 2 \text{ for } 3 \leq k \leq 6$$
$$\nu(2, \omega_k) = 2 \text{ for all } 1 \leq k \leq 6$$

and the splitting index of this information structure is $\nu = 2$.

The splitting function of an information structure can be read off a graphic representation of the information structure. Such a graphic representation, called an information tree, has vertices and branches. There is a vertex for every date $0 \leq t \leq T$ and every set of each partition $\mathbf{f}_t$. A vertex that represents date t and partition set $\mathbf{f}_t(\omega)$ is connected with branches to all the vertices at time $t+1$ that represent the sets of the partition $\mathbf{f}_{t+1}$ that are subsets of $\mathbf{f}_t(\omega)$. The vertices at the end of the branches that originate from a common vertex are said to descend from that common vertex.

Figure 3.1 shows the tree of the information structure in Example 3.5. The number of branches at a vertex is the value of the splitting function at that vertex.

Each vertex of the information tree, taken together with the branches that originate from it, can be seen in isolation as a one-period model. Looking at it this way the reader may realize that a necessary and sufficient condition for the completeness of a price system is that the matrix of prices

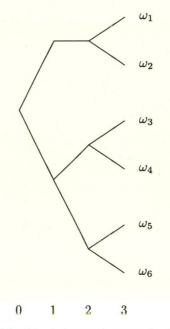

Figure 3.1: The information tree in Example 3.5.

that descend from each vertex has a rank equal to the value of the splitting function at that vertex.

To make this clear, it is helpful to continue with the preceding example by introducing securities, and working through all the details of computing the trading strategies that attain certain special consumption processes.

Example 3.6 This is a continuation of Example 3.5. Consider the two securities with the terminal payouts

$$d_1(\omega_k) = 1 \quad \text{for } k = 1, \dots, 6$$

$$d_2(\omega_k) = \begin{cases} k & \text{for } k = 1, 2, 3 \\ 6 & \text{for } k = 4 \\ 4 & \text{for } k = 5 \\ 5 & \text{for } k = 6 \end{cases}$$

Figures 3.2 and 3.3 show two adapted price systems in this market. The trees of the price systems follow the tree of the information structure

p_1	ω_1	ω_2	ω_3	ω_4	ω_5	ω_6
$t = 0$	0.729	0.729	0.729	0.729	0.729	0.729
$t = 1$	0.81	0.81	0.81	0.81	0.81	0.81
$t = 2$	0.9	0.9	0.9	0.9	0.909	0.909
$t = 3$	1	1	1	1	1	1

p_2	ω_1	ω_2	ω_3	ω_4	ω_5	ω_6
$t = 0$	2.4	2.4	2.4	2.4	2.4	2.4
$t = 1$	1.26	1.26	3.75	3.75	3.75	3.75
$t = 2$	1.4	1.4	4.2	4.2	4.2	4.2
$t = 3$	1	2	3	6	4	5

Table 3.1: Price system A in Example 3.6.

precisely because the price systems are adapted. For $t = 0, 1, 2$ the column vectors at the vertices are

$$\begin{pmatrix} p_1(t, \omega) \\ p_2(t, \omega) \end{pmatrix}$$

whereas for $t = 3$ they are

$$\begin{pmatrix} d_1(\omega) \\ d_2(\omega) \end{pmatrix}$$

The two price systems A and B differ only at the vertex $(2, \{\omega_5, \omega_6\})$. The terminal payouts of the two securities and the price systems A and B can also be presented in table format as in Tables 3.1 and 3.2. Observe that the tables show that each $p_n(t)$ is constant on the sets of the partition $\mathbf{f}_t$, that is, the price systems A and B are adapted.

It turns out that the price system A is complete, and the price system B is not complete. To see this, denote the partition sets in the given information structure

$$f_{11} = \{\omega_1, \omega_2\}, \quad f_{12} = \{\omega_3, \ldots, \omega_6\}$$
$$f_{21} = \{\omega_1, \omega_2\}, \quad f_{22} = \{\omega_3, \omega_4\}, \quad f_{23} = \{\omega_5, \omega_6\}$$

and examine first the special adapted consumption processes called elementary adapted consumption processes. There is an elementary adapted consumption process associated with each vertex of the information structure. For each $0 \leq t \leq T$ and $f \in \mathbf{f}_t$, the elementary consumption process associated with $\{t, f\}$ is denoted $\chi_{\{t, f\}}$ and is equal to zero everywhere except at the vertex $\{t, f\}$, that is

p_1	ω_1	ω_2	ω_3	ω_4	ω_5	ω_6
$t = 0$	0.729	0.729	0.729	0.729	0.729	0.729
$t = 1$	0.81	0.81	0.81	0.81	0.81	0.81
$t = 2$	0.9	0.9	0.9	0.9	0.909	0.909
$t = 3$	1	1	1	1	1	1

p_2	ω_1	ω_2	ω_3	ω_4	ω_5	ω_6
$t = 0$	2.4	2.4	2.4	2.4	2.4	2.4
$t = 1$	1.26	1.26	3.75	3.75	3.75	3.75
$t = 2$	1.4	1.4	4.2	4.2	4.242	4.242
$t = 3$	1	2	3	6	4	5

Table 3.2: Price system B in Example 3.6.

$$\chi_{\{t,\,f\}}(\tau, \omega) = \begin{cases} 1 & \text{if } \tau = t \text{ and } \omega \in f \\ 0 & \text{otherwise} \end{cases}$$

The elementary adapted consumption processes form a basis for all the adapted consumption processes. Therefore, a price system is complete if and only if all the elementary adapted consumption processes are attainable. Focusing on the price system A, consider the elementary adapted consumption process $\chi_{\{2,\,f_{22}\}}$. To attain this consumption process, a trading strategy $\theta_n(t, f)$ must satisfy

$$\theta_1(3, f_{21}) + \theta_2(3, f_{21}) = 0 \tag{3.2}$$
$$\theta_1(3, f_{21}) + 2\theta_2(3, f_{21}) = 0 \tag{3.3}$$
$$\theta_1(3, f_{22}) + 3\theta_2(3, f_{22}) = 0 \tag{3.4}$$
$$\theta_1(3, f_{22}) + 6\theta_2(3, f_{22}) = 0 \tag{3.5}$$
$$\theta_1(3, f_{23}) + 4\theta_2(3, f_{23}) = 0 \tag{3.6}$$
$$\theta_1(3, f_{23}) + 5\theta_2(3, f_{23}) = 0 \tag{3.7}$$

$$0.9[\theta_1(2, f_{11}) - \theta_1(3, f_{21})] + 1.4[\theta_2(2, f_{11}) - \theta_2(3, f_{11})] = 0 \tag{3.8}$$
$$0.9[\theta_1(2, f_{12}) - \theta_1(3, f_{22})] + 4.2[\theta_2(2, f_{12}) - \theta_2(3, f_{22})] = 1 \tag{3.9}$$
$$0.909[\theta_1(2, f_{12}) - \theta_1(3, f_{23})] + 4.2[\theta_2(2, f_{12}) - \theta_2(3, f_{23})] = 0 \tag{3.10}$$
$$0.81[\theta_1(1) - \theta_1(2, f_{11})] + 1.26[\theta_2(1) - \theta_2(2, f_{11})] = 0 \tag{3.11}$$
$$0.81[\theta_1(1) - \theta_1(2, f_{12})] + 3.75[\theta_2(1) - \theta_2(2, f_{12})] = 0 \tag{3.12}$$

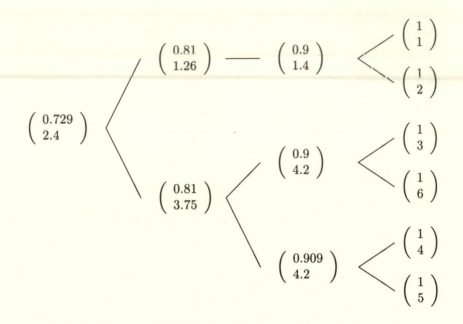

Figure 3.2: Price system A in Example 3.6.

There is one equation here for each intermediate and terminal vertex of the information tree. Equations 3.2 to 3.7 determine $\theta_n(3, f) = 0$ for all $f \in \mathbf{f}_2$. Substituting these values into Equations 3.8 to 3.10 yields

$$0.9\theta_1(2, f_{11}) + 1.4\theta_2(2, f_{11}) \;=\; 0 \qquad (3.13)$$
$$0.9\theta_1(2, f_{12}) + 4.2\theta_2(2, f_{12}) \;=\; 1 \qquad (3.14)$$
$$0.909\theta_1(2, f_{12}) + 4.2\theta_2(2, f_{12}) \;=\; 0 \qquad (3.15)$$

Equations 3.14 and 3.15 have the solution

$$\theta_1(2, f_{12}) \;=\; -111.1111$$
$$\theta_2(2, f_{12}) \;=\; 24.0476$$

Substitution of these values into Equations 3.11 and 3.12 then yields

$$0.81\theta_1(1) + 1.26\theta_2(1) \;=\; 0.81\theta_1(2, f_{11}) + 1.26\theta_2(2, f_{11}) \qquad (3.16)$$
$$0.81\theta_1(1) + 3.75\theta_2(1) \;=\; 0.1786 \qquad (3.17)$$

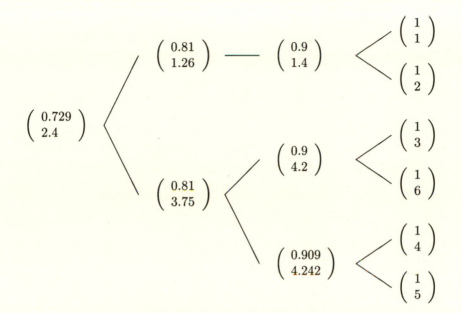

Figure 3.3: Price system B in Example 3.6.

Notice that the right side of Equation 3.16 is 0.9 times the left side of Equation 3.13, and therefore, zero. Thus

$$\theta_1(1) = -0.1116$$
$$\theta_2(1) = 0.0717$$

It does not matter what $\theta_1(2, f_{11})$ and $\theta_2(2, f_{11})$ are as long as they satisfy

$$0.9\theta_1(2, f_{11}) + 1.4\theta_2(2, f_{11}) = 0$$

Thus, given price system A, the elementary adapted consumption process $X_{\{2, f_{22}\}}$ is attainable, and its initial cost is

$$0.729\theta_1(1) + 2.4\theta_2(1) = 0.0908$$

Reviewing this solution procedure it becomes apparent that a necessary and sufficient condition for the existence of the attaining trading strategy is that each one of the systems 3.2 – 3.3, 3.4 – 3.5, 3.6 – 3.7, 3.9 – 3.10, and 3.11 – 3.12 has a solution. In this regard, problems will arise with systems like 3.14 and 3.15 only when the matrix of the system has a rank of 1. To require that this does not happen is to require that the two price vectors that descend from $(1, f_{12})$ be linearly independent. This is precisely the difference between price systems A and B. With price system B the two price vectors

$$\begin{pmatrix} 0.9 \\ 4.2 \end{pmatrix} \text{ and } \begin{pmatrix} 0.909 \\ 4.242 \end{pmatrix}$$

that descend from $(1, f_{12})$ are not linearly independent. Consequently, the following analog of Equations 3.14 and 3.15 does not have a solution

$$0.9\theta_1(2, f_{12}) + 4.2\theta_2(2, f_{12}) = 1$$
$$0.909\theta_1(2, f_{12}) + 4.242\theta_2(2, f_{12}) = 0$$

It follows that the consumption process $\chi_{\{2, f_{22}\}}$ is unattainable and the price system B is incomplete.

Are all elementary adapted consumption processes attainable at the price system A? It is clear now that this happens if and only if every set of vectors of prices or terminal payouts that descend from a common vertex is linearly independent. The price system A has this property and, therefore, the price system A is complete.

Notice that without intermediate trading the market in this example would be incomplete. In fact, there are $K = 6$ states and only rank$(D) = 2$ linearly independent securities. This is the main difference between the one period model and the multiperiod model: intermediate trading may make all adapted consumption processes attainable with fewer linearly independent securities than would be required without intermediate trading.

The generalization of this example leads to a theorem that characterizes complete multiperiod price systems. We adopt the following additional notation: for each $1 \leq t \leq T$ and $\omega \in \Omega$ denote by $D(t, \omega)$ the matrix

$$D(t, \omega) = \begin{pmatrix} p_1[t, \mathbf{f}_{t-1}^1(\omega)] & \cdots & p_N[t, \mathbf{f}_{t-1}^1(\omega)] \\ \cdots\cdots\cdots\cdots\cdots & \cdots & \cdots\cdots\cdots\cdots\cdots \\ p_1[t, \mathbf{f}_{t-1}^{\nu(t-1,\omega)}(\omega)] & \cdots & p_N[t, \mathbf{f}_{t-1}^{\nu(t-1,\omega)}(\omega)] \end{pmatrix}$$

where $\mathbf{f}_{t-1}^1(\omega), \ldots, \mathbf{f}_{t-1}^{\nu(t-1,\omega)}(\omega)$ are the sets of the partition $\mathbf{f}_t$ that are subsets of $\mathbf{f}_{t-1}(\omega)$.

Theorem 3.3 *An adapted price system $p_n(t)$ is complete if and only if for each $1 \leq t \leq T$ and $\omega \in \Omega$, rank$[D(t, \omega)] = \nu(t - 1, \omega)$.*

The proof consists of finding the trading strategies $\theta_n^{(t,\omega)}(\tau, \xi)$ that attain the elementary adapted consumption processes $\chi_{\{l,\mathbf{f}_t(\omega)\}}$, $1 \leq t \leq T$, $\omega \in \Omega$, that is, trading strategies that satisfy

$$\sum_{n=1}^{N} [\theta_n^{(t,\omega)}(\tau, \xi) - \theta_n^{(t,\omega)}(\tau+1, \xi)] p_n(\tau, \xi) = \chi_{\{t, \mathbf{f}_t(\omega)\}}(\tau, \xi)$$

$$\text{for all } 1 \leq \tau \leq T, \ \xi \in \Omega$$

The solution follows the logic of Example 3.6 and the discussion there makes it clear that $\text{rank}[D(t, \omega)] = \nu(t-1, \omega)$ is a necessary and sufficient condition for the existence of a solution.

Corollary 3.2 *A necessary condition for any adapted price system to be complete is that the number of securities be at least as large as the splitting index of the information structure, $N \geq \nu$.*

It is worth repeating here that the main difference between the one-period model and the multiperiod model is: intermediate trading may make all adapted consumption processes attainable with fewer linearly independent securities than would be required without intermediate trading.

3.6 Value Processes

In this section we introduce several new concepts and their basic properties. These concepts are used here and in subsequent chapters to characterize trading strategies that do not affect intermediate consumption, to define budget sets, and to characterize attainable consumption processes. The new concepts described here include the cumulative endowment process, the discounted cumulative endowment process, the cumulative consumption process, the discounted cumulative consumption process, the value process, the discounted value process, the gain process, and the discounted gain process. From now on we assume that one of the securities is a bond with a constant rate of interest r, that is

$$d_j = (1+r)^T$$
$$p_{jt} = (1+r)^t$$

Also, as before, $\theta_n(0) = \theta_n(T+1) = 0$ for all $1 \leq n \leq N$.

Definition 3.17 Suppose that $p = \{p_n(0), \ldots, p_n(T)\}$ is a price system, $e = \{e(0), \ldots, e(T)\}$ is an endowment process, $\theta = \{\theta_n(1), \ldots, \theta_n(T)\}$ is a trading strategy, and $c = \{c(0), \ldots, c(T)\}$ is the consumption process generated by the endowment process e and the trading strategy θ given the price system p. We define the following concepts:

1. The cumulative endowment process is the sequence of sums $\sum_{s=0}^{t} e(s)$.

2. The discounted cumulative endowment process is the sequence of sums $\sum_{s=0}^{t} \frac{e(s)}{(1+r)^s}$. This process is also called the present value of endowment.

3. The cumulative consumption process is the sequence of sums $\sum_{s=0}^{t} c(s)$.

4. The discounted cumulative consumption process is the sequence of sums $\sum_{s=0}^{t} \frac{c(s)}{(1+r)^s}$. This process is also called the present value of consumption.

5. The preconsumption value process is the sequence of sums

$$\sum_{n=1}^{N} \theta_n(t) p_n(t)$$

6. The postconsumption value process is the sequence of sums

$$\sum_{n=1}^{N} \theta_n(t+1) p_n(t)$$

7. The discounted preconsumption value process is the sequence of sums

$$\sum_{n=1}^{N} \frac{\theta_n(t) p_n(t)}{(1+r)^t}$$

8. The discounted postconsumption value process is the sequence of sums

$$\sum_{n=1}^{N} \frac{\theta_n(t+1) p_n(t)}{(1+r)^t}$$

9. The gain process is the sequence of double sums

$$\sum_{s=1}^{t} \sum_{n=1}^{N} \theta_n(s)[p_n(s) - p_n(s-1)]$$

10. The discounted gain process is the sequence of double sums

$$\sum_{s=1}^{t}\sum_{n=1}^{N}\theta_n(s)\left[\frac{p_n(s)}{(1+r)^s} - \frac{p_n(s-1)}{(1+r)^{s-1}}\right]$$

Except for the value and gain processes, all the definitions above are self-explanatory. The preconsumption value process at time t is the value of the trading strategy before consumption at time t. The postconsumption value process at time t is the value of the trading strategy after consumption at time t. To explain the definition of the gain process it is enough to notice that $\theta_n(s)[p_n(s) - p_n(s-1)]$ is the gain or loss on security n from time $s-1$ after consumption to time s before consumption. Similarly, $\theta_n(s)\left[\dfrac{p_n(s)}{(1+r)^s} - \dfrac{p_n(s-1)}{(1+r)^{s-1}}\right]$ is the change in the present value of the position in security n between the dates $s-1$ and s. By adding together Equations 3.1 for dates $0 \leq s \leq t$ we get that cumulative consumption plus value equals cumulative endowment plus gain from trade.

Theorem 3.4 *We have the following accounting identities. For all* $1 \leq t \leq T$

$$\sum_{s=0}^{t-1} c(s) + \sum_{n=1}^{N}\theta_n(t)p_n(t) = \sum_{s=0}^{t-1} e(s) + \sum_{s=1}^{t}\sum_{n=1}^{N}\theta_n(s)[p_n(s) - p_n(s-1)]$$

$$\sum_{s=0}^{t} c(s) + \sum_{n=1}^{N}\theta_n(t+1)p_n(t) = \sum_{s=0}^{t} e(s) + \sum_{s=1}^{t}\sum_{n=1}^{N}\theta_n(s)[p_n(s) - p_n(s-1)]$$

Similarly, by adding together the discounted Equations 3.1 for $0 \leq s \leq t$ we get the discounted version of the preceding theorem.

Theorem 3.5 *We have the following accounting identities. For all* $1 \leq t \leq T$

$$\sum_{s=0}^{t-1}\frac{c(s)}{(1+r)^s} + \sum_{n=1}^{N}\frac{\theta_n(t)p_n(t)}{(1+r)^t}$$

$$= \sum_{s=0}^{t-1}\frac{e(s)}{(1+r)^s} + \sum_{s=1}^{t}\sum_{n=1}^{N}\theta_n(s)\left[\frac{p_n(s)}{(1+r)^s} - \frac{p_n(s-1)}{(1+r)^{s-1}}\right]$$

$$\sum_{s=0}^{t}\frac{c(s)}{(1+r)^s} + \sum_{n=1}^{N}\frac{\theta_n(t+1)p_n(t)}{(1+r)^t}$$

$$= \sum_{s=0}^{t}\frac{e(s)}{(1+r)^s} + \sum_{s=1}^{t}\sum_{n=1}^{N}\theta_n(s)\left[\frac{p_n(s)}{(1+r)^s} - \frac{p_n(s-1)}{(1+r)^{s-1}}\right]$$

Setting $e(1) = e(2) = \ldots = e(T) = 0$ in the preceding two theorems and using the fact that $c(0) = e(0) - \sum_{n=1}^{N} \theta_n(1)p_n(0)$ we get Corollary 3.3. This corollary is central to the alternative characterization of complete price systems in Chapter 6, and also serves as the definition of attainable consumption processes in the continuous multiperiod model in Chapters 9 and 12.

Corollary 3.3 *A consumption process* $\{c(0), \ldots, c(T)\}$ *is attainable if and only if it satisfies one of the two following equivalent conditions:*

1. *For every* $2 \leq t \leq T$

$$\sum_{s=1}^{t-1} c(s) + \sum_{n=1}^{N} \theta_n(t)p_n(t)$$

$$= \sum_{n=1}^{N} \theta_n(1)p_n(0) + \sum_{s=1}^{t}\sum_{n=1}^{N} \theta_n(s)[p_n(s) - p_n(s-1)]$$

2. *For every* $2 \leq t \leq T$

$$\sum_{s=1}^{t-1} \frac{c(s)}{(1+r)^s} + \sum_{n=1}^{N} \frac{\theta_n(t)p_n(t)}{(1+r)^t}$$

$$= \sum_{n=1}^{N} \theta_n(1)p_n(0) + \sum_{s=1}^{t}\sum_{n=1}^{N} \theta_n(s)\left[\frac{p_n(s)}{(1+r)^s} - \frac{p_n(s-1)}{(1+r)^{s-1}}\right]$$

In particular, an attainable consumption process satisfies

$$\sum_{s=1}^{T} c(s) = \sum_{n=1}^{N} \theta_n(1)p_n(0) + \sum_{s=1}^{T}\sum_{n=1}^{N} \theta_n(s)[p_n(s) - p_n(s-1)]$$

and

$$\sum_{s=1}^{T} \frac{c(s)}{(1+r)^s} = \sum_{n=1}^{N} \theta_n(1)p_n(0) + \sum_{s=1}^{T}\sum_{n=1}^{N} \theta_n(s)\left[\frac{p_n(s)}{(1+r)^s} - \frac{p_n(s-1)}{(1+r)^{s-1}}\right]$$

Stated in words, the total (discounted) cumulative consumption equals initial value plus the total (discounted) gain from trade.

3.7 Self-Financing Strategies

The final two concepts of this chapter are arbitrage trading strategies and
self-financing trading strategies. The definition of an arbitrage strategy is
just a restatement of Definition 1.6: an arbitrage trading strategy gives a
trader with a zero endowment process a nonnegative, nonzero, consumption process. Because consumption preferences of traders are increasing,
arbitrage strategies do not exist in a multiperiod equilibrium. The second
concept of this section is a self-financing trading strategy. Such a strategy
involves intermediate trading but does not affect intermediate consumption.
The formal definition is as follows.

Definition 3.18 A trading strategy $\theta_n(t)$ is self-financing at prices $p_n(t)$
if and only if for all $1 \leq t \leq T - 1$

$$\sum_{n=1}^{N} [\theta_n(t) - \theta_n(t+1)]p_n(t) = 0$$

A trader who uses a self-financing trading strategy consumes at intermediate times exactly his or her intermediate endowments. A simple buy and
hold strategy is a self-financing strategy. Example 3.7 illustrates a more
complicated self-financing trading strategy.

If the terminal payout of a security can be duplicated in equilibrium by
a self-financing trading strategy

$$d_{N+1} = \sum_{n=1}^{N} \theta_n(T)d_n$$

then the initial price of that security, $p_{N+1}(0)$, must equal the initial cost
of the trading strategy

$$p_{N+1}(0) = \sum_{n=1}^{N} \theta_n(1)p_n(0)$$

Otherwise, just as in the one-period model, there exists an arbitrage strategy, contrary to the underlying equilibrium situation. In this reasoning it is
crucial that the self-financing strategy, like a security, has no intermediate
payouts.

Example 3.7 $\Omega = \{\omega_1, \ldots, \omega_8\}$, $T = 3$, and $N = 3$. Securities 1 and 2
are defined by

$$
\begin{aligned}
d_1(\omega_k) &= 1.1^3 &&= 1.331 &&\text{for all } 1 \leq k \leq 8 \\
d_2(\omega_k) &= 1.2^3 &&= 1.728 &&\text{for } k = 1 \\
d_2(\omega_k) &= 1.2^2 0.8^1 &&= 1.152 &&\text{for } k = 2, 3, 5 \\
d_2(\omega_k) &= 1.2^1 0.8^2 &&= 0.768 &&\text{for } k = 4, 6, 7 \\
d_2(\omega_k) &= 0.8^3 &&= 0.512 &&\text{for } k = 8
\end{aligned}
$$

and security 3 is a call option on security 2

$$d_3 = \max(0, d_2 - 1)$$

The evolution of information is given by the information structure

$$\mathbf{f}_1 = \{\{\omega_1, \omega_2, \omega_3, \omega_4\}, \{\omega_5, \omega_6, \omega_7, \omega_8\}\} = \{f_{11}, f_{12}\}$$
$$\mathbf{f}_2 = \{\{\omega_1, \omega_2\}, \{\omega_3, \omega_4\}, \{\omega_5, \omega_6\}, \{\omega_7, \omega_8\}\} = \{f_{21}, f_{22}, f_{23}, f_{24}\}$$

Suppose that equilibrium prices for securities 1 and 2 are as follows

$$
\begin{array}{llll}
p_1(0)   & = 1   & p_2(0)   & = 1 \\
p_1(1, f_{11}) & = 1.1 & p_2(1, f_{11}) & = 1.2 \\
p_1(1, f_{12}) & = 1.1 & p_2(1, f_{12}) & = 0.8 \\
p_1(2, f_{21}) & = 1.21 & p_2(2, f_{21}) & = 1.44 \\
p_1(2, f_{22}) & = 1.21 & p_2(2, f_{22}) & = 0.96 \\
p_1(2, f_{23}) & = 1.21 & p_2(2, f_{23}) & = 0.96 \\
p_1(2, f_{24}) & = 1.21 & p_2(2, f_{24}) & = 0.64
\end{array}
$$

It is easy to verify that every two price vectors that descend from the same vertex are independent, and that, therefore, this price system is complete. The consumption process represented by the call option is then attainable by a self-financing trading strategy that is the solution of fourteen equations. There are eight equations at $t = 3$

$$
\begin{array}{rcl}
1.331\theta_1(3, f_{21}) + 1.728\theta_2(3, f_{21}) & = & 0.728 \\
1.331\theta_1(3, f_{21}) + 1.152\theta_2(3, f_{21}) & = & 0.152 \\
1.331\theta_1(3, f_{22}) + 1.152\theta_2(3, f_{22}) & = & 0.152 \\
1.331\theta_1(3, f_{22}) + 0.768\theta_2(3, f_{22}) & = & 0 \\
1.331\theta_1(3, f_{23}) + 1.152\theta_2(3, f_{23}) & = & 0.152 \\
1.331\theta_1(3, f_{23}) + 0.768\theta_2(3, f_{23}) & = & 0 \\
1.331\theta_1(3, f_{24}) + 0.768\theta_2(3, f_{24}) & = & 0 \\
1.331\theta_1(3, f_{24}) + 0.512\theta_2(3, f_{24}) & = & 0
\end{array}
$$

with the solution

$$
\begin{array}{llll}
\theta_1(3, f_{21}) & = & -0.7513 & \quad \theta_2(3, f_{21}) = 1 \\
\theta_1(3, f_{22}) & = & -0.2284 & \quad \theta_2(3, f_{22}) = 0.3958 \\
\theta_1(3, f_{23}) & = & -0.2284 & \quad \theta_2(3, f_{23}) = 0.3958 \\
\theta_1(3, f_{24}) & = & 0   & \quad \theta_2(3, f_{24}) = 0
\end{array}
$$

When this solution is substituted into the four equations at $t = 2$, these equations become

$$1.21\theta_1(2, f_{11}) + 1.44\theta_2(2, f_{11}) = 0.5309$$
$$1.21\theta_1(2, f_{11}) + 0.96\theta_2(2, f_{11}) = 0.1036$$
$$1.21\theta_1(2, f_{12}) + 0.96\theta_2(2, f_{12}) = 0.1036$$
$$1.21\theta_1(2, f_{12}) + 0.64\theta_2(2, f_{12}) = 0$$

and the solution is

$$\theta_1(2, f_{11}) = -0.6206 \qquad \theta_2(2, f_{11}) = 0.8902$$
$$\theta_1(2, f_{12}) = -0.1713 \qquad \theta_2(2, f_{12}) = 0.3239$$

Finally, the two equations at $t = 1$ and their solutions are

$$1.1\theta_1(1) + 1.2\theta_2(1) = 0.3855$$
$$1.1\theta_1(1) + 0.8\theta_2(1) = 0.0707$$

and

$$\theta_1(1) = -0.5083, \quad \theta_2(1) = 0.7872$$

Because this self-financing trading strategy duplicates the call option, the initial equilibrium price of the option equals the initial cost of this trading strategy

$$p_3(0) = -0.5083 \times 1 + 0.7872 \times 1 = 0.2789$$

Theorems 3.4 and 3.5 imply the following alternative characterization of self-financing trading strategies.

Theorem 3.6 *Self-financing trading strategies can be characterized in the following two equivalent ways:*

1. *A trading strategy $\theta_n(t)$ is self-financing at prices $p_n(t)$ if and only if for each $1 \le t \le T$*

$$\sum_{n=1}^{N} \theta_n(t)p_n(t) = \sum_{n=1}^{N} \theta_n(1)p_n(0) + \sum_{s=1}^{t}\sum_{n=1}^{N} \theta_n(s)[p_n(s) - p_n(s-1)]$$

2. *A trading strategy $\theta_n(t)$ is self-financing at prices $p_n(t)$ if and only if for each $1 \le t \le T$*

$$\sum_{n=1}^{N} \theta_n(t)\frac{p_n(t)}{(1+r)^t}$$

$$= \sum_{n=1}^{N} \theta_n(1)p_n(0) + \sum_{s=1}^{t}\sum_{n=1}^{N} \theta_n(s)\left[\frac{p_n(s)}{(1+r)^s} - \frac{p_n(s-1)}{(1+r)^{s-1}}\right]$$

Proof. The proof follows immediately from substituting

$$c(0) = e(0) - \sum_{n=1}^{N} \theta_n(1)p_n(0)$$

and

$$c(1) = c(2) = \ldots = c(T-1) = 0$$

in Theorems 3.4 and 3.5. ∎

Problems

1. Prove that if a partition $\mathbf{g}$ is finer than a partition $\mathbf{f}$, then any union of sets of $\mathbf{f}$ is a union of sets of $\mathbf{g}$.

2. Prove that if a random variable y is measurable on $\mathbf{f}^x$, then there exists a function $h : \mathcal{R} \to \mathcal{R}$ such that for all $\omega \in \Omega$

$$y(\omega) = h[x(\omega)]$$

3. The meet of the partitions $\mathbf{f}^1, \ldots, \mathbf{f}^I$ is the finest partition that is coarser than each $\mathbf{f}^i$. The join of the partitions $\mathbf{f}^1, \ldots, \mathbf{f}^I$ is the coarsest partition that is finer than each $\mathbf{f}^i$. The meet of partitions is denoted $\bigwedge_{i=1}^{I} \mathbf{f}^i$, and the join is denoted $\bigvee_{i=1}^{I} \mathbf{f}^i$.

   (a) If $\mathbf{f}^1, \ldots, \mathbf{f}^I$ represent the information of the different traders, what do the meet and the join represent?

   (b) For

$$\mathbf{f}^1 = \{\{\omega_1\}, \{\omega_2, \omega_3, \omega_4\}, \{\omega_5, \omega_6, \omega_7\}\}$$

$$\mathbf{f}^2 = \{\{\omega_1, \omega_2, \omega_3\}, \{\omega_4\}, \{\omega_5, \omega_6\}, \{\omega_7\}\}$$

   compute the meet $\mathbf{f}^1 \wedge \mathbf{f}^2$ and the join $\mathbf{f}^1 \vee \mathbf{f}^2$.

4. Consider the following market: $K = 5$, $N = 4$, $T = 2$

$$f_{11} = \{\omega_1, \omega_2\}, \ f_{12} = \{\omega_3, \omega_4\}, \ f_{13} = \{\omega_5\}$$

   matrix of terminal payouts

$$D = \begin{pmatrix} 2 & 4 & 5 & 1 \\ 1 & 1 & 2 & 1 \\ 3 & 2 & 4 & 1 \\ 4 & 5 & 7 & 1 \\ 5 & 6 & 10 & 1 \end{pmatrix}$$

and prices

$$p_1(0) = 3.6, \ p_2(0) = 4, \ p_3(0) = 6.6, \ p_4(0) = 1$$
$$p_1(1, f_{11}) = 1.5, \ p_2(1, f_{11}) = 2.5, \ p_3(1, f_{11}) = 3.5, \ p_4(1, f_{11}) = 1$$
$$p_1(1, f_{12}) = 3.25, \ p_2(1, f_{12}) = 2.75, \ p_3(1, f_{12}) = 4.75, \ p_4(1, f_{12}) = 1$$
$$p_1(1, f_{13}) = 5, \ p_2(1, f_{13}) = 6, \ p_3(1, f_{13}) = 10, \ p_4(1, f_{13}) = 1$$

(a) Is this an equilibrium price system?

(b) Is this a complete price system?

(c) Compute the initial equilibrium price of the following three securities

    i. A call option on security 1 with an exercise price $a = 3.50$.

    ii. A down-and-under call option on security 1 with an exercise price $a = 3.50$. This is a call option with an extra provision — if the price of security 1 ever drops below the exercise price, then the option becomes worthless.

    iii. A convertible security that in each state pays at the terminal time the largest payout of the securities 1 — 4 in that state.

Notes

The general outline of the discrete multiperiod model appears in [4] and [19]. Example 3.6 and the characterization of completeness in Theorem 3.3 are due to [53]. The characterization of self-financing trading strategies in Theorem 3.6 is an adaptation to discrete time of a formula in [61]. The existence of equilibrium in this model is established by [29].

Chapter 4

Multiperiod Equilibrium Price Measures

4.1   Equilibrium Price Measures

An equilibrium price measure in the multiperiod model is an extension of the same concept in the one-period model. As before, equilibrium price measures are derived from the given price system and constitute artificial probability measures. An equilibrium price measure exists if and only if the given price system does not permit arbitrage strategies. If an equilibrium price measure exists, then it is unique if and only if the given price system is complete. Relative to an equilibrium price measure all prices are conditional expected terminal payouts, given available information, discounted at the rate of interest.

The construction of equilibrium price measures in the multiperiod model is a natural modification of the one-period procedure. The multiperiod model is broken into a collection of one-period models, and an equilibrium price measure is defined for each one-period model in this collection. The multiperiod equilibrium price measure is then defined as a product of the one-period measures, so that the one-period measures become conditional values of this multiperiod measure. Unless stated otherwise, we assume that the bond is security number 1, that is, $p_1(t) = (1 + r)^t$ for $0 \leq t \leq T - 1$ and $d_1 = (1 + r)^T$. Also, as in the preceding chapters, consider prices and trading strategies as vectors in the appropriate real linear spaces, and denote transposed vectors and matrices with a prime. Specifically, $p(t)$ is the N-dimensional vector of security prices at time t

$$p(t) = \begin{pmatrix} p_1(t) \\ \ldots \\ p_N(t) \end{pmatrix}$$

74

$D(t, \omega)$ is the matrix

$$
D(t,\omega) = \begin{pmatrix} p_1[t, \mathbf{f}_t^1 \ _1(\omega)] & \cdots & p_N[t, \mathbf{f}_{t-1}^1(\omega)] \\ \cdots\cdots\cdots\cdots & \cdots & \cdots\cdots\cdots\cdots \\ p_1[t, \mathbf{f}_{t-1}^{\nu(t-1,\omega)}(\omega)] & \cdots & p_N[t, \mathbf{f}_{t-1}^{\nu(t-1,\omega)}(\omega)] \end{pmatrix}
$$

and $Q[t, \mathcal{S}_{t-1}(\omega)]$ is a vector (of unknowns) of dimension $\nu(t-1,\omega)$ whose elements are associated with the partition sets $\mathbf{f}_{t-1}^1(\omega), \ldots, \mathbf{f}_{t-1}^{\nu(t-1,\omega)}(\omega)$

$$
Q[t, \mathcal{S}_{t-1}(\omega)] = \begin{pmatrix} Q[t, \mathbf{f}_{t-1}^1(\omega)] \\ \cdots\cdots\cdots\cdots \\ Q[t, \mathbf{f}_{t-1}^{\nu(t-1,\omega)}(\omega)] \end{pmatrix}
$$

The symbol $\mathcal{S}_{t-1}(\omega)$ denotes the split of $\mathbf{f}_{t-1}(\omega)$, that is, the set of sets of the partition $\mathbf{f}_t$ that are subsets of $\mathbf{f}_{t-1}(\omega)$

$$
\mathcal{S}_{t-1}(\omega) = \{\mathbf{f}_{t-1}^1(\omega), \ldots, \mathbf{f}_{t-1}^{\nu(t-1,\omega)}(\omega)\}
$$

Definition 4.1 If for a given price system p and for every $1 \le t \le T$ the system of linear equations

$$
D'(t, \omega)Q[t, \mathcal{S}_{t-1}(\omega)] = (1 + r)p(t - 1, \omega)
$$

has positive solutions, $Q[t, \mathbf{f}_{t-1}^j(\omega)] > 0$ for all $1 \le j \le \nu(t - 1, \omega)$, then

$$
Q(\omega) = \prod_{t=1}^{T} Q[t, \mathbf{f}_t(\omega)]
$$

is called an equilibrium price measure for the price system p.

In the preceding definition, notice that the set $\mathbf{f}_t(\omega)$ is one of the sets $\mathbf{f}_{t-1}^j(\omega)$.

Example 4.1 The number of states is $K = 7$, the terminal date is $T = 3$, the number of securities is $N = 3$, and the information structure is

$$
\mathbf{f}_1 = \{\{\omega_1, \omega_2, \omega_3, \omega_4, \omega_5\}, \{\omega_6, \omega_7\}\} = \{f_{11}, f_{12}\}
$$
$$
\mathbf{f}_2 = \{\{\omega_1, \omega_2, \omega_3\}, \{\omega_4, \omega_5\}, \{\omega_6, \omega_7\}\} = \{f_{21}, f_{22}, f_{23}\}
$$

The terminal payouts of the three securities are

$$
D = \begin{pmatrix} 1.331 & 60 & 120 \\ 1.331 & 30 & 48 \\ 1.331 & 20 & 60 \\ 1.331 & 40 & 50 \\ 1.331 & 40 & 40 \\ 1.331 & 21 & 24 \\ 1.331 & 24 & 21 \end{pmatrix}
$$

and their prices are

$$p_1(0) = 1, \quad p_2(0) = 21.64, \quad p_3(0) = 25.02$$
$$p_1(1, f_{11}) = 1.1, \quad p_2(1, f_{11}) = 30.99, \quad p_3(1, f_{11}) = 41.53$$
$$p_1(1, f_{12}) = 1.1, \quad p_2(1, f_{12}) = 19.01, \quad p_3(1, f_{12}) = 18.18$$
$$p_1(2, f_{21}) = 1.21, \quad p_2(2, f_{21}) = 27.27, \quad p_3(2, f_{21}) = 60$$
$$p_1(2, f_{22}) = 1.21, \quad p_2(2, f_{22}) = 36.36, \quad p_3(2, f_{22}) = 40.91$$
$$p_1(2, f_{23}) = 1.21, \quad p_2(2, f_{23}) = 20.91, \quad p_3(2, f_{23}) = 20$$

Security 1 is a bond and the rate of interest is $r = 10$ percent. The split of the partition set $f_0(\omega)$ is $S_0(\omega) = \{f_{11}, f_{12}\}$ for all $\omega \in \Omega$. For $\omega \in f_{11}$ the split of $f_1(\omega)$ is $S_1(\omega) = \{f_{21}, f_{22}\}$, and for $\omega \in f_{12}$ we have $S_1(\omega) = \{f_{23}\}$. The matrix $D(1, \omega)$ is the same for all ω

$$D(1, \omega) = \begin{pmatrix} 1.1 & 30.99 & 41.53 \\ 1.1 & 19.01 & 18.18 \end{pmatrix}$$

and the system of equations for

$$Q[1, S_0(\omega)] = \begin{pmatrix} Q(1, f_{11}) \\ Q(1, f_{12}) \end{pmatrix}$$

is

$$\begin{pmatrix} 1.10 & 1.10 \\ 30.99 & 19.01 \\ 41.53 & 18.18 \end{pmatrix} \begin{pmatrix} Q(1, f_{11}) \\ Q(1, f_{12}) \end{pmatrix} = 1.1 \begin{pmatrix} 1.00 \\ 21.64 \\ 25.02 \end{pmatrix}$$

with the solution

$$Q(1, f_{11}) = \frac{2}{5}, \quad Q(1, f_{12}) = \frac{3}{5}$$

Proceeding with the solution for $t = 2$ and $t = 3$ yields

$$Q(2, f_{21}) = \tfrac{1}{4}, \quad Q(2, f_{22}) = \tfrac{3}{4}$$
$$Q(2, f_{23}) = 1$$
$$Q(3, \omega_1) = \tfrac{1}{6}, \quad Q(3, \omega_2) = \tfrac{1}{3}, \quad Q(3, \omega_3) = \tfrac{1}{2}$$
$$Q(3, \omega_4) = \tfrac{1}{2}, \quad Q(3, \omega_5) = \tfrac{1}{2}$$
$$Q(3, \omega_6) = \tfrac{1}{3}, \quad Q(3, \omega_7) = \tfrac{2}{3}$$

Because all the solutions are positive, an equilibrium price measure exists and is equal to

$$
\begin{aligned}
Q(\omega_1) &= \tfrac{2}{5} \times \tfrac{1}{4} \times \tfrac{1}{6} &= \tfrac{1}{60} \\
Q(\omega_2) &= \tfrac{2}{5} \times \tfrac{1}{4} \times \tfrac{1}{3} &= \tfrac{1}{30} \\
Q(\omega_3) &= \tfrac{2}{5} \times \tfrac{1}{4} \times \tfrac{1}{2} &= \tfrac{1}{20} \\
Q(\omega_4) &= \tfrac{2}{5} \times \tfrac{3}{4} \times \tfrac{1}{2} &= \tfrac{3}{20} \\
Q(\omega_5) &= \tfrac{2}{5} \times \tfrac{3}{4} \times \tfrac{1}{2} &= \tfrac{3}{20} \\
Q(\omega_6) &= \tfrac{3}{5} \times 1 \times \tfrac{1}{3} &= \tfrac{1}{5} \\
Q(\omega_7) &= \tfrac{3}{5} \times 1 \times \tfrac{2}{3} &= \tfrac{2}{5}
\end{aligned}
$$

Notice that $\displaystyle\sum_{k=1}^{7} Q(\omega_k) = 1.$

As in the one-period model, all equilibrium price measures are artificial probability measures on the sample space Ω. Because the rate of interest at which the bond appreciates is constant, the first equation in each one of the linear systems in Definition 4.1 is

$$
\sum_{j=1}^{\nu(t-1,\omega)} Q[t, \mathbf{f}_{t-1}^{j}(\omega)] = 1
$$

and therefore, also $\displaystyle\sum_{k=1}^{K} Q(\omega_k) = 1$. To verify that an equilibrium price measure is a product of conditional probabilities, formalize the definition of conditional probability as follows.

Definition 4.2 *For an event A on the probability space (Ω, P) and a partition $\mathbf{f}$ of Ω, the conditional probability $P(A|\mathbf{f})$ is the random variable*

$$
P(A|\mathbf{f})(\omega) = \frac{P[A \cap \mathbf{f}(\omega)]}{P[\mathbf{f}(\omega)]}
$$

Notice that the conditional probability is measurable on $\mathbf{f}$ and that this concept of conditional probability defines simultaneously the conditional probabilities $P(A|f_j)$ for all the sets f_j of the partition $\mathbf{f}$.

Example 4.2 $\Omega = \{\omega_1, \ldots, \omega_5\}$, $P(\omega_k) = \tfrac{1}{5}$ for $k = 1, \ldots, 5$

$\mathbf{f} = \{\{\omega_1, \omega_2, \omega_3, \omega_5\}, \{\omega_4\}\} = \{f_1, f_2\}$, and $A = \{\omega_4, \omega_5\}$. Then

$$
P(A|\mathbf{f})(\omega) =
\begin{cases}
\dfrac{P(\omega_5)}{P(f_1)} = \tfrac{1}{4} & \text{if } \omega \in f_1 \\[2ex]
\dfrac{P(\omega_4)}{P(f_2)} = 1 & \text{if } \omega = \omega_4
\end{cases}
$$

The next theorem confirms that a multiperiod equilibrium price measure is a product of conditional probabilities.

Theorem 4.1 *For all* $1 \leq t \leq T$ *and* $\omega \in \Omega$

$$Q[\mathbf{f}_t(\omega)|\mathbf{f}_{t-1}](\omega) = Q[t, \mathbf{f}_t(\omega)]$$

Proof. From Definition 4.1

$$Q[\mathbf{f}_t(\omega)|\mathbf{f}_{t-1}](\omega) = \frac{\displaystyle\sum_{\xi \in \mathbf{f}_t(\omega)} \prod_{s=1}^{T} Q[s, \mathbf{f}_s(\xi)]}{\displaystyle\sum_{\eta \in \mathbf{f}_{t-1}(\omega)} \prod_{s=1}^{T} Q[s, \mathbf{f}_s(\eta)]}$$

$$= \frac{\displaystyle\sum_{\xi \in \mathbf{f}_t(\omega)} \prod_{s=1}^{t} Q[s, \mathbf{f}_s(\xi)]}{\displaystyle\sum_{\eta \in \mathbf{f}_{t-1}(\omega)} \prod_{s=1}^{t-1} Q[s, \mathbf{f}_s(\eta)]}$$

Now, for $1 \leq s \leq t-1$, we have $\mathbf{f}_s(\xi) = \mathbf{f}_s(\eta) = \mathbf{f}_s(\omega)$ and, therefore, all but one term cancel in the preceding ratio yielding $Q[t, \mathbf{f}_t(\omega)]$. ∎

The important properties of equilibrium price measures in the one-period model carry over to the multiperiod model. To verify this keep in mind that each vertex of the information tree, taken together with the branches that originate from it, can be seen in isolation as a one-period model. Definition 4.1 says that an equilibrium price measure exists for the multiperiod market if and only if it exists for each one of the isolated one-period markets. This implies the following analogs of Theorem 2.1, Corollary 2.1, and Theorem 2.2.

Theorem 4.2 *An equilibrium price measure exists if and only if the given price system p does not permit arbitrage strategies.*

Corollary 4.1 *An equilibrium price measure exists if and only if the given price system p is an equilibrium price system for some population of traders with continuous, increasing, and convex preferences.*

Theorem 4.3 *If an equilibrium price measure exists, then it is unique if and only if the given price system is complete.*

Example 4.3 $K = 3$, $N = 3$, and $T = 2$. The information structure of traders is

$$f_{11} = \{\omega_1, \omega_2\}, \ f_{12} = \{\omega_3\}$$

Security 3 is a bond, and $r = 0$. The terminal payouts are

$$D = \begin{pmatrix} 32 & 22 & 10 \\ 16 & 12 & 10 \\ 12 & 14 & 10 \end{pmatrix}$$

and the prices are

$$p_1(0) = 16, \ p_2(0) = 15, \ p_3(0) = 10$$
$$p_1(1, f_{11}) = 24, \ p_2(1, f_{11}) = 16, \ p_3(1, f_{11}) = 10$$
$$p_1(1, f_{12}) = 12, \ p_2(1, f_{12}) = 14, \ p_3(1, f_{12}) = 10$$

The given price system is not an equilibrium price system and every consumption process is attainable. Indeed, the trading strategy

$$\theta_1(2, f_{11}) = -\tfrac{3}{8}, \ \theta_2(2, f_{11}) = \tfrac{1}{2}, \ \theta_3(2, f_{11}) = \tfrac{1}{10}$$
$$\text{all other } \theta_n(t, \omega) = 0$$

is an arbitrage strategy because

$$-\tfrac{3}{8} \times 24 + \tfrac{1}{2} \times 16 + \tfrac{1}{10} \times 10 = 0$$
$$-\tfrac{3}{8} \times 32 + \tfrac{1}{2} \times 22 + \tfrac{1}{10} \times 10 = 0$$
$$-\tfrac{3}{8} \times 16 + \tfrac{1}{2} \times 12 + \tfrac{1}{10} \times 10 = 1$$

Every consumption process is attainable because the two price vectors at time 1 are linearly independent and the three payout vectors at time 2 are linearly independent. An equilibrium price measure does not exist because the system of equations

$$32Q(2, \omega_1) + 16Q(2, \omega_2) = 24$$
$$22Q(2, \omega_1) + 12Q(2, \omega_2) = 16$$
$$10Q(2, \omega_1) + 10Q(2, \omega_2) = 10$$

does not have a solution.

Example 4.4 In Example 4.3 change $p_2(1, f_{11})$ from 16 to 17. Then, an equilibrium price measure exists and is unique. To verify this, examine the linear systems of equations

$$24Q(1, f_{11}) + 12Q(1, f_{12}) = 16$$
$$17Q(1, f_{11}) + 14Q(1, f_{12}) = 15$$
$$10Q(1, f_{11}) + 10Q(1, f_{12}) = 10$$

$$32Q(2, \omega_1) + 16Q(2, \omega_2) = 24$$
$$22Q(2, \omega_1) + 12Q(2, \omega_2) = 17$$
$$10Q(2, \omega_1) + 10Q(2, \omega_3) = 10$$

$$12Q(2, \omega_3) = 12$$
$$14Q(2, \omega_3) = 14$$
$$10Q(2, \omega_3) = 10$$

The unique solution of these systems is

$$Q(1, f_{11}) = \tfrac{1}{3}, \ Q(1, f_{12}) = \tfrac{2}{3}$$
$$Q(2, \omega_1) = \tfrac{1}{2}, \ Q(2, \omega_2) = \tfrac{1}{2}$$
$$Q(2, \omega_3) = 1$$

Therefore

$$Q(\omega_1) = \tfrac{1}{3} \times \tfrac{1}{2} = \tfrac{1}{6}$$
$$Q(\omega_2) = \tfrac{1}{3} \times \tfrac{1}{2} = \tfrac{1}{6}$$
$$Q(\omega_3) = \tfrac{2}{3} \times 1 = \tfrac{2}{3}$$

The equilibrium price measure exists and is unique, the prices are equilibrium prices for some population of traders, there are no arbitrage opportunities, and every adapted consumption process is attainable.

Relative to an equilibrium price measure, all prices are discounted expected terminal payouts conditional on available information. These conditional expectations are defined as follows.

Definition 4.3 For a random variable x on a probability space (Ω, P) and a partition $\mathbf{f}$ of Ω, the conditional expectation $E_P(x|\mathbf{f})$ is the random variable

$$E_P(x|\mathbf{f})(\omega) = \frac{\displaystyle\sum_{\xi \in \mathbf{f}(\omega)} P(\xi) x(\xi)}{\displaystyle\sum_{\xi \in \mathbf{f}(\omega)} P(\xi)}$$

Notice that the conditional expectation is measurable on $\mathbf{f}$.

Example 4.5 $\Omega = \{\omega_1, \ldots, \omega_5\}$, $P(\omega_k) = \frac{1}{5}$ for $k = 1, \ldots, 5$

$$\mathbf{f} = \{\{\omega_1, \omega_2, \omega_3, \omega_5\}, \{\omega_4\}\} = \{f_1, f_2\}$$

$$x(\omega_1) = 1, \ x(\omega_2) = 1, \ x(\omega_3) = 2, \ x(\omega_4) = 3, \ x(\omega_5) = 2$$

Then

$$E_P(x|\mathbf{f})(\omega_1) = \frac{\frac{1+1+2+2}{5}}{\frac{4}{5}} = \frac{3}{2}$$

$$E_P(x|\mathbf{f})(\omega_4) = \frac{\frac{3}{5}}{\frac{1}{5}} = 3$$

The value of $E_P(x|\mathbf{f})(\omega_k)$ for $k = 2, 3, 5$ is the same as $E_P(x|\mathbf{f})(\omega_1)$.

The next theorem says that averaging with respect to a fine partition and then again with respect to a coarse partition is the same as averaging just once with respect to the coarse partition.

Theorem 4.4 (The Law of Iterated Expectations) *If a partition $\mathbf{f}$ is coarser than a partition $\mathbf{g}$, then for any random variable x*

$$E_P[E_P(x|\mathbf{g})|\mathbf{f}] = E_P(x|\mathbf{f})$$

The law of iterated expectations is frequently used in the subsequent analysis. The proof of this theorem is left to the reader (Problem 2.) With this preparation the representation of prices by the equilibrium price measure can be stated as follows.

Theorem 4.5 *If Q is an equilibrium price measure, then for each $1 \leq n \leq N$ and $0 \leq t \leq T$*

$$p_n(t) = \frac{E_Q(d_n|\mathbf{f}_t)}{(1+r)^{T-t}}$$

Proof. To prove the theorem notice that Definition 4.1 and Theorem 4.1 together imply that

$$p_n(t) = \frac{E_Q[p_n(t+1)|\mathbf{f}_t]}{1+r}$$

and

$$p_n(t+1) = \frac{E_Q[p_n(t+2)|\mathbf{f}_{t+1}]}{1+r}$$

Substituting the second equation into the first and using the fact that $\mathbf{f}_t$ is coarser than $\mathbf{f}_{t+1}$ and the law of iterated expectations yields

$$p_n(t) = \frac{E_Q[p_n(t+2)|\mathbf{f}_t]}{(1+r)^2}$$

This procedure, when continued, produces the assertion of the theorem. ∎

The proof of Theorem 4.5 suggests an additional characterization of equilibrium prices in terms of an equilibrium price measure Q. First a definition.

Definition 4.4 A sequence of random variables $x(t)$ for $0 \le t \le T$ is a martingale on the information structure $\{\mathbf{f}_t\}$ and a probability measure P if and only if for all $0 \le s \le t \le T$

$$E_P[x(t)|\mathbf{f}_s] = x(s)$$

The definition says that at any time and state the expectation of the future value of x is its current value. Notice that, by definition, a martingale on the information structure $\{\mathbf{f}_t\}$ is adapted to $\{\mathbf{f}_t\}$.

Theorem 4.6 *For each security the sequence of its discounted prices is a Q-martingale, that is, for all $0 \le s \le t \le T$*

$$E_Q\left[\frac{p_n(t)}{(1+r)^t}\Big|\mathbf{f}_s\right] = \frac{p_n(s)}{(1+r)^s}$$

Proof. Indeed

$$E_Q\left[\frac{p_n(t)}{(1+r)^t}\Big|\mathbf{f}_s\right] = \frac{E_Q[E_Q(d_n|\mathbf{f}_t)|\mathbf{f}_s]}{(1+r)^T}$$

$$= \frac{E_Q(d_n|\mathbf{f}_s)}{(1+r)^T} = \frac{p_n(s)}{(1+r)^s}$$

The second equality above follows from fact that $\mathbf{f}_s$ is coarser than $\mathbf{f}_t$. ∎

The next theorem is a consequence of Theorem 4.6, Corollary 3.3, and Theorem 3.6.

Theorem 4.7 *In general, the sum of the discounted cumulative consumption process and the preconsumption discounted value process*

$$\sum_{s=0}^{t-1}\frac{c(s)}{(1+r)^s} + \frac{\sum_{n=1}^{N}\theta_n(t)p_n(t)}{(1+r)^t}$$

for $1 \leq t \leq T$ is a Q-martingale. If the trading strategy θ is self-financing, then the discounted value process

$$\frac{\sum_{n=1}^{N} \theta_n(t)p_n(t)}{(1+r)^t}$$

for $1 \leq t \leq T$ is a Q-martingale.

Reviewing the list of recent results suggests that, paralleling the one-period model, any equilibrium price measure Q is a risk-adjusted probability measure in the multiperiod model. For the actual probability measure P, the representation of prices as discounted expected terminal payouts and the martingale property would hold in a market populated by risk-neutral traders. The risk-adjusting property of Q makes this representation true with respect to Q even when traders are not risk-neutral. In addition, Theorem 4.7 tells us that, after adjustment for risk, the expected rate of return on any trading strategy is exactly the riskless rate of interest.

4.2   The Price Functional

An equilibrium price measure produces a very simple representation of the price functional. As in the one-period model, the price functional is defined as the initial cost of an attainable consumption process.

Definition 4.5 The price functional $\phi : M(p) \rightarrow \mathcal{R}$ is such that for every $c \in M(p)$

$$\phi(c) = c(0) + \sum_{n=1}^{N} \theta_n(1)p_n(0)$$

for any trading strategy $\theta_n(t)$ such that for all $1 \leq t \leq T$

$$\sum_{n=1}^{N} [\theta_n(t) - \theta_n(t+1)]p_n(t) = c(t)$$

where, as usual, $\theta_n(T+1) = 0$ and $p_n(T) = d_n$.

As in the one-period model, the set of attainable consumption processes $M(p)$ is a linear space of real vectors and ϕ is a linear functional on $M(p)$. The price functional has the following representation in terms of any equilibrium price measure Q.

Theorem 4.8 *If the price system p does not permit arbitrage strategies, then for every $c \in M(p)$ and every equilibrium price measure Q*

$$\phi(c) = \sum_{t=0}^{T} \frac{E_Q[c(t)]}{(1+r)^t}$$

Proof. From the definition of the price functional and Theorem 4.5

$$\frac{c(t)}{(1+r)^t} = \frac{1}{(1+r)^T} \sum_{n=1}^{N} [\theta_n(t) - \theta_n(t+1)] E_Q(d_n | \mathbf{f}_t)$$

$$= \frac{1}{(1+r)^T} \sum_{n=1}^{N} E_Q\{[\theta_n(t) - \theta_n(t+1)]d_n | \mathbf{f}_t]\}$$

because $\theta_n(t)$ is predictable. Taking expectations of both sides in the preceding equation and summing over t produces

$$\sum_{t=0}^{T} \frac{E_Q[c(t)]}{(1+r)^t} = c(0) + \sum_{n=1}^{N} \theta_n(1) \frac{E_Q(d_n)}{(1+r)^T} = c(0) + \sum_{n=1}^{N} \theta_n(1)p_n(0)$$

and the theorem follows. ∎

The representation of the price functional in terms of an equilibrium price measure simplifies the calculation of equilibrium prices of various attainable securities. For example, when the price system is complete, the equilibrium price measure Q is unique. For any security $1 \leq n \leq N$ and any positive number a the call option on security n with the exercise price a is attainable and its initial equilibrium price

$$(1+r)^{-T} E_Q[\max(0, d_n - a)]$$

resembles a risk-neutral valuation formula.

Example 4.6 In the market of Example 4.4 consider securities 4, 5, and 6 with the terminal payouts

$$d_4 = \max(0, d_2 - 13)$$
$$d_5 = \max(d_1, d_2)$$
$$d_6 = \max(p_2, d_2)$$

Security 4 is a call option on security 2, security 5 is a convertible security that allows a switch between securities 1 and 2, and security 6 delivers the outcome of the advice "sell at the high" for security 2. Notice that, unlike securities 4 and 5, the terminal payout of security 6 depends on the price history of security 2 and not just on its terminal payout.

The explicit payouts of securities 4, 5, and 6 are

$$d_4(\omega_1) = 9, \ d_4(\omega_2) = 0, \ d_4(\omega_3) = 1$$
$$d_5(\omega_1) = 32, \ d_5(\omega_2) = 16, \ d_5(\omega_3) = 14$$
$$d_6(\omega_1) = 22, \ d_6(\omega_2) = 17, \ d_6(\omega_3) = 14$$

The representation of the price functional in terms of the equilibrium price measure, as computed in Example 4.4, determines the initial equilibrium prices of these three securities as follows

$$p_4(0) = \tfrac{1}{6} \times 9 + \tfrac{1}{6} \times 0 + \tfrac{2}{3} \times 1 = 2\tfrac{1}{6}$$
$$p_5(0) = \tfrac{1}{6} \times 32 + \tfrac{1}{6} \times 16 + \tfrac{2}{3} \times 14 = 17\tfrac{1}{3}$$
$$p_6(0) = \tfrac{1}{6} \times 22 + \tfrac{1}{6} \times 17 + \tfrac{2}{3} \times 14 = 15\tfrac{5}{6}$$

Theorem 4.8 defines a positive extension of the price functional from its domain, $M(p)$, to the whole consumption set X. Conversely, any positive extension ψ of the price functional ϕ defines an equilibrium price measure Q

$$Q(\omega) = (1 + r)^T \psi \left(\chi_{\{T, \omega\}} \right)$$

For each state ω, the positive number $Q(\omega)$ is the future value of the initial cost of consuming exactly nothing until the terminal time T, and then consuming one unit if and only if the prevailing state is ω. As in the one-period model, there is a one-to-one correspondence between equilibrium price measures Q and positive extensions ψ of the price functional ϕ.

Theorem 4.9 *The formulas:*

1. $\psi(c) = \displaystyle\sum_{t=0}^{T} \frac{E_Q[c(t)]}{(1+r)^t}$

2. $Q(\omega) = (1 + r)^T \psi \left(\chi_{\{T, \omega\}} \right)$

establish a one-to-one correspondence between equilibrium price measures Q and positive extensions $\psi : \ X \to \mathcal{R}$ of the price functional.

Proof. Theorem 4.8 implies that ψ defined by item 1 is an extension of the price functional ϕ. That this ψ is positive follows immediately from the fact that the expected value of a nonnegative random variable is nonnegative and that if, in addition, this random variable is positive with positive probability, then the expected value is positive.

Conversely, each $Q(\omega)$ defined by item 2 is positive because ψ is a positive functional. Second, Q is a probability measure on Ω because

$$\sum_{k=1}^{K} Q(\omega) = (1+r)^{T}\psi\left(\chi_{\{T,\omega\}}\right) = (1+r)^{T}\frac{1}{(1+r)^{T}} = 1$$

Third, discounted prices are martingales relative to this probability measure Q. To show this, fix a security n other than the bond, that is, $n \neq 1$, and any $0 \leq s \leq t \leq T$ and $\omega \in \Omega$. Let $\theta_n(t)$ be the following trading strategy: do not trade until time s, then buy one unit of security n if and only if the prevailing state is indistinguishable from ω, financing the purchase with the sale of an appropriate amount of security 1. Hold this position until time t, then liquidate it and invest the proceeds in security 1, and hold until the terminal time T. Formally

$$\theta_n(s+\tau,\xi) = 1$$
$$\theta_1(s+\tau,\xi) = -\frac{p_n(s,\xi)}{(1+r)^s}$$

for $\zeta \in \mathbf{f}_s(\omega)$, and $1 \leq r \leq t - s$, and

$$\theta_1(t+\tau,\xi) = \frac{p_n(t,\xi)}{(1+r)^t} - \frac{p_n(s,\xi)}{(1+r)^s}$$

for $\xi \in \mathbf{f}_s(\omega)$ and $1 \leq \tau \leq T - t$. All other $\theta_m(u,\xi) = 0$.

This trading strategy is self-financing, and at time T it produces the terminal consumption

$$c(T,\xi) = \left[\frac{p_n(t,\xi)}{(1+r)^t} - \frac{p_n(s,\xi)}{(1+r)^s}\right](1+r)^{T}\chi_{\{\mathbf{f}_s(\omega)\}}(\xi)$$

The initial cost of this trading strategy is zero, therefore $\psi[0,\ldots,c(T)] = 0$. From the definition of Q it follows immediately that

$$E_Q[c(T)] = (1+r)^{T}\psi[0,\ldots,c(T)]$$

that is, $E_Q[c(T)] = 0$. In other words

$$E_Q\left[\frac{p_n(t)}{(1+r)^t}\chi_{\{\mathbf{f}_s(\omega)\}}\right] = E_Q\left[\frac{p_n(s)}{(1+r)^s}\chi_{\{\mathbf{f}_s(\omega)\}}\right]$$

Using the definition of expectation, the preceding equation can be written

$$\sum_{\xi \in \mathbf{f}_s(\omega)} Q(\xi) \frac{p_n(t, \xi)}{(1+r)^t} = \sum_{\xi \in \mathbf{f}_s(\omega)} Q(\xi) \frac{p_n(s, \xi)}{(1+r)^s}$$

and, because $p_n(s)$ is constant on the set $\mathbf{f}_s(\omega)$, the preceding equation implies that

$$\frac{p_n(s, \omega)}{(1+r)^s} = \frac{\displaystyle\sum_{\xi \in \mathbf{f}_s(\omega)} Q(\xi) \frac{p_n(t, \xi)}{(1+r)^t}}{\displaystyle\sum_{\xi \in \mathbf{f}_s(\omega)} Q(\xi)} = E_Q \left[\frac{p_n(t)}{(1+r)^t} \middle| \mathbf{f}_s \right] (\omega)$$

which proves that $\dfrac{p_n(t)}{(1+r)^t}$ is a martingale with respect to Q.

Finally, to show that the correspondence between Q and ψ is one-to-one, suppose that Q_1 and Q_2 are two equilibrium price measures, and ψ_1 and ψ_2 are the corresponding extensions of the price functional. If $\psi_1 = \psi_2$, then consider the consumption process $\chi_{\{T, \omega\}}$. Then

$$\psi_1 \left(\chi_{\{T, \omega\}} \right) = (1+r)^{-T} Q_1(\omega)$$

$$\psi_2 \left(\chi_{\{T, \omega\}} \right) = (1+r)^{-T} Q_2(\omega)$$

which implies that $Q_1 = Q_2$. ∎

4.3   Attainable Set and Budget Sets

In this section we extend Theorems 2.4 and 2.6 to the discrete multiperiod model. First, notice that for every adapted endowment process e the set $B(e, p) - e$ of net trades, that is processes $c - e$ such that $c \in B(e, p)$, is equal to $B(0, p)$ and we have the following result.

Theorem 4.10 *Suppose that e is an adapted endowment process, p is a price system, and c is an adapted consumption process. Then $c \in B(e, p)$ if and only if $c - e \in B(0, p)$.*

This theorem states that the adapted consumption process c is in the budget set $B(e, p)$ if and only if the net trade $c - e$ is attainable at zero initial cost.

Second, recall that a trading strategy in the discrete multiperiod model is an N-dimensional vector of predictable sequences of random variables on the finite sample space Ω

$$\theta_n(1,\omega),\ldots,\theta_n(T,\omega)$$

The set Θ of trading strategies is a linear space of finite dimension. On the space Θ define a linear operator, called the consumption operator

$$H : \Theta \to X$$

such that $H(\theta)$ is the consumption process generated by the trading strategy θ with a zero endowment process. Then H is a linear operator, rank(H) is finite, and im(H) = $B(0,p)$. Consequently, there exists a linear operator G

$$\Theta \xrightarrow{H} X \xrightarrow{G} \mathcal{R}^{\dim(X)-\text{rank}(H)}$$

such that $B(0,p) = \text{im}(H) = \ker(G)$. This proves the following extension of Theorem 2.4.

Theorem 4.11 *If the price system p does not permit arbitrage strategies, then there exists a linear operator*

$$G : X \to \mathcal{R}^{\dim(X)-\text{rank}(H)}$$

such that $c \in B(e,p)$ if and only if $G(c-e) = 0$.

    The linear operator G that satisfies $\ker(G) = B(0,p)$ need not be unique. If the price system p does not permit arbitrage strategies, then G is unique if and only if the price system p is complete. We call G a budget operator. The budget operator generalizes the concept of the price functional.

    Theorem 4.11 identifies a finite number of linear budget constraints. In particular, for the one-period model $X = \mathcal{R}^{K+1}$ and, in the notation of Section 1.4, rank(H) = rank(D), and the budget operator G is equal to the operator $\begin{pmatrix} F \\ \phi \end{pmatrix}$.

Example 4.7 Consider a market with $K = 3$, $T = 2$, the information structure

$$\mathbf{f}_1 = \{\{\omega_1,\omega_2\},\{\omega_3\}\} = \{f_{11}, f_{12}\}$$

the terminal payouts

$$D = \begin{pmatrix} 22 & 10 \\ 12 & 10 \\ 14 & 10 \end{pmatrix}$$

and prices

$$p_1(0) = 14, \quad p_2(0) = 10$$

$$p_1(1, f_{11}) = p_1(1, f_{12}) = 14, \quad p_2(1, f_{11}) = p_2(1, f_{12}) = 10$$

It is easy to verify that this price system does not permit arbitrage strategies and that it is incomplete. Also, we have that $\Theta = \mathcal{R}^6$ and $X = \mathcal{R}^6$. Denote

$$\theta = \begin{pmatrix} \theta_1(1) \\ \theta_2(1) \\ \theta_1(2, f_{11}) \\ \theta_2(2, f_{11}) \\ \theta_1(2, f_{12}) \\ \theta_2(2, f_{12}) \end{pmatrix} \qquad c = \begin{pmatrix} c(0) \\ c(1, f_{11}) \\ c(1, f_{12}) \\ c(2, \omega_1) \\ c(2, \omega_2) \\ c(2, \omega_3) \end{pmatrix}$$

Then the consumption operator $H : \mathcal{R}^6 \to \mathcal{R}^6$ is

$$H = \begin{pmatrix} -14 & -10 & 0 & 0 & 0 & 0 \\ 14 & 10 & -14 & -10 & 0 & 0 \\ 14 & 10 & 0 & 0 & -14 & -10 \\ 0 & 0 & 22 & 10 & 0 & 0 \\ 0 & 0 & 12 & 10 & 0 & 0 \\ 0 & 0 & 0 & 0 & 14 & 10 \end{pmatrix}$$

For any $0 < \alpha < 1$ multiply the first row by 1, the second row by α, the third row by $1 - \alpha$, the fourth row by $\dfrac{\alpha}{5}$, the fifth row by $\dfrac{4\alpha}{5}$, the sixth row by $1 - \alpha$, and add. Also, add the first, third, and sixth rows. Both additions yield zero. On the other hand

$$\begin{vmatrix} 14 & -14 & -10 & 0 \\ 0 & 22 & 10 & 0 \\ 0 & 12 & 10 & 0 \\ 0 & 0 & 0 & 10 \end{vmatrix} \neq 0$$

so that $\mathrm{rank}(H) = 4$. Consider the linear operator $G_\alpha : \mathcal{R}^6 \to \mathcal{R}^2$ given by

$$G_\alpha = \begin{pmatrix} 1 & \alpha & 1 - \alpha & \frac{\alpha}{5} & \frac{4\alpha}{5} & 1 - \alpha \\ 1 & 0 & 1 & 0 & 0 & 1 \end{pmatrix}$$

Notice that the first row of G_α is a representation of the price functional that corresponds to the equilibrium price measure

$$Q(\omega_1) = \frac{\alpha}{5}, \quad Q(\omega_2) = \frac{4\alpha}{5}, \quad \text{and} \quad Q(\omega_3) = 1 - \alpha$$

The lack of uniqueness of the budget operator corresponds to the lack of uniqueness of the equilibrium price measure. For any $0 < \alpha', \alpha'' < 1$ we have $G_{\alpha'}(z) = 0$ if and only if $G_{\alpha''}(z) = 0$. This follows immediately from the fact that for any $0 < \alpha < 1$ and $z \in \mathcal{R}^6$ we have $G_\alpha(z) = 0$ if and only if $z_1 + z_3 + z_6 = 0$ and $\alpha \left(z_1 + z_2 + \frac{1}{5}z_4 + \frac{4}{5}z_5 \right) = 0$. Therefore, any choice of a budget operator describes all the budget constraints, that is, for any $0 < \alpha < 1$ we have $\text{im}(H) = \ker(G_\alpha) = B(0,p)$ and for any adapted endowment process e the budget constraints are $G_\alpha(c - e) = 0$.

For instance, if $\alpha = \frac{1}{2}$ and

$$e = \begin{pmatrix} 10 \\ 20 \\ 30 \\ 10 \\ 15 \\ 20 \end{pmatrix}$$

then the budget constraints are

$$c(0) + \frac{1}{2}c(1, f_{11}) + \frac{1}{2}c(1, f_{12}) + \frac{1}{10}c(2, \omega_1) + \frac{4}{10}c(2, \omega_2) + \frac{1}{2}c(2, \omega_3) = 52$$
$$c(0) + c(1, f_{12}) + c(2, \omega_3) = 60$$

The characterization of budget sets in Theorem 2.6 extends unchanged to the discrete multiperiod model.

Theorem 4.12 *Suppose that the price system p does not permit arbitrage strategies. Then for any adapted consumption process c we have $c \in B(e,p)$ if and only if $\psi(c - e) = 0$ for every positive extension ψ of the price functional ϕ.*

Problems

1. For an equilibrium price measure Q prove that for any $0 \leq t \leq T$ and $\omega, \xi \in \Omega$

$$Q(\xi|\mathbf{f}_t)(\omega) = \begin{cases} \prod_{s=t+1}^{T} Q[s, \mathbf{f}_s(\xi)] & \text{if } \xi \in \mathbf{f}_t(\omega) \\ 0 & \text{otherwise} \end{cases}$$

2. Prove that if a partition $\mathbf{f}$ is coarser than a partition $\mathbf{g}$, then for any random variable x, we have $E_P[E_P(x|\mathbf{g})|\mathbf{f}] = E_P(x|\mathbf{f})$ (the law of iterated expectations).

3. Solve again Problem 4 from Chapter 3.

4. Consider the following market: $K = 6$, $N = 3$, $T = 2$

$$f_{11} = \{\omega_1, \omega_2\}, \quad f_{12} = \{\omega_3, \omega_4\}, \quad f_{13} = \{\omega_5, \omega_6\}$$

matrix of terminal payouts

$$D = \begin{pmatrix} 1 & 0 & 1 \\ 1 & 1 & 0 \\ 1 & 0 & 2 \\ 1 & 2 & 1 \\ 1 & 0.82 & 0.1 \\ 1 & 0.64 & 0.09 \end{pmatrix}$$

and prices

$$p_1(0) = 1.0, \quad p_2(0) = 1.129, \quad p_3(0) = 0.6935$$
$$p_1(1, f_{11}) = 1.0, \quad p_2(1, f_{11}) = 0.8, \quad p_3(1, f_{11}) = 0.2$$
$$p_1(1, f_{12}) = 1.0, \quad p_2(1, f_{12}) = 1.5, \quad p_3(1, f_{12}) = 1.25$$
$$p_1(1, f_{13}) = 1.0, \quad p_2(1, f_{13}) = 0.73, \quad p_3(1, f_{13}) = 0.095$$

(a) Is this an equilibrium price system?

(b) What is the dimension of the space $M(p)$ of attainable consumption processes?

(c) What is the initial equilibrium price of a call option on security 2 with the exercise price $a = 0.7$?

5. Prove that for any adapted endowment process e, the set $B(e, p) - e$ is a linear subspace of the attainable set M.

6. Prove Theorem 4.12.

7. Compute the budget operators in Problem 4.

Notes

Corollary 4.1 is extended in [29]. The martingale property of discounted prices with respect to an equilibrium price measure, Theorem 4.6, is implicit in [4] and [19]. The systematic use of the martingale property to characterize financial markets is due to [39]. Theorem 4.9, like Theorem 2.4, is an adaptation to discrete time of a corresponding theorem in [39]. The characterization of budget sets in Theorem 4.11 is new. An alternative derivation of a finite number of linear budget constraints appears in [44]. Budget operators in both discrete time and continuous time, and their application to problems of optimal portfolio choice, are developed in [23].

Chapter 5

Discrete Stochastic Calculus

5.1 Introduction

This chapter introduces a discrete analog of continuous time stochastic calculus. The concepts in this chapter include quadratic covariation processes, orthogonal martingales, stochastic integrals, stochastic exponentials, likelihood ratio processes, and orthogonal martingale bases. The theorems include a discrete version of Itô's formula, a discrete version of Girsanov's theorem on the transformation of martingales under a change of the probability measure, a theorem on the existence of orthogonal martingale bases, a representation of nonzero martingales as stochastic exponentials, and Doob's decomposition theorem for discrete stochastic processes.

The theory in this chapter is used in Chapter 6 to deliver a representation of the equilibrium price measure for a complete price system, and to design practical applications of the discrete multiperiod model. In addition, the techniques of this chapter offer a new characterization of complete price systems, and permit an easy derivation of a linear relationship between risk and expected return in the discrete multiperiod model. Finally, the discussion here serves as an intuitive and instructive introduction to the mathematical techniques of the continuous multiperiod model.

Throughout this chapter Ω is a finite sample space, $\{\mathbf{f}_t\}$ is an information structure on Ω, $t = 0, \ldots, T$, and P and Q are two probability measures on Ω such that $P(\omega), Q(\omega) > 0$ for all $\omega \in \Omega$. A discrete stochastic process x is a sequence $x(0), \ldots, x(T)$ of random variables, abbreviated as $\{x_t\}$. To simplify the appearance of formulas, the two forms of notation for elements of a stochastic process x, $x(t)$ and x_t, are used interchangeably. Similarly, the realization of the stochastic process x at time t and state ω, $x(t, \omega)$, is denoted — when convenient — by $x_t(\omega)$.

5.2 Covariation Processes and Orthogonal Martingales

Quadratic Covariation Processes

For any two processes x and y, whether adapted or not, we define the optional and predictable quadratic covariation processes.

Definition 5.1 The optional quadratic covariation process of $x = \{x_t\}$ and $y = \{y_t\}$, denoted $\{[x, y]_t\}$, is the process

$$[x, y]_0 = x(0)y(0)$$

$$[x, y]_t = x(0)y(0) + \sum_{s=1}^{t} [x(s) - x(s-1)][y(s) - y(s-1)]$$

$$\text{for } 1 \leq t \leq T$$

The optional quadratic covariation process of x with itself, $\{[x, x]_t\}$, is called the optional quadratic variation process of x.

It is easy to see that the optional quadratic variation process is increasing.

Example 5.1 $\Omega = \{\omega_1, \ldots, \omega_6\}$, $T = 3$, and the stochastic processes x and y are

x	ω_1	ω_2	ω_3	ω_4	ω_5	ω_6
$t = 0$	0	1	2	1	0	−1
$t = 1$	2	3	1	2	1	0
$t = 2$	−1	0	−1	0	−1	0
$t = 3$	−2	2	2	1	3	2

y	ω_1	ω_2	ω_3	ω_4	ω_5	ω_6
$t = 0$	0	2	−1	−2	0	1
$t = 1$	1	3	0	2	−1	3
$t = 2$	2	1	−1	−2	−1	0
$t = 3$	1	2	0	1	0	2

Then

$[x, y]$	ω_1	ω_2	ω_3	ω_4	ω_5	ω_6
$t = 0$	0	2	-2	-2	0	-1
$t = 1$	2	4	-3	2	-1	1
$t = 2$	-1	10	-1	10	-1	1
$t = 3$	0	12	2	13	3	5

Definition 5.2 The predictable quadratic covariation process of $x = \{x_t\}$ and $y = \{y_t\}$ relative to the information structure $\{\mathbf{f}_t\}$ and probability measure P, denoted $\{\langle x, y \rangle_t\}$, is the process

$$\langle x, y \rangle_0 = E_P[x(0)y(0)]$$

$$\langle x, y \rangle_t = E_P[x(0)y(0)] + \sum_{s=1}^{t} E_P\{[x(s) - x(s-1)][y(s) - y(s-1)]|\mathbf{f}_{s-1}\}$$

$$\text{for } 1 \leq t \leq T$$

The predictable quadratic covariation process of x with itself, $\{\langle x, x \rangle_t\}$, is called the predictable quadratic variation process of x.

Notice that the predictable quadratic covariation process $\{\langle x, y \rangle_t\}$, $1 \leq t \leq T$, is predictable, and the predictable quadratic variation process $\{\langle x, x \rangle_t\}$, $1 \leq t \leq T$, is predictable and increasing.

Example 5.2 In Example 5.1 add the probability measure $P(\omega) = \frac{1}{6}$ for all $\omega \in \Omega$ and the information structure

$$\mathbf{f}_1 = \{\{\omega_1, \omega_2\}, \{\omega_3, \omega_4, \omega_5, \omega_6\}\}$$
$$\mathbf{f}_2 = \{\{\omega_1, \omega_2\}, \{\omega_3, \omega_4\}, \{\omega_5, \omega_6\}\}$$

Then the predictable quadratic covariation process of x and y is

$\langle x, y \rangle$	ω_1	ω_2	ω_3	ω_4	ω_5	ω_6
$t = 0$	$-\frac{1}{2}$	$-\frac{1}{2}$	$-\frac{1}{2}$	$-\frac{1}{2}$	$-\frac{1}{2}$	$-\frac{1}{2}$
$t = 1$	$\frac{5}{6}$	$\frac{5}{6}$	$\frac{5}{6}$	$\frac{5}{6}$	$\frac{5}{6}$	$\frac{5}{6}$
$t = 2$	$\frac{7}{3}$	$\frac{7}{3}$	$\frac{10}{3}$	$\frac{10}{3}$	$\frac{10}{3}$	$\frac{10}{3}$
$t = 3$	$\frac{23}{6}$	$\frac{23}{6}$	$\frac{19}{3}$	$\frac{19}{3}$	$\frac{22}{3}$	$\frac{22}{3}$

Independent Partitions

This subsection presents a definition of independent partitions that generalizes the concept of independent random variables.

Definition 5.3 Partitions **f** and **g** are independent relative to a probability measure P if and only if for every $f \in \mathbf{f}$ and $g \in \mathbf{g}$

$$P(f \cap g) = P(f)P(g)$$

Example 5.3 The partitions $\mathbf{f}_1$ and $\mathbf{f}_2$ in Example 5.2 are not independent relative to the given probability measure P, whereas the partitions

$$\mathbf{f} = \{\{\omega_1, \omega_2, \omega_3\}, \{\omega_4, \omega_5, \omega_6\}\}$$
$$\mathbf{g} = \{\{\omega_1, \omega_4\}, \{\omega_2, \omega_5\}, \{\omega_3, \omega_6\}\}$$

are independent relative to P.

The independence of random variables is defined in terms of independence of the partitions generated by these random variables.

Definition 5.4 A random variable x and a partition **f** are independent relative to a probability measure P if and only if the partitions $\mathbf{f}^x$ and $\mathbf{f}$ are independent. Random variables x and y are independent if and only if the partitions $\mathbf{f}^x$ and $\mathbf{f}^y$ are independent.

Example 5.4 In the previous example define the random variable

$$x(\omega_1) = x(\omega_2) = x(\omega_3) = 1$$
$$x(\omega_4) = x(\omega_5) = x(\omega_6) = 2$$

Then $\mathbf{f}^x = \mathbf{f}$ and x is independent of **g** and for all $\omega \in \Omega$

$$E_P(x|\mathbf{g})(\omega) = \frac{\frac{1+2}{6}}{\frac{2}{6}} = \frac{3}{2} = E_P(x)$$

The next theorem says that this is true whenever x and **g** are independent.

Theorem 5.1 *If a random variable x and a partition* **g** *are independent, then*

$$E_P(x|\mathbf{g}) = E_P(x)$$

Proof. By definition

$$E_P(x|\mathbf{g})(\omega) \;=\; \frac{\displaystyle\sum_{\xi \in \mathbf{g}(\omega)} P(\xi)x(\xi)}{\displaystyle\sum_{\xi \in \mathbf{g}(\omega)} P(\xi)}$$

$$= \sum_{\xi \in \Omega} P(\xi|\mathbf{g})(\omega)x(\xi)$$

Suppose $\mathbf{f}^x = \{f_1^x, \ldots, f_u^x\}$. Then

$$E_P(x|\mathbf{g})(\omega) \;=\; \sum_{j=1}^{u} \sum_{\xi \in f_j^x} P(\xi|\mathbf{g})(\omega)x(\xi) \;=\; \sum_{j=1}^{u} x(f_j^x) \sum_{\xi \in f_j^x} P(\xi|\mathbf{g})(\omega)$$

$$= \sum_{j=1}^{u} x(f_j^x)P(f_j^x|\mathbf{g})(\omega) \;=\; \sum_{j=1}^{u} x(f_j^x)P(f_j^x) = E_P(x)$$

This completes the proof. ∎

Example 5.5 Suppose that for $0 \le t \le T$

$$x_t = \sum_{s=0}^{t} a_s$$

where for all $0 \le t \le T$ we have $E_P(a_t) = 0$ and for all $1 \le t \le T$ the random variable a_t is independent of $\mathbf{f}_{t-1}$. Denote $\text{var}(a_t) = \sigma_t^2$, then

$$[x,x]_t = \sum_{s=0}^{t} a_s^2$$

$$\langle x,x \rangle_t = \sum_{s=0}^{t} \sigma_s^2$$

Orthogonal Martingales

This subsection describes a property of the quadratic covariation processes and introduces the notion of orthogonal martingales.

Theorem 5.2 *If $\{x_t\}$ and $\{y_t\}$ are martingales, then $\{x_t y_t - [x,y]_t\}$ and $\{x_t y_t - \langle x,y \rangle_t\}$ are martingales.*

Proof. For any $1 \le t \le T$ the conditional expectation $E_P(x_t y_t - [x,y]_t|\mathbf{f}_{t-1})$ is equal to

$E_P[x_t y_t - (x_t - x_{t-1})(y_t - y_{t-1})|\mathbf{f}_{t-1}] - [x,y]_{t-1}$

$$= E_P(x_t y_t - x_t y_t + x_t y_{t-1} + x_{t-1} y_t - x_{t-1} y_{t-1}|\mathbf{f}_{t-1}) - [x,y]_{t-1}$$
$$= x_{t-1} y_{t-1} - [x,y]_{t-1}$$

and similarly, the conditional expectation $E_P(x_t y_t - \langle x,y \rangle_t|\mathbf{f}_{t-1})$ is equal to

$E_P[x_t y_t - (x_t - x_{t-1})(y_t - y_{t-1})|\mathbf{f}_{t-1}] - \langle x,y \rangle_{t-1}$

$$= E_P(x_t y_t - x_t y_t + x_t y_{t-1} + x_{t-1} y_t - x_{t-1} y_{t-1}|\mathbf{f}_{t-1}) - \langle x,y \rangle_{t-1}$$
$$= x_{t-1} y_{t-1} - \langle x,y \rangle_{t-1}$$

The rest of the proof follows from the law of iterated expectations. ∎

Definition 5.5 Two martingales $\{x_t\}$ and $\{y_t\}$ are orthogonal if and only if $\langle x,y \rangle_t = 0$ for all $0 \le t \le T$.

Theorem 5.3 *If the two martingales $\{x_t\}$ and $\{y_t\}$ are orthogonal, then $x_0 y_0 = 0$ and the process $\{x_t y_t\}$ is a martingale. Conversely, if $x_0 y_0 = 0$ and $\{x_t y_t\}$ is a martingale, then the two martingales $\{x_t\}$ and $\{y_t\}$ are orthogonal.*

Proof. If $\{x_t\}$ and $\{y_t\}$ are orthogonal, then $x_0 y_0 = \langle x,y \rangle_0 = 0$ and, from Theorem 5.2, $\{x_t y_t\}$ is a martingale. Conversely, observe first that if $\{x_t y_t\}$ is a martingale, then Theorem 5.2 implies that the predictable quadratic covariation process $\{\langle x,y \rangle_t\}$ is a martingale and, second, that the process $\{\langle x,y \rangle_t\}$ is predictable. Consequently, it is constant and for all $0 \le t \le T$

$$\langle x,y \rangle_t = \langle x,y \rangle_0 = x_0 y_0 = 0$$

This completes the proof. ∎

The proof of the next theorem is left as an exercise for the reader.

Theorem 5.4 *The martingales $\{x\}$ and $\{y\}$ are orthogonal if and only if for every $0 \le s \le t \le T$*

$$E_P(x_t y_t|\mathbf{f}_s) = E_P(x_t|\mathbf{f}_s) E_P(y_t|\mathbf{f}_s)$$

5.3   Stochastic Integrals

The notion of a stochastic integral has fundamental importance in the theory of martingales and in models of prices in financial markets. The importance of stochastic integrals in models of financial markets follows from the earlier observation that the trading gain generated by a predictable trading strategy $\{\theta_{1t}, \ldots, \theta_{nt}\}$ at prices $\{p_{1t}, \ldots, p_{nt}\}$ is

$$\sum_{n=1}^{N} \sum_{s=1}^{t} \theta_{ns}(p_{ns} - p_{n,s-1})$$

Definition 5.6 For any processes $\{\alpha_t\}$ and $\{x_t\}$ the stochastic integral $\int_0^t \alpha_s dx_s$ is the process

$$\int_0^t \alpha_s dx_s = \begin{cases} 0 & \text{if } t = 0 \\ \displaystyle\sum_{s=1}^{t} \alpha_s(x_s - x_{s-1}) & \text{if } 1 \leq t \leq T \end{cases}$$

The integral $\int_0^t \alpha_s dx_s$ is also called the transform of the process $\{x_t\}$ by the process $\{\alpha_t\}$ and denoted $\{(\alpha \bullet x)_t\}$.

For any process $\alpha = \{\alpha_t\}$ define the process $\alpha_- = \{\alpha_{t-}\}$ by setting $\alpha_{t-} = \alpha_{t-1}$ for $1 \leq t \leq T$. The stochastic integral $\int_0^t \alpha_{s-} dx_s$, also denoted $\{(\alpha_- \bullet x)_t\}$, is then

$$\int_0^t \alpha_{s-} dx_s = \begin{cases} 0 & \text{if } t = 0 \\ \displaystyle\sum_{s=1}^{t} \alpha_{s-1}(x_s - x_{s-1}) & \text{if } 1 \leq t \leq T \end{cases}$$

The stochastic integral has four fundamental properties that, suitably modified, extend to the general continuous time theory of stochastic integration. The first property is extremely simple. Define the change at time t in a process $\{v_t\}$ as the backward difference

$$\Delta v_t = v_t - v_{t-} = v_t - v_{t-1}$$

Then $\Delta(\alpha \bullet x) = \alpha \Delta x$ for any processes α and x. The second property is the preservation of martingales.

Theorem 5.5 *If the process $\{\alpha_t\}$ is predictable and the process $\{x_t\}$ is a martingale, then the integral $\int_0^t \alpha_s dx_s$ is a martingale.*

Proof. For any $1 \leq t \leq T$

$$E_P[\sum_{s=1}^{t} \alpha_s(x_s - x_{s-1})|\mathbf{f}_{t-1}] = E_P[\alpha_t(x_t - x_{t-1})|\mathbf{f}_{t-1}] + \sum_{s=1}^{t-1} \alpha_s(x_s - x_{s-1})$$

Because α_t is measurable on $\mathbf{f}_{t-1}$ and $\{x_t\}$ is a martingale

$$E_P[\alpha_t(x_t - x_{t-1})|\mathbf{f}_{t-1}] = 0$$

and the rest follows from the law of iterated expectations. ∎

The third fundamental property of the stochastic integral is associativity.

Theorem 5.6 *For any processes α, β, and x*

$$\alpha \bullet (\beta \bullet x) = (\alpha\beta) \bullet x$$

Proof. Denote $y_t = (\beta \bullet x)_t$. Then

$$[\alpha \bullet (\beta \bullet x)]_t = \sum_{s=1}^{t} \alpha_s\beta_s(x_s - x_{s-1}) = [(\alpha\beta) \bullet x]_t$$

which proves the theorem. ∎

Stochastic Integrals and Covariation Processes

The fourth fundamental property of the stochastic integral is associativity with respect to the quadratic covariation processes.

Theorem 5.7 *We have the following properties:*

1. For any stochastic processes α, x, and y

$$[\alpha \bullet x, y] = \alpha \bullet [x, y]$$

2. For a predictable process α and any processes x and y

$$\langle \alpha \bullet x, y \rangle = \alpha \bullet \langle x, y \rangle$$

Proof. For $t = 0$, both sides of item 1 are zero. Suppose that $t \geq 1$, then

$$(\alpha \bullet x)_t = \sum_{s=1}^{t} \alpha_s(x_s - x_{s-1})$$

and therefore

$$\lfloor\alpha\bullet x,y\rfloor_t = \sum_{s=1}^{t}\alpha_s(x_s-x_{s-1})(y_s-y_{s-1})$$

On the other hand

$$[x,y]_t = x_0y_0 + \sum_{s=1}^{t}(x_s-x_{s-1})(y_s-y_{s-1})$$

and thus

$$(\alpha\bullet[x,y])_t = \sum_{s=1}^{t}\alpha_s(x_s-x_{s-1})(y_s-y_{s-1})$$

The proof of item 2 is similar. ∎

Next, we calculate the integral $\int_0^t x_{s-}dx_s$.

Theorem 5.8 *We have*

$$\int_0^t x_{s-}dx_s = \frac{1}{2}\left(x_t^2 - [x,x]_t\right)$$

Proof. The proof is based on the following identity that is easy to verify directly

$$2\sum_{s=1}^{t}x_{s-1}(x_s-x_{s-1}) = \sum_{s=1}^{t}(x_s^2-x_{s-1}^2) - \sum_{s=1}^{t}(x_s-x_{s-1})^2$$

The first sum on the right side telescopes into $x_t^2 - x_0^2$ and the theorem follows from the definition of the optional quadratic variation process. ∎

It is important to notice that the definition of the stochastic integral can be modified to yield the familiar formula for the integral $\int_0^t x_s dx_s$. If we define

$$\int_0^t x_s dx_s = \sum_{s=1}^{t}\frac{x_{s-1}+x_s}{2}(x_s-x_{s-1})$$

then

$$\int_0^t x_s dx_s = \frac{1}{2}\left(x_t^2 - x_0^2\right)$$

but such a definition of the stochastic integral does not preserve the martingale property. Next, Theorem 5.8 implies the following formula for integration by parts.

Theorem 5.9

$$\int_0^t x_{s-} dy_s = x_t y_t - \int_0^t y_{s-} dx_s - [x, y]_t$$

Proof. The proof is based on the following identity that follows immediately from the definition of the optional quadratic covariation process

$$[x, y]_t = \frac{1}{2}([x + y, x + y]_t - [x, x]_t - [y, y]_t)$$

Using this identity and Theorem 5.8 we get

$$\begin{aligned}
[x, y]_t &= \frac{1}{2}\left[(x_t + y_t)^2 - 2\int_0^t (x_{s-} + y_{s-})d(x_s + y_s)\right.\\
&\qquad \left. - x_t^2 + 2\int_0^t x_{s-} dx_s - y_t^2 + \int_0^t y_{s-} dy_s\right]\\
&= \frac{1}{2}\left(2x_t y_t - 2\int_0^t x_{s-} dy_s - 2\int_0^t y_{s-} dx_s\right)
\end{aligned}$$

This ends the proof. ∎

Theorem 5.9 can be written in shorthand notation

$$d(x_t y_t) = x_{t-} dy_t + y_{t-} dx_t + d[x, y]_t$$

where the differential of a process $\{v_t\}$ is defined as the backward difference

$$dv_t = \Delta v_t$$

Using this shorthand notation we can write the definition of the optional quadratic covariation process

$$d[x, y]_t = dx_t dy_t$$

and the definition of the predictable quadratic covariation process

$$d\langle x, y\rangle_t = E_P(dx_t dy_t | \mathbf{f}_{t-1})$$

Itô's Formula

The next theorem is a trivial identity in the finite framework of this chapter. The continuous version of this identity is the celebrated formula of K. Itô for the change of variables in a stochastic integral. As an introduction to Itô's formula consider the Stieltjes integral

$$I = \int_0^t 2x_s \exp\left(x_s^2\right) dx_s$$

This integral is easily computed by substituting $f(x_s) = \exp(x_s^2)$ so that

$$I = \int_0^t f'(x_s)dx_s = f(x_t) - f(x_0) = \exp(x_t^2) - \exp(x_0^2)$$

The formula

$$f(x_t) = f(x_0) + \int_0^t f'(x_s)dx_s$$

for a continuously differentiable function $f : \mathcal{R} \to \mathcal{R}$ is called the formula for a change of variables in a Stieltjes integral. For the discrete stochastic integrals in this chapter the formula for a change of variables has an extra term. The significance of this fact is that such correction terms appear in the formula for a change of variables in the continuous stochastic integrals in subsequent chapters.

Theorem 5.10 (Itô's formula) *If the function $f : \mathcal{R} \to \mathcal{R}$ is differentiable, then for all $1 \le t \le T$*

$$f(x_t) = f(x_0) + \int_0^t f'(x_{s-})dx_s + \sum_{s=1}^t [f(x_s) - f(x_{s-}) - f'(x_{s-})\Delta x_s]$$

The proof is left as an exercise for the reader.

Stochastic Exponentials

A stochastic exponential of an adapted process w is a product of suitably adjusted increments of w. Heuristically, the stochastic exponential $\{x_t\}$ of $\{w_t\}$ is the solution of the stochastic differential equation

$$dx_t = x_{t-}dw_t$$

This is formalized in the next theorem.

Theorem 5.11 *Let $\{w_t\}$ be an adapted process and x_0 an arbitrary constant. Then there exists a unique adapted process $\{x_t\}$ such that*

$$x_t = x_0 + \int_0^t x_{s-}dw_s$$

For $1 \le t \le T$ the process $\{x_t\}$ is given by the formula

$$x_t = x_0 \prod_{s=1}^t (1 + w_s - w_{s-1})$$

If the process $\{w_t\}$ is a martingale, then the process $\{x_t\}$ is a martingale.

Proof. Substitute $t = 1, \ldots, T$ in the equation

$$x_t = x_0 + \int_0^t x_{s-} \, dw_s$$

This procedure defines $x_1, \ldots, x_T$ as

$$
\begin{aligned}
x_1 &= x_0(1 + w_1 - w_0) \\
x_2 &= x_0(1 + w_1 - w_0)(1 + w_2 - w_1)
\end{aligned}
$$

and so on. If $\{w_t\}$ is a martingale, then for every $1 \leq t \leq T$

$$E_P(x_t|\mathbf{f}_{t-1}) = x_{t-1} E_P(1 + w_t - w_{t-1}|\mathbf{f}_{t-1}) = x_{t-1}$$

and $\{x_t\}$ is a martingale. ∎

By analogy with the Stieltjes integral

$$e^{w_t} = e^{w_0} + \int_0^t e^{w_s} \, dw_s$$

the process $\{x_t\}$ in Theorem 5.11 is called a stochastic exponential.

Definition 5.7 The unique process $\{x_t\}$ such that

$$x_t = 1 + \int_0^t x_{s-} \, dw_s$$

is called the stochastic exponential of the process $\{w_t\}$ and is denoted

$$x_t = \mathcal{E}_t(w)$$

The preceding definition and Theorem 5.11 imply that the solution of the integral equation

$$x_t = x_0 + \int_0^t x_{s-} \, dw_s$$

is $x_t = x_0 \mathcal{E}_t(w)$. Similarly, if $\{\alpha_t\}$ is predictable, then the solution of the integral equation

$$x_t = x_0 + \int_0^t \alpha_s x_{s-} \, dw_s$$

is $x_t = x_0 \mathcal{E}_t(\alpha \bullet w)$ given by the formula

$$x_t = x_0 \prod_{s=1}^t [1 + \alpha_s(w_s - w_{s-1})]$$

This section ends with a multiplication formula for stochastic exponentials.

Theorem 5.12

$$\mathcal{E}_t(x)\mathcal{E}_t(y) = \mathcal{E}_t(x + y + [x, y])$$

Proof. Denote $f_t = \mathcal{E}_t(x)$ and $g_t = \mathcal{E}_t(y)$. Then

$$
\begin{aligned}
df_t &= f_{t-}dx_t \\
dg_t &= g_{t-}dy_t \\
d[f, g]_t &= f_{t-}g_{t-}d[x, y]_t
\end{aligned}
$$

The third equation follows from the definition of the optional quadratic covariation process

$$d[u, v]_t = du_t dv_t$$

Next, the formula for integration by parts implies that

$$
\begin{aligned}
d(f_t g_t) &= f_{t-}dg_t + g_{t-}df_t + d[f, g]_t \\
&= f_{t-}g_{t-}dy_t + f_{t-}g_{t-}dx_t + f_{t-}g_{t-}d[x, y]_t \\
&= f_{t-}g_{t-}d(x_t + y_t + [x, y]_t)
\end{aligned}
$$

This completes the proof. ∎

5.4   Change of Measure and Girsanov's Theorem

The next concept is a special martingale generated by the ratio of the two probability measures P and Q.

The Likelihood Ratio Process

Definition 5.8 The likelihood ratio process is

$$z_t = E_P\left(\left.\frac{Q}{P}\right| f_t\right)$$

The likelihood ratio process is a positive martingale. The assertion that the process $\{z_t\}$ is a martingale follows immediately from the law of iterated expectations. It is positive because $\dfrac{Q}{P}$ is positive.

Example 5.6 $\Omega = \{\omega_1, \ldots, \omega_6\}$, $P(\omega) = \frac{1}{6}$ for all $\omega \in \Omega$

$$Q(\omega_1) = Q(\omega_6) = \tfrac{1}{4}$$
$$Q(\omega_2) = Q(\omega_3) = Q(\omega_4) = Q(\omega_5) = \tfrac{1}{8}$$

$$\mathbf{f}_1 = \{\{\omega_1, \omega_2\}, \{\omega_3, \omega_4, \omega_5, \omega_6\}\}$$
$$\mathbf{f}_2 = \{\{\omega_1, \omega_2\}, \{\omega_3, \omega_4\}, \{\omega_5, \omega_6\}\}$$

Then

$$\frac{Q}{P}(\omega) = \begin{cases} \tfrac{3}{2} & \text{if } \omega = \omega_1 \\ \tfrac{3}{4} & \text{if } \omega \in \{\omega_2, \omega_3, \omega_4, \omega_5\} \\ \tfrac{3}{2} & \text{if } \omega = \omega_6 \end{cases}$$

and the likelihood ratio process is

z	ω_1	ω_2	ω_3	ω_4	ω_5	ω_6
$t = 0$	1	1	1	1	1	1
$t = 1$	$\tfrac{9}{8}$	$\tfrac{9}{8}$	$\tfrac{15}{16}$	$\tfrac{15}{16}$	$\tfrac{15}{16}$	$\tfrac{15}{16}$
$t = 2$	$\tfrac{9}{8}$	$\tfrac{9}{8}$	$\tfrac{3}{4}$	$\tfrac{3}{4}$	$\tfrac{9}{8}$	$\tfrac{9}{8}$
$t = 3$	$\tfrac{3}{2}$	$\tfrac{3}{4}$	$\tfrac{3}{4}$	$\tfrac{3}{4}$	$\tfrac{3}{4}$	$\tfrac{3}{2}$

The next theorem relates the likelihood ratio process to conditional expectations relative to the probability measures P and Q.

Theorem 5.13 *For any adapted process $\{x_t\}$ and any $0 \le s \le t \le T$*

$$\frac{E_P(z_t x_t | \mathbf{f}_s)}{E_P(z_t | \mathbf{f}_s)} = E_Q(x_t | \mathbf{f}_s)$$

Proof. First, from the definition of conditional expectation

$$E_P(z_t x_t | \mathbf{f}_s) = \frac{\displaystyle\sum_{\xi \in \mathbf{f}_s(\omega)} P(\xi) z_t(\xi) x_t(\xi)}{\displaystyle\sum_{\xi \in \mathbf{f}_s(\omega)} P(\xi)}$$

$$E_P(z_t | \mathbf{f}_s) = \frac{\displaystyle\sum_{\xi \in \mathbf{f}_s(\omega)} P(\xi) z_t(\xi)}{\displaystyle\sum_{\xi \in \mathbf{f}_s(\omega)} P(\xi)}$$

Therefore

$$\frac{E_P(z_t x_t | \mathbf{f}_s)(\omega)}{E_P(z_t | \mathbf{f}_s)(\omega)} = \frac{\displaystyle\sum_{\xi \in \mathbf{f}_s(\omega)} P(\xi) z_t(\xi) x_t(\xi)}{\displaystyle\sum_{\xi \in \mathbf{f}_s(\omega)} P(\xi) z_t(\xi)}$$

Second, from the definition of the likelihood ratio process

$$z_t(\xi) = \frac{Q[\mathbf{f}_t(\xi)]}{P[\mathbf{f}_t(\xi)]}$$

Let the sets of $\mathbf{f}_t$ that are subsets of $\mathbf{f}_s(\omega)$ be $f_1, \ldots, f_u$. Then

$$\frac{E_P(z_t x_t | \mathbf{f}_s)(\omega)}{E_P(z_t | \mathbf{f}_s)(\omega)} = \frac{\displaystyle\sum_{j=1}^{u} \sum_{\xi \in f_j} P(\xi) z_t(\xi) x_t(\xi)}{\displaystyle\sum_{j=1}^{u} \frac{Q(f_j)}{P(f_j)} P(f_j)}$$

$$= \frac{\displaystyle\sum_{j=1}^{u} \frac{Q(f_j)}{P(f_j)} P(f_j) x_t(f_j)}{\displaystyle\sum_{j=1}^{u} Q(f_j)}$$

$$= E_Q(x_t | \mathbf{f}_s)(\omega)$$

This completes the proof. ∎

Corollary 5.1 *An adapted process $\{x_t\}$ is a Q-martingale if and only if the process $\{z_t x_t\}$ is a P-martingale.*

The proof of the corollary is left as an exercise for the reader.

Girsanov's Theorem

In this subsection we consider three stochastic integrals associated with the likelihood ratio process

$$\int_0^t \frac{dz_s}{z_{s-}}, \quad \int_0^t \frac{d[x, z]_s}{z_s}, \quad \text{and} \quad \int_0^t \frac{d\langle x, z \rangle_s}{z_{s-}}$$

From the definition of a stochastic integral, the integral $\displaystyle\int_0^t \frac{dz_s}{z_{s-}}$ is the process

$$\int_0^t \frac{dz_s}{z_{s-}} = \begin{cases} 0 & \text{if } t = 0 \\ \sum_{s=1}^t \dfrac{z_s - z_{s-1}}{z_{s-1}} & \text{if } 1 \le t \le T \end{cases}$$

Theorem 5.5 and the fact that the process $\{z_t\}$ is a P-martingale together imply that the integral $\int_0^t \dfrac{dz_s}{z_{s-}}$ is a P-martingale.

Example 5.7 Compute $\int_0^t \dfrac{dz_s}{z_{s-}}$ in Example 5.6.

$\int_0^t \frac{dz_s}{z_{s-}}$	ω_1	ω_2	ω_3	ω_4	ω_5	ω_6
$t = 0$	0	0	0	0	0	0
$t = 1$	$\frac{1}{8}$	$\frac{1}{8}$	$-\frac{1}{16}$	$-\frac{1}{16}$	$-\frac{1}{16}$	$-\frac{1}{16}$
$t = 2$	$\frac{1}{8}$	$\frac{1}{8}$	$-\frac{21}{80}$	$-\frac{21}{80}$	$\frac{11}{80}$	$\frac{11}{80}$
$t = 3$	$\frac{11}{24}$	$-\frac{5}{24}$	$-\frac{21}{80}$	$-\frac{21}{80}$	$-\frac{47}{240}$	$\frac{113}{240}$

From the definition of a stochastic integral, the integral $\int_0^t \dfrac{d[x,z]_s}{z_s}$ is

$$\int_0^t \frac{d[x,z]_s}{z_s} = \begin{cases} 0 & \text{if } t = 0 \\ \sum_{s=1}^t \dfrac{[x,z]_s - [x,z]_{s-1}}{z_s} & \text{if } 1 \le t \le T \end{cases}$$

and the integral $\int_0^t \dfrac{d\langle x,z \rangle_s}{z_{s-}}$ is

$$\int_0^t \frac{d\langle x,z \rangle_s}{z_{s-}} = \begin{cases} 0 & \text{if } t = 0 \\ \sum_{s=1}^t \dfrac{\langle x,z \rangle_s - \langle x,z \rangle_{s-1}}{z_{s-1}} & \text{if } 1 \le t \le T \end{cases}$$

Example 5.8 In Example 5.6 add the stochastic process x

x	ω_1	ω_2	ω_3	ω_4	ω_5	ω_6
$t = 0$	0	0	0	0	0	0
$t = 1$	10	10	-5	-5	-5	-5
$t = 2$	10	10	-21	-21	11	11
$t = 3$	$\frac{110}{3}$	$-\frac{50}{3}$	-21	-21	$-\frac{47}{3}$	$\frac{113}{3}$

Then the processes $[x,z]_t$, $A_t = \int_0^t \dfrac{d[x,z]_s}{z_s}$, $x_t - A_t$, $B_t = \int_0^t \dfrac{d\langle x,z \rangle_s}{z_{s-}}$, and $x_t - B_t$ are as follows.

$[x, z]_t$	ω_1	ω_2	ω_3	ω_4	ω_5	ω_6
$t = 0$	0	0	0	0	0	0
$t = 1$	$\frac{5}{4}$	$\frac{5}{4}$	$\frac{5}{16}$	$\frac{5}{16}$	$\frac{5}{16}$	$\frac{5}{16}$
$t = 2$	$\frac{5}{4}$	$\frac{5}{4}$	$\frac{53}{16}$	$\frac{53}{16}$	$\frac{53}{16}$	$\frac{53}{16}$
$t = 3$	$\frac{45}{4}$	$\frac{45}{4}$	$\frac{53}{16}$	$\frac{53}{16}$	$\frac{213}{16}$	$\frac{213}{16}$

A_t	ω_1	ω_2	ω_3	ω_4	ω_5	ω_6
$t = 0$	0	0	0	0	0	0
$t = 1$	$\frac{10}{9}$	$\frac{10}{9}$	$\frac{1}{3}$	$\frac{1}{3}$	$\frac{1}{3}$	$\frac{1}{3}$
$t = 2$	$\frac{10}{9}$	$\frac{10}{9}$	$\frac{13}{3}$	$\frac{13}{3}$	3	3
$t = 3$	$\frac{70}{9}$	$\frac{130}{9}$	$\frac{13}{3}$	$\frac{13}{3}$	$\frac{49}{3}$	$\frac{29}{3}$

$x_t - A_t$	ω_1	ω_2	ω_3	ω_4	ω_5	ω_6
$t = 0$	0	0	0	0	0	0
$t = 1$	$\frac{80}{9}$	$\frac{80}{9}$	$-\frac{16}{3}$	$-\frac{16}{3}$	$-\frac{16}{3}$	$-\frac{16}{3}$
$t = 2$	$\frac{80}{9}$	$\frac{80}{9}$	$-\frac{76}{3}$	$-\frac{76}{3}$	8	8
$t = 3$	$\frac{260}{9}$	$-\frac{280}{9}$	$-\frac{76}{3}$	$-\frac{76}{3}$	-32	28

$\langle x, z \rangle_t$	ω_1	ω_2	ω_3	ω_4	ω_5	ω_6
$t = 0$	0	0	0	0	0	0
$t = 1$	$\frac{5}{8}$	$\frac{5}{8}$	$\frac{5}{8}$	$\frac{5}{8}$	$\frac{5}{8}$	$\frac{5}{8}$
$t = 2$	$\frac{5}{8}$	$\frac{5}{8}$	$\frac{29}{8}$	$\frac{29}{8}$	$\frac{29}{8}$	$\frac{29}{8}$
$t = 3$	$\frac{85}{8}$	$\frac{85}{8}$	$\frac{29}{8}$	$\frac{29}{8}$	$\frac{109}{8}$	$\frac{109}{8}$

B_t	ω_1	ω_2	ω_3	ω_4	ω_5	ω_6
$t = 0$	0	0	0	0	0	0
$t = 1$	$\frac{5}{8}$	$\frac{5}{8}$	$\frac{5}{8}$	$\frac{5}{8}$	$\frac{5}{8}$	$\frac{5}{8}$
$t = 2$	$\frac{5}{8}$	$\frac{5}{8}$	$\frac{153}{40}$	$\frac{153}{40}$	$\frac{153}{40}$	$\frac{153}{40}$
$t = 3$	$\frac{685}{72}$	$\frac{685}{72}$	$\frac{153}{40}$	$\frac{153}{40}$	$\frac{4577}{360}$	$\frac{4577}{360}$

$x_t - B_t$	ω_1	ω_2	ω_3	ω_4	ω_5	ω_6
$t = 0$	0	0	0	0	0	0
$t = 1$	$\frac{75}{8}$	$\frac{75}{8}$	$-\frac{45}{8}$	$-\frac{45}{8}$	$-\frac{45}{8}$	$-\frac{45}{8}$
$t = 2$	$\frac{75}{8}$	$\frac{75}{8}$	$-\frac{993}{40}$	$-\frac{993}{40}$	$\frac{287}{40}$	$\frac{287}{40}$
$t = 3$	$\frac{1955}{72}$	$-\frac{1885}{72}$	$-\frac{993}{40}$	$-\frac{993}{40}$	$-\frac{10217}{360}$	$\frac{8983}{360}$

An inspection of the processes $\{x_t\}$, $\{x_t - A_t\}$, and $\{x_t - B_t\}$ in the preceding example reveals that the first is a P-martingale and the second and third are Q-martingales. This is Girsanov's theorem.

Theorem 5.14 *If $\{x_t\}$ is a P-martingale, then*

$$x_t - \int_0^t \frac{d[x, z]_s}{z_s} \quad \text{and} \quad x_t - \int_0^t \frac{d\langle x, z\rangle_s}{z_{s-}}$$

are Q-martingales.

Proof. Consider first the process $x_t - \int_0^t \frac{d[x, z]_s}{z_s}$. For $1 \leq t \leq T$ the conditional expectation $E_Q\left(x_t - \int_0^t \frac{d[x, z]_s}{z_s} \,\middle|\, \mathbf{f}_{t-1}\right)$ is equal to

$$E_Q(x_t|\mathbf{f}_{t-1}) - \int_0^{t-1} \frac{d[x, z]_s}{z_s} - E_Q\left\{\frac{(x_t - x_{t-1})(z_t - z_{t-1})}{z_t} \,\middle|\, \mathbf{f}_{t-1}\right\}$$

From Theorem 5.13 the last term in the preceding equation is

$$E_Q\left\{\frac{(x_t - x_{t-1})(z_t - z_{t-1})}{z_t} \,\middle|\, \mathbf{f}_{t-1}\right\} = \frac{E_P\{(x_t - x_{t-1})(z_t - z_{t-1})|\mathbf{f}_{t-1}\}}{z_{t-1}}$$

which is equal to

$$E_P\left\{(x_t - x_{t-1})\left(\frac{z_t}{z_{t-1}} - 1\right)\,\middle|\, \mathbf{f}_{t-1}\right\} = \frac{E_P(x_t z_t|\mathbf{f}_{t-1})}{z_{t-1}} - x_{t-1}$$

Therefore

$$E_Q\left(x_t - \int_0^t \frac{d[x, z]_s}{z_s}\,\middle|\, \mathbf{f}_{t-1}\right) = x_{t-1} - \int_0^{t-1} \frac{d[x, z]_s}{z_s}$$

and the martingale property follows from the law of iterated expectations.

Now consider the process $x_t - \int_0^t \frac{d\langle x, z\rangle_s}{z_{s-}}$. For $1 \leq t \leq T$ the conditional expectation

$$E_Q\left(x_t - \int_0^t \frac{d\langle x, z\rangle_s}{z_{s-}}\,\middle|\, \mathbf{f}_{t-1}\right)$$

is equal to

$$E_Q(x_t|\mathbf{f}_{t-1}) - \int_0^{t-1} \frac{d\langle x, z\rangle_s}{z_{s-}} - \frac{\langle x, z\rangle_t - \langle x, z\rangle_{t-1}}{z_{t-1}}$$

The last term in the preceding equation is

$$\frac{\langle x, z\rangle_t - \langle x, z\rangle_{t-1}}{z_{t-1}} = \frac{E_\Gamma[(x_t - x_{t-1})(z_t - z_{t-1})|\mathbf{f}_{t-1}]}{E_P(z_t|\mathbf{f}_{t-1})}$$

which is equal to

$$\frac{E_P[z_t(x_t - x_{t-1})(1 - \frac{z_{t-1}}{z_t})|\mathbf{f}_{t-1}]}{E_P(z_t|\mathbf{f}_{t-1})} = E_Q\left[(x_t - x_{t-1})\left(1 - \frac{z_{t-1}}{z_t}\right)\bigg|\mathbf{f}_{t-1}\right]$$

and to

$$E_Q(x_t|\mathbf{f}_{t-1}) - x_{t-1} + z_{t-1}E_Q\left(\frac{x_t - x_{t-1}}{z_t}\bigg|\mathbf{f}_{t-1}\right) = E_Q(x_t|\mathbf{f}_{t-1}) - x_{t-1}$$

Therefore

$$E_Q\left(x_t - \int_0^t \frac{d\langle x, z\rangle_s}{z_{s-}}\bigg|\mathbf{f}_{t-1}\right) = x_{t-1} - \int_0^{t-1} \frac{d\langle x, z\rangle_s}{z_{s-}}$$

and the proof is completed by applying the law of iterated expectations. ∎

The next section deals with the representation of martingales as stochastic integrals and stochastic exponentials.

5.5   Representation of Martingales

This section establishes Theorem 5.15 on the representation of any martingale $\{x_t\}$ as a sum of stochastic integrals with respect to the $\nu - 1$ special martingales

$$\{w_{1t}\}, \ldots, \{w_{\nu-1,t}\}$$

As usual, ν is the splitting index of the information structure $\{\mathbf{f}_t\}$. In addition, any martingale that is always different from zero can be represented as a stochastic exponential of the processes $\{w_{1t}\}, \ldots, \{w_{\nu-1,t}\}$. To introduce this theorem consider the following example.

Example 5.9 The probability space is $\Omega = \{\omega_1, \omega_2, \omega_3, \omega_4\}$, the probability measure is $P(\omega) = \frac{1}{4}$ for all $\omega \in \Omega$, $T = 2$, and the information structure is

$$\mathbf{f}_1 = \{\{\omega_1\}, \{\omega_2, \omega_3, \omega_4\}\}$$

Consider the random variables $e_1, \ldots, e_4$

$$e_h(\omega_k) = \begin{cases} 1 & \text{if } k = h \\ 0 & \text{if } k \neq h \end{cases}$$

and the martingales $e_{ht} = E_P(e_h|\mathbf{f}_t)$. These martingales are shown below.

e_1	ω_1	ω_2	ω_3	ω_4
$t = 0$	$\frac{1}{4}$	$\frac{1}{4}$	$\frac{1}{4}$	$\frac{1}{4}$
$t = 1$	1	0	0	0
$t = 2$	1	0	0	0

e_2	ω_1	ω_2	ω_3	ω_4
$t = 0$	$\frac{1}{4}$	$\frac{1}{4}$	$\frac{1}{4}$	$\frac{1}{4}$
$t = 1$	0	$\frac{1}{3}$	$\frac{1}{3}$	$\frac{1}{3}$
$t = 2$	0	1	0	0

e_3	ω_1	ω_2	ω_3	ω_4
$t = 0$	$\frac{1}{4}$	$\frac{1}{4}$	$\frac{1}{4}$	$\frac{1}{4}$
$t = 1$	0	$\frac{1}{3}$	$\frac{1}{3}$	$\frac{1}{3}$
$t = 2$	0	0	1	0

e_4	ω_1	ω_2	ω_3	ω_4
$t = 0$	$\frac{1}{4}$	$\frac{1}{4}$	$\frac{1}{4}$	$\frac{1}{4}$
$t = 1$	0	$\frac{1}{3}$	$\frac{1}{3}$	$\frac{1}{3}$
$t = 2$	0	0	0	1

Every martingale $\{x_t\}$ has a representation

$$x_t(\omega_k) = \sum_{h=1}^{4} x_t(\omega_h) e_{ht}(\omega_k) \tag{5.1}$$

for $t = 0, 1, 2$. For example, the martingale

x	ω_1	ω_2	ω_3	ω_4
$t = 0$	1	1	1	1
$t = 1$	16	-4	-4	-4
$t = 2$	16	3	-24	9

has the representation

$$x_t = 16e_{1t} + 3e_{2t} - 24e_{3t} + 9e_{4t}$$

Notice that in this representation the coordinates $16, 3, -24, 9$ do not depend on t.

This representation of martingales matches the representation of vectors in a vector basis. The four martingales $\{e_{ht}\}$ for $h = 1, 2, 3, 4$ form what might be called a basis. In general, this example suggests that if the sample space Ω has K elements, then there exists a basis of K martingales in the sense of Equation 5.1.

It is fruitful to consider the martingales on the given information structure as a combination of their restrictions to the vertices of the information structure, just as we considered the discrete multiperiod model as a combination of discrete one-period models. This perspective suggests looking for a basis of m martingales $\{w_{ht}\}$ that allow the representation of the increments of any martingale $\{x_t\}$ in terms of the increments of the basis martingales

$$dx_t = \sum_{h=1}^{m} \alpha_{ht} dw_{ht} \qquad (5.2)$$

where the coordinates α_{ht} are predictable processes. Theorem 5.15 asserts that for a basis in the sense of Equation 5.2 the required number of martingales is one less than the splitting index of the information structure, $m = \nu - 1$, and that the basis martingales can be chosen to be pairwise orthogonal. In the present example $\nu = 3$ and there is a two-dimensional orthogonal basis

w_1	ω_1	ω_2	ω_3	ω_4
$t=0$	0	0	0	0
$t=1$	1	$-\frac{1}{3}$	$-\frac{1}{3}$	$-\frac{1}{3}$
$t=2$	1	$\frac{2}{3}$	$-\frac{1}{3}$	$-\frac{4}{3}$

w_2	ω_1	ω_2	ω_3	ω_4
$t=0$	0	0	0	0
$t=1$	0	0	0	0
$t=2$	0	1	-2	1

The construction of such an orthogonal basis and the computation of coordinates in such a basis are shown in the proof of Theorem 5.15. See also Example 5.10.

The precise definition of a basis in the sense of Equation 5.2 is as follows.

Definition 5.9 A finite set of martingales $\{w_{1t}\}, \ldots, \{w_{mt}\}$ is called a basis if and only if for every martingale $\{x_t\}$ there are predictable processes

$$\{\alpha_{1t}\}, \ldots, \{\alpha_{mt}\}$$

such that for every $1 \leq t \leq T$

$$x_t = x_0 + \sum_{h=1}^{m} \int_0^t \alpha_{hs} dw_{hs}$$

If the martingales $\{w_{1t}\}, \ldots, \{w_{mt}\}$ are pairwise orthogonal, that is, for every $1 \leq j \leq m$, $1 \leq h \leq m$, $j \neq h$, and every $0 \leq t \leq T$, $\langle w_j, w_h \rangle_t = 0$, then the basis $\{w_{1t}\}, \ldots, \{w_{mt}\}$ is called orthogonal.

We call

$$x_t = x_0 + \sum_{h=1}^{m} \int_0^t \alpha_{hs} dw_{hs}$$

a predictable representation of the martingale $\{x_t\}$. Because every martingale has a predictable representation in a basis, the information represented by a basis cannot be less than $\{f_t\}$. To formalize this, define the information structure generated by a set of stochastic processes as follows.

Definition 5.10 The information structure $\{f_t^{v_1,\ldots,v_m}\}$ generated by the stochastic processes $\{v_{1t}\},\ldots,\{v_{mt}\}$ is such that:

1. The partition $f_0^{v_1,\ldots,v_m}$ is the coarsest partition on which the random variables $v_{10},\ldots,v_{m0}$ are measurable.

2. For every $1 \leq t \leq T$ the partition $f_t^{v_1,\ldots,v_m}$ is the coarsest partition that is finer than $f_{t-1}^{v_1,\ldots,v_m}$ and on which the random variables $v_{1t},\ldots,v_{mt}$ are measurable.

Every orthogonal basis has the property that $\{f_t^{w_1,\ldots,w_m}\} = \{f_t\}$.

Theorem 5.15 *Let the splitting index of the information structure $\{f_t\}$ be ν. Then there exists an orthogonal basis of $\nu - 1$ martingales*

$$\{w_{1t}\}, \quad , \{w_{\nu-1,t}\}$$

If, in addition, the process $\{x_t\}$ is such that $x_t(\omega) \neq 0$ for all t and ω, then there are predictable processes $\{\beta_{1t}\},\ldots,\{\beta_{\nu-1,t}\}$ such that for every $1 \leq t \leq T$

$$x_t = x_0 \mathcal{E}_t \left(\sum_{h=1}^{\nu-1} \beta_h \bullet w_h \right)$$

Proof. For all $1 \leq h \leq \nu - 1$ and $1 \leq t \leq T$ denote the increments of the basis martingales $\{w_{1t}\},\ldots,\{w_{\nu-1,t}\}$ by

$$dw_{ht} = w_{ht} - w_{h,t-1}$$

The construction of a basis is done in steps, with each step corresponding to a vertex of the information structure. The number of the basis martingales that have non-zero values at some vertex depends on the value of the splitting function at that vertex. To assist the reader's intuition the construction below shows explicitly how the basis martingales are defined at $t = 0$ and $t = 1$ for possible values of the splitting function at $t = 0$: $\nu(0) = 1, 2, \ldots, \nu$.

Figure 5.1: The values of dw_{h1} for $\nu(0) = 1$ in the proof of Theorem 5.15.

Define $w_{j0} = 0$ for all $1 \leq j \leq \nu - 1$ and consider first the case $\nu(0) = 1$. In this case, for all $1 \leq h \leq \nu - 1$ define $dw_{h1} = 0$. Figure 5.1 shows the initial segment of the information structure and the basis martingales when $\nu(0) = 1$.

Because $\nu(0) = 1$, $\mathbf{f}_1 = \mathbf{f}_0$, and consequently $\mathbf{f}_1^{w_1,\ldots,w_{\nu-1}} = \mathbf{f}_1$. Because $\{x_t\}$ is a martingale on this information structure, then $x_1 = x_0$ and the processes $\{\alpha_{1t}\}, \ldots, \{\alpha_{\nu-1,t}\}$ and $\{\beta_{1t}\}, \ldots, \{\beta_{\nu-1,t}\}$ are arbitrary predictable processes. Next consider the case $\nu(0) = 2$ and define

$$
\begin{aligned}
dw_{11}(f_{11}) &= 1 \\
dw_{11}(f_{12}) &= -\frac{P(f_{11})}{P(f_{12})}
\end{aligned}
$$

$$dw_{h1} = 0 \text{ for } 2 \leq h \leq \nu - 1$$

Figure 5.2 shows the initial segment of the information structure and the basis martingales when $\nu(0) = 2$.

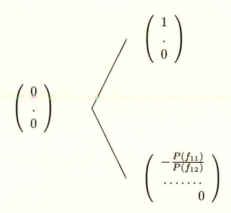

Figure 5.2: The values of dw_{h1} for $\nu(0) = 2$ in the proof of Theorem 5.15.

In this case $\mathbf{f}_1 = \{f_{11}, f_{12}\}$. Because $1 \neq -\dfrac{P(f_{11})}{P(f_{12})}$, we have $\mathbf{f}_1^{w_1,\ldots,w_{\nu-1}} = \mathbf{f}_1^{w_1} = \mathbf{f}_1$. Consider the two systems of equations

$$\alpha_{11}[w_{11}(f_{11}) - w_{10}] = x(f_{11}) - x_0 \tag{5.3}$$
$$\alpha_{11}[w_{11}(f_{12}) - w_{10}] = x(f_{12}) - x_0 \tag{5.4}$$

and

$$1 + \beta_{11}[w_{11}(f_{11}) - w_{10}] = \frac{x(f_{11})}{x_0} \tag{5.5}$$

$$1 + \beta_{11}[w_{11}(f_{12}) - w_{10}] = \frac{x(f_{12})}{x_0} \tag{5.6}$$

The martingale property of the processes w_1 and x implies that Equations 5.3 and 5.4 are linearly dependent and, therefore, the system 5.3 – 5.4 has a solution α_{11}. Similarly, Equations 5.5 and 5.6 are linearly dependent and have a solution β_{11}. The reader should note that $\alpha_{11} = x_0\beta_{11}$. Next, consider the case $\nu(0) = 3$. Define

$$dw_{11}(f_{11}) = 1$$
$$dw_{11}(f_{12}) = 0$$
$$dw_{11}(f_{13}) = -\frac{P(f_{11})}{P(f_{13})}$$
$$dw_{21}(f_{11}) = 1$$
$$dw_{21}(f_{12}) = -\frac{P(f_{11}) + P(f_{13})}{P(f_{12})}$$
$$dw_{21}(f_{13}) = 1$$

$$dw_{h1} = 0 \text{ for } 3 \leq h \leq \nu - 1$$

Figure 5.3 shows the initial segment of the information structure and the basis martingales when $\nu(0) = 3$. In this case

$$\mathbf{f}_1^{w_1} = \{f_{11}, f_{12}, f_{13}\}$$
$$\mathbf{f}_1^{w_2} = \{f_{11} \cup f_{13}, f_{12}\}$$

and, therefore

$$\mathbf{f}_1^{w_1, w_2} = \{f_{11}, f_{12}, f_{13}\} = \mathbf{f}_1$$

The martingales $\{w_{10}, w_{11}\}$ and $\{w_{20}, w_{21}\}$ are orthogonal because

$$w_{10}w_{20} \qquad\qquad = 0$$

$$P(f_{11}) \cdot 1 \cdot 1 + P(f_{12}) \cdot 0 \cdot [-\frac{P(f_{11}) + P(f_{13})}{P(f_{12})}]$$
$$+ P(f_{13}) \cdot [-\frac{P(f_{11})}{P(f_{13})}] \cdot 1 \qquad\qquad = 0$$

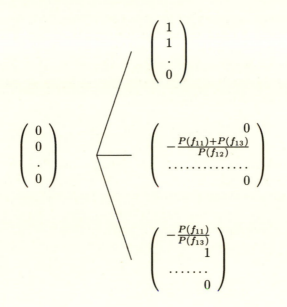

Figure 5.3: The values of dw_{h1} for $\nu(0) = 3$ in the proof of Theorem 5.15.

Now consider the two systems of equations

$$\alpha_{11}[w_{11}(f_{11}) - w_{10}] + \alpha_{21}[w_{21}(f_{11}) - w_{20}] = x(f_{11}) - x_0 \quad (5.7)$$
$$\alpha_{11}[w_{11}(f_{12}) - w_{10}] + \alpha_{21}[w_{21}(f_{12}) - w_{20}] = x(f_{12}) - x_0 \quad (5.8)$$
$$\alpha_{11}[w_{11}(f_{13}) - w_{10}] + \alpha_{21}[w_{21}(f_{13}) - w_{20}] = x(f_{13}) - x_0 \quad (5.9)$$

and

$$1 + \beta_{11}[w_{11}(f_{11}) - w_{10}] + \beta_{21}[w_{21}(f_{11}) - w_{20}] = \frac{x(f_{11})}{x_0} \quad (5.10)$$

$$1 + \beta_{11}[w_{11}(f_{12}) - w_{10}] + \beta_{21}[w_{21}(f_{12}) - w_{20}] = \frac{x(f_{12})}{x_0} \quad (5.11)$$

$$1 + \beta_{11}[w_{11}(f_{13}) - w_{10}] + \beta_{21}[w_{21}(f_{13}) - w_{20}] = \frac{x(f_{12})}{x_0} \quad (5.12)$$

The system of Equations 5.7 and 5.8 has a solution because the determinant of this system is different from zero

$$\begin{vmatrix} 1 & 0 \\ 1 & -\dfrac{P(f_{11})+P(f_{13})}{P(f_{12})} \end{vmatrix} \neq 0$$

The martingale property of the processes $\{w_{10}, w_{11}\}$, $\{w_{20}, w_{21}\}$, and $\{x_0, x_1\}$ implies that Equation 5.9 is a linear combination of Equations 5.7 and 5.8. Therefore, the system 5.7 – 5.9 has a solution α_{11}, α_{21}. Similarly, the system of Equations 5.10 – 5.12 has a solution β_{11}, β_{21}. Notice that the two systems of equations are such that $\alpha_{h1} = x_0 \beta_{h1}$ for $h = 1, 2$.

This construction of the processes

$$\{w_{1t}\}, \ldots, \{w_{\nu-1,t}\}$$

is continued for all the possible values of $\nu(0) \leq \nu$, and then the construction is repeated for subsequent $t \leq T$. As one more instance of this procedure consider $\nu(0) = 4$ and define

$$
\begin{aligned}
dw_{11}(f_{11}) &= 1 \\
dw_{11}(f_{12}) &= 0 \\
dw_{11}(f_{13}) &= 0 \\
dw_{11}(f_{14}) &= -\frac{P(f_{11})}{P(f_{14})} \\
dw_{21}(f_{11}) &= 1 \\
dw_{21}(f_{12}) &= 0 \\
dw_{21}(f_{13}) &= -\frac{P(f_{11}) + P(f_{14})}{P(f_{13})} \\
dw_{21}(f_{14}) &= 1 \\
dw_{31}(f_{11}) &= 1 \\
dw_{21}(f_{12}) &= -\frac{P(f_{11}) + P(f_{13}) + P(f_{14})}{P(f_{12})} \\
dw_{31}(f_{13}) &= 1 \\
dw_{31}(f_{14}) &= 1
\end{aligned}
$$

$$dw_{h1} = 0 \text{ for } 4 \leq h \leq \nu - 1$$

It is easy to check that the processes

$$\{w_{10}, w_{11}\}, \{w_{20}, w_{21}\}, \text{ and } \{w_{30}, w_{31}\}$$

are pairwise orthogonal martingales. Furthermore, the partitions generated by the random variables w_{11}, w_{21}, w_{31} are

$$
\begin{aligned}
\mathbf{f}_1^{w_1} &= \{f_{11}, f_{12} \cup f_{13}, f_{14}\} & (5.13) \\
\mathbf{f}_1^{w_2} &= \{f_{11} \cup f_{14}, f_{12}, f_{13}\} & (5.14) \\
\mathbf{f}_1^{w_3} &= \{f_{11} \cup f_{13} \cup f_{14}, f_{12}\} & (5.15)
\end{aligned}
$$

so that $\mathbf{f}_1^{w_1, w_2, w_3} = \{f_{11}, f_{12}, f_{13}, f_{14}\} = \mathbf{f}_1$. Finally, the determinant

$$
\begin{vmatrix}
1 & 0 & 0 \\
1 & 0 & -\dfrac{P(f_{11})+P(f_{14})}{P(f_{13})} \\
1 & -\dfrac{P(f_{11})+P(f_{13})+P(f_{14})}{P(f_{12})} & 1
\end{vmatrix}
$$

is different from zero, and therefore, the linear systems for α_{h1} and β_{h1} for $h = 1, 2, 3$ have a solution. ∎

The proof of Theorem 5.15 suggests that there is a simple relationship between the predictable processes in the representation of a martingale as a sum of stochastic integrals and the representation of a martingale as a stochastic exponential. Indeed, if $x_t(\omega) \neq 0$ for all t and ω and

$$
x_t = x_0 + \sum_{h=1}^{m} \int_0^t \alpha_{hs} dw_{hs}
$$

then

$$
x_t = x_0 + \sum_{h=1}^{m} \int_0^t \frac{\alpha_{hs}}{x_{s-}} x_{s-} dw_{hs}
$$

and, therefore

$$
x_t = x_0 \mathcal{E}_t \left(\sum_{h=1}^{m} \beta_h \bullet w_h \right)
$$

with $\beta_h = \dfrac{\alpha_{hs}}{x_{s-}}$. Conversely, if a martingale $\{x_t\}$ has this representation as a stochastic exponential, then the processes $\alpha_{hs} = \beta_h x_{s-}$ define a predictable representation of $\{x_t\}$ as a sum of stochastic integrals.

Example 5.10 This is a continuation of Example 5.9. The construction in the proof of Theorem 5.15 produces the two-dimensional orthogonal basis $\{w_{1t}\}$, $\{w_{2t}\}$. Figure 5.4 shows the increments of the basis processes. The probabilities and conditional probabilities used to compute these increments are as follows

$$
P(f_{11}) = \frac{1}{4}, \quad P(f_{12}) = \frac{3}{4}
$$

$$
P(\omega_1|\mathbf{f}_1)(f_{11}) = 1, \quad \text{and} \quad P(\omega_h|\mathbf{f}_1)(f_{12}) = \frac{1}{3} \quad \text{for} \quad h = 2, 3, 4
$$

The orthogonal basis computed from the increments in Figure 5.4 follows.

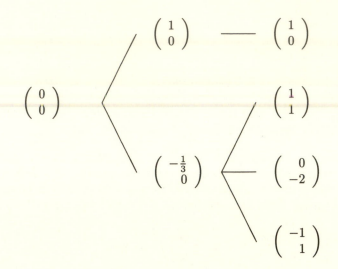

Figure 5.4: The martingale increments dw_1 and dw_2 in Example 5.10.

w_1	ω_1	ω_2	ω_3	ω_4
$t = 0$	0	0	0	0
$t = 1$	1	$-\frac{1}{3}$	$-\frac{1}{3}$	$-\frac{1}{3}$
$t = 2$	1	$\frac{2}{3}$	$-\frac{1}{3}$	$-\frac{4}{3}$

w_2	ω_1	ω_2	ω_3	ω_4
$t = 0$	0	0	0	0
$t = 1$	0	0	0	0
$t = 2$	0	1	-2	1

Notice that $\mathbf{f}_t^{w_1,w_2} = \mathbf{f}_t$ for each $t = 0, 1, 2$. Next, consider the martingale

x	ω_1	ω_2	ω_3	ω_4
$t = 0$	1	1	1	1
$t = 1$	16	-4	-4	-4
$t = 2$	16	3	-24	9

The predictable processes $\{\alpha_{ht}\}$ and $\{\beta_{ht}\}$ ($h = 1, 2$) that determine the representation of the martingale $\{x_t\}$ as a sum of stochastic integrals and a stochastic exponential follow; the entry n/a means that $\alpha_{ht}(\omega)$ and $\beta_{ht}(\omega)$ are arbitrary there.

α_1	ω_1	ω_2	ω_3	ω_4
$t = 0$	n/a	n/a	n/a	n/a
$t = 1$	15	15	15	15
$t = 2$	n/a	-3	-3	-3

α_2	ω_1	ω_2	ω_3	ω_4
$t = 0$	n/a	n/a	n/a	n/a
$t = 1$	n/a	n/a	n/a	n/a
$t = 2$	n/a	10	10	10

β_1	ω_1	ω_2	ω_3	ω_4		β_2	ω_1	ω_2	ω_3	ω_4
$t=0$	n/a	n/a	n/a	n/a		$t=0$	n/a	n/a	n/a	n/a
$t=1$	n/a	n/a	n/a	n/a		$t=1$	n/a	n/a	n/a	n/a
$t=2$	n/a	$\frac{3}{4}$	$\frac{3}{4}$	$\frac{3}{4}$		$t=2$	n/a	$-\frac{5}{2}$	$-\frac{5}{2}$	$-\frac{5}{2}$

5.6   The Doob Decomposition

The final result from the theory of discrete martingale processes that appears in this chapter is Doob's decomposition of adapted processes as sums of martingales and predictable processes.

Theorem 5.16 (Doob) *Given a real number a, every adapted process x has a unique decomposition*

$$x_t = a_t + w_t$$

where $\{a_t\}$ is a predictable process such that $a_0 = a$ and $\{w_t\}$ is a martingale.

Proof. Define

$$a_t = \begin{cases} a & \text{if } t = 0 \\ a_{t-1} - x_{t-1} + E_P(x_t|\mathbf{f}_{t-1}) & \text{if } 1 \le t \le T \end{cases}$$

$$w_t = \begin{cases} x_0 - a & \text{if } t = 0 \\ w_{t-1} + x_t - E_P(x_t|\mathbf{f}_{t-1}) & \text{if } 1 \le t \le T \end{cases}$$

This is the desired decomposition. To prove uniqueness suppose that there is a predictable process $\{a'_t\}$ such that $a'_0 = a$ and a martingale $\{w'_t\}$ such that

$$x_t = a'_t + w'_t$$

Then

$$x_t - x_{t-1} = a'_t - a'_{t-1} + w'_t - w'_{t-1}$$

and taking conditional expectations

$$a_t - a_{t-1} = E_P(x_t|\mathbf{f}_{t-1}) - x_{t-1} = a'_t - a'_{t-1}$$

Because $a'_0 = a_0 = a$, $a'_t = a_t$ for all $0 \le t \le T$ and uniqueness follows. ∎

In this decomposition of the process $\{x_t\}$, the processes $\{a_t\}$ and $\{w_t\}$ have descriptive names.

Definition 5.11 In the Doob decomposition of the process $\{x_t\}$

$$x_t = a_t + w_t$$

the process $\{a_t\}$ is called the predictable part of $\{x_t\}$ and the martingale $\{w_t\}$ is called the innovation part of $\{x_t\}$.

The predictable component represents the part of x_t that is anticipated at time $t - 1$, whereas the innovation component represents the part of x_t that is not anticipated at time $t - 1$.

If the process $\{x_t\}$ is such that its conditional expected value is no less than its current value, then the predictable process $\{a_t\}$ is increasing. A process $\{x_t\}$ with this property is called a submartingale.

Definition 5.12 An adapted process $\{x_t\}$ is called a submartingale relative to the probability measure P if and only if for any $0 \leq s \leq t \leq T$

$$E_P(x_t|\mathbf{f}_s) \geq x_s$$

The assertion that the predictable part of a submartingale is increasing follows immediately from the definition of a submartingale and the construction of the predictable part of a process in the proof of Theorem 5.16.

Example 5.11 $\Omega = \{\omega_1, \ldots, \omega_6\}$, $T - 3$, $P(\omega) = \frac{1}{6}$ for all $\omega \in \Omega$, the information structure is

$$\mathbf{f}_1 = \{\{\omega_1, \omega_2\}, \{\omega_3, \omega_4, \omega_5, \omega_6\}\}$$
$$\mathbf{f}_2 = \{\{\omega_1, \omega_2\}, \{\omega_3, \omega_4\}, \{\omega_5, \omega_6\}\}$$

and x is the submartingale

x	ω_1	ω_2	ω_3	ω_4	ω_5	ω_6
$t = 0$	1	1	1	1	1	1
$t = 1$	3	3	2	2	2	2
$t = 2$	4	4	3	3	2	2
$t = 3$	4	5	6	2	1	3

Then Doob's decomposition of x with $a = 0$ is

a	ω_1	ω_2	ω_3	ω_4	ω_5	ω_6
$t = 0$	0	0	0	0	0	0
$t = 1$	$\frac{4}{3}$	$\frac{4}{3}$	$\frac{4}{3}$	$\frac{4}{3}$	$\frac{4}{3}$	$\frac{4}{3}$
$t = 2$	$\frac{7}{3}$	$\frac{7}{3}$	$\frac{11}{6}$	$\frac{11}{6}$	$\frac{11}{6}$	$\frac{11}{6}$
$t = 3$	$\frac{17}{6}$	$\frac{17}{6}$	$\frac{17}{6}$	$\frac{17}{6}$	$\frac{11}{6}$	$\frac{11}{6}$

w	ω_1	ω_2	ω_3	ω_4	ω_5	ω_6
$t = 0$	1	1	1	1	1	1
$t = 1$	$\frac{5}{3}$	$\frac{5}{3}$	$\frac{2}{3}$	$\frac{2}{3}$	$\frac{2}{3}$	$\frac{2}{3}$
$t = 2$	$\frac{5}{3}$	$\frac{5}{3}$	$\frac{7}{6}$	$\frac{7}{6}$	$\frac{1}{6}$	$\frac{1}{6}$
$t = 3$	$\frac{7}{6}$	$\frac{13}{6}$	$\frac{19}{6}$	$-\frac{5}{6}$	$-\frac{5}{6}$	$\frac{7}{6}$

An adapted process $\{x_t\}$ is called a supermartingale if and only if the process $\{-x_t\}$ is a submartingale. It is easy to see that the predictable part of a supermartingale is decreasing.

We now establish two additional results related to the Doob decomposition of an adapted process. The first result is stated in terms of the dual predictable projection process which is introduced in Definition 5.13. This result is that the predictable component of a process is its dual predictable projection. The second result concerns the Doob decomposition of a P-martingale, when the decomposition is done with respect to another probability measure Q. This result is just a restatement of Girsanov's theorem.

Definition 5.13 For a stochastic process x define the predictable projection of x as the process

$$(\pi x)_t = \begin{cases} x_0 & \text{if } t = 0 \\ E_P(x_t | \mathbf{f}_{t-1}) & \text{otherwise} \end{cases}$$

and the dual predictable projection of x as the process

$$(\pi^* x)_t = \begin{cases} x_0 & \text{if } t = 0 \\ x_0 + \sum_{s=1}^{t} E_P(x_s - x_{s-1} | \mathbf{f}_{s-1}) & \text{otherwise} \end{cases}$$

It is easy to see that the projection processes in the preceding definition are predictable. For an explanation of the duality relationship between the two projection processes see Problem 11.

Theorem 5.17 *Suppose that the process x is adapted. Then the process $x - \pi^* x$ is a martingale.*

Proof. We have

$$
\begin{aligned}
E_P[x_t - (\pi^* x)_t | \mathbf{f}_{t-1}] &= E_P(x_t | \mathbf{f}_{t-1}) - (\pi^* x)_t \\
&= E_P(x_t | \mathbf{f}_{t-1}) - E_P(x_t - x_{t-1} | \mathbf{f}_{t-1}) - (\pi^* x)_{t-1} \\
&= x_{t-1} - (\pi^* x)_{t-1}
\end{aligned}
$$

This completes the proof. ∎

The following is a simple corollary to Theorem 5.16.

Corollary 5.2 *If the process x is adapted, then*

$$x - \pi^* x + (x - \pi^* x)$$

is the Doob decomposition of x with the initial value of the predictable part equal to x_0.

Notice that the initial value of the predictable part is equal to x_0 if and only if the innovation component is null at zero. Finally, suppose that Q is a probability measure on the probability space Ω such that $Q(\omega) > 0$ for all $\omega \in \Omega$. Then we have the following corollary to Girsanov's theorem.

Corollary 5.3 *Let x be a P-martingale. Then the Doob decomposition of x with respect to Q such that the innovation component is null at zero is*

$$x_t = x_0 + \int_0^t \frac{d\langle x, z\rangle_s}{z_{s-}} + \left(x_t - x_0 - \int_0^t \frac{d\langle x, z\rangle_s}{z_{s-}} \right)$$

Problems

1. Prove that for any three processes x, y, and z

$$[[x, y], z] = [x, [y, z]]$$

2. Prove that any partition is independent of the trivial partition.

3. Prove that if **f** and **g** are independent partitions and **h** is coarser than **g**, then **h** and **f** are independent.

4. Prove Theorem 5.4.

5. Prove the polarization formulas

$$[x, y] = \frac{1}{2}([x + y, x + y] - [x, x] - [y, y])$$
$$\langle x, y \rangle = \frac{1}{2}(\langle x + y, x + y \rangle - \langle x, x \rangle - \langle y, y \rangle)$$

6. Prove that for any processes $\{\alpha_t\}, \{\beta_t\}, \{x_t\}, \{y_t\}$

$$[\alpha \bullet x, \beta \bullet y]_t = \int_0^t \alpha_s \beta_s d[x, y]_s$$

7. Prove that the likelihood ratio process $\{z_t\}$ is a positive P-martingale.

8. Prove that the reciprocal of the likelihood ratio process, $\left\{\frac{1}{z_t}\right\}$, is a Q-martingale.

9. Prove the following representation of the likelihood ratio process as a stochastic exponential

$$z = \mathcal{E}(\frac{1}{z_-} \bullet z)$$

10. Prove that if $\{x_t\}$ is a P-martingale, then given the initial value $a = x_0^2$ the predictable part of the process $\{x_t^2\}$ is $\langle x, x \rangle_t$.

11. For any processes $\{x_t\}$ and $\{y_t\}$, prove the following equality which explains the name dual predictable projection for the process $\{(\pi^*x)_t\}$

$$E_P[\int_0^t (\pi x)_s dy_s] = E_P[\int_0^t x_s d(\pi^* y)_s]$$

12. Prove that a process $\{x_t\}$ is predictable if and only if $\pi^* x = x$.

13. Prove that for any processes $\{x_t\}$ and $\{y_t\}$

$$\pi^*[x, y] = \langle x, y \rangle$$

14. Prove that if x is a martingale and y is adapted, then for all $0 \leq t \leq T$

$$(\pi^* xy)_t = \langle x, y \rangle_t + \int_0^t x_{s-} d(\pi^* y)_s$$

15. Let x be a P-martingale, w an adapted process, and suppose that the probability measure Q is such that

$$Q = P\mathcal{E}_T(w)$$

Prove that the Doob decomposition of x with respect to Q with null initial value of the predictable component is

$$x = \langle x, w \rangle + (x - \langle x, w \rangle)$$

16. A random variable $\tau : \Omega \to \{0, \ldots, T\}$ is called a stopping time if and only if for each $0 \le t \le T$ the event $\{\omega \mid \tau(\omega) = t\}$ is either empty or is a union of sets of the partition $\mathbf{f}_t$. This definition says that for any $0 \le t \le T$ the event $\{\tau = t\}$ is decidable at time t, that is, each trader knows at each time t whether or not $\tau = t$. A stopping time τ is called predictable if and only if $\tau \equiv 0$ or for each $1 \le t \le T$ the event $\{\tau = t\}$ is either empty or is a union of sets of the partition $\mathbf{f}_{t-1}$. Prove that for any process $\{x_t\}$ and predictable stopping time τ

$$E_P(x_\tau) = E_P[(\pi x)_\tau]$$

Notes

The development of discrete stochastic calculus in this chapter parallels the corresponding theorems in Chapters 10 and 11. The decomposition of an adapted process in Theorem 5.16 is due to [22].

Chapter 6

Extensions of the Discrete Multiperiod Model

6.1 Introduction

This chapter uses the discrete stochastic calculus of Chapter 5 to deliver further results in the discrete multiperiod model. For any equilibrium price measure, we justify for the likelihood ratio process of this measure with respect to the given probability measure the name *risk adjustment process*. Starting with a complete price system, we obtain a representation of the risk adjustment process as a stochastic exponential. As an example of using this representation, we compute an explicit call pricing formula that involves the binomial distribution function. The limiting form of this formula anticipates the introduction of the Black-Scholes call pricing model in Chapter 9.

Section 6.5 offers a new characterization of a complete price system. We show there that a price system p that does not permit arbitrage strategies is complete if and only if the discounted prices $\dfrac{p_{2t}}{(1+r)^t}, \ldots, \dfrac{p_{nt}}{(1+r)^t}$ form a basis for martingales with respect to some equilibrium price measure. Suitably modified, this characterization of complete price systems remains true in the general continuous model in Chapter 12.

The last section of this chapter describes an interpretation of the risk adjustment process as the single risk factor in the discrete multiperiod model. We demonstrate there that the Doob decomposition and Girsanov's theorem imply a relationship between the predictable and innovation components of the rate of return of every security. Specifically, the risk premium of every security is proportional to the conditional covariance between the likelihood

127

ratio process and the innovation part of the rate of return of that security.

6.2　A Simple Option Pricing Model

This section deals with a discrete multiperiod model with two securities and an information structure $\{\mathbf{f}_t\}$ that has a splitting index $\nu = 2$. Security 1 is a bond with a constant rate of interest, that is, the terminal payout and prices are

$$d_1 = (1+r)^T$$

$$p_{1t} = (1+r)^t$$

By assumption, the price of security 2, p_{2t}, is different from zero for all t and ω, and for all $0 \le t \le T$ we have $\mathbf{f}_t^{p2} = \mathbf{f}_t$, that is, the price of security 2 represents all the information available to the traders. For $1 \le t \le T$ define

$$\mu_t = E_P\left(\frac{p_{2t}}{p_{2,t-1}}\bigg| \mathbf{f}_{t-1}\right) - 1$$

$$w_t = w_{t-1} + \frac{p_{2t}}{p_{2,t-1}} - E_P\left(\frac{p_{2t}}{p_{2,t-1}}\bigg| \mathbf{f}_{t-1}\right)$$

where w_0 is an arbitrary constant and $p_{2T} = d_2$. The predictable process $\{\mu_t\}$ represents the conditional expected net rate of return of security 2 during the time interval $[t-1,t]$, that is, the predictable component. The process $\{w_t\}$ is a martingale and represents the innovation component of the rate of return of security 2 during the time period $[t-1,t]$. The realized rate of return of security 2 during $[t-1,t]$ is

$$\frac{p_{2t}}{p_{2,t-1}} = 1 + \mu_t + w_t - w_{t-1}$$

This representation of the rate of return, based on the Doob decomposition, as a sum of a predictable component and an innovation component is unique for each w_0. Indeed, suppose that there is another such representation

$$\frac{p_{2t}}{p_{2,t-1}} = 1 + \mu_t' + w_t' - w_{t-1}'$$

Then $\mu_t' + w_t' - w_{t-1}' = \mu_t + w_t - w_{t-1}$ and taking conditional expectations

$$E_P(\mu_t'|\mathbf{f}_{t-1}) = E_P(\mu_t|\mathbf{f}_{t-1})$$

Therefore, $\mu'_t = \mu_t$ for all $1 \le t \le T$ and

$$w'_t - w'_{t-1} = w_t - w_{t-1}$$

and if $w'_0 = w_0$, then $w'_t = w_t$ for all $0 \le t \le T$. From the preceding representation of the realized rates of return of security 2 we get the following representation of prices for every $0 \le t \le T$

$$p_{2t} = p_{20} \prod_{s=1}^{t} (1 + \mu_s + w_s - w_{s-1})$$

Notice that using shorthand notation the preceding representation of the price of security 2 can be written

$$dp_t = \mu_t p_{t-} dt + \sigma_t p_{t-} dw_t$$

where $dt = 1$. To determine the existence and uniqueness of an equilibrium price measure in this market consider a second probability measure Q on the sample space Ω such that $Q(\omega) > 0$ for all $\omega \in \Omega$. Let $\{z_t\}$ be the likelihood ratio process for $\dfrac{Q}{P}$ and define

$$v_t = w_t - \int_0^t \frac{d\langle w, z \rangle_s}{z_{s-}}$$

In terms of the process $\{v_t\}$ the price of security 2 has the representation

$$p_{2t} = p_{20} \prod_{s=1}^{t} \left(1 + \mu_s + v_s - v_{s-1} + \frac{\langle w, z \rangle_s - \langle w, z \rangle_{s-1}}{z_{s-1}} \right) \qquad (6.1)$$

and

$$\frac{p_{2t}}{(1+r)^t} = p_{20} \prod_{s=1}^{t} \frac{1 + \mu_s + v_s - v_{s-1} + \dfrac{\langle w, z \rangle_s - \langle w, z \rangle_{s-1}}{z_{s-1}}}{1 + r} \qquad (6.2)$$

The probability measure Q is an equilibrium price measure only if the process $\left\{ \dfrac{p_{2t}}{(1+r)^t} \right\}$ is a Q-martingale. The necessary and sufficient condition for this is that for all $1 \le t \le T$

$$E_Q \left(\frac{1 + \mu_t + v_t - v_{t-1} + \dfrac{\langle w, z \rangle_t - \langle w, z \rangle_{t-1}}{z_{t-1}}}{1 + r} \,\middle|\, f_{t-1} \right) = 1$$

From Girsanov's theorem, Theorem 5.14, the process $\{v_t\}$ is a Q-martingale and, therefore, the preceding equation is equivalent to

$$
E_Q \left(\left. \frac{1 + \mu_t + \dfrac{\langle w, z \rangle_t - \langle w, z \rangle_{t-1}}{z_{t-1}}}{1 + r} \right| \mathbf{f}_{t-1} \right) = 1 \tag{6.3}
$$

Because the process inside the expectation is predictable the preceding condition is equivalent to

$$
1 + \mu_t + \frac{\langle w, z \rangle_t - \langle w, z \rangle_{t-1}}{z_{t-1}} = 1 + r \tag{6.4}
$$

or, for all $1 \leq t \leq T$

$$
\frac{\langle w, z \rangle_t - \langle w, z \rangle_{t-1}}{z_{t-1}} = -(\mu_t - r) \tag{6.5}
$$

Because the martingale $\{w_t\}$ is such that $\mathbf{f}_t^w = \mathbf{f}_t$ for all $0 \leq t \leq T$ and $\nu = 2$, it follows from Theorem 5.15 that the P-martingale $\{z_t\}$ has a representation as the stochastic exponential

$$
z_t = \mathcal{E}_t(\beta \bullet w) = \prod_{s=1}^{t} [1 + \beta_s(w_s - w_{s-1})]
$$

where the process $\{\beta_t\}$ is predictable. Therefore

$$
z_t - z_{t-1} = z_{t-1} \beta_t (w_t - w_{t-1})
$$

and from Equation 6.5

$$
\frac{E_P[(w_t - w_{t-1})(z_t - z_{t-1})|\mathbf{f}_{t-1}]}{z_{t-1}} = -(\mu_t - r) \tag{6.6}
$$

so that if Q is an equilibrium price measure and $\langle w, w \rangle_t - \langle w, w \rangle_{t-1} \neq 0$, then

$$
\beta_t = -\frac{\mu_t - r}{\langle w, w \rangle_t - \langle w, w \rangle_{t-1}}
$$

If $\langle w, w \rangle_t - \langle w, w \rangle_{t-1} = 0$, then $z_t = z_{t-1}$ and β_t is arbitrary. Let $\{\sigma_t^2\}$ be the conditional variance process for the rate of return

$$
\sigma_t^2 = \mathrm{var}_P(w_t|\mathbf{f}_{t-1}) = E_P[(w_t - w_{t-1})^2|\mathbf{f}_{t-1}] = \langle w, w \rangle_t - \langle w, w \rangle_{t-1}
$$

Then

$$\beta_t = -\frac{\mu_t - r}{\sigma_t^2}$$

and the likelihood ratio process has the representation

$$z_t(\omega) = \prod_{s=1}^{t} \left[1 - \frac{\mu_s - r}{\sigma_s^2}(w_s - w_{s-1}) \right] \tag{6.7}$$

Therefore, if for every $1 \leq t \leq T$

$$\frac{\mu_t - r}{\sigma_t^2}(w_t - w_{t-1}) \quad < \quad 1 \tag{6.8}$$

then the equilibrium price measure Q exists, is unique, and is given by

$$Q(\omega) = P(\omega)z_T(\omega) = P(\omega) \prod_{t=1}^{T} \left[1 - \frac{\mu_t - r}{\sigma_t^2}(w_t - w_{t-1}) \right]$$

or, equivalently

$$Q \;=\; P\mathcal{E}_T\left(-\frac{\mu - r}{\sigma^2} \bullet w \right) \tag{6.9}$$

There are no arbitrage strategies and the price system $\{p_{1t}, p_{2t}\}$ is complete. Equation 6.9 is a representation of the equilibrium price measure and the key to risk adjustment and the representation of the price functional in this market. In addition, the likelihood ratio process has the representation

$$z_t = \mathcal{E}_t\left(-\frac{\mu - r}{\sigma^2} \bullet w \right)$$

Because the process $\left\{ z_t \dfrac{p_{2t}}{(1+r)^t} \right\}$ is a P-martingale, the likelihood ratio process z_t is also called the risk adjustment process for this market.

The preceding discussion has the following implications. First, the condition for existence of an equilibrium price measure is the inequality in Equation 6.8, with the interpretation that for security 2 the risk premium per unit of risk times the rate of return innovation is always less than unity. Second, the condition for uniqueness of the equilibrium price measure in this market is that the price of security 2 represents all the information available to the traders. This latter condition is equivalent to the condition for completeness in Theorem 3.3, that is, the condition that rank$[D(t,\omega)] = \nu(t-1,\omega)$. Third, because the discounted price of security 2 is a martingale relative to Q, Equation 6.6 and Theorem 5.13 imply that

$$E_Q(w_t - w_{t-1}|\mathbf{f}_{t-1}) = -(\mu_t - r)$$

so that, relative to Q, the conditional expected innovation in the rate of return on security 2 equals minus its risk premium. Finally, if Q is an equilibrium price measure, then Equations 6.2 and 6.4 imply that the discounted price of security 2 has a representation as the stochastic exponential

$$p_{2t} = p_{20}\mathcal{E}_t\left(\frac{1}{1+r}\bullet v\right)$$

Equipped with Equation 6.9 for the equilibrium price measure Q we can finally deliver a formula for the initial price of an option on security 2. A call option on security 2 with any exercise price a is attainable and has the initial price

$$p_{30} = \frac{E_P[\max(0, p_{2T} - a)z_T]}{(1+r)^T} \tag{6.10}$$

$$= \frac{E_P\left[\max(0, p_{2T} - a)\mathcal{E}_T\left(-\frac{\mu-r}{\sigma^2}\bullet w\right)\right]}{(1+r)^T} \tag{6.11}$$

Example 6.1 The number of states is $K = 3$, the probability measure is $P(\omega) = \frac{1}{3}$ for all ω, the terminal time is $T = 2$, the number of securities is $N = 3$, the information structure is

$$\mathbf{f}_1 = \{\{\omega_1, \omega_2\}, \{\omega_3\}\}$$

the rate of interest is $r = 0$, the terminal payoffs are

$$D = \begin{pmatrix} 10 & 32 & 22 \\ 10 & 16 & 6 \\ 10 & 12 & 2 \end{pmatrix}$$

and the prices of securities 1 and 2 are

p_1	ω_1	ω_2	ω_3		p_2	ω_1	ω_2	ω_3
$t=0$	10	10	10		$t=0$	16	16	16
$t=1$	10	10	10		$t=1$	24	24	12
$t=2$	10	10	10		$t=2$	32	16	12

It is easy to verify that security 3 is a call option on security 2 with an exercise price $a = 10$, and that security 2 represents all the information available to traders: $\mathbf{f}_0^{p_2} = \mathbf{f}_0$, $\mathbf{f}_1^{p_2} = \mathbf{f}_1$, and $\mathbf{f}_2^{p_2} = \mathbf{f}_2$. The predictable and innovation components of the rate of return on security 2 are

μ	ω_1	ω_2	ω_3
$t=0$	n/a	n/a	n/a
$t=1$	$\frac{1}{4}$	$\frac{1}{4}$	$\frac{1}{4}$
$t=2$	0	0	0

w	ω_1	ω_2	ω_3
$t=0$	0	0	0
$t=1$	$\frac{1}{4}$	$\frac{1}{4}$	$-\frac{1}{2}$
$t=2$	$\frac{7}{12}$	$-\frac{1}{12}$	$-\frac{1}{2}$

and the conditional variance process for the rate of return is

σ^2	ω_1	ω_2	ω_3
$t=0$	n/a	n/a	n/a
$t=1$	$\frac{1}{8}$	$\frac{1}{8}$	$\frac{1}{8}$
$t=2$	$\frac{1}{9}$	$\frac{1}{9}$	0

From Equation 6.7 the likelihood ratio process is

z	ω_1	ω_2	ω_3
$t=0$	1	1	1
$t=1$	$\frac{1}{2}$	$\frac{1}{2}$	2
$t=2$	$\frac{1}{2}$	$\frac{1}{2}$	2

and, therefore, security 3 is attainable by trading in securities 1 and 2. From Equation 6.11 the initial price of security 3 is

$$p_{30} = \frac{1}{3} \times 22 \times \frac{1}{2} + \frac{1}{3} \times 6 \times \frac{1}{2} + \frac{1}{3} \times 2 \times 2 = 6$$

Of course, the same value for the price p_{30} can be obtained by the method of Chapter 4.

6.3 An Explicit Option Pricing Formula

As another example of using Equation 6.11, consider a model in which the innovation part of the rate of return of security 2 is a symmetric random walk on a line. It is important to remember that this example is just a special case of the model in Section 6.2.

A symmetric random walk on a line is a description of a particle moving along the integer-valued points $0, \pm1, \pm2, \ldots$ stepping to the left or to the right at equal time intervals. The probabilities of a movement in either direction are equal and do not depend on the position of the particle. The random walk starts at time 0 and ends at time T.

At time $t = 1$ the particle can be in one of two positions, either 1 or -1 with the probabilities $P(x_1 = 1) = \frac{1}{2}$ and $P(x_1 = -1) = \frac{1}{2}$. At time $t = 2$, after two steps, the particle can be in one of three positions, $-2, 0, 2$, with the probabilities

$$P(x_2 = -2) = \frac{1}{4}, \ P(x_2 = 0) = \frac{1}{2}, \ P(x_2 = 2) = \frac{1}{4}$$

At time t the particle can be in one of $t+1$ positions

$$-t, -t+2, -t+4, \ldots, t-4, t-2, t$$

with the probabilities

$$P(x_t = t - 2j) = \left(\begin{array}{c} t \\ j \end{array} \right) 2^{-t}, \ 0 \le j \le t$$

The sample space Ω for such a random walk consists of 2^T elements with the probabilities $P(\omega_k) = 2^{-T}$ for each $1 \le k \le 2^T$. Let $\{\mathbf{f}_t\}$ be the information structure generated by the stochastic process $\{x_t\}$, that is, $\{\mathbf{f}_t\} = \{\mathbf{f}_t^x\}$. On this information structure the process $\{x_t\}$ is a martingale with mean $E_P(x_t) = 0$ and variance $E_P(x_t^2) = t$. Suppose that r, μ, and σ are positive constants such that

$$1 + \mu + \sigma > 1, \ 0 < 1 + \mu - \sigma < 1, \ r - \sigma < \mu < r + \sigma \qquad (6.12)$$

and consider a market with the following three securities. Security 1 is a bond with a constant rate of interest r, the predictable component of the rate of return on security 2 is constant, $\mu_t = \mu$, and the innovation component of the rate of return on security 2 is the martingale $w_t = \sigma x_t$. Therefore

$$d_1 = (1 + r)^T$$

$$d_2 = p_{20} \prod_{t=1}^{T} [1 + \mu + \sigma(x_t - x_{t-1})]$$

$$p_{1t} = (1 + r)^t$$

$$p_{2t} = p_{20} \prod_{s=1}^{t} [1 + \mu + \sigma(x_s - x_{s-1})]$$

Security 3 is a call option on security 2 with the exercise price a, and the information structure of the traders is $\{\mathbf{f}_t\}$. The assumptions about the rate of return innovation imply that

$$\sigma_t^2 = E_P[(w_t - w_{t-1})^2 | \mathfrak{f}_{t-1}] = \sigma^2$$

Denote

$$\lambda = \frac{\mu - r}{\sigma^2}$$

then $z_T = \prod_{t=1}^{T} [1 - \lambda\sigma(x_t - x_{t-1})]$.   Condition 6.8 for the absence of arbitrage strategies is $\lambda\sigma(x_t - x_{t-1}) < 1$ for all $1 \leq t \leq T$.   Because $x_t - x_{t-1} = \pm 1$, this is equivalent to the third condition in Equation 6.12, that is, $r - \sigma < \mu < r + \sigma$. The terminal payout, d_2, of security 2 is of the form

$$p_{20}(1 + \mu + \sigma)^{T-j}(1 + \mu - \sigma)^j$$

for $0 \leq j \leq T$ and

$$P\left[d_2 = p_{20}(1 + \mu + \sigma)^{T-j}(1 + \mu - \sigma)^j\right] = \left(\begin{array}{c} T \\ j \end{array}\right) 2^{-T}$$

Suppose that $a < (1 + \mu + \sigma)^T$, otherwise the price of the call is zero. To relate the exercise price a to the terminal payout of security 2 denote

$$\kappa(a) = \text{argmax}\left\{j \mid 0 \leq j \leq T \text{ and } (1 + \mu + \sigma)^{T-j}(1 + \mu - \sigma)^j > a\right\}$$

that is, $\kappa(a)$ is such that

$$(1 + \mu + \sigma)^{T-\kappa(a)-1}(1 + \mu - \sigma)^{\kappa(a)+1} \leq a < (1 + \mu + \sigma)^{T-\kappa(a)}(1 + \mu - \sigma)^{\kappa(a)}$$

Using formula 6.11 we get that the price of the call option p_{30} is equal to

$$\frac{2^{-T}}{(1 + r)^T} \sum_{j=0}^{\kappa(a)} \left(\begin{array}{c} T \\ j \end{array}\right) (1 + \mu + \sigma)^{T-j}(1 + \mu - \sigma)^j(1 - \lambda\sigma)^{T-j}(1 + \lambda\sigma)^j$$

$$- \frac{a}{(1 + r)^T} 2^{-T} \sum_{j=0}^{\kappa(a)} \left(\begin{array}{c} T \\ j \end{array}\right) (1 - \lambda\sigma)^{T-j}(1 + \lambda\sigma)^j$$

The call pricing formula above can be written more succinctly in terms of the binomial distribution function. Consider a random variable y defined as the number of successes in a sequence of m random experiments such that the result of each experiment is either success or failure. The probability of success is always π and the results of the m experiments are independent. Then y can have one of the values $0, 1, \ldots, m$ and its distribution is

$$P(y = j) = \binom{m}{j} \pi^j (1 - \pi)^{m-j}$$

The distribution function of y, denoted $B_m(j, \pi)$, is

$$B_m(j, \pi) = P(y \le j) = \sum_{h=0}^{j} \binom{m}{h} \pi^h (1 - \pi)^{m-h}$$

Conditions 6.12 guarantee that

$$0 < \frac{(1 + \mu - \sigma)(1 + \lambda\sigma)}{2(1 + r)} < 1 \quad \text{and} \quad 0 < \frac{1 + \lambda\sigma}{2} < 1$$

and in terms of the binomial distribution function the price of the call option is

$$p_{30} = p_{20} B_T \left[\kappa(a), \frac{(1 + \mu - \sigma)(1 + \lambda\sigma)}{2(1 + r)} \right]$$

$$- \frac{a}{(1 + r)^T} B_T \left[\kappa(a), \frac{1 + \lambda\sigma}{2} \right] \tag{6.13}$$

Equation 6.13 offers an explicit formula for the pricing of a call option in this example. In addition to its intrinsic interest, this formula converges to the Black-Scholes call pricing formula that will be developed systematically in Chapter 9. To obtain the limit of Equation 6.13 divide the time period $[0, T]$ into m equal time intervals of length T/m and denote

$$R = \frac{mr}{T}, \quad M = \frac{m\mu}{T}, \quad \Sigma = \frac{\sqrt{m}\sigma}{\sqrt{T}}$$

The mean and variance of the natural logarithm of the price ratio $\dfrac{p_{2T}}{p_{20}}$ are then

$$E_P \left[\log \left(\frac{p_{2T}}{p_{20}} \right) \right] = \frac{m}{2} \log \left[\left(1 + \frac{MT}{m} \right)^2 - \frac{\Sigma^2 T}{m} \right]$$

$$\text{var}_P \left[\log \left(\frac{p_{2T}}{p_{20}} \right) \right] = \frac{m}{2} \left[\log \left(1 + \frac{MT}{m} + \Sigma\sqrt{\frac{T}{m}} \right) \right]^2$$

$$+ \frac{m}{2} \left[\log \left(1 + \frac{MT}{m} - \Sigma\sqrt{\frac{T}{m}} \right) \right]^2$$

$$- \frac{m}{2} \left\{ \log \left[\left(1 + \frac{MT}{m} \right)^2 - \frac{\Sigma^2 T}{m} \right] \right\}^2$$

and if r, μ, and σ go to zero as m goes to infinity such that R, M, and Σ remain constant, then the mean and variance above converge to

$$\lim_{m \to \infty} \; E_P \left[\log \left(\frac{p_{2T}}{p_{20}} \right) \right] = MT - \frac{1}{2}\Sigma^2 T$$

$$\lim_{m \to \infty} \; \text{var}_P \left[\log \left(\frac{p_{2T}}{p_{20}} \right) \right] = \Sigma^2 T$$

By the Moivre-Laplace central limit theorem the binomial distribution functions in Equation 6.13 converge to the normal distribution function

$$\lim_{m \to \infty} B_T \left[\kappa(a), \frac{(1 + \mu - \sigma)(1 + \lambda\sigma)}{2(1 + r)} \right] = N \left[\frac{\log \left(\frac{p_{20}}{a} \right) + (R + \frac{1}{2}\Sigma^2)T}{\Sigma\sqrt{T}} \right]$$

$$\lim_{m \to \infty} B_T \left[\kappa(a), \frac{1 + \lambda\sigma}{2} \right] = N \left[\frac{\log \left(\frac{p_{20}}{a} \right) + (R - \frac{1}{2}\Sigma^2)T}{\Sigma\sqrt{T}} \right]$$

Finally, the present value factor converges to the negative exponential

$$\lim_{m \to \infty} \left(\frac{1}{1 + \dfrac{RT}{m}} \right)^m = e^{-RT}$$

Together, these observations imply that the limit of Equation 6.13 is

$$p_{30} = p_{20} N \left[\frac{\log \left(\frac{p_{20}}{a} \right) + (R + \frac{1}{2}\Sigma^2)T}{\Sigma\sqrt{T}} \right]$$

$$- a e^{-RT} N \left[\frac{\log \left(\frac{p_{20}}{a} \right) + (R - \frac{1}{2}\Sigma^2)T}{\Sigma\sqrt{T}} \right] \qquad (6.14)$$

Equation 6.14 is the Black-Scholes call pricing formula. The Black-Scholes formula is an approximation to the binomial formula, Equation 6.13, when the number of intermediate periods m is large. It is also the exact formula in the simple continuous multiperiod model in Chapter 9.

The Black-Scholes formula allows an easy examination of the comparative statics of the price of a call option in this market. The following table lists the signs of the partial derivatives of p_{30} in Equation 6.14.

x	p_{20}	a	T	Σ^2	R
$\dfrac{\partial p_{30}}{\partial x}$	$+$	$-$	$+$	$+$	$+$

The price of the call option is a decreasing function of the exercise price and an increasing function of the price of the underlying security, terminal time, variance of return on the underlying security, and the rate of interest on the bond.

6.4   Representation of Equilibrium Price Measures

In this section we consider the discrete multiperiod model with N securities and an information structure $\{\mathbf{f}_t\}$ that has a splitting index $\nu = N$. Security 1 is a bond with a constant rate of interest, that is

$$d_{1T} = (1+r)^T$$

$$p_{1t} = (1+r)^t$$

By assumption, the prices of securities $2, \ldots, N$ are different from zero for all t and ω, and for all $0 \le t \le T$ we have $\mathbf{f}_t^{p_2, \ldots, p_N} = \mathbf{f}_t$, that is, the prices of securities $2, \ldots, N$ represent all the information available to the traders. For $2 \le n \le N$ and $1 \le t \le T$ define

$$\mu_{nt} \; = \; E_P \left(\frac{p_{nt}}{p_{n,t-1}} \middle| \mathbf{f}_{t-1} \right) - 1$$

$$x_{nt} \; = \; x_{n,t-1} + \frac{p_{nt}}{p_{n,t-1}} - E_P \left(\frac{p_{nt}}{p_{n,t-1}} \middle| \mathbf{f}_{t-1} \right)$$

where x_{n0} are arbitrary constants and $p_{nT} = d_n$. For each $2 \le n \le N$ the predictable process $\{\mu_{nt}\}$ represents the conditional expected net rate of return of security n during the time interval $[t-1, t]$, that is, the predictable component. The process $\{x_{nt}\}$ is a martingale and represents the innovation component of the rate of return of security n during the time period $[t-1, t]$. The realized rate of return of security n during $[t-1, t]$ is

$$\frac{p_{nt}}{p_{n,t-1}} = 1 + \mu_{nt} + x_{nt} - x_{n,t-1}$$

From this representation of the realized rates of return of securities $2, \ldots, N$ we get the following representation of prices for $1 \le t \le T$

$$p_{nt} \; = \; p_{n0} \prod_{s=1}^{t} (1 + \mu_{ns} + x_{ns} - x_{n,s-1}) \qquad (6.15)$$

or, in shorthand notation

$$dp_{nt} = \mu_{nt}p_{nt-}dt + p_{nt-}dx_{nt}$$

Defining the cumulative predictable part of the rate of return

$$\kappa_{nt} = \sum_{s=1}^{t} \mu_{ns}$$

gives the representation of prices as stochastic exponentials

$$p_{nt} = p_{n0}\mathcal{E}_t(\kappa_n + x_n)$$

From Theorem 5.11 there exists an orthogonal basis

$$\{w_{1t}\}, \ldots, \{w_{\nu-1,t}\}$$

so that there exist predictable processes $\{\alpha_{nht}\}$ such that for each $2 \leq n \leq N$ and $0 \leq t \leq T$

$$x_{nt} = x_{n0} + \sum_{h=1}^{\nu-1} \int_0^t \alpha_{nhs}dw_{hs}$$

This representation of the martingales $\{x_{nt}\}$ implies that for each $2 \leq n \leq N$ and $1 \leq t \leq T$

$$x_{nt} - x_{n,t-1} = \sum_{h=1}^{\nu-1} \alpha_{nht}(w_{ht} - w_{h,t-1}) \qquad (6.16)$$

Substituting the representation of rate of return innovations in Equation 6.16 into the representation of prices in Equation 6.15, we get for all $1 \leq t \leq T$

$$p_{nt} = p_{n0} \prod_{s=1}^{t} \left[1 + \mu_{ns} + \sum_{h=1}^{\nu-1} \alpha_{nhs}(w_{hs} - w_{h,s-1}) \right]$$

To determine the existence and uniqueness of an equilibrium price measure in this market consider a second probability measure Q on the sample space Ω such that $Q(\omega) > 0$ for all $\omega \in \Omega$. Let $\{z_t\}$ be the likelihood ratio process for $\dfrac{Q}{P}$ and define

$$v_{ht} = w_{ht} - \int_0^t \frac{d\langle w_h, z \rangle_s}{z_{s-}}$$

In terms of the processes $\{v_{ht}\}$ the price of security n has the representation

$$p_{nt} = p_{n0} \prod_{s=1}^{t} \left[1 + \mu_{ns} + \sum_{h=1}^{\nu-1} \alpha_{nhs} \left(v_{hs} - v_{h,s-1} + \frac{\langle w_h, z \rangle_s - \langle w_h, z \rangle_{s-1}}{z_{s-1}} \right) \right]$$

and the discounted price $\dfrac{p_{nt}}{(1+r)^t}$ has the representation

$$p_{n0} \prod_{s=1}^{t} \frac{1 + \mu_{ns} + \sum_{h=1}^{\nu-1} \alpha_{nhs} \left(v_{hs} - v_{h,s-1} + \frac{\langle w_h, z \rangle_s - \langle w_h, z \rangle_{s-1}}{z_{s-1}} \right)}{1+r}$$

The probability measure Q is an equilibrium price measure only if the processes $\left\{ \dfrac{p_{nt}}{(1+r)^t} \right\}$ are Q-martingales. The necessary and sufficient condition for this is that for all $2 \leq n \leq N$ and $1 \leq t \leq T$ the conditional expectation

$$E_Q \left[\frac{1 + \mu_{nt} + \sum_{h=1}^{\nu-1} \alpha_{nhs} \left(v_{ht} - v_{h,t-1} + \frac{\langle w_h, z \rangle_t - \langle w_h, z \rangle_{t-1}}{z_{t-1}} \right)}{1+r} \middle| \mathbf{f}_{t-1} \right]$$

is equal to one. The processes $\{\alpha_{nht}\}$ are predictable, and from Girsanov's theorem, Theorem 5.14, the processes $\{v_{nt}\}$ are Q-martingales. Therefore, the preceding condition is equivalent to

$$E_Q \left(\frac{1 + \mu_{nt} + \sum_{h=1}^{\nu-1} \alpha_{nhs} \frac{\langle w_h, z \rangle_t - \langle w_h, z \rangle_{t-1}}{z_{t-1}}}{1+r} \middle| \mathbf{f}_{t-1} \right) = 1$$

Because for each $2 \leq n \leq N$ the process inside the expectation is predictable, the preceding condition is equivalent to

$$1 + \mu_{nt} + \sum_{h=1}^{\nu-1} \alpha_{nht} \frac{\langle w_h, z \rangle_t - \langle w_h, z \rangle_{t-1}}{z_{t-1}} = 1 + r$$

or, for all $2 \leq n \leq N$ and $1 \leq t \leq T$

$$\sum_{h=1}^{\nu-1} \alpha_{nht} \frac{\langle w_h, z \rangle_t - \langle w_h, z \rangle_{t-1}}{z_{t-1}} = -(\mu_{nt} - r) \qquad (6.17)$$

Theorem 5.15 and the fact that $z_0 = 1$ imply that the P-martingale $\{z_t\}$ has a representation as the stochastic exponential

$$z_t = \mathcal{E}_t \left(\sum_{h=1}^{\nu-1} \beta_h \bullet w_h \right)$$

$$= \prod_{s=1}^{t} \left[1 + \sum_{h=1}^{\nu-1} \beta_{hs}(w_{hs} - w_{h,s-1}) \right]$$

where the processes $\{\beta_{ht}\}$ are predictable. Therefore

$$z_t - z_{t-1} = z_{t-1} \sum_{h=1}^{\nu-1} \beta_{ht}(w_{ht} - w_{h,t-1})$$

and from Equation 6.17

$$\sum_{h=1}^{\nu-1} \alpha_{nht} E_P \left[(w_{ht} - w_{h,t-1}) \sum_{j=1}^{\nu-1} \beta_{jt}(w_{jt} - w_{j,t-1}) \middle| \mathbf{f}_{t-1} \right] = -(\mu_{nt} - r)$$

Because the basis martingales $\{w_{ht}\}$ are orthogonal, the preceding equation is equivalent to

$$\sum_{h=1}^{\nu-1} \alpha_{nht} \beta_{ht} E_P \left[(w_{ht} - w_{h,t-1})^2 \middle| \mathbf{f}_{t-1} \right] = -(\mu_{nt} - r) \qquad (6.18)$$

Introduce the notation

$$\Gamma_{nht} = \text{covar}_P(x_{nt}, w_{ht} | \mathbf{f}_{t-1})$$

Then Equation 6.16 implies that

$$\Gamma_{nht} = E_P[(x_{nt} - x_{n,t-1})(w_{ht} - w_{h,t-1}) | \mathbf{f}_{t-1}]$$

$$= \alpha_{nht} E_P \left[(w_{ht} - w_{h,t-1})^2 \middle| \mathbf{f}_{t-1} \right]$$

and therefore the system in Equation 6.18 can be written

$$\sum_{h=1}^{\nu-1} \Gamma_{nht} \beta_{ht} = -(\mu_{nt} - r)$$

or, in matrix form

$$\Gamma_t \beta_t = -(\mu_t - r1)$$

where Γ_t denotes the $(N-1) \times (N-1)$ matrix $\{\Gamma_{nht}\}$, $2 \le n \le N$, $1 \le h \le \nu - 1$, β_t denotes the vector $\{\beta_{nt}\}$ for $2 \le n \le N$, μ_t denotes the vector $\{\mu_{nt}\}$ for $2 \le n \le N$, and 1 denotes the $N-1$-dimensional vector $\begin{pmatrix} 1 \\ \cdots \\ 1 \end{pmatrix}$.

Suppose that securities $2, \ldots, N$ are such that the matrix Γ_t is nonsingular for all $1 \le t \le T$ and denote its inverse by $\{\delta_{hnt}\}$. Then for all $1 \le h \le \nu - 1$ and $1 \le t \le T$

$$\beta_{ht} = -\sum_{n=2}^{N} \delta_{hnt}(\mu_{nt} - r) \tag{6.19}$$

and the likelihood ratio process has the representation

$$z_t(\omega) = \prod_{s=1}^{t} \left[1 - \sum_{h=1}^{\nu-1} \sum_{n=2}^{N} \delta_{hns}(\mu_{ns} - r)(w_{hs} - w_{h,s-1}) \right] \tag{6.20}$$

Therefore, if for every $1 \le t \le T$

$$\sum_{h=1}^{\nu-1} \sum_{n=2}^{N} \delta_{hns}(\mu_{ns} - r)(w_{hs} - w_{h,s-1}) < 1 \tag{6.21}$$

then the equilibrium price measure Q exists, is unique, and is given by

$$Q(\omega) = P(\omega)z_T(\omega) = P(\omega) \prod_{s=1}^{T} \left[1 - \sum_{h=1}^{\nu-1} \sum_{n=2}^{N} \delta_{hns}(\mu_{ns} - r)(w_{hs} - w_{h,s-1}) \right]$$

or, equivalently

$$Q = P\mathcal{E}_T \left[-\sum_{h=1}^{\nu-1} \sum_{n=2}^{N} \delta_{hn}(\mu_n - r) \bullet w_h \right] \tag{6.22}$$

There are no arbitrage strategies and the price system $\{p_{nt}\}$ is complete. Equation 6.22 is a representation of the equilibrium price measure and implies a similar representation of the likelihood ratio process

$$z_t = \mathcal{E}_t \left[-\sum_{h=1}^{\nu-1} \sum_{n=2}^{N} \delta_{hn}(\mu_n - r) \bullet w_h \right]$$

The role of the likelihood ratio process in this model is formalized in the following definition.

Definition 6.1 A stochastic process $\{y_t\}$ is called a risk adjustment process if and only if for each $1 \leq n \leq N$ the process $\left\{ y_t \dfrac{p_{nt}}{1+r)^t} \right\}$ is a P-martingale.

Suppose that the price system p does not permit arbitrage strategies and let Q be an equilibrium price measure. Then the likelihood ratio process

$$z_t = E_P \left(\frac{Q}{P} \middle| \mathbf{f}_t \right)$$

is a risk adjustment process.

Example 6.2 This is an example of pricing an option on a security with a stochastic volatility. The number of states is $K = 16$, the probability measure is $P(\omega) = \frac{1}{16}$ for all ω, the terminal time is $T = 2$, the number of securities is $N = 5$, the partition at time $t = 1$ is

$$\{\{\omega_1, \omega_2, \omega_3, \omega_4\}, \{\omega_5, \omega_6, \omega_7, \omega_8\}, \{\omega_9, \omega_{10}, \omega_{11}, \omega_{12}\}, \{\omega_{13}, \omega_{14}, \omega_{15}, \omega_{16}\}\}$$

the rate of interest is r, and the prices and terminal payouts of securities 1 – 4 are given below. For $t = 1$ prices are given by the formulas

$$p_{nt} = p_{n0} \prod_{s=1}^{t} (1 + \mu_{ns} + x_{ns} - x_{n,s-1})$$

and terminal payouts are given by the same formulas with $t = 2$

$$d_n = p_{n2}$$

For $t = 1, 2$, the predictable and innovation components in the preceding formulas are given by

$$\mu_{1t} = r$$
$$\mu_{2t} = 3r$$
$$\mu_{3t} = 2r$$
$$\mu_{4t} = 4r$$

$$
\begin{aligned}
dx_{1t} &= 0 \\
dx_{2t} &= 2\xi_{t-1}dw_{1t} & & - 2\xi_{t-1}dw_{3t} \\
dx_{3t} &= & \xi_{t-1}dw_{2t} & - \xi_{t-1}dw_{3t} \\
dx_{4t} &= \xi_{t-1}dw_{1t} & +3\xi_{t-1}dw_{2t} & - \xi_{t-1}dw_{3t}
\end{aligned}
$$

where, as before, the differential of any process $\{v_t\}$ is the backward difference

$$dv_t = v_t - v_{t-1}$$

Alternatively, the defining formulas above can be seen as a shorthand notation for the corresponding integral representation formulas. For instance, the definition of $\{x_{2t}\}$ above is shorthand for the representation

$$x_{2t} = x_{20} + 2 \int_0^t \xi_{s-} dw_{1s} - 2 \int_0^t \xi_{s-} dw_{3s}$$

The initial values $\{x_{n0}\}$ are arbitrary. The process $\{\xi_t\}$ is

$$\xi_t = \xi_0 \prod_{s=1}^t (1 + \nu + y_t - y_{t-1})$$

where

$$dy_t = -\frac{3}{2}\tau dw_{1t} - \frac{1}{2}\tau dw_{2t}$$

and ξ_0, ν, τ are positive constants such that

$$\frac{r}{\xi_0} + 2\tau < 1 + \nu < \frac{1+3r}{4\xi_0} - 2\tau \quad \text{and} \quad \frac{r}{\xi_0} < 1 \qquad (6.23)$$

The processes $\{w_{1t}\}$ and $\{w_{2t}\}$ are independent symmetric random walks, and for $t = 1, 2$, the process $\{w_{3t}\}$ is given by

$$w_{30} = 0, \quad dw_{3t} = dw_{1t}dw_{2t}$$

The multiperiod tree of the vectors

$$\begin{pmatrix} dw_{1t} \\ dw_{2t} \\ dw_{3t} \end{pmatrix}$$

consists of the repeated one-period segment shown in Figure 6.11. Finally, security 5 is a call option on security 2

$$d_5 = \max(0, d_{22} - a)$$

It is easy to verify that $\{w_{1t}, w_{2t}, w_{3t}\}$ is an orthogonal basis for the given information structure and probability measure. The conditional covariance matrix Γ_t is

$$\Gamma_t = E_P(dw_{ht}dx_{jt}|f_{t-1}) = \begin{pmatrix} 2 & 0 & -2 \\ 0 & 1 & -1 \\ 1 & 3 & -1 \end{pmatrix} \xi_{t-1}$$

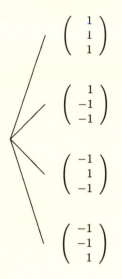

Figure 6.1: A one-period segment of increments of the random walks in Example 6.2.

and the conditional return covariance matrix for securities $2 - 4$ is

$$\Gamma_t \Gamma_t' = \begin{pmatrix} 8 & 2 & 4 \\ 2 & 2 & 4 \\ 4 & 4 & 11 \end{pmatrix} \xi_{t-1}^2$$

The preceding formula for the conditional return covariance matrix follows from the fact that

$$\mathrm{covar}_P \left(\frac{p_{nt}}{p_{n,t-1}}, \frac{p_{mt}}{p_{m,t-1}} \bigg| \mathbf{f}_{t-1} \right) = E_P(dx_{nt} dx_{mt} | \mathbf{f}_{t-1})$$

and the definition of the martingales $\{x_{nt}\}$. Therefore, the process $\{\xi_t\}$ has an interpretation as a common volatility factor for securities $2 - 4$, and the definition of this process implies the following values at time $t = 1$

$$
\begin{aligned}
\xi_1(f_{11}) &= \xi_0(1 + \nu - 2\tau) \\
\xi_1(f_{12}) &= \xi_0(1 + \nu - \tau) \\
\xi_1(f_{13}) &= \xi_0(1 + \nu + \tau) \\
\xi_1(f_{14}) &= \xi_0(1 + \nu + 2\tau)
\end{aligned}
$$

In this example the securities have stochastic conditional variances or volatilities of return. For instance, if the prevailing state is ω_7, then the conditional variance of return on security 2 for $t = 2$ is $8\xi_0^2(1 + \nu - \tau)^2$, and if the prevailing state is ω_{16}, then this variance is $8\xi_0^2(1 + \nu + 2\tau)^2$.

k	$z_2(\omega_k)$	k	$z_2(\omega_k)$
1	$\left(1 - \frac{r}{\xi_0}\right)\left[1 - \frac{r}{\xi_0(1+\nu-2\tau)}\right]$	9	$\left(1 - \frac{r}{3\xi_0}\right)\left[1 - \frac{r}{\xi_0(1+\nu+\tau)}\right]$
2	$\left(1 - \frac{r}{\xi_0}\right)\left[1 - \frac{r}{3\xi_0(1+\nu-2\tau)}\right]$	10	$\left(1 - \frac{r}{3\xi_0}\right)\left[1 - \frac{r}{3\xi_0(1+\nu+\tau)}\right]$
3	$\left(1 - \frac{r}{\xi_0}\right)\left[1 - \frac{r}{3\xi_0(1+\nu-2\tau)}\right]$	11	$\left(1 - \frac{r}{3\xi_0}\right)\left[1 - \frac{r}{3\xi_0(1+\nu+\tau)}\right]$
4	$\left(1 - \frac{r}{\xi_0}\right)\left[1 + \frac{r}{\xi_0(1+\nu-2\tau)}\right]$	12	$\left(1 - \frac{r}{3\xi_0}\right)\left[1 + \frac{r}{\xi_0(1+\nu+\tau)}\right]$
5	$\left(1 - \frac{r}{3\xi_0}\right)\left[1 - \frac{r}{\xi_0(1+\nu-\tau)}\right]$	13	$\left(1 + \frac{5r}{3\xi_0}\right)\left[1 - \frac{r}{\xi_0(1+\nu+2\tau)}\right]$
6	$\left(1 - \frac{r}{3\xi_0}\right)\left[1 - \frac{r}{3\xi_0(1+\nu-\tau)}\right]$	14	$\left(1 + \frac{5r}{3\xi_0}\right)\left[1 - \frac{r}{3\xi_0(1+\nu+2\tau)}\right]$
7	$\left(1 - \frac{r}{3\xi_0}\right)\left[1 - \frac{r}{3\xi_0(1+\nu-\tau)}\right]$	15	$\left(1 + \frac{5r}{3\xi_0}\right)\left[1 - \frac{r}{3\xi_0(1+\nu+2\tau)}\right]$
8	$\left(1 - \frac{r}{3\xi_0}\right)\left[1 + \frac{r}{\xi_0(1+\nu-\tau)}\right]$	16	$\left(1 + \frac{5r}{3\xi_0}\right)\left[1 + \frac{r}{\xi_0(1+\nu+2\tau)}\right]$

Table 6.1. The risk adjustment process in Example 6.2.

The terminal value of the risk adjustment process is

$$z_2 = \prod_{t=1}^{2} [1 + \beta_{1t}(w_{1t} - w_{1,t-1}) + \beta_{2t}(w_{2t} - w_{2,t-1}) + \beta_{3t}(w_{3t} - w_{3,t-1})]$$

The processes $\{\beta_{ht}\}$ are determined from Equation 6.19. Notice that

$$\Gamma_t^{-1} = \begin{pmatrix} \frac{1}{3} & -1 & \frac{1}{3} \\ -\frac{1}{6} & 0 & \frac{1}{3} \\ -\frac{1}{6} & -1 & \frac{1}{3} \end{pmatrix} \xi_{t-1}^{-1}$$

and, therefore

$$\beta_{1t} = -\frac{1}{\xi_{t-1}}[\ \tfrac{1}{3}(\mu_{2t} - r)\ -(\mu_{3t} - r)\ +\tfrac{1}{3}(\mu_{4t} - r)] = -\frac{2r}{3\xi_{t-1}}$$

$$\beta_{2t} = -\frac{1}{\xi_{t-1}}[-\tfrac{1}{6}(\mu_{2t} - r)\ \qquad\ +\tfrac{1}{3}(\mu_{4t} - r)] = -\frac{2r}{3\xi_{t-1}}$$

$$\beta_{3t} = -\frac{1}{\xi_{t-1}}[-\tfrac{1}{6}(\mu_{2t} - r)\ -(\mu_{3t} - r)\ +\tfrac{1}{3}(\mu_{4t} - r)] = \frac{r}{3\xi_{t-1}}$$

k	$d_{22}(\omega_k)$
1	$p_{20}(1+3r)^2$
2	$p_{20}(1+3r)[1+3r+4\xi_0(1+\nu-2\tau)]$
3	$p_{20}(1+3r)^2$
4	$p_{20}(1+3r)[1+3r-4\xi_0(1+\nu-2\tau)]$
5	$p_{20}(1+3r+4\xi_0)(1+3r)$
6	$p_{20}(1+3r+4\xi_0)[1+3r+4\xi_0(1+\nu-\tau)]$
7	$p_{20}(1+3r+4\xi_0)(1+3r)$
8	$p_{20}(1+3r+4\xi_0)[1+3r-4\xi_0(1+\nu-\tau)]$
9	$p_{20}(1+3r)^2$
10	$p_{20}(1+3r)[1+3r+4\xi_0(1+\nu+2\tau)]$
11	$p_{20}(1+3r)^2$
12	$p_{20}(1+3r)[1+3r-4\xi_0(1+\nu+2\tau)]$
13	$p_{20}(1+3r-4\xi_0)(1+3r)$
14	$p_{20}(1+3r-4\xi_0)[1+3r+4\xi_0(1+\nu+\tau)]$
15	$p_{20}(1+3r-4\xi_0)(1+3r)$
16	$p_{20}(1+3r-4\xi_0)[1+3r-4\xi_0(1+\nu+\tau)]$

Table 6.2: The terminal payout of security 2 in Example 6.2.

The explicit values of z_2 are given in Table 6.1. Conditions 6.23 guarantee that all $z_2(\omega) > 0$. From the given representation of prices and terminal payouts, the explicit values of the terminal payouts of security 2 are computed in Table 6.2. Combining the explicit values of $d_{22}(\omega_k)$ and $z_2(\omega_k)$, we get the initial price of security 5

$$p_{50} = \frac{\sum_{k=1}^{16} \max[0, d_{22}(\omega_k) - a]z_2(\omega_k)}{16(1+r)^2}$$

6.5   Completeness

In this section we continue with the discrete multiperiod model with N securities and an information structure $\{\mathfrak{f}_t\}$. Security 1 is a bond with a constant rate of interest

$$d_1 = (1+r)^T$$
$$p_{1t} = (1+r)^t$$

We begin with a characterization of attainable consumption processes that says that a consumption process is attainable if and only if its present value can be represented as a sum of stochastic integrals with respect to discounted prices. To simplify the equations we adopt the following vector notation. If $\{\alpha_{1t}, \ldots, \alpha_{Nt}\}$ and $\{x_{1t}, \ldots, x_{Nt}\}$ are two vectors of stochastic processes, then we write $\alpha_t' x_t$ for $\sum_{n=1}^{N} \alpha_{nt} x_{nt}$ and $\int_0^t \alpha_s' dx_s$ for

$$\sum_{n=1}^{N} \int_0^t \alpha_{ns}' dx_{ns}.$$

Theorem 6.1 *Suppose that the price system p does not permit arbitrage strategies and let Q be an equilibrium price measure. Then a consumption process $c = \{c_0, \ldots, c_T\} \in X$ is attainable if and only if there exists a vector of predictable processes $\alpha_t = \{\alpha_{1t}, \ldots, \alpha_{Nt}\}$ such that we have the predictable representation, for all $0 \leq t \leq T$*

$$E_Q \left(\sum_{s=1}^{T} \frac{c_s}{p_{1s}} \middle| \mathbf{f}_t \right) = E_Q \left(\sum_{s=1}^{T} \frac{c_s}{p_{1s}} \right) + \int_0^t \alpha_s' d \left(\frac{p_s}{p_{1s}} \right)$$

Proof. Suppose that the consumption process c is attainable. Then there is a trading strategy θ such that

$$\sum_{s=1}^{T} \frac{c_s}{p_{1s}} = \theta_1' p_0 + \int_0^T \theta_s' d \left(\frac{p_s}{p_{1s}} \right)$$

Because θ is predictable, the stochastic integral on the right side of the preceding equation is a Q-martingale. Therefore

$$E_Q \left(\sum_{s=1}^{T} \frac{c_s}{p_{1s}} \middle| \mathbf{f}_t \right) = \theta_1' p_0 + \int_0^t \theta_s' d \left(\frac{p_s}{p_{1s}} \right)$$

Taking expectations

$$E_Q \left(\sum_{s=1}^{T} \frac{c_s}{p_{1s}} \right) = \theta_1' p_0$$

Conversely, suppose that

$$E_Q \left(\sum_{s=1}^{T} \frac{c_s}{p_{1s}} \middle| \mathbf{f}_t \right) = E_Q \left(\sum_{s=1}^{T} \frac{c_s}{p_{1s}} \right) + \int_0^t \alpha_s' d \left(\frac{p_s}{p_{1s}} \right) \tag{6.24}$$

For $2 \leq n \leq N$ and $1 \leq t \leq T$ define

$$\theta_{nt} = \alpha_{nt}$$

and for $n = 1$ and $1 \le t \le T - 1$ define

$$\theta_{1,t+1} = E_Q \left(\sum_{s=1}^{T} \frac{c_s}{p_{1s}} \right) + \int_0^t \alpha_s' d \left(\frac{p_s}{p_{1s}} \right) - \sum_{s=1}^{t} \frac{c_s}{p_{1s}} - \sum_{n=2}^{N} \frac{\theta_{n,t+1} p_{nt}}{p_{1t}}$$

and

$$\theta_{11} = E_Q \left(\sum_{s=1}^{T} \frac{c_s}{p_{1s}} \right) - \sum_{n=2}^{N} \theta_{n1} p_{n0}$$

Then for $1 \le t \le T - 1$

$$\sum_{s=1}^{t} \frac{c_s}{p_{1s}} = E_Q \left(\sum_{s=1}^{T} \frac{c_s}{p_{1s}} \right) + \int_0^t \alpha_s' d \left(\frac{p_s}{p_{1s}} \right) - \frac{\theta_{t+1}' p_t}{p_{1t}}$$

and

$$\theta_1' p_0 = E_Q \left(\sum_{s=1}^{T} \frac{c_s}{p_{1s}} \right)$$

Next, we need to show that

$$\int_0^t \theta' s d \left(\frac{p_s}{p_{1s}} \right) = \int_0^t \alpha' s d \left(\frac{p_s}{p_{1s}} \right)$$

The idea here is to notice that because $\frac{p_1}{p_1} = 1$, we have

$$\int_0^t \theta_s' d \left(\frac{p_s}{p_{1s}} \right) = \sum_{n=2}^{N} \int_0^t \theta_{ns} d \left(\frac{p_{ns}}{p_{1s}} \right)$$

$$= \sum_{n=2}^{N} \int_0^t \alpha_{ns} d \left(\frac{p_{ns}}{p_{1s}} \right)$$

$$= \int_0^t \alpha_s' d \left(\frac{p_s}{p_{1s}} \right)$$

Finally, substituting $t = T$ in Equation 6.24 shows that

$$\sum_{s=1}^{T} \frac{c_s}{p_{1s}} = E_Q \left(\sum_{s=1}^{T} \frac{c_s}{p_{1s}} \right) + \int_0^T \theta_s' d \left(\frac{p_s}{p_{1s}} \right)$$

This completes the proof. ∎

We have the following corollary.

Corollary 6.1 *Suppose that the price system p does not permit arbitrage strategies and let Q be an equilibrium price measure. Then p is complete if and only if every Q-martingale x on $\{\mathbf{f}_t\}$ has a predictable representation*

$$x_t = x_0 + \int_0^t \alpha'_s d\left(\frac{p_{ns}}{p_{1s}}\right)$$

Proof. Suppose that every Q-martingale has a predictable representation and let $c = \{c_0, \ldots, c_T\} \in X$. Then the Q-martingale $E_Q\left(\sum_{s=1}^{T} \frac{c_s}{p_{1s}} \middle| \mathbf{f}_t\right)$ has a predictable representation, and therefore, c is attainable. Conversely, let x be a Q-martingale and consider the consumption process $c_t = 0$ for $1 \le t < T$ and $c_T = x_T p_{1T}$. Then $x_t = E_Q(x_T | \mathbf{f}_t) = E_Q\left(\sum_{s=1}^{T} \frac{c_s}{p_{1s}} \middle| \mathbf{f}_t\right)$ and x has a predictable representation. ∎

We can summarize our characterization of complete price systems as follows.

Theorem 6.2 *Suppose that the price system p does not permit arbitrage strategies and let Q be an equilibrium price measure. Then the following statements are equivalent:*

1. *The price system p is complete.*

2. *The equilibrium price measure Q is unique.*

3. *The discounted price processes $\dfrac{p_2}{p_1}, \ldots, \dfrac{p_N}{p_1}$ form a basis for Q-martingales.*

6.6   Risk and Return

In this section we describe an interpretation of the risk adjustment process as the single risk factor in the discrete multiperiod model. We deliver this interpretation by establishing a linear relationship between risk and expected return, when risk is defined as the conditional covariance between the innovation component of the rate of return and the risk adjustment process. For a complete price system, we have already used this relationship in Equations 6.5 and 6.17, but because of the importance of this relationship, and because it holds also for incomplete price systems, we present here a more comprehensive discussion of this subject.

Suppose that Q is an equilibrium price measure in this model. We do not assume that the price system is complete, therefore, Q need not be unique. Let

$$z_t = E_P\left(\frac{Q}{P}\,\middle|\,\mathbf{f}_t\right)$$

be the risk adjustment process of the equilibrium price measure Q with respect to the probability measure P. It follows immediately from the definition of conditional expectation that for every $\omega \in \Omega$

$$z_t(\omega) = \frac{Q[\mathbf{f}_t(\omega)]}{P[\mathbf{f}_t(\omega)]}$$

Therefore

$$\frac{1}{z_t(\omega)} = \frac{P[\mathbf{f}_t(\omega)]}{Q[\mathbf{f}_t(\omega)]} = E_Q\left(\frac{P}{Q}\,\middle|\,\mathbf{f}_t\right)(\omega)$$

is the risk adjustment process of the probability measure P with respect to the equilibrium price measure Q.

The next theorem establishes a relationship between the risk and expected return of the N securities in this market. This interpretation will be made clear in the subsequent discussion. The notation π^*, introduced in Chapter 5, stands for the dual predictable projection operator. Because the context involves two probability measures, P and Q, we add to the notation for the dual predictable projection and the predictable quadratic covariation a superscript of either P or Q to distinguish between dual predictable projections and predictable quadratic covariation processes with respect to the probability measures P and Q.

Theorem 6.3 *Suppose that the price system p does not permit arbitrage strategies and let Q be an equilibrium price measure. Then for any security $1 \le n \le N$ and any $0 \le t \le T$*

$$\left[\pi^*\left(\frac{p_n}{p_1}\right)\right]_t^P = p_{n0} - \int_0^t \frac{d\left\langle \frac{p_n}{p_1}, z\right\rangle_s^P}{z_{s-}}$$

Proof. The theorem can be proved either directly or as a consequence of the Doob decomposition and Girsanov's theorem, as stated in Corollaries 5.2 and 5.3. In the application of Corollary 5.3 we reverse the roles of the probability measures P and Q. Because the process $\dfrac{p_{nt}}{p_{1t}}$ is a Q-martingale, its predictable part with respect to the probability measure P and the initial value $\dfrac{p_{n0}}{p_{10}} = p_{n0}$ is

$$p_{n0} + \int_0^t z_{s-} d\left\langle \frac{p_n}{p_1}, z^{-1}\right\rangle_s^Q$$

On the other hand, this predictable part is the dual predictable projection

$$\left[\pi^*\left(\frac{p_n}{p_1}\right)\right]_t^P$$

and because the predictable component with a given initial value is unique

$$\left[\pi^*\left(\frac{p_n}{p_1}\right)\right]_t^P = p_{n0} + \int_0^t z_{s-} d\left\langle \frac{p_n}{p_1}, z^{-1}\right\rangle_s^Q$$

Next, using Theorem 5.13, the conditional expectation

$$E_Q\left[\left(\frac{p_{nt}}{p_{1t}} - \frac{p_{n,t-1}}{p_{1,t-1}}\right)\left(\frac{1}{z_t} - \frac{1}{z_{t-1}}\right)\bigg| \mathbf{f}_{t-1}\right]$$

is equal to

$$-\frac{E_P\left[\left(\frac{p_{nt}}{p_{1t}} - \frac{p_{n,t-1}}{p_{1,t-1}}\right)(z_t - z_{t-1})\bigg| \mathbf{f}_{t-1}\right]}{z_{t-1}^2}$$

so that

$$z_{t-}d\left\langle \frac{p_n}{p_1}, \frac{1}{z}\right\rangle_t^Q = -\frac{E_P\left[\left(\frac{p_{nt}}{p_{1t}} - \frac{p_{n,t-1}}{p_{1,t-1}}\right)(z_t - z_{t-1})\bigg| \mathbf{f}_{t-1}\right]}{z_{t-1}}$$

$$= -\frac{d\left\langle \frac{p_n}{p_1}, z\right\rangle_t^P}{z_{t-1}}$$

and consequently

$$\int_0^t z_{s-}d\left\langle \frac{p_n}{p_1}, \frac{1}{z}\right\rangle_s^Q = -\int_0^t \frac{d\left\langle \frac{p_n}{p_1}, z\right\rangle_s^P}{z_{s-}}$$

This completes the proof. ∎

Theorem 6.3 may be easier to interpret in its differential form, for every $0 \leq t \leq T$

$$d\left[\pi^*\left(\frac{p_n}{p_1}\right)\right]_t^P = -\frac{d\left\langle \frac{p_n}{p_1}, z\right\rangle_t^P}{z_{t-1}}$$

From Definition 5.13 of dual predictable projection

$$d\left[\pi^*\left(\frac{p_n}{p_1}\right)\right]_t^P = E_P\left(\frac{p_{nt}}{p_{1t}} - \frac{p_{n,t-1}}{p_{1,t-1}}\bigg| \mathbf{f}_{t-1}\right)$$

and from the definition of the predictable quadratic covariation process

$$d \left\langle \frac{p_n}{p_1}, z \right\rangle_t^P = E_P \left[\left(\frac{p_{nt}}{p_{1t}} - \frac{p_{n,t-1}}{p_{1,t-1}} \right) (z_t - z_{t-1}) \bigg| \mathbf{f}_{t-1} \right]$$

Consider the Doob decomposition of the rate of return of security $2 \leq n \leq N$ for $1 \leq t \leq T$

$$\mu_{nt} = E_P \left(\frac{p_{nt}}{p_{n,t-1}} \bigg| \mathbf{f}_{t-1} \right) - 1$$

$$x_{nt} = x_{n,t-1} + \frac{p_{nt}}{p_{n,t-1}} - E_P \left(\frac{p_{nt}}{p_{n,t-1}} \bigg| \mathbf{f}_{t-1} \right)$$

where x_{n0} are arbitrary constants and $p_{nT} = d_n$. As before, for every $2 \leq n \leq N$, the predictable process $\{\mu_{nt}\}$ represents the conditional expected net rate of return of security n during the time interval $[t-1, t]$, and the martingale $\{x_{nt}\}$ represents the innovation part of the rate of return of security n during the same time period. It is easy to see that

$$\frac{p_{nt}}{p_{1t}} - \frac{p_{n,t-1}}{p_{1,t-1}} = \frac{p_{n,t-1}}{p_{1t}} (\mu_{nt} - r + x_{nt} - x_{n,t-1})$$

and, therefore

$$d \left[\pi^* \left(\frac{p_n}{p_1} \right) \right]_t^P = \frac{p_{n,t-1}}{p_{1t}} (\mu_{nt} - r)$$

Furthermore, the product

$$\left(\frac{p_{nt}}{p_{1t}} - \frac{p_{n,t-1}}{p_{1,t-1}} \right) (z_t - z_{t-1})$$

is equal to

$$\frac{p_{n,t-1}}{p_{1t}} (\mu_{nt} - r + x_{nt} - x_{n,t-1}) (z_t - z_{t-1})$$

and because $\{z_t\}$ is a P-martingale, the conditional expectation

$$E_P \left[\left(\frac{p_{nt}}{p_{1t}} - \frac{p_{n,t-1}}{p_{1,t-1}} \right) (z_t - z_{t-1}) \bigg| \mathbf{f}_{t-1} \right]$$

is equal to

$$\frac{p_{n,t-1}}{p_{1t}} E_P \left[(x_{nt} - x_{n,t-1}) (z_t - z_{t-1}) \big| \mathbf{f}_{t-1} \right]$$

We have proved the following theorem.

Theorem 6.4 *Suppose that the price system p does not permit arbitrage strategies and let Q be an equilibrium price measure. Then for each security $1 \leq n \leq N$ and each time $1 \leq t \leq T$*

$$\mu_{nt} - r = -\frac{1}{z_{t-1}}\text{covar}_P(x_{nt}, z_t|\mathbf{f}_{t-1})$$

Theorem 6.4 says that the risk premium of a security is proportional to the conditional covariance of the innovation part of the rate of return for that security and the risk adjustment process. Accepting this conditional covariance as the measure of risk produces a linear relationship between expected return and risk of securities. Notice that when the price system p is not complete, the risk factor z is not unique.

Problems

1. Suppose that the price system p does not permit arbitrage strategies and let Q be an equilibrium price measure. Show that for each security $1 \leq n \leq N$ and each time $0 \leq t \leq T$

$$p_{n0} = \left\langle \frac{p_n}{p_1}, z \right\rangle_t + \int_0^t z_{s-}d\left[\pi^*\left(\frac{p_n}{p_1}\right)\right]_s$$

2. Consider a discrete one-period model with prices that do not permit arbitrage strategies and let Q be an equilibrium price measure in this model. To introduce multi-period trading into this model, consider the intermediate dates $1, \ldots, T-1$, an information structure $\{\mathbf{f}_t\}$ with a splitting index ν, and a basis $w_1, \ldots, w_{\nu-1}$ for Q-martingales on $\{\mathbf{f}_t\}$. Furthermore, suppose that the original securities are replaced with ν securities, which are traded at times $0 \leq t < T$ and have the terminal payouts

$$d_n = \begin{cases} 1 & \text{if } n = 1 \\ w_{n-1,T} & \text{if } 2 \leq n \leq \nu \end{cases}$$

Show that Q is an equilibrium price measure in the resulting discrete multiperiod model. What are the equilibrium prices in the multiperiod model? How does the equilibrium allocation of consumption in the multiperiod model differ from the allocation of consumption in the original one-period model?

3. Produce a direct proof of Theorem 6.3.

Notes

Section 6.2 extends and formalizes an idea of [72] and [17]. The main results of [17] are presented here as Section 6.3. The representation of equilibrium price measures in Sections 6.2 and 6.4 is new. In Section 6.5, both the characterization of attainable consumption processes in Theorem 6.1 and the characterization of complete price systems in Theorem 6.2 are patterned after the general results of [41] and [42]. An approximation to the limit of the pricing formula in Example 6.2 appears in [24]. Section 6.6 is new.

Chapter 7

The Wiener Process

7.1 Introduction

This chapter introduces the Wiener process, which is a special stochastic process in continuous time. The Wiener process is central to Itô calculus, which is a special case of continuous time stochastic calculus.

Itô calculus provides a mathematical introduction to the Black-Scholes option pricing model. The Black-Scholes model is a simple continuous multiperiod model with an infinite number of states, continuous arrival of information, and continuous trading in securities. This model demonstrates how continuous trading expands the set that is attainable with a finite number of securities from a linear space of finite dimension to a linear space of infinite dimension. All the concepts in this model are suitable modifications of the corresponding concepts in the discrete model. Observing these analogies helps with the intuitive understanding of the Black-Scholes model.

A precise description of the Black-Scholes model requires concepts from Itô calculus. Starting with the following partial description, the model is introduced in stages as the necessary concepts are acquired. The first description of the framework for this model is as follows:

- Initial date 0, terminal date T, intermediate trading dates $0 < t < T$.

- States belong to an infinite sample space Ω.

- There is only one, perishable, consumption good.

- There are $N = 2$ endogenous securities and no exogenous securities. The two securities are infinitely divisible, and there are no taxes or other costs associated with trading. The securities make only terminal payouts d_1 and d_2.

- There is a finite number I of traders. The resolution of uncertainty over time is common to all traders and is described by a given information structure.

- Traders receive endowments of the consumption good only at times 0 and T. The endowment process of trader i is denoted $e^i = \{e_0^i, e_T^i\}$.

- Traders consume only at times 0 and T. The consumption process of trader i is denoted $c^i = \{c_0^i, c_T^i\}$.

- On the consumption set X traders have complete preference orderings that are continuous, increasing, and convex. The description of the consumption set is postponed to Chapter 8.

Notice that, unlike the discrete multiperiod model, this model excludes intermediate endowments and intermediate consumption. At intermediate dates economic activity is restricted to exchanging securities at their relative prices. We reintroduce intermediate consumption in the general continuous model in Chapter 12.

The prices p_{1t}, p_{2t} and the trading strategies θ_{1t}, θ_{2t} determine the consumption of traders at times 0 and T. Whereas in the discrete model θ_{nt} denotes the number of units of security n held in the time interval $[t-1, t)$, in the continuous model θ_{nt} denotes the instantaneous position in security n at time $0 \leq t \leq T$. In particular, θ_{n0} describes the postconsumption portfolio at time 0, and θ_{nT} describes the preconsumption portfolio at time T. For trader i

$$c_0^i = e_0^i - \sum_{n=1}^{2} \theta_{n0}^i p_{n0}$$

$$c_T^i = e_T^i + \sum_{n=1}^{2} \theta_{nT}^i d_n$$

Furthermore, the characterization of self-financing trading strategies

$$\sum_{n=1}^{2} \theta_{nt} p_{nt} = \sum_{n=1}^{2} \theta_{n1} p_{n0} + \sum_{s=1}^{t} \sum_{n=1}^{2} \theta_{ns} \left(p_{ns} - p_{n,s-1} \right)$$

for all $1 \leq t \leq T$ lends itself to a convenient extension to the continuous model. In this extension, the gain process

$$\sum_{s=1}^{t} \sum_{n=1}^{2} \theta_{ns} \left(p_{ns} - p_{n,s-1} \right)$$

turns into a sum of integrals in continuous time, one of which is the Itô integral. The Itô integral extends the concept of a stochastic integral introduced in Chapter 5.

Section 7.2 recasts discrete information structures into a more general concept that fits conveniently into the continuous time framework. Section 7.3 deals with the Wiener process and its properties.

7.2   General Information Structures

When the sample space Ω is finite, it is convenient to represent information through partitions of Ω. On an infinite sample space it is convenient to represent information through σ-fields. Whereas a partition of a sample space is a set of special decidable events, a σ-field is the set of all the decidable events. To see the transition from a partition to a σ-field it helps to look first at fields and σ-fields on a finite sample space.

Definition 7.1 A set **F** of subsets of a sample space Ω is called a field if and only if:

1. The sample space is in **F**, that is, $\Omega \in \mathbf{F}$.

2. For every $A \in \mathbf{F}$ also $\Omega - A \in \mathbf{F}$.

3. For every $A, B \in \mathbf{F}$ also $A \cup B \in \mathbf{F}$.

Notice that this definition implies that a field contains the empty set, and that if $A, B \in \mathbf{F}$, then also $A \cap B \in \mathbf{F}$.

There is a very simple relationship between partitions and fields. Starting with a partition **f**, consider the set **F** of all the unions of sets of **f** (including the empty union), this set **F** is a field. Indeed, the sample space Ω is the union of all the sets in **f** and, therefore, belongs to **F**. If $A \in \mathbf{F}$, then A is a union of some sets of **f** and $\Omega - A$ is the union of the remaining sets of **f**. Finally, if both A and B are unions of sets of **f**, so is $A \cup B$.

Example 7.1 Suppose that

$$\Omega = \{\omega_1, \omega_2, \omega_3, \omega_4\} \text{ and } \mathbf{f} = \{\{\omega_1\}, \{\omega_2, \omega_3\}, \{\omega_4\}\}$$

Then

$$\mathbf{F} = \{\emptyset, \{\omega_1\}, \{\omega_4\}, \{\omega_2, \omega_3\}, \{\omega_1, \omega_4\}, \{\omega_1, \omega_2, \omega_3\}, \{\omega_2, \omega_3, \omega_4\}, \Omega\}$$

The field **F** represents the same information that is represented by the partition **f**. The partition lists special decidable events: when the prevailing state is ω, then $\mathbf{f}(\omega)$ is known to have occurred and all the other partition sets are known not to have occurred. These are not all the decidable events, however, it is precisely the field **F** that contains, together with all the sets of the partition, all the other decidable events, that is, all the events known to have occurred or not to have occurred. The field **F** contains more events than the partition **f**, but it does not represent any more information than **f** does.

When the sample space is finite, every field is generated by some partition. To recover the partition from the field discard all the sets that are unions of other sets in the field.

Example 7.2 In the previous example discard the empty set that is an empty union of other sets, the set $\{\omega_1, \omega_4\}$ that is a union of $\{\omega_1\}$ and $\{\omega_4\}$, the set $\{\omega_1, \omega_2, \omega_3\}$ that is a union of $\{\omega_1\}$ and $\{\omega_2, \omega_3\}$, the set $\{\omega_2, \omega_3, \omega_4\}$ that is a union of $\{\omega_2, \omega_3\}$ and $\{\omega_4\}$, and Ω that is a union of $\{\omega_1\}$, $\{\omega_2, \omega_3\}$, and $\{\omega_4\}$. The remaining sets form a partition of Ω.

The comparative fineness of partitions translates into inclusion of fields. The field generated by the finer of two partitions has all the decidable events of the other field, and also additional decidable events that the other field does not contain. In other words, a partition **f** is finer than a partition **g** if and only if the field **F** contains the field **G**, that is, every set of **G** belongs to **F**. The bigger field represents more information.

On a finite sample space, a partition **f** and a field **F** are two equivalent ways of representing the same information. On infinite sample spaces partitions and fields are not sufficient to represent information in all practical situations. The difficulty with fields is that they are tailored specifically to finite sample spaces. This motivates the following definition of a σ-field as the formal representation of information on an infinite sample space.

Definition 7.2 A set **F** of subsets of a sample space Ω is called a σ-field if and only if:

1. The sample space is in **F**, that is, $\Omega \in \mathbf{F}$.

2. For every $A \in \mathbf{F}$ also $\Omega - A \in \mathbf{F}$.

3. For every sequence $\{A_m\}_{m=1}^{\infty}$ such that $A_m \in \mathbf{F}$ for every $m \geq 1$ we have $\bigcup_{m=1}^{\infty} A_m \in \mathbf{F}$.

This definition says that a σ-field is a field that contains not only all finite unions but also all countable unions of its elements. On a finite sample space every field is a σ-field, but on infinite sample spaces there are fields that are not σ-fields. Notice that a σ-field contains all countable intersections of its elements.

To give a precise definition of an information structure in the continuous model requires the formal concepts of a probability space and a filtration.

Definition 7.3 A probability space is a triple $\{\Omega, \mathbf{F}, P\}$ where Ω is a sample space, $\mathbf{F}$ is a σ-field of subsets of Ω, and P is a probability measure on $\mathbf{F}$. The elements of $\mathbf{F}$ are called events. The probability measure P assigns to each event A a nonnegative number $P(A)$ such that $P(\Omega) = 1$ and for any sequence $\{A_m\}_{m=1}^{\infty}$ of disjoint events the probability of their union is the sum of their probabilities

$$P(\bigcup_{m=1}^{\infty} A_m) = \sum_{m=1}^{\infty} P(A_m)$$

In general, it is impossible to define a probability measure on the set of all the subsets of an uncountably infinite sample space. Therefore, in Definition 7.3 of a probability space, it is generally impossible for every subset of the sample space to be an event. Also, notice that the foregoing definition implies that if $A \subset B$, then $P(A) \leq P(B)$.

Definition 7.4 A filtration of the probability space $\{\Omega, \mathbf{F}, P\}$ is a family of σ-fields $\{\mathbf{F}_t\}$, $0 \leq t \leq T$, such that:

1. For all $0 \leq s \leq t \leq T$ we have $\mathbf{F}_s \subset \mathbf{F}_t$.

2. $\mathbf{F}_0$ contains all the events of probability zero.

3. For every $0 \leq t < T$ we have $\mathbf{F}_t = \bigcap_{u > t} \mathbf{F}_u$.

In Definition 7.4 of a filtration, (1) says that a filtration is an increasing family of σ-fields, (2) says that all the impossible events are known at the initial time and, therefore, always, and (3) says that a filtration is right continuous, that is, new information at time t arrives precisely at t and not an instant after t.

Definition 7.5 A filtered probability space is the quadruple

$$\{\Omega, \mathbf{F}, P, \{\mathbf{F}_t\}\}$$

where $\{\Omega, \mathbf{F}, P\}$ is a probability space and $\{\mathbf{F}_t\}$ is a filtration of $\{\Omega, \mathbf{F}, P\}$.

The definition of an information structure is now as follows.

Definition 7.6 An information structure on a probability space $\{\Omega, \mathbf{F}, P\}$ is a filtration $\{\mathbf{F}_t\}$ such that:

1. $A \in \mathbf{F}_0$ if and only if $P(A) = 0$ or $P(A) = 1$.

2. The terminal σ-field $\mathbf{F}_T = \mathbf{F}$.

As in the discrete case, the information of traders is standardized at the initial and terminal time to be trivial and complete, respectively.

To formulate the notion of informational consistency with an information structure in the continuous context requires the concept of information represented by a random variable in the continuous context. This in turn requires the introduction of special sets of real numbers called Borel sets, after the French mathematician E. Borel. Consider the set $\mathbf{B_0}$ of countable unions of open intervals in $\mathcal{R}$. The set $\mathbf{B_0}$ satisfies conditions (1) and (3) in the definition of a σ-field. As the following example shows, however, $A \in \mathbf{B_0}$ does not guarantee that $\mathcal{R} - A \in \mathbf{B_0}$.

Example 7.3 Let $r_1, r_2, \ldots$ be the enumeration of rational numbers. For each $m \geq 1$ choose an open interval E_m such that $r_m \in E_m$ and put $A = \bigcup_{m=1}^{\infty} E_m$. If E is an open interval, then E contains a rational number and, therefore, E intersects one of the intervals E_m so that $A \cap E \neq \emptyset$. As a countable union of open intervals the set A belongs to $\mathbf{B_0}$. The set $\mathcal{R} - A$, however, does not belong to $\mathbf{B_0}$. If it did, it would be a union of open intervals, and each one of these intervals would intersect A, which is a contradiction.

Notice that including in a set all the countable unions of open intervals and complements of these unions produces a σ-field. This motivates the following definition.

Definition 7.7 The Borel σ-field $\mathbf{B}$ of $\mathcal{R}$ is the set of all the countable unions of open intervals and the complements of countable unions of open intervals. Any set in $\mathbf{B}$ is called a Borel set.

There are sets of real numbers that are not Borel sets, but those sets do not play any role in ordinary probability and analysis. The Borel σ-field is large enough for all practical purposes.

The immediate reason for considering Borel sets is to define a real random variable on a general probability space $\{\Omega, \mathbf{F}, P\}$. When the sample space Ω is finite, every function $x : \Omega \to \mathcal{R}$ is a random variable. When Ω is infinite, then to be a random variable a function $x : \Omega \to \mathcal{R}$ has to satisfy a special condition: for any Borel set B, the set of states $\omega \in \Omega$ such that $x(\omega) \in B$ has to be in $\mathbf{F}$. If this condition is satisfied, then for every Borel set B the probability that $x(\omega) \in B$ is defined as

$$P\{x(\omega) \in B\} = P\{\omega \mid x(\omega) \in B\}$$

If this condition is not satisfied, then the right side of the preceding formula may be meaningless and simple questions about the distribution of x cannot be answered.

Fortunately, the preceding special condition is not entirely new. Rather, it is a suitably modified concept of measurability of a random variable on a partition. The fact is, that on a finite sample space a random variable x is measurable on a partition $\mathbf{f}$ if and only if for every Borel set B the set $\{\omega | x(\omega) \in B\}$, denoted $x^{-1}(B)$, belongs to the field $\mathbf{F}$ generated by the partition $\mathbf{f}$.

To see this, consider a random variable x that is measurable on the partition $\mathbf{f} = \{f_1, f_2, \ldots, f_u\}$, that is, constant on the sets $f_1, f_2, \ldots, f_u$. Denote $x(f_j) = \alpha_j$, and let B be a Borel set. If B does not contain any of the numbers $\alpha_1, \ldots, \alpha_u$, then $x^{-1}(B) = \emptyset \in \mathbf{F}$. If $\alpha_{j_1}, \ldots, \alpha_{j_v} \in B$, then $x^{-1}(B) = f_{j_1} \cup \ldots \cup f_{j_v} \in \mathbf{F}$.

Conversely, if for every Borel set B we have $x^{-1}(B) \in \mathbf{F}$, then pick a number α from the range of x and a Borel set B such that $\alpha \in B$ and B does not contain any other numbers from the range of x. Then $x^{-1}(B)$ contains a subset of some partition set f_j. Because $x^{-1}(B) \in \mathbf{F}$, we have that $x^{-1}(B)$ is a union of partition sets and, therefore, $x^{-1}(B)$ contains all of f_j, so that x is constant on f_j.

The equivalence of the measurability of a random variable on a partition $\mathbf{f}$ and the condition that $x^{-1}(B) \in \mathbf{F}$ for every Borel set B motivates the following definition of measurability of a function on a σ-field.

Definition 7.8 A function $x : \Omega \to \mathcal{R}$ is measurable on a σ-field $\mathbf{F}$ if and only if for every Borel set B the set $x^{-1}(B)$ belongs to $\mathbf{F}$.

Hence the formal definition of a random variable.

Definition 7.9 A function $x : \Omega \to \mathcal{R}$ is called a random variable on the probability space $\{\Omega, \mathbf{F}, P\}$ if and only if x is measurable on $\mathbf{F}$.

As before, a random variable represents information. On a finite sample space, this information is the coarsest partition on which x is measurable. On an infinite sample space, this information is the smallest σ-field on which x is measurable.

Definition 7.10 For a random variable x on a probability space $\{\Omega, \mathbf{F}, P\}$, the smallest σ-field on which x is measurable is called the σ-field generated by x and denoted $\mathbf{F}^x$.

In the discrete multiperiod model, prices p_{nt} and trading strategies θ_{nt} are sequences of random variables with t running through the integer values $1, \ldots, T$. In the continuous multiperiod model, prices and trading strategies are sets of random variables with t running through all the real values $0 \le t \le T$. Such sets of random variables are called stochastic processes.

Definition 7.11 A stochastic process on the probability space $\{\Omega, \mathbf{F}, P\}$ is a function $x : [0, T] \times \Omega \to \mathcal{R}$ such that for every $0 \leq t \leq T$, $x(t, \cdot)$ is a random variable on $\{\Omega, \mathbf{F}, P\}$. For a fixed $\omega \in \Omega$, the function $x(\cdot, \omega) :$ $[0, T] \to \mathcal{R}$ is called a sample path of the process x. The realization of the stochastic process x at time t and state ω, $x(t, \omega)$, is also denoted $x_t(\omega)$. The stochastic process x is also denoted $\{x_t\}$.

A stochastic process is a set of real-valued random variables. Sometimes a stochastic process can also be interpreted as a single random variable whose values are functions of time, that is, the sample paths of the process. Notice that to make the second interpretation precise, the set of all the real functions on $[0, T]$ has to be endowed with a σ-field. This is done in Section 7.3.

The requirement of informational consistency for endowments and consumptions is that the terminal endowment and consumption of each trader be random variables on the given probability space $\{\Omega, \mathbf{F}, P\}$. The requirement of informational consistency for prices and trading strategies is that for all $1 \leq i \leq I$, $1 \leq n \leq N$, and $0 \leq t \leq T$, p_{nt} and θ_{nt}^i be measurable on $\mathbf{F}_t$. This analogy with the discrete model suggests the following definition.

Definition 7.12 A stochastic process x on a filtered probability space

$$\{\Omega, \mathbf{F}, P, \{\mathbf{F}_t\}\}$$

is adapted to the filtration $\{\mathbf{F}_t\}$ if and only if each x_t is measurable on $\mathbf{F}_t$.

With these modifications of the old concepts, a more accurate statement of the framework for the Black-Scholes model is as follows:

- A time interval $[0, T]$.

- A filtered probability space $\{\Omega, \mathbf{F}, P, \{\mathbf{F}_t\}\}$.

- A single, perishable, consumption good.

- Two endogenous securities whose terminal payouts d_1 and d_2 are random variables on $\{\Omega, \mathbf{F}\}$.

- A finite number I of traders. The information structure of traders is $\{\mathbf{F}_t\}$.

- The initial endowment of trader i is a number e_0^i and his or her terminal endowment is a random variable e_T^i, measurable on $\mathbf{F}_T$. Traders do not receive intermediate endowments.

- The initial consumption of trader i is a number c_0^i and his or her terminal consumption is a random variable c_T^i, measurable on $\mathbf{F}_T$. Traders do not consume at intermediate times.

- On the consumption set X traders have complete preference orderings that are continuous, increasing, and convex.

The information structure in the Black-Scholes model is generated by an important stochastic process named after the American mathematician N. Wiener. The construction of a Wiener process is the subject of the next section.

7.3   The Wiener Process

The Wiener process is a formalization of the limiting case of a symmetric random walk on a line that was introduced in Chapter 6. The Wiener process W starts at the origin, has independent increments, and every increment $W_t - W_s$ is distributed normally with mean 0 and variance $t - s$. The sample paths of the Wiener process are series of short sharp turns.

The formal description of the Wiener process involves the construction of a sample space, a σ-field of events, and a probability measure. The sample space Ω is the set of all the continuous functions $\omega : [0, \infty) \to \mathcal{R}$, the σ-field of events $\mathbf{F}$ is the smallest σ-field that contains all the sets of continuous functions ω such that for some times $0 < t_1 < \ldots < t_m$ and Borel sets $B_1, \ldots, B_m$, all $\omega(t_j) \in B_j$. The Wiener process is then the function $W : [0, \infty) \times \Omega \to \mathcal{R}$ given by $W(t, \omega) = \omega(t)$. The sample paths of the Wiener process are the elements of the sample space Ω. Because of this, all the sample paths of the Wiener process are continuous.

The following theorem guarantees the existence and uniqueness of a probability measure P on $\{\Omega, \mathbf{F}\}$ that starts the Wiener process at the origin, gives it independent increments, and imposes on every increment $W_t - W_s$ a normal distribution with mean 0 and variance $t - s$. To state the theorem denote by $p(t, x, y)$ the normal density function

$$p(t, x, y) = (2\pi t)^{-\frac{1}{2}} \exp\left[-\frac{(y - x)^2}{2t} \right]$$

Theorem 7.1 (Wiener) *There exists a unique probability measure P on the measurable space $\{\Omega, \mathbf{F}\}$ such that for any $0 < t_1 < \ldots < t_m$ and any Borel sets $B_1, \ldots, B_m$ the probability $P\left\{ \omega \mid \omega(t_1) \in B_1, \ldots, \omega(t_m) \in B_m \right\}$ is equal to*

$$\int_{B_1} \cdots \int_{B_m} p(t_1, 0, x_1) p(t_2 - t_1, x_1, x_2) \ldots$$

$$p(t_m - t_{m-1}, x_{m-1}, x_m) dx_m dx_{m-1} \ldots dx_1$$

Definition 7.13 We say that the triple $\{\Omega, \mathbf{F}, P\}$ is the Wiener probability space. The function $W : [0, \infty) \times \Omega \to \mathcal{R}$ given by $W(t, \omega) = \omega(t)$ is called the Wiener process on the Wiener probability space.

This definition of the Wiener process implies that on $\{\Omega, \mathbf{F}, P\}$ its multidimensional distribution

$$P\{W_{t_1} \in B_1, \ldots, W_{t_m} \in B_m\} = P\left\{\omega \mid \omega(t_1) \in B_1, \ldots, \omega(t_m) \in B_m\right\}$$

is equal to

$$\int_{B_1} \cdots \int_{B_m} p(t_1, 0, x_1) p(t_2 - t_1, x_1, x_2) \ldots$$

$$p(t_m - t_{m-1}, x_{m-1}, x_m) dx_m dx_{m-1} \ldots dx_1$$

In particular, $P\{W_t \in B\} = \int_B p(t, 0, x) dx$, so that

$$E_P(W_t) = \int_{-\infty}^{\infty} x p(t, 0, x) dx = 0$$

$$E_P(W_t^2) = \int_{-\infty}^{\infty} x^2 p(t, 0, x) dx = t$$

Furthermore

$$P\{W_{t_1} \in B_1, W_{t_2} \in B_2\} = \int_{B_1} \int_{B_2} p(t_1, 0, x_1) p(t_2 - t_1, x_1, x_2) dx_2 dx_1$$

which implies that the expectation $E_P(W_{t_2} - W_{t_1})$ is equal to

$$\int_{-\infty}^{\infty} \int_{-\infty}^{\infty} (x_2 - x_1) p(t_1, 0, x_1) p(t_2 - t_1, x_1, x_2) dx_2 dx_1 = 0$$

and the variance $E_P\left[(W_{t_2} - W_{t_1})^2\right]$ is equal to

$$\int_{-\infty}^{\infty} \int_{-\infty}^{\infty} (x_2 - x_1)^2 p(t_1, 0, x_1) p(t_2 - t_1, x_1, x_2) dx_2 dx_1 = t_2 - t_1$$

Finally

$$P\{W_0 = 0\} = P\{\omega \mid \omega(0) = 0\} = 1$$

so that the probability measure P assigns probability one to the set of all the continuous functions in Ω that start at the origin. This means that the measure P "discards," by assigning probability zero, the set of all the continuous functions in Ω that do not start at the origin. Stated still differently, the Wiener process starts at the origin with probability one.

Convergence

To prepare for the definition of the quadratic variation processes and the Itô integral, this subsection reviews convergence with probability one and convergence in probability.

Definition 7.14 The sequence of random variables $\{x_m\}$ converges to a random variable x with probability one if and only if

$$P\left\{\omega \mid \lim_{m \to \infty} x_m(\omega) = x(\omega)\right\} = 1$$

Definition 7.15 We say that the sequence of random variables $\{x_m\}$ converges in probability to a random variable x if and only if for every $\epsilon > 0$

$$\lim_{m \to \infty} P\{\omega \mid |x_m - x| \geq \epsilon\} = 0$$

The sequence $x_m(\omega)$ converges to $x(\omega)$ for some $\omega \in \Omega$ if and only if for every $k \geq 1$ there is a $u \geq 1$ such that for every $m \geq u$ we have

$$|x_m(\omega) - x(\omega)| < \frac{1}{k}$$

Therefore, the event $\left\{\omega \mid \lim_{m \to \infty} x_m(\omega) = x(\omega)\right\}$ is equal to the event

$$\bigcap_{k \geq 1} \bigcup_{u \geq 1} \bigcap_{m \geq u} \left\{\omega \mid |x_m(\omega) - x(\omega)| < \frac{1}{k}\right\} \tag{7.1}$$

Let $\{A_m\}$ be a sequence of events, then we use the following notation.

Definition 7.16 We denote

$$\liminf_{m \to \infty} A_m = \bigcup_{u \geq 1} \bigcap_{m \geq u} A_m$$

$$\limsup_{m \to \infty} A_m = \bigcap_{u \geq 1} \bigcup_{m \geq u} A_m$$

The event $\liminf_{m \to \infty} A_m$ is called the lower limit of the sequence of events $\{A_m\}$, and the event $\limsup_{m \to \infty} A_m$ is called the upper limit of the sequence of events $\{A_m\}$.

The lower and upper limits of a sequence of events have the following simple interpretation. The lower limit of a sequence of events $\{A_m\}$ is the set of sample points that belong to almost all the events A_m. The upper limit of a sequence of events A_m is the set of sample points that belong to infinitely many events A_m.

Using the concept of a lower limit of a sequence of events we can rewrite Equation 7.1 as

$$\left\{ \omega \,\middle|\, \lim_{m\to\infty} x_m(\omega) = x(\omega) \right\}$$

$$= \bigcap_{k\geq 1} \liminf_{m\to\infty} \left\{ \omega \,\middle|\, |x_m(\omega) - x(\omega)| < \frac{1}{k} \right\} \qquad (7.2)$$

Next, we introduce the lower limit and the upper limit of a sequence of real numbers.

Definition 7.17 Let $\{a_m\}$ be a sequence of real numbers. The sequence

$$\left\{ \inf_{k\geq 1} a_{m+k} \right\}$$

is increasing and its limit

$$\lim_{m\to\infty} \inf_{k\geq 1} a_{m+k}$$

is called the lower limit of the sequence $\{a_m\}$ and is denoted $\liminf\limits_{m\to\infty} a_m$. Similarly, we define the upper limit of the sequence $\{a_m\}$

$$\limsup_{m\to\infty} a_m = \lim_{m\to\infty} \sup_{k\geq 1} a_{m+k}$$

There is an alternative characterization of the lower and upper limits of a sequence $\{a_m\}$. A necessary and sufficient condition for $\gamma = \liminf\limits_{m\to\infty} a_m$ is that γ satisfy the two following conditions:

1. If $\gamma' > \gamma$, then $a_m < \gamma'$ for infinitely many m.

2. If $\gamma'' < \gamma$, then $a_m > \gamma''$ for almost all m.

Similarly, a necessary and sufficient condition for $\gamma = \limsup\limits_{m\to\infty} a_m$ is that γ satisfy the two following conditions:

1. If $\gamma' > \gamma$, then $a_m < \gamma'$ for almost all m.

2. If $\gamma'' < \gamma$, then $a_m > \gamma''$ for infinitely many m.

For completeness and future reference we also define the lower limit and the upper limit of a function at a point.

Definition 7.18 The lower limit and the upper limit of a real function f at a point ξ are defined as follows:

1. $\displaystyle\liminf_{x\to\xi} f(x) = \inf\left\{\lim_{m\to\infty} f(x_m) \;\middle|\; x_m \neq \xi \text{ and } \lim_{m\to\infty} x_m = \xi\right\}$

2. $\displaystyle\limsup_{x\to\xi} f(x) = \sup\left\{\lim_{m\to\infty} f(x_m) \;\middle|\; x_m \neq \xi \text{ and } \lim_{m\to\infty} x_m = \xi\right\}$

It is easy to see that the sequence $\{a_m\}$ converges to a limit a if and only if

$$\liminf_{m\to\infty} a_m = \limsup_{m\to\infty} a_m = a$$

Similarly, the function f has a limit a at a point ξ if and only if

$$\liminf_{x\to\xi} f(x) = \limsup_{x\to\xi} f(x) = a$$

We use the following property of lower and upper limits.

Theorem 7.2 *For any sequence $\{A_m\}$ of events*

$$P\left(\liminf_{m\to\infty} A_m\right) \leq \liminf_{m\to\infty} P(A_m) \leq \limsup_{m\to\infty} P(A_m) \leq P\left(\limsup_{m\to\infty} A_m\right)$$

We can easily show that convergence with probability one implies convergence in probability.

Theorem 7.3

$$P\left\{\omega \;\middle|\; \lim_{m\to\infty} x_m(\omega) = x(\omega)\right\} = 1$$

implies that for every $\epsilon > 0$

$$\lim_{m\to\infty} P\left\{\omega \mid |x_m - x| > \epsilon\right\} = 0$$

Proof. Convergence with probability one and Equation 7.2 imply that

$$P\left\{\bigcup_{k\geq 1} \limsup_{m\to\infty}\left\{\omega \;\middle|\; |x_m(\omega) - x(\omega)| \geq \frac{1}{k}\right\}\right\} = 0$$

Together, the preceding equation and Theorem 7.2 indicate that for every $k \geq 1$

$$\liminf_{m\to\infty} P\left\{\omega \;\middle|\; |x_m(\omega) - x(\omega)| \geq \frac{1}{k}\right\}$$

$$= \limsup_{m \to \infty} P \left\{ \omega \;\middle|\; |x_m(\omega) - x(\omega)| \ge \frac{1}{k} \right\} = 0$$

This completes the proof. ∎

We end this subsection with a theorem on the probability of the event "A_m infinitely often."

Theorem 7.4 (Borel-Cantelli) *Let $\{A_m\}$ be a sequence of events such that $\sum\limits_{m=1}^{\infty} P(A_m) < \infty$. Then $P\left(\limsup\limits_{m \to \infty} A_m \right) = 0$.*

Quadratic Variation Processes

To characterize further the sample paths of the Wiener process and to prepare for the introduction of the Itô integral, consider a natural extension of the quadratic variation processes in Chapter 5. Intuitively, the optional quadratic variation process of a stochastic process is the limit of the sum of squared changes of the stochastic process, and the predictable quadratic variation process of a stochastic process is the limit of the sum of conditional expected squared changes of the stochastic process. Both the optional and the predictable variation processes are increasing.

The subsequent definitions of the quadratic variation processes use the sequence of dyadic partitions of the intervals $[0, t]$ for all $0 \le t \le T$. A dyadic partition of the interval $[0, t]$ is the sequence of points $t_{m,j} \wedge t$, where $t_{m,j} = j2^{-m}$ and m and j are nonnegative integers. In this notation the wedge denotes a minimum, $t_{m,j} \wedge t = \min(t_{m,j}, t)$, so that a dyadic partition of the interval $[0, t]$ consists of the endpoints 0 and t of this interval and interior points of this interval that have the form $j2^{-m}$. The convergence of the sum of squared changes of a stochastic process on a general sequence of partitions is discussed after Theorem 7.6.

Definition 7.19 Let $\{x_t\}$ be a stochastic process on the probability space $\{\Omega, \mathbf{F}, P\}$ and time interval $[0, T]$. Corresponding to dyadic partitions of the intervals $[0, t]$, where $0 \le t \le T$, consider sequences of sums of squared changes of the process $\{x_t\}$

$$S_m(x)(t, \omega) = x^2(0, \omega) + \sum_{j=1}^{\infty} [x(t_{m,j} \wedge t, \omega) - x(t_{m,j-1} \wedge t, \omega)]^2$$

If there exists a stochastic process, denoted $\{[x,x]_t\}$, such that for every $0 \le t \le T$ and every $\epsilon > 0$

$$\lim_{m\to\infty} P\left\{ \sup_{0\leq u\leq t} |S_m(x)(u,\omega) - [x,x](u,\omega)| \geq \epsilon \right\} = 0$$

then we say that $[x,x]$ is the optional quadratic variation process of x. In that case we also say that $[x,x]$ is the limit of the sum of squared changes of the process x in the topology of uniform convergence on compacts in probability.

Notice that the infinite sums in the preceding definition have only a finite number of nonzero terms. This is true because for all sufficiently large j the minimum $t_{m,j} \wedge t = t$ and the corresponding terms of the sum are zero.

The following explains the term *uniform convergence on compacts in probability* in the definition of the optional quadratic variation process. For any $0 \leq u \leq t$ and $m \geq 1$ the event

$$\left\{ |S_m(x)(u,\omega) - [x,x](u,\omega)| \geq \epsilon \right\}$$

is included in the event

$$\left\{ \sup_{0\leq u\leq t} |S_m(x)(u,\omega) - [x,x](u,\omega)| \geq \epsilon \right\}$$

Therefore, the uniform convergence

$$\lim_{m\to\infty} P\left\{ \sup_{0\leq u\leq t} |S_m(x)(u,\omega) - [x,x](u,\omega)| \geq \epsilon \right\} = 0$$

means that for every $\delta > 0$ there is a $v \geq 1$ such that for all $m \geq v$ and all $0 \leq u \leq t$

$$P\left\{ |S_m(x)(u,\omega) - [x,x](u,\omega)| \geq \epsilon \right\} < \delta$$

By contrast, ordinary convergence means that for every $0 \leq u \leq t$ and $\delta > 0$ there is a $v \geq 1$ such that for all $m \geq v$

$$P\left\{ |S_m(x)(u,\omega) - [x,x](u,\omega)| \geq \epsilon \right\} < \delta$$

With ordinary convergence, the integer v may depend on both δ and u. When convergence is uniform, the integer v may depend on δ, but does not depend on u as long as $0 \leq u \leq t$. Finally, the definition of the optional quadratic variation process implies that it is an increasing process.

A precise statement of the next definition requires the concept of a conditional expectation on an infinite probability space. Recall that for a random variable x on a finite probability space $\{\Omega, P\}$, and a partition $\mathbf{f}$ of Ω the conditional expectation $E_P(x|\mathbf{f})$ is a random variable, measurable on $\mathbf{f}$, such that for all $\omega \in \Omega$

$$\sum_{\xi \in \mathbf{f}(\omega)} P(\xi) E_P(x|\mathbf{f})(\xi) = \sum_{\xi \in \mathbf{f}(\omega)} P(\xi) x(\xi)$$

Therefore, the following definition.

Definition 7.20 Suppose that x is a random variable on the probability space $\{\Omega, \mathbf{F}, P\}$ and a σ-field $\mathbf{G}$ is such that $\mathbf{G} \subset \mathbf{F}$. Then the conditional expectation $E_P(x|\mathbf{G})$ is a random variable such that:

1. The conditional expectation is integrable, $E_P(|E_P(x|\mathbf{G})|) < \infty$.

2. The random variable $E_P(x|\mathbf{G})$ is measurable on $\mathbf{G}$.

3. For every $A \in \mathbf{G}$

$$\int_A E_P(x|\mathbf{G}) dP = \int_A x \, dP$$

The definition of the predictable quadratic variation process is now as follows.

Definition 7.21 Let $\{x_t\}$ be a stochastic process on the filtered probability space $\{\Omega, \mathbf{F}, P, \{\mathbf{F}_t\}\}$ and time interval $[0, T]$. Corresponding to dyadic partitions of the intervals $[0, t]$, where $0 \leq t \leq T$, consider sequences of sums of conditional expected squared changes, $S_m(x)(t, \omega)$, of the process $\{x_t\}$

$$x^2(0) + \sum_{j=1}^{\infty} E_P \left\{ [x(t_{m,j} \wedge t) - x(t_{m,j-1} \wedge t)]^2 \mid \mathbf{F}_{t_{m,j-1} \wedge t} \right\} (\omega)$$

If there exists a stochastic process, denoted $\{\langle x, x \rangle_t\}$, such that, for every $0 \leq t \leq T$ and every $\epsilon > 0$

$$\lim_{m \to \infty} P \left\{ \sup_{0 \leq u \leq t} |S_m(x)(u, \omega) - \langle x, x \rangle(u, \omega)| \geq \epsilon \right\} = 0$$

then we say that $\langle x, x \rangle$ is the predictable quadratic variation process of x. In that case we also say that $\langle x, x \rangle$ is the limit of the sum of conditional expected squared changes of the process x in the topology of uniform convergence on compacts in probability.

Like the optional quadratic variation process, the predictable quadratic variation process is increasing. The two preceding definitions have intuitive shorthand counterparts that are both suggestive and easy to remember. For the optional quadratic variation process we write

$$d[x,x]_t = (dx_t)^2$$

and for the predictable quadratic variation process we write

$$d\langle x,x\rangle_t = E_P\left[(dx_t)^2|\mathbf{F}_t\right]$$

We show next that the elementary properties of the Wiener process imply that, relative to the natural filtration of the Wiener process, the predictable quadratic variation of the Wiener process is time. We start with a definition of the σ-field generated by a stochastic process and the natural filtration of the Wiener process.

Definition 7.22 For a stochastic process $\{x_t\}$ on the probability space

$$\{\Omega, \mathbf{F}, P\}$$

the smallest σ-field that contains all the events of probability 0 and on which all the random variables x_s for $0 \le s \le t$ are measurable is denoted $\mathbf{F}_t^x$ and called the σ-field generated by the stochastic process x up to time t.

Notice that the family $\{\mathbf{F}_t^W \mid 0 \le t \le T\}$ is a filtration on the Wiener probability space, called the natural filtration of the Wiener process.

Theorem 7.5

$$\langle W, W\rangle_t = t$$

Proof. Indeed, the conditional expectation

$$E_P\left\{[W(t_{m,j} \wedge t) - W(t_{m,j-1} \wedge t)]^2 \;\middle|\; \mathbf{F}_{t_{m,j-1} \wedge t}^W\right\}$$

is equal to

$$E_P\left\{[W(t_{m,j} \wedge t) - W(t_{m,j-1} \wedge t)]^2\right\} = t_{m,j} \wedge t - t_{m,j-1} \wedge t$$

Therefore

$$\langle W, W\rangle_t = \lim_{m\to\infty} \sum_{j=1}^{\infty}(t_{m,j} \wedge t - t_{m,j-1} \wedge t) = t$$

This completes the proof. ∎

More surprisingly, the optional quadratic variation of the Wiener process is also time. This is a property of the Wiener probability measure that "discards" all the continuous functions in the sample space Ω that do not have this characteristic. In fact, we prove the following stronger result.

Theorem 7.6

$$P\left\{\omega \;\middle|\; \lim_{m\to\infty} \sum_{j=1}^{\infty} [W(t_{m,j} \wedge t, \omega) - W(t_{m,j-1} \wedge t, \omega)]^2 = t \right\} = 1$$

Proof. The proof proceeds in three steps.

- Fix m and j and denote

$$
\begin{aligned}
z(\omega) &= W(t_{m,j} \wedge t, \omega) - W(t_{m,j-1} \wedge t, \omega) \\
k &= t_{m,j} \wedge t - t_{m,j-1} \wedge t \\
\Delta_{m,j}(\omega) &= z^2(\omega) - k
\end{aligned}
$$

Because $z(\omega) \sim N(0, k)$

$$E_P\left(z^2\right) = k \quad \text{and} \quad E_P\left(\Delta_{m,j}\right) = 0$$

Also

$$\Delta_{m,j}^2 = \left(z^2 - k\right)^2 = z^4 - 2kz^2 + k^2$$

so that

$$E_P\left(\Delta_{m,j}^2\right) = E_P\left(z^4\right) - 2k^2 + k^2 = 2k^2$$

- Fix $\epsilon > 0$ and apply Chebyshev's inequality to $\sum_{j=1}^{\infty} \Delta_{m,j}$. For a random variable x with mean μ and variance σ^2 Chebyshev's inequality asserts that

$$P\{|x - \mu| \geq \epsilon\} \leq \frac{\sigma^2}{\epsilon^2}$$

Therefore, using the independence of the increments of the Wiener process and the results of the preceding step

$$P\left\{\left|\sum_{j=1}^{\infty}\Delta_{m,j}\right|\geq\epsilon\right\}\leq\frac{2\sum_{j=1}^{\infty}(t_{m,j}\wedge t-t_{m,j-1}\wedge t)^2}{\epsilon^2}\leq\frac{2(t+1)}{\epsilon^2 2^m}$$

and

$$\sum_{m=1}^{\infty}P\left\{\left|\sum_{j=1}^{\infty}\Delta_{m,j}\right|\geq\epsilon\right\}\leq\sum_{m=1}^{\infty}\frac{2(t+1)}{\epsilon^2 2^m}=\frac{2(t+1)}{\epsilon^2}<\infty$$

- Apply the Borel-Cantelli lemma to the events

$$A_{m,k}=\left\{\left|\sum_{j=1}^{\infty}\Delta_{m,j}\right|\geq\frac{1}{k}\right\}$$

First, $P\left\{\bigcup_{k\geq 1}\limsup_{m\to\infty}A_{m,k}\right\}=0$. Therefore

$$P\left\{\bigcap_{k\geq 1}\liminf_{m\to\infty}\left\{\left|\sum_{j=1}^{\infty}\Delta_{m,j}\right|<\frac{1}{k}\right\}\right\}=1$$

Equation 7.2 now implies that, with probability one

$$\lim_{m\to\infty}\sum_{j=1}^{\infty}\Delta_{m,j}=0$$

and from the definition of $\Delta_{m,j}$, we have, with probability one

$$\lim_{m\to\infty}\sum_{j=1}^{\infty}[W(t_{m,j}\wedge t,\omega)-W(t_{m,j-1}\wedge t,\omega)]^2=t$$

This completes the proof. ∎

Corollary 7.1

$$[W,W]_t=t$$

Using the shorthand notation, Theorems 7.5 and 7.6 can be written

$$(dW_t)^2 = E_P \left[(dW_t)^2 \mid \mathbf{F}_t^W \right] = dt$$

Theorem 7.6 can be extended in several directions. We now state some of these extensions without proof. First, for the sequence of dyadic partitions, the sum of squared changes of the Wiener process not only converges but also converges uniformly to time, that is, if

$$S_m(W)(t, \omega) = \sum_{j=1}^{\infty} [W(t_{m,j} \wedge t, \omega) - W(t_{m,j-1} \wedge t, \omega)]^2$$

then, with probability one

$$\lim_{m \to \infty} \sup_{0 \le t \le T} |S_m(W)(t, \omega) - t| = 0$$

Second, consider a general sequence of partitions

$$\Pi_{t,m} = \{\lambda_{t,m,0}, \ldots, \lambda_{t,m,u(t,m)}\}$$

where $0 = \lambda_{t,m,0} < \lambda_{t,m,1} \cdots < \lambda_{t,m,u(t,m)} = t$. The mesh of a partition $\Pi_{t,m}$ is the size of the longest interval of that partition

$$\mu(\Pi_{t,m}) = \max_{1 \le j \le u(t,m)} |\lambda_{t,m,j} - \lambda_{t,m,j-1}|$$

The sum of squared changes of the Wiener process converges, with probability one, to time, for every sequence of partitions whose mesh converges to zero. Third, for every sample path of the Wiener process, there is a sequence of partitions whose mesh converges to zero, and for which the sum of squared changes of that sample path converges to zero. Fourth, for almost every sample path of the Wiener process, there is a sequence of partitions whose mesh converges to zero, and for which the sum of squared changes of that sample path converges to infinity.

Variation of Wiener Sample Paths

Like quadratic variation, the concept of variation also helps characterize the fluctuations of the sample paths of the Wiener process. The Wiener probability measure discards the set of all the sample paths that do not fluctuate wildly and retains only those whose sum of the absolute values of changes is infinite.

Definition 7.23 Let $f : [a, b] \to \mathcal{R}$ be a real function on the closed interval $[a, b]$, and let $\Pi = \{\lambda_0, \ldots, \lambda_m\}$ be a partition of the interval $[a, b]$. Denote

$$\int_a^b |df| = \sup_\Pi \sum_{j=1}^m |f(\lambda_j) - f(\lambda_{j-1})|$$

where the supremum is taken over all the finite partitions Π of the interval $[a, b]$. This supremum, $\int_a^b |df|$, is called the variation of the function f on the interval $[a, b]$. If $\int_a^b |df| < \infty$, then we say that the function f has finite variation on the interval $[a, b]$. If $\int_a^b |df| = \infty$, then we say that f has infinite variation on the interval $[a, b]$.

Intuitively, a continuous function of infinite variation fluctuates a lot.

Example 7.4 The following are examples of functions that have finite variation and functions that have infinite variation on compact intervals:

1. If f is monotone on $[a, b]$, then

$$\int_a^b |df| = |f(b) - f(a)|$$

2. If f is differentiable on $[a, b]$ and f' is bounded, then f has finite variation on $[a, b]$. Indeed, from the mean value theorem, for each $1 \le j \le m$ there is a $\lambda_{j-1} \le \tau_j \le \lambda_j$ such that

$$f(\lambda_j) - f(\lambda_{j-1}) = f'(\tau_j)(\lambda_j - \lambda_{j-1})$$

and because $|f'(\tau_j)| \le M$

$$|f(\lambda_j) - f(\lambda_{j-1})| \le M(\lambda_j - \lambda_{j-1})$$

and

$$\sum_{j=1}^m |f(\lambda_j) - f(\lambda_{j-1})| \le M(b - a)$$

3. If f is integrable on $[a, b]$ and

$$F(t) = \int_a^t f(s)ds$$

then

$$\int_a^b |dF| \le \int_a^b |f(s)|ds$$

Indeed, let $\{\lambda_0, \ldots, \lambda_m\}$ be a partition of the interval $[a, b]$. For all $1 \le j \le m$

$$|F(\lambda_j) - F(\lambda_{j-1})| = \left| \int_{\lambda_{j-1}}^{\lambda_j} f(s)ds \right| \le \int_{\lambda_{j-1}}^{\lambda_j} |f(s)|ds$$

so that

$$\sum_{j=1}^m |F(\lambda_j) - F(\lambda_{j-1})| \le \sum_{j=1}^m \int_{\lambda_{j-1}}^{\lambda_j} |f(s)|ds = \int_a^b |f(s)|ds$$

4. The function

$$f(t) = \begin{cases} 0 & \text{for } t = 0 \\ t \sin\left(\dfrac{\pi}{t}\right) & \text{for } 0 < t \le 2 \end{cases}$$

shown in Figure 7.1, is continuous on the interval $[0, 2]$ and has there infinite variation. To see this consider the sequence of partitions of $[0, 2]$

$$\Pi_m = \left\{ 0, \frac{2}{2m - 1}, \ldots, \frac{2}{2(m - j) + 1}, \ldots, 2 \right\}$$

The function f is 0 at the 0-th point of these partitions, then as j runs through the values $1, \ldots, m$ the function f alternates in sign, and has the absolute value $\dfrac{2}{2(m - j) + 1}$ at the j-th point. Consequently, the sum

$$\sum_{j=1}^m |f(\lambda_{m,j}) - f(\lambda_{m,j-1})|$$

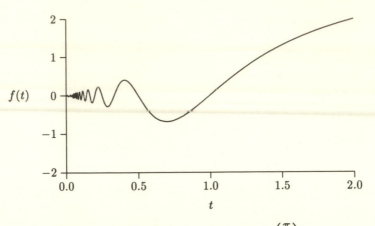

Figure 7.1: The function $f(t) = t \sin\left(\dfrac{\pi}{t}\right)$.

is equal to

$$\frac{2}{2m-1} + \sum_{j=1}^{m-1}\left[\frac{2}{2(m-j)-1} + \frac{2}{2(m-j)+1}\right]$$

Now, for every $1 \le j \le m-1$

$$\frac{2}{2(m-j)-1} > \frac{1}{m-j} \quad \text{and} \quad \frac{2}{2(m-j)+1} > \frac{1}{m-j+1}$$

and, therefore

$$\sum_{j=1}^{m}|f(\lambda_{m,j}) - f(\lambda_{m,j-1})| > 2\sum_{j=2}^{m}\frac{1}{j}$$

Because $\displaystyle\sum_{j=1}^{m}\frac{1}{j}$ tends to infinity, this function has infinite variation on $[0,2]$.

Theorem 7.7 implies that, with probability one, the sample paths of the Wiener process have infinite variation on finite intervals.

Theorem 7.7 *For every $t > 0$*

$$\int_0^t |dW_s| = \infty$$

Proof. The proof is based on the obvious inequality

$$\sum_{j=1}^{m} |W(\lambda_j) - W(\lambda_{j-1})| \geq \frac{\displaystyle\sum_{j=1}^{m} [W(\lambda_j) - W(\lambda_{j-1})]^2}{\displaystyle\max_{1 \leq j \leq m} |W(\lambda_j) - W(\lambda_{j-1})|}$$

First, the numerator of the fraction on the right side has a positive limit as $m \to \infty$. Second, the sample paths of the Wiener process are continuous and, therefore, uniformly continuous on the interval $[0, t]$. Consequently, the denominator tends to zero, the whole fraction goes to infinity, and the left side also goes to infinity. ∎

The following property of the Wiener process is interpreted later as the local risk of prices in the Black-Scholes model and its extensions.

Theorem 7.8 *The set Λ of sample paths W_t of the Wiener process that are differentiable at some point $t \geq 0$ is contained in a set $A \in \mathbf{F}$ such that $P(A) = 0$.*

This theorem says that almost all the sample paths of the Wiener process are nowhere differentiable. The somewhat oblique statement of the theorem avoids the need to determine if the set Λ itself belongs to $\mathbf{F}$.

Equipped with the Wiener probability space and the Wiener process, we can take one more step toward the complete specification of the Black-Scholes model. The first two elements of the model are:

- A time interval $[0, T]$.

- The Wiener probability space $\{\Omega, \mathbf{F}, P\}$ with the filtration $\{\mathbf{F}_t^W\}$.

To define the gain process in the Black-Scholes model requires the concept of the integral $\int_0^t x_s dW_s$ for certain stochastic processes $\{x_t\}$ on the Wiener probability space. The meaning of this integral is the subject of the next chapter.

Problems

1. Prove that if $\mathbf{F}$ is a field, then $\emptyset \in \mathbf{F}$, and if $A, B \in \mathbf{F}$, then $A \bigcap B \in \mathbf{F}$.

2. Suppose that $\Omega \in \mathbf{F}$ and that $A, B \in \mathbf{F}$ implies that $A - B \in \mathbf{F}$. Show that $\mathbf{F}$ is a field.

3. Suppose that $\Omega \in \mathbf{F}$ and that $\mathbf{F}$ is closed under the formation of complements and finite disjoint unions. Show that $\mathbf{F}$ need not be a field.

4. Show that a σ-field cannot be countably infinite, it is either finite or uncountably infinite.

5. Show that a random variable x is measurable on the field $\{\emptyset, \Omega\}$ if and only if x is constant.

6. Prove that if $A \in \mathbf{F}$ if and only if $P(A) = 0$ or $P(A) = 1$, then $\mathbf{F}$ is a σ-field.

7. Prove that if x and y are random variables such that y is measurable on $\mathbf{F}^x$, then there exists a measurable function f such that $y(\omega) = f[x(\omega)]$.

8. Prove that if $W(t)$ is a Wiener process and c is a positive constant, then $Z(t) = cW\left(\dfrac{t}{c^2}\right)$ is also a Wiener process.

9. Show that the normal transition density

$$p(t, x, y) = \frac{1}{\sqrt{2\pi t}} \exp\left[-\frac{(x-y)^2}{2t}\right]$$

satisfies the partial differential equation

$$\frac{\partial p}{\partial t} = \frac{1}{2}\frac{\partial^2 p}{\partial x^2}$$

10. Let $x_t = \displaystyle\int_0^t W_s ds$. Prove that $E_P(x_t) = 0$ and $E_P(x_t) = \dfrac{t^3}{3}$.

11. Prove that if f is a function of finite variation on the interval $[a, b]$ and $a \le c \le b$, then

$$\int_a^b |df| = \int_a^c |df| + \int_c^b |df|$$

12. Prove that if f is continuous and has finite variation on the interval $[a, b]$, then the function

$$g(t) = \int_a^t |df|$$

is continuous on $[a, b]$.

13. Suppose that the function f has finite variation on the interval $[a, b]$. Prove that the two functions

$$g(t) = \int_a^t |df| + f(t) - f(a)$$

$$h(t) = \int_a^t |df| - f(t) + f(a)$$

are monotonic. Conclude that every function of finite variation is a difference of two monotonic functions.

Notes

The material in this chapter is standard in the mathematical probability literature. References to the properties of the Wiener process include [52], [51], [36], [1], [47], [50], [58], [54], [65], and [70], and represent a variety of detail and rigor.

Chapter 8

Itô Calculus

8.1 Introduction

In this chapter we offer two definitions of the Itô integral. The first definition describes the Itô integral as a limit of sums. This definition is not very elegant but it offers more intuition about what is involved in constructing a stochastic integral than the second, abstract, definition. It is the procedure in the second definition, however, that we use in Chapter 11 to lead us to the general concept of a stochastic integral.

The remainder of the chapter describes Itô's formula for the change of variables in an Itô integral, and defines the stochastic exponential of an Itô process. All the concepts and results in this chapter are special cases of the more general theory. The presentation of these results is designed to prepare the reader for the Black-Scholes model in Chapter 9 and the material on continuous time martingales, general stochastic integrals, and the general continuous multiperiod model in Chapters 10, 11, and 12.

8.2 The Itô Integral

An Example

Consider again the sequence of dyadic partitions of the interval $[0, t]$ and the two sequences of simple function approximations to the Wiener process on this interval

$$W_m^-(s) = \sum_{j=1}^{\infty} W(t_{m,j-1} \wedge t) \chi_{[t_{m,j-1} \wedge t, t_{m,j} \wedge t)}(s)$$

$$W_m^+(s) \; = \; \sum_{j=1}^{\infty} W(t_{m,j} \wedge t) \chi_{[t_{m,j-1} \wedge t, \, t_{m,j} \wedge t)}(s)$$

In the preceding formulas $\chi_{[u, \, v)}$ denotes the indicator function of the left closed, right open interval $[u, v)$. The processes W_m^- and W_m^+ are constant on the left closed, right open intervals $[t_{m,j-1} \wedge t, t_{m,j} \wedge t)$ and, therefore, are right continuous. Both W_m^- and W_m^+ approximate the Wiener process W on the interval $[0, t]$ in the sense that

$$\lim_{m \to \infty} \int_0^t \left(W_s - W_{ms}^- \right)^2 ds = 0$$

and

$$\lim_{m \to \infty} \int_0^t \left(W_s - W_{ms}^+ \right)^2 ds = 0$$

The difference between the simple functions W_m^- and W_m^+ is in the choice of the value of the function in the interval $[t_{m,j-1} \wedge t, t_{m,j} \wedge t)$. In the function W_m^- it is the value of the Wiener process W at the left end point of the interval, whereas in the function W_m^+ it is the value of the Wiener process W at the right end point of the interval. It turns out that the choice of the constant values of the simple functions in the intervals $[t_{m,j-1} \wedge t, t_{m,j} \wedge t)$ is material.

In analogy with the discrete case in Chapter 5 we define the Itô integrals of simple functions as the sums

$$\int_0^t W_{ms}^- dW_s \; = \; \sum_{j=1}^{\infty} W(t_{m,j-1} \wedge t) \left[W(t_{m,j} \wedge t) - W(t_{m,j-1} \wedge t) \right]$$

$$\int_0^t W_{ms}^+ dW_s \; = \; \sum_{j=1}^{\infty} W(t_{m,j} \wedge t) \left[W(t_{m,j} \wedge t) - W(t_{m,j-1} \wedge t) \right]$$

As in the proof of Theorem 5.8, the integral $\int_0^t W_{ms}^- dW_s$ can be written

$$\int_0^t W_{ms}^- dW_s \; = \; \frac{1}{2} \sum_{j=1}^{\infty} \left[W^2(t_{m,j} \wedge t) - W^2(t_{m,j-1} \wedge t) \right]$$

$$- \frac{1}{2} \sum_{j=1}^{\infty} \left[W(t_{m,j} \wedge t) - W(t_{m,j-1} \wedge t) \right]^2$$

The first sum on the right side telescopes into W_t^2, and by Theorem 7.6, the second sum converges, with probability one, to

$$\lim_{m \to \infty} \sum_{j=1}^{\infty} [W(t_{m,j} \wedge t) - W(t_{m,j-1} \wedge t)]^2 = [W, W]_t = t$$

Therefore, with probability one

$$\lim_{m \to \infty} \int_0^t W_{ms}^- dW_s = \frac{1}{2} \left(W_t^2 - t \right)$$

To compute the limit of the integrals $\int_0^t W_{ms}^+ dW_s$ notice that

$$\int_0^t W_{m,s}^+ dW_s = \int_0^t W_{m,s}^- dW_s + \sum_{j=1}^{\infty} [W(t_{m,j} \wedge t) - W(t_{m,j-1} \wedge t)]^2$$

so that, with probability one

$$\lim_{m \to \infty} \int_0^t W_{ms}^+ dW_s = \frac{1}{2} \left(W_t^2 - t \right) + [W, W]_t = \frac{1}{2} \left(W_t^2 + t \right)$$

Even though both sequences of simple functions W_{mt}^- and W_{mt}^+ approximate the continuous function W_t and the corresponding sequences of integrals $\int_0^t W_{ms}^- dW_s$ and $\int_0^t W_{ms}^+ dW_s$ approximate the intuitive concept of the integral $\int_0^t W_s dW_s$, the limits of the sequences of integrals are not even close. This result reflects the fact that the fluctuations of the paths of the Wiener process are too large to define the integral $\int_0^t W_s dW_s$ as a Stieltjes integral, that is, as the limit

$$\lim_{m \to \infty} \sum_{j=1}^{\infty} W(\tau_j) [W(t_{m,j} \wedge t) - W(t_{m,j-1} \wedge t)]$$

with an arbitrary choice of $t_{m,j-1} \wedge t \le \tau_j \le t_{m,j} \wedge t$. To arrive at a successful definition of the Itô integral $\int_0^t W_s dW_s$ we must restrict the selection of the points $t_{m,j-1} \wedge t \le \tau_j \le t_{m,j} \wedge t$. To make this Itô integral a martingale, we reason in analogy with Theorem 5.5 and approximate the Wiener process W with the sequence W_m^- of functions whose value $W(t_{m,j-1} \wedge t)$ on each partition interval is the value of the Wiener process W at the left end point of that interval. Consequently, we define

$$\int_0^t W_s dW_s = \lim_{m \to \infty} \int_0^t W_{ms}^- dW_s = \frac{1}{2} \left(W_t^2 - t \right)$$

This definition of the integral $\int_0^t W_s dW_s$ indeed produces a martingale, as shown in Example 8.1. On the other hand, it follows from the same example that

$$E_P\left(W_t^2 + t \,\middle|\, \mathbf{F}_s^W\right) = W_s^2 - s + 2t$$

so that the alternative candidate for the definition of the integral $\int_0^t W_s dW_s$

$$\lim_{m \to \infty} \int_0^t W_{ms}^+ dW_s = \frac{1}{2}\left(W_t^2 + t\right)$$

does not produce a martingale. We start with the formal definition of a continuous time martingale.

Definition 8.1 An adapted process $\{x_t\}$ on a filtered probability space

$$\{\Omega, \mathbf{F}, P, \{\mathbf{F}_t\}\}$$

is called a martingale on $[0, T]$ if and only if:

1. For each $0 \leq t \leq T$ we have $E_P(|x_t|) < \infty$.

2. For each $0 \leq u \leq t \leq T$, with probability one, $E_P(x_t|\mathbf{F}_u) = x_u$.

Example 8.1 The following two processes are martingales on the natural filtration of the Wiener process:

1. The Wiener process. Indeed

$$E_P(|W_t|) = \frac{1}{\sqrt{2\pi}} \int_{-\infty}^{\infty} |a| \exp(-\frac{a^2}{2t}) da = \frac{\sqrt{t}}{2} < \infty$$

and

$$
\begin{aligned}
E_P(W_t|\mathbf{F}_u^W) &= E_P(W_t - W_u + W_u|\mathbf{F}_u^W) \\
&= E_P(W_t - W_u|\mathbf{F}_u^W) + E_P(W_u|\mathbf{F}_u^W) \\
&= W_u
\end{aligned}
$$

because $W_t - W_u$ is independent of $\mathbf{F}_u^W$ and W_u is measurable on $\mathbf{F}_u^W$.

2. The process $W_t^2 - t$. First

$$E_P(|W_t^2 - t|) \le E_P(W_t^2 + t) = 2t < \infty$$

Second

$$
\begin{aligned}
E_P\left(W_t^2 - t \,\middle|\, \mathbf{F}_u^W\right) &= E_P\left[(W_t - W_u)^2 + 2W_t W_u - W_u^2 - t \,\middle|\, \mathbf{F}_u^W\right] \\
&= t - u + 2W_u^2 - W_u^2 - t \\
&= W_u^2 - u
\end{aligned}
$$

A First Definition of the Itô Integral

The preceding discussion may lead the reader to expect that the definition of the integral $\int_0^t x_s dW_s$ proceeds as follows. First, approximate the integrand $\{x_t\}$ on the interval $[0, t]$ by a sequence of simple functions

$$x_m^-(s) = \sum_{j=1}^{\infty} x(t_{m,j-1} \wedge t) \chi_{[t_{m,j-1} \wedge t, \, t_{m,j} \wedge t)}(s)$$

Second, define the Itô integral of a simple function

$$\int_0^t x_{ms}^- dW_s = \sum_{j=1}^{\infty} x(t_{m,j-1} \wedge t)\left[W(t_{m,j} \wedge t) - W(t_{m,j-1} \wedge t)\right]$$

and finally, define the integral $\int_0^t x_s dW_s$ as the limit

$$\int_0^t x_s dW_s = \lim_{m \to \infty} \int_0^t x_{ms}^- dW_s$$

This indeed is the case when the integrand $\{x_t\}$ is adapted and continuous (*i.e.*, with probability one has continuous sample paths). When the process $\{x_t\}$, however, is not continuous, then the sequence of simple functions $\{x_{mt}^-\}$, as defined previously, is not a good approximation to the process $\{x_t\}$ in the sense that the integrals $\int_0^t (x_s - x_{ms}^-)^2 ds$ need not be small even for large m. To overcome this problem, and to define the Itô integral for certain discontinuous integrands $\{x_t\}$, consider a different construction of the simple processes $\{x_{mt}^-\}$ such that

$$\lim_{m \to \infty} \int_0^T \left(x_t - x_{mt}^-\right)^2 dt = 0$$

The proposed construction is carried out in three steps. First, approximate the integrand $\{x_t\}$ with a sequence of bounded processes $\{x^*_{mt}\}$. Second, approximate the bounded processes $\{x^*_{mt}\}$ with continuous bounded processes $\{x_{mt}\}$. Third, define the simple function approximation to the integrand $\{x_t\}$ off the continuous process approximation $\{x_{mt}\}$. Specifically, for every $0 \le t \le T$ define

$$x^*_m(t) \;=\; x(t)\chi_{\{|x| \le m\}}(t)$$

$$x_m(t) \;=\; m \int_0^t e^{m(s-t)} x^*_m(s)\,ds$$

and

$$x^-_m(t) = \sum_{j=1}^{\infty} x_m(t_{m,j-1} \wedge T)\chi_{[t_{m,j-1} \wedge T,\, t_{m,j} \wedge T)}(t)$$

For each $m \ge 1$, the process x^*_m coincides with the process x whenever the latter does not exceed m, and is zero otherwise. This definition of the process x^*_m means that $|x^*_m| \le m$. In addition, for each $m \ge 1$, the value of the process x_m at time t is a continuous weighted average of the values of x^*_m to the left of t. This weighted average is such that with increasing m the weights used in the calculation of $x_m(t)$ concentrate on progressively smaller left neighborhoods of t. This explains why, given some regularity assumptions stated later, the sequence of processes x_m is a continuous bounded approximation to the process x.

This procedure is formalized in Theorem 8.1. The procedure works when the integrand $\{x_t\}$ is adapted, measurable, and satisfies, with probability one

$$\int_0^T x_t^2\, dt < \infty$$

The next definition describes the concept of a measurable stochastic process.

Definition 8.2 The first item below is the definition of a product σ-field and the second item is the definition of a measurable process:

- If $\mathbf{F}$ is a σ-field on the sample space Ω and $\mathbf{G}$ is a σ-field on the sample space Ξ, then the product σ-field $\mathbf{F} \bigotimes \mathbf{G}$ is the smallest σ-field on the sample space $\Omega \times \Xi$ that contains all the sets of the form $F \times G$, where $F \in \mathbf{F}$ and $G \in \mathbf{G}$.

- A stochastic process $\{x_t\}$, where $0 \le t \le T$, on the space $\{\Omega, \mathbf{F}\}$, is measurable if and only if the function

$$x : [0, T] \times \Omega \to \mathcal{R}$$

is measurable on the product σ-field $\mathbf{B}([0, T]) \otimes \mathbf{F}$, where $\mathbf{B}([0, T])$ is the Borel σ-field of the interval $[0, T]$.

The definition says that a stochastic process is measurable when it is a measurable function of both of its arguments. Recall that in Definition 7.11 a stochastic process

$$x : [0, T] \times \Omega \to \mathcal{R}$$

has to be measurable only as a function of the argument ω for any fixed $0 \le t \le T$.

Example 8.2 If the sample paths of a stochastic process are right continuous (left continuous) with probability one, then the process is called right continuous (left continuous.) An adapted right continuous (left continuous) process is measurable. To see this, consider for instance the case of a right continuous process and define an approximating sequence of right continuous simple processes

$$x_m(t, \omega) = x(t_{m,j}, \omega)$$

for $t_{m,j-1} \le t < t_{m,j}$. Because each one of the simple processes $\{x_{mt}\}$ is measurable, letting m go to infinity establishes that the process $\{x_t\}$ is measurable.

Theorem 8.1 *Suppose that $\{x_t\}$ is a stochastic process on the interval $[0, T]$, adapted to the filtration $\{\mathbf{F}_t^W\}$, measurable, and such that, with probability one*

$$\int_0^T x_t^2 dt < \infty$$

Then there exists a sequence of adapted, measurable, simple stochastic processes $\{x_{mt}\}$ such that, with probability one

$$\int_0^T x_{mt}^2 dt \;\; < \;\; \infty$$

$$\lim_{m \to \infty} \int_0^T (x_t - x_{mt})^2 \, dt \;\; = \;\; 0$$

and, with probability one, the sequence of integrals $\int_0^t x_{ms} dW_s$ converges uniformly on the interval $[0, T]$. Furthermore, the limit

$$\lim_{m \to \infty} \int_0^t x_{ms} dW_s$$

does not depend on the choice of the approximating sequence of adapted, measurable, simple processes $\{x_{mt}\}$ such that $\int_0^T x_{mt}^2 dt < \infty$.

Definition 8.3 For a stochastic process $\{x_t\}$ in the preceding theorem define

$$\int_0^t x_s dW_s = \lim_{m \to \infty} \int_0^t x_{ms} dW_s$$

The left side of the preceding equation is called the Itô integral of the process $\{x_t\}$. The Itô integral is also called the transform of the process $\{x_t\}$ by the Wiener process $\{W_t\}$ and denoted $\{(x \bullet W)_t\}$. For $0 \le u \le t$ define the integral

$$\int_u^t x_s dW_s = \int_0^t x_s \chi_{[u,\, t]}(s) dW_s$$

where $\chi_{[u,\, t]}$ is the indicator function of the interval $[u, t]$.

Notice that the simple processes above approximate the given integrand $\{x_t\}$ on the whole interval $[0, T]$ and, therefore, the Itô integral is defined simultaneously for all $0 \le t \le T$.

8.3   Properties of the Itô Integral

Because of the uniform convergence of the approximating integrals

$$\int_0^t x_{ms} dW_s$$

the Itô integral is a continuous function of t on the interval $[0, T]$. Theorem 8.2 shows that the simple properties of the Itô integral are identical to the simple properties of ordinary integrals. Despite the care that went into its definition, the Itô integral is not in general a martingale. This defect is remedied in Theorem 8.4, which asserts that a suitable further restriction of the integrands makes the Itô integral a martingale.

Theorem 8.2 *If the adapted, measurable, processes $\{x_t\}$ and $\{y_t\}$ are such that $\int_0^T x_t^2 dt < \infty$ and $\int_0^T y_t^2 dt < \infty$, then:*

1. *For any constants α, β*

$$\int_0^t (\alpha x_s + \beta y_s) dW_s = \alpha \int_0^t x_s dW_s + \beta \int_0^t y_s dW_s$$

2. *For any $0 \le u \le t$*

$$\int_0^t x_s dW_s = \int_0^u x_s dW_s + \int_u^t x_s dW_s$$

Using the identity

$$ab = \frac{1}{2}\left[(a+b)^2 - a^2 - b^2\right]$$

we define the optional and predictable quadratic covariation of two processes.

Definition 8.4 We define quadratic covariation processes by polarization:

$$[x, y]_t = \frac{1}{2}\left([x+y, x+y]_t - [x, x]_t - [y, y]_t\right)$$

$$\langle x, y \rangle_t = \frac{1}{2}\left(\langle x+y, x+y \rangle_t - \langle x, x \rangle_t - \langle y, y \rangle_t\right)$$

Because each quadratic covariation process is defined as a difference of two increasing processes, each is a process of finite variation on compacts.

Theorem 8.3 *If the adapted, measurable, processes $\{x_t\}$ and $\{y_t\}$ are such that $\int_0^T x_t^2 dt < \infty$ and $\int_0^T y_t^2 dt < \infty$, then:*

1. *The optional quadratic variation of the Itô integral is*

$$[x \bullet W, x \bullet W]_t = \langle x \bullet W, x \bullet W \rangle_t = \int_0^t x_s^2 ds$$

2. *The optional quadratic covariation of two Itô integrals is*

$$[x \bullet W, y \bullet W]_t = \langle x \bullet W, y \bullet W \rangle_t = \int_0^t x_s y_s ds$$

Using the shorthand notation, the preceding theorem can be written

$$d[x \bullet W, y \bullet W]_t \;=\; d(x \bullet W)_t d(y \bullet W)_t \qquad\qquad = \; x_t y_t dt$$
$$d\langle x \bullet W, y \bullet W \rangle_t \;=\; E_P\left[d(x \bullet W)_t d(y \bullet W)_t \,\big|\, \mathbf{F}_t^W\right] \;=\; x_t y_t dt$$

A further restriction of the integrand $\{x_t\}$ such that

$$E_P\left(\int_0^T x_t^2 dt\right) < \infty$$

guarantees that the Itô integral is a martingale. This requirement is stronger than the condition

$$\int_0^T x_t^2 dt < \infty$$

for the existence of the Itô integral $\int_0^t x_s dW_s$ in Theorem 8.1. Indeed, because the random variable $\int_0^T x_t^2 dt$ is nonnegative, if

$$P\left\{\int_0^T x_t^2 dt = \infty\right\} > 0$$

then

$$E_P\left(\int_0^T x_t^2 dt\right) = \infty$$

Theorem 8.4 *If the adapted, measurable, processes $\{x_t\}$ and $\{y_t\}$ are such that*

$$E_P\left(\int_0^T x_t^2 dt\right) < \infty \quad \text{and} \quad E_P\left(\int_0^T y_t^2 dt\right) < \infty$$

then:

1. *For any $0 \leq t \leq T$*

$$E_P\left(\left|\int_0^t x_s dW_s\right|\right) < \infty$$

2. *For any $0 \leq u \leq t \leq T$*

$$E_P\left(\int_0^t x_s dW_s \,\bigg|\, \mathbf{F}_u^W\right) = \int_0^u x_s dW_s$$

3. For any $0 \leq u \leq t \leq T$

$$E_P \left(\int_0^t x_s dW_s \int_0^t y_s dW_s \, \bigg| \, \mathbf{F}_u^W \right) = E_P \left(\int_0^t x_s y_s ds \, \bigg| \, \mathbf{F}_u^W \right)$$

In Theorem 8.4, items 1 and 2 say that the Itô integral is a martingale, and imply in particular that

$$E_P \left(\int_0^t x_s dW_s \right) = E_P \left(\int_0^t x_s dW_s \, | \mathbf{F}_0 \right) = \int_0^0 x_s dW_s = 0$$

Item 3 of Theorem 8.4 identifies the variance of an Itô integral, and the covariance of two Itô integrals, and implies in particular that

$$E_P \left[\left(\int_0^t x_s dW_s \right)^2 \right] = E_P \left([x \bullet W, x \bullet W]_t \right) = E_P \left(\int_0^t x_s^2 ds \right) < \infty$$

Paralleling the shorthand notation for quadratic variation processes, the integral notation in this section has an intuitive shorthand counterpart that is both suggestive and easy to remember. The Itô integral

$$I_t = \int_0^t x_s dW_s$$

is written in the shorthand notation

$$dI_t = x_t dW_t$$

For example, the integral

$$W_t^2 - t = 2 \int_0^t W_s dW_s$$

is written in the shorthand notation

$$d(W_t^2 - t) = 2W_t dW_t$$

or, equivalently

$$dW_t^2 = 2W_t dW_t + dt$$

The shorthand notation is particularly useful for writing Itô's formula for the Wiener process.

8.4   Itô's Formula for the Wiener Process

This section describes Itô's formula for the change of variables in an Itô integral. For a twice continuously differentiable function $f : \mathcal{R} \to \mathcal{R}$ Itô's formula says that for every $t \geq 0$

$$f(W_t) = f(W_0) + \int_0^t f'(W_s)dW_s + \frac{1}{2}\int_0^t f''(W_s)ds$$

In the shorthand notation Itô's formula is written

$$df(W_t) = f'(W_t)dW_t + \frac{1}{2}f''(W_t)dt$$

and can be regarded as a Taylor expansion

$$df(W_t) = f'(W_t)dW_t + \frac{1}{2}f''(W_t)(dW_t)^2$$

with the rules (compare with the formula for the optional quadratic variation of a Wiener process in Corollary 7.1)

$$(dW_t)^2 = dt, \ (dW_t)^3 = 0$$

The following is a useful extension of this version of Itô's formula. A still more general version and a proof are given in Theorem 8.10.

Theorem 8.5 *If $f : [0, T] \times \mathcal{R} \to \mathcal{R}$ is continuously differentiable in the first argument and twice continuously differentiable in the second argument, then for every $0 \leq t \leq T$*

$$f(t, W_t) = f(0, W_0) + \int_0^t \frac{\partial f(s, W_s)}{\partial W_s}dW_s + \int_0^t \left[\frac{\partial f(s, W_s)}{\partial s}\right.$$
$$\left. + \frac{1}{2}\frac{\partial^2 f(s, W_s)}{\partial W_s^2}\right] ds$$

Using the shorthand notation, this version of Itô's formula is written

$$df(t, W_t) = \frac{\partial f(t, W_t)}{\partial W_t}dW_t + \left[\frac{\partial f(t, W_t)}{\partial t} + \frac{1}{2}\frac{\partial^2 f(t, W_t)}{\partial W_t^2}\right] dt$$

and can be regarded as a Taylor expansion

$$df(t, W_t) = \frac{\partial f(t, W_t)}{\partial W_t}dW_t + \frac{\partial f(t, W_t)}{\partial t}dt + \frac{1}{2}\frac{\partial^2 f(t, W_t)}{\partial W_t^2}(dW_t)^2$$

with the rules

$$(dW_t)^2 = dt, \ (dW_t)^3 = 0, \ (dt)^2 = 0, \ dtdW_t = 0$$

Example 8.3 Let $f(t, W_t) = \exp\left(W_t - \frac{1}{2}t\right)$. Then

$$\frac{\partial f(t, W_t)}{\partial t} + \frac{1}{2}\frac{\partial^2 f(t, W_t)}{\partial W_t^2} = 0$$

and therefore Itô's formula implies that

$$\int_0^t \exp\left(W_s - \frac{1}{2}s\right) dW_s = \exp\left(W_t - \frac{1}{2}t\right) - 1$$

Consequently, the function $\exp\left(W_t - \frac{1}{2}t\right)$ plays the role of the exponential function in Itô integrals. Because

$$E_P\left\{\int_0^T \left[\exp\left(W_t - \frac{1}{2}t\right)\right]^2 dt\right\} < \infty$$

the Itô integral above is a martingale, and thus the process

$$x_t = \exp\left(W_t - \frac{1}{2}t\right)$$

is a martingale.

8.5 Representation of Martingales

This section establishes the representation of certain martingales on the natural filtration of the Wiener process as Itô integrals. In the language of Chapter 5, the Wiener process is a basis for certain martingales on the Wiener filtration. The reader should compare this subsection with Theorem 5.15 on the representation of martingales in discrete time.

Consider the Itô integral $x_t = \int_0^t \alpha_s dW_s$. Theorem 8.4 implies that if

$$E_P\left(\int_0^T \alpha_s^2 ds\right) < \infty,$$ then the integral x_t is a continuous martingale and for all $0 \le t \le T$

$$E_P\left(x_t^2\right) \le E_P\left(\int_0^T \alpha_s^2 ds\right) < \infty$$

This property of the Itô integral is formalized in the following definition.

Definition 8.5 A square integrable martingale on the time interval $[0, T]$ is a right continuous martingale $\{x_t\}$ such that

$$\sup_{0 \le t \le T} E_P\left(x_t^2\right) < \infty$$

Thus, the following corollary.

Corollary 8.1 *If x is an adapted, measurable, process such that*

$$E_P \left(\int_0^T x_t^2 dt \right) < \infty$$

then the Itô integral $\int_0^t x_s dW_s$ is a square integrable martingale.

The representation theorem below says that Itô integrals are the only square integrable martingales on the natural filtration of the Wiener process. Stated differently, a square integrable martingale that has a representation as a Borel measurable function of Wiener sample paths is an Itô integral. Before the precise statement of the representation theorem consider the following special case.

Let $f : [0, T] \times \mathcal{R} \to \mathcal{R}$ be continuously differentiable in the first argument and twice continuously differentiable in the second argument, and such that

$$\frac{\partial f(t, W_t)}{\partial t} + \frac{1}{2} \frac{\partial^2 f(t, W_t)}{\partial W_t^2} = 0$$

and

$$E_P \left\{ \int_0^T \left[\frac{\partial f(t, W_t)}{\partial W_t} \right]^2 dt \right\} < \infty$$

Then for the process $f_t = f(t, W_t)$ for $0 \le t \le T$ Itô's formula implies that $\{f_t\}$ is a martingale with the integral representation

$$f_t = f_0 + \int_0^t \frac{\partial f(s, W_s)}{\partial W_s} dW_s$$

Theorem 8.6 of H. Kunita and S. Watanabe generalizes this representation of martingales on the natural filtration of the Wiener process as Itô integrals.

Theorem 8.6 (Kunita-Watanabe) *If $\{x_t\}$ is a square integrable martingale on the filtration $\{\mathbf{F}_t^W\}$, then there exists an adapted measurable process $\{\alpha_t\}$ such that $E_P \left(\int_0^T \alpha_t^2 dt \right) < \infty$ and for all $0 \le t \le T$*

$$x_t = x_0 + \int_0^t \alpha_s dW_s$$

8.6   A Second Definition of the Itô Integral

In this section we present a second, abstract, definition of the Itô integral. This definition relies on a property of the Itô integral that we now derive from the constructive definition of this integral. Let x and η be two adapted, measurable processes, such that

$$E_P \left(\int_0^T x_t^2 dt \right) < \infty$$

$$E_P \left(\int_0^T \eta_t^2 dt \right) < \infty$$

Denote $y_t = \int_0^t \eta_s dW_s$. First, we have from Theorem 8.3

$$[W, y]_t = \int_0^t \eta_s ds$$

Second, we have from Theorem 8.4

$$E_P \left(\int_0^T x_t dW_t \int_0^T \eta_t dW_t \right) = E_P \left(\int_0^T x_t \eta_t dt \right) = E_P \left(\int_0^T x_t d[W, y]_t \right)$$

Notice that the optional quadratic covariation process $[W, y]$ has finite variation on compacts and, therefore, the integral on the right side of the preceding equation is the familiar Stieltjes integral. From the theorem of Kunita and Watanabe, every square integrable martingale y can be represented as

$$y_t = y_0 + \int_0^t \eta_s dW_s$$

where $E_P \left(\int_0^T \eta_t^2 dt \right) < \infty$. Therefore, for every square integrable martingale y

$$E_P \left[\left(\int_0^T x_t dW_t \right) y_T \right] = E_P \left(\int_0^T x_t d[W, y]_t \right)$$

We show later that if $E_P \left(\int_0^T x_t^2 dt \right) < \infty$, then the Itô integral $z_t = \int_0^t x_s dW_s$ is the unique square integrable martingale such that

$$E_P\left(z_T y_T\right) = E_P\left(\int_0^T x_t d[W, y]_t\right)$$

The preceding equation then serves as an abstract definition of the integral $\int_0^t x_s dW_s$. This definition proceeds as follows.

The set of square integrable martingales on the interval $[0, T]$ is a Hilbert space with the scalar product

$$(x, y) = E_P(x_T y_T)$$

Suppose that $E_P\left(\int_0^T x_t^2 dt\right) < \infty$ and consider the following linear functional on the space of square integrable martingales

$$f(y) = E_P\left(\int_0^T x_t d[W, y]_t\right)$$

Recall the Riesz representation theorem, Theorem 2.9, that says that if $g : \mathcal{R}^m \to \mathcal{R}$ is a linear functional, then there is a unique $z \in \mathcal{R}^m$ such that $g(y) = (y, z)$ for all $y \in \mathcal{R}^m$. This theorem can be extended to say that if $g : X \to \mathcal{R}$ is a continuous linear functional on a Hilbert space X, then there is a unique $z \in X$ such that $g(y) = (y, z)$ for all $y \in X$. Because the set of square integrable martingales is a Hilbert space, and the functional f is continuous, there is a unique square integrable martingale z such that

$$E_P(y_T z_T) = E_P\left(\int_0^T x_t d[W, y]_t\right)$$

We define

$$\int_0^t x_s dW_s = z_t$$

Notice that this definition of the Itô integral is good only for adapted, measurable, integrands x such that $E_P\left(\int_0^T x_t^2 dt\right) < \infty$.

8.7   Itô Processes

Definition 8.6 A stochastic process $\{x_t\}$ $(0 \le t \le T)$ on the filtered Wiener probability space $\{\Omega, \mathbf{F}, P, \{\mathbf{F}_t^W\}\}$ is called an Itô process if and only if there exist adapted measurable processes $\{\alpha_t\}$ and $\{\sigma_t\}$ such that, with probability one:

1. The time integral $\int_0^T |\alpha_t| dt < \infty$.

2. The time integral $\int_0^T \sigma_t^2 dt < \infty$.

3. For all $0 \leq t \leq T$

$$x_t = x_0 + \int_0^t \alpha_s ds + \int_0^t \sigma_s dW_s$$

The shorthand notation for an Itô process is

$$dx_t = \alpha_t dt + \sigma_t dW_t$$

The quadratic variation of an Itô process is the same as the quadratic variation of its Itô integral component.

Theorem 8.7 *If $\{x_t\}$ and $\{y_t\}$ are the Itô processes*

$$x_t = x_0 + \int_0^t \alpha_s ds + \int_0^t \sigma_s dW_s$$

$$y_t = y_0 + \int_0^t \beta_s ds + \int_0^t \tau_s dW_s$$

then

$$[x, y]_t = \langle x, y \rangle_t = x_0^2 + \int_0^t \sigma_s \tau_s ds$$

In particular, the representation $dx_t = \alpha_t dt + \sigma_t dW_t$ implies $(dx_t)^2 = \sigma_t^2 dt$. Theorem 8.10 shows the role of $(dx_t)^2$ in the representation of a differentiable function of an Itô process. First, we introduce a definition of a stochastic integral relative to an Itô process.

Definition 8.7 Consider the Itô process

$$x_t = x_0 + \int_0^t \alpha_s ds + \int_0^t \sigma_s dW_s$$

and an adapted, measurable, process $\{y_t\}$ such that with probability one

$$\int_0^T |y_t \alpha_t| dt < \infty \quad \text{and} \quad \int_0^T (y_t \sigma_t)^2 dt < \infty$$

Then, we define

$$\int_0^t y_s dx_s = \int_0^t y_s \alpha_s ds + \int_0^t y_s \sigma_s dW_s$$

It follows immediately from the definition of an Itô process that the stochastic integral $\int_0^t y_s dx_s$ is an Itô process. Furthermore, the definition of this integral is associative, that is

$$\int_0^t z_s d\left(\int_0^s y_u dx_u\right) = \int_0^t z_s y_s dx_s$$

Paralleling the discrete case of Theorem 5.9 we can prove for such stochastic integrals a formula for integration by parts.

Theorem 8.8 *If $\{x_t\}$ and $\{y_t\}$ are Itô processes, then*

$$\int_0^t x_s dy_s = x_t y_t - \int_0^t y_s dx_s - [x, y]_t$$

The proof of Itô's formula uses the following result on the representation of optional quadratic covariation processes.

Theorem 8.9 *Let $\{x_t\}$ be an Itô process and $f, g : \mathcal{R} \to \mathcal{R}$ be continuously differentiable functions. Define the processes*

$$f_t = f(x_t) \quad and \quad g_t = g(x_t)$$

Then

$$[f, g]_t = [f, g]_0 + \int_0^t f'(x_s) g'(x_s) d[x, x]_s$$

Proof. Denote

$$S_{mt} = f_0 g_0 + \sum_{j=1}^{\infty} \left(f_{t_{m,j} \wedge t} - f_{t_{m,j-1} \wedge t}\right)\left(g_{t_{m,j} \wedge t} - g_{t_{m,j-1} \wedge t}\right)$$

Then S_{mt} is equal to

$$f_0 g_0 + \sum_{j=1}^{\infty} \frac{f_{t_{m,j} \wedge t} - f_{t_{m,j-1} \wedge t}}{x_{t_{m,j} \wedge t} - x_{t_{m,j-1} \wedge t}} \frac{g_{t_{m,j} \wedge t} - g_{t_{m,j-1} \wedge t}}{x_{t_{m,j} \wedge t} - x_{t_{m,j-1} \wedge t}} \left(x_{t_{m,j} \wedge t} - x_{t_{m,j-1} \wedge t}\right)^2$$

and

$$[f, g]_t = \lim_{m \to \infty} S_{mt} = [f, g]_0 + \int_0^t f'(x_s) g'(x_s) d[x, x]_s$$

This completes the proof. ∎

With this preparation Itô's formula is as follows.

Theorem 8.10 (Itô's formula) *If $\{x_t\}$ is an Itô process and $f : \mathcal{R} \to \mathcal{R}$ is twice continuously differentiable, then for every $0 \le t \le T$*

$$f(x_t) = f(x_0) + \int_0^t f'(x_s)dx_s + \frac{1}{2}\int_0^t f''(x_s)d[x,x]_s$$

Proof. The formula is obviously correct for the function $f(x_t) = x_t$. We show that if it holds for two twice continuously differentiable functions f and g, then it also holds for their product fg. Indeed, suppose that

$$df_t = f'_t dx_t + \frac{1}{2}f''_t d[x,x]_t$$

$$dg_t = g'_t dx_t + \frac{1}{2}g''_t d[x,x]_t$$

Combining these with the formula for integration by parts

$$d(f_t g_t) = f_t dg_t + g_t df_t + d[f,g]_t$$

and the representation of optional quadratic covariation processes in Theorem 8.9

$$d[f,g]_t = f'_t g'_t d[x,x]_t$$

yields

$$d(f_t g_t) = (f_t g_t)'dx_t + \frac{1}{2}(f_t g_t)''d[x,x]_t$$

It follows that Itô's formula holds for all polynomials in x_t. The result for any twice continuously differentiable function f follows from approximating the function f with polynomials. ∎

A useful generalization of the preceding theorem is as follows. Let $f : [0,T] \times \mathcal{R} \to \mathcal{R}$ be continuously differentiable in the first argument and twice continuously differentiable in the second argument. Then, for every $0 \le t \le T$

$$f(t,x_t) = f(0,x_0) + \int_0^t \frac{\partial f(s,x_s)}{\partial x_s}dx_s + \int_0^t \frac{\partial f(s,x_s)}{\partial s}ds$$
$$+\frac{1}{2}\int_0^t \frac{\partial^2 f(s,x_s)}{\partial x_s^2}d[x,x]_s$$

If $\{x_t\}$ is the Itô process

$$x_t = x_0 + \int_0^t \alpha_s ds + \int_0^t \sigma_s dW_s$$

then this formula can also be written

$$f(t, x_t) = f(0, x_0) + \int_0^t \sigma_s \frac{\partial f(s, x_s)}{\partial x_s} dW_s$$
$$+ \int_0^t \left[\frac{\partial f(s, x_s)}{\partial s} + \alpha_s \frac{\partial f(s, x_s)}{\partial x_s} + \frac{1}{2} \sigma_s^2 \frac{\partial^2 f(s, x_s)}{\partial x_s^2} \right] ds$$

Using the shorthand notation this version of Itô's formula is written

$$df(t, x_t) = \sigma_t \frac{\partial f(t, x_t)}{\partial x_t} dW_t + \left[\frac{\partial f(t, x_t)}{\partial t} + \alpha_t \frac{\partial f(t, x_t)}{\partial x_t} + \frac{1}{2} \sigma_t^2 \frac{\partial^2 f(t, x_t)}{\partial x_t^2} \right] dt$$

and can be regarded as a Taylor expansion

$$df(t, x_t) = \frac{\partial f(t, x_t)}{\partial x_t} dx_t + \frac{\partial f(t, x_t)}{\partial t} dt + \frac{1}{2} \frac{\partial^2 f(t, x_t)}{\partial x_t^2} (dx_t)^2$$

with the rules (compare with the formula for the optional quadratic variation of an Itô process in Theorem 8.7)

$$(dx_t)^2 = \sigma_t^2 dt, \ (dx_t)^3 = 0, \ (dt)^2 = 0, \ dt dx_t = 0$$

Example 8.4 This is an example of solving a stochastic differential equation. Find an adapted, measurable, process $\{x_t\}$ such that

$$E_P \left(\int_0^T x_t^2 dt \right) < \infty$$

and

$$dx_t = \mu x_t dt + \delta x_t dW_t$$

where μ and δ are real numbers. Proceeding formally, apply Itô's formula to the function $f(x_t) = \log x_t$. Then the process $\{\log x_t\}$ has the representation

$$d \log x_t = \left(\mu x_t \frac{1}{x_t} - \frac{1}{2} \delta^2 x_t^2 \frac{1}{x_t^2} \right) dt + \delta x_t \frac{1}{x_t} dW_t = \left(\mu - \frac{1}{2} \delta^2 \right) dt + \delta dW_t$$

Therefore

$$\log x_t - \log x_0 = \left(\mu - \frac{1}{2} \delta^2 \right) t + \delta W_t$$

or, equivalently

$$x_t = x_0 \exp\left[\left(\mu - \frac{1}{2}\delta^2\right)t + \delta W_t\right]$$

The process $\{x_t\}$ is adapted because it is a Borel measurable function of W_t. In addition, the process $\{x_t\}$ is continuous and therefore measurable in the sense of Definition 8.2. A direct calculation reveals that

$$x_t^2 = x_0^2 \exp\left(\delta^2 t\right) \exp\left\{\left[2\mu - \frac{1}{2}(2\delta)^2\right]t + 2\delta W_t\right\}$$

so that

$$E_P\left(x_t^2\right) = x_0^2 \exp\left[\left(2\mu + \delta^2\right)t\right]$$

Consequently

$$E_P\left(\int_0^T x_t^2 dt\right) = \int_0^T E_P\left(x_t^2\right) dt$$

$$= x_0^2 \int_0^T \exp\left[\left(2\mu + \delta^2\right)t\right] dt < \infty$$

8.8   Stochastic Exponentials

The stochastic exponential of a Wiener process is a suitable modification of the stochastic exponential in Chapter 5. By definition, the stochastic exponential $x_t = \mathcal{E}_t(W)$ is the solution of the integral equation

$$x_t = 1 + \int_0^t x_s dW_s$$

or, equivalently, the stochastic differential equation

$$dx_t = x_t dW_t$$

Substituting $\mu = 0$ and $\delta = 1$ in Example 8.4 implies that

$$\mathcal{E}_t(W) = \exp\left(W_t - \frac{1}{2}t\right)$$

Similarly, if the process $\{\sigma_t\}$ is such that $\int_0^T \sigma_t^2 dt < \infty$ with probability one, then the Itô integral $x_t = \int_0^t \sigma_s dW_s$ exists and the integral equation

$$y_t = 1 + \int_0^t y_s dx_s$$

has the solution

$$
\begin{aligned}
y_t &= \mathcal{E}_t(x) \\
&= \mathcal{E}_t(\sigma \bullet W) \\
&= \exp\left(\int_0^t \sigma_s dW_s - \frac{1}{2} \int_0^t \sigma_s^2 ds \right) \\
&= \exp\left(x_t - \frac{1}{2}[x,x]_t \right)
\end{aligned}
$$

It can be shown that if there is a $\lambda > 1$ such that

$$E_P\left[\exp\left(\lambda \int_0^T \sigma_t^2 dt \right) \right] < \infty$$

then the stochastic exponential $\{\mathcal{E}_t(x)\}$ is a martingale.

Definition 8.8 If $\{x_t\}$ is the Itô process

$$x_t = \int_0^t \alpha_s ds + \int_0^t \sigma_s dW_s$$

then the unique solution

$$\mathcal{E}_t(x) = \exp\left[\int_0^t \sigma_s dW_s + \int_0^t \left(\alpha_s - \frac{1}{2}\sigma_s^2 \right) ds \right] = \exp\left(x_t - \frac{1}{2}[x,x]_t \right)$$

of the integral equation

$$y_t = 1 + \int_0^t y_s dx_s$$

is called the stochastic exponential of the Itô process $\{x_t\}$.

Problems

1. Show that if $\int_0^a x_s^2 ds = 0$ with probability one, then $\int_0^a x_s dW_s = 0$.

2. Prove that $\int_0^a (a-t)dW_t = \int_0^a W_t dt$.

3. Show that if $f(t)$ is a function of time alone and $\int_0^t f^2(s)ds < \infty$, then $\int_0^t f(s)dW_s$ is distributed normally $N\left(0, \int_0^t f^2(s)ds\right)$.

4. Prove that $\int_0^t \left(W_s^2 - s\right)dW_s = \frac{1}{3}W_t^3 - tW_t$.

5. Use Itô's formula to compute $E_P\left[\left(\int_0^t W_s dW_s\right)^3\right]$.

6. Consider the Itô process $\{x_t\}$ with the representation

$$dx_t = (ax_t + b)dt + cdW_t$$

where $a \neq 0$, b, and c are constants. Let

$$f(t, x_t) = e^{-at}x_t - \frac{b}{a}\left(1 - e^{-at}\right)$$

   (a) Find the representation of $f(t, x_t)$ as an Itô process.
   (b) Show that

$$x_t = x_0 e^{at} + \frac{b}{a}(e^{at} - 1) + ce^{at}\int_0^t e^{-as}dW_s$$

   (c) Calculate $E_P(x_t)$ and $\mathrm{var}_P(x_t)$.

7. Prove that for an Itô process $\{x_t\}$

$$[x, x]_t = x_t^2 - 2\int_0^t x_s dx_s$$

8. Prove that for Itô processes $\{x_t\}$ and $\{y_t\}$

$$\mathcal{E}_t(x)\mathcal{E}_t(y) = \mathcal{E}_t(x + y + [x, y])$$

Notes

The material in this chapter is standard in the mathematical probability literature. References to the properties of the Itô integral include [1], [36], [38], [57], [58], [50], [51], [54], [65], and [70], and represent a variety of detail and rigor.

Chapter 9

The Black-Scholes Model

9.1 Elements of the Model

Equipped with the concepts of Itô calculus we can undertake a complete specification of the Black-Scholes model. This specification consists of a description of the available information, the traded securities, the consumption set, the traders' budget sets, and a definition of equilibrium. We start with some preliminary matters.

Definition 9.1 Given a probability space $\{\Omega, \mathbf{F}, P\}$ and a number $1 \leq k < \infty$, the set $\mathcal{L}^k (\Omega, \mathbf{F}, P)$ consists of all the random variables x on $\{\Omega, \mathbf{F}, P\}$ such that $E_P \left(|x|^k \right) < \infty$. The set $\mathcal{L}^\infty (\Omega, \mathbf{F}, P)$ consists of all the random variables that are bounded, except on a set of probability measure zero.

In particular, $\mathcal{L}^1 (\Omega, \mathbf{F}, P)$ is the set of all the random variables whose absolute value has a finite expectation, and $\mathcal{L}^2 (\Omega, \mathbf{F}, P)$ is the set of all the random variables with a finite expectation and variance. The sets $\mathcal{L}^k (\Omega, \mathbf{F}, P)$ are linear spaces. For $1 \leq k < \infty$ this follows immediately from Minkowski's inequality

$$\left[E_P \left(|x + y|^k \right) \right]^{\frac{1}{k}} \leq \left[E_P \left(|x|^k \right) \right]^{\frac{1}{k}} + \left[E_P \left(|y|^k \right) \right]^{\frac{1}{k}}$$

Speaking loosely, the size of the space $\mathcal{L}^k(\Omega, \mathbf{F}, P)$ is a decreasing function of the exponent k. This follows easily from Hölder's inequality

$$E_P(|xy|) \leq \left[E_P \left(|x|^k \right) \right]^{\frac{1}{k}} \left[E_P \left(|y|^l \right) \right]^{\frac{1}{l}}$$

where $1 < k < \infty$ and $1 < l < \infty$ are such that $\dfrac{1}{k} + \dfrac{1}{l} = 1$. The precise meaning of the statement on the size of the space $\mathcal{L}^k(\Omega, \mathbf{F}, P)$ is as follows.

Theorem 9.1 *If* $1 \leq k' \leq k'' \leq \infty$, *then*

$$\mathcal{L}^{k''}(\Omega, \mathbf{F}, P) \subset \mathcal{L}^{k'}(\Omega, \mathbf{F}, P)$$

Proof. First, suppose that $1 \leq k' < k'' < \infty$ and apply Hölder's inequality to the random variables $|x|^{k'}$ and 1 and the exponent $k = \dfrac{k''}{k'}$. We get

$$E_P\left(|x|^{k'}\right) \leq \left\{ E_P\left[\left(|x|^{k'}\right)^{\frac{k''}{k'}} \right] \right\}^{\frac{k'}{k''}}$$

Therefore

$$\left[E_P\left(|x|^{k'}\right) \right]^{\frac{1}{k'}} \leq \left[E_P\left(|x|^{k''}\right) \right]^{\frac{1}{k''}}$$

This establishes the claim for $1 \leq k' < k'' < \infty$. The extension to $1 \leq k' \leq k'' \leq \infty$ is obvious. ∎

For any random variable $x \in \mathcal{L}^k(\Omega, \mathbf{F}, P)$ we set

$$\|x\|_k = \left[E_P\left(|x|^k\right) \right]^{\frac{1}{k}}$$

for $1 \leq k < \infty$ and

$$\|x\|_\infty = \operatorname*{ess\,sup}_{\omega \in \Omega} |x(\omega)|$$

where the essential supremum is

$$\operatorname*{ess\,sup}_{\omega \in A} x(\omega) = \inf \left\{ \alpha \in \mathcal{R} \mid P\{\omega \in A | x(\omega) > \alpha\} = 0 \right\}$$

It follows that for $1 \leq k \leq \infty$ the set $\mathcal{L}^k(\Omega, \mathbf{F}, P)$ is a normed linear space and that for $1 \leq k' \leq k'' \leq \infty$ we have $\|x\|_{k''} \leq \|x\|_{k'}$. By assumption, for each trader in the Black-Scholes model, the endowment process $e^i = \{e^i_0, e^i_T\}$ and the consumption process $c^i = \{c^i_0, c^i_T\}$ are such that

$$e^i_T, c^i_T \in \mathcal{L}^2\left(\Omega, \mathbf{F}^W_T, P\right)$$

where $\{\Omega, \mathbf{F}, P\}$ is the Wiener probability space and $\{\mathbf{F}^W_t\}$ is the natural filtration of the Wiener process. This specifies the consumption set as

$$X = \mathcal{R} \times \mathcal{L}^2\left(\Omega, \mathbf{F}^W_T, P\right)$$

Although intuitively attractive, this specification of the consumption set fails to deliver completeness of the Black-Scholes model. We return to this problem and an alternative specification of the consumption set in Section 9.2.

The terminal payouts of the two securities in the Black-Scholes model are

$$d_1 = e^{rT}$$
$$d_2 = p_{20}\mathcal{E}_T(x)$$

where $x_t = \mu t + \sigma W_t$ is the return process for security 2 and r, μ, σ are positive constants. The reader should recall that $\mathcal{E}_t(x) = \exp[(\mu - \frac{1}{2}\sigma^2)t + \sigma W_t]$. Before the terminal time, the prices of the two securities are

$$p_{1t} = e^{rt}$$
$$p_{2t} = p_{20}\mathcal{E}_t(x)$$

Notice that the price $\{p_{2t}\}$ is an Itô process. To make sense, the Black-Scholes model requires a proof that these prices are indeed equilibrium prices for some population of traders with continuous, increasing, and convex preferences.

Security 1 is a bond that appreciates at a constant rate of interest r. Security 2 is a stock whose price, like the Wiener process $\{W_t\}$, is nowhere differentiable with probability one. This property of the price implies local risk, traders do not even know in which instantaneous direction the price will move next. Notice that both prices are continuous and adapted to the Wiener filtration $\{\mathbf{F}_t^W\}$ and that for each $0 \le t \le T$ the information carried by prices is identical to the information carried by the Wiener process $\{W_t\}$, that is $\mathbf{F}_t^{p_1,p_2} = \mathbf{F}_t^{p_2} = \mathbf{F}_t^W$. This equality of the Wiener and price filtrations justifies the exogenous specification that traders observe $\{\mathbf{F}_t^W\}$.

To validate Black-Scholes prices as equilibrium prices requires that we impose a certain restriction on the trading strategies in this model. This restriction is stated in terms of the (unique) equilibrium price measure and, therefore, a discussion of change of measure, the likelihood ratio process, and Girsanov's theorem precedes the definition of a budget set and an equilibrium.

The Likelihood Ratio Process

In this subsection we define a continuous time analog of the discrete likelihood ratio process in Chapter 5. The basic properties of the likelihood ratio process in discrete time extend to the continuous time framework. In particular, the likelihood ratio process is the risk adjustment process in this model. Consider a nonnegative random variable ρ on $\{\Omega, \mathbf{F}, P\}$ such that $E_P(\rho) = 1$ and define a set function Q on $\mathbf{F}$

$$Q(A) = \int_A \rho\, dP$$

It is easy to see that Q is a probability measure on $\{\Omega, \mathbf{F}\}$ and that $P(A) = 0$ implies that $Q(A) = 0$. Moreover, if $P\{\rho > 0\} = 1$, then $Q(A) = 0$ implies that $P(A) = 0$. This relationship between the measures P and Q is important enough to deserve a name.

Definition 9.2 A probability measure Q on $\{\Omega, \mathbf{F}\}$ is absolutely continuous with respect to a probability measure P on $\{\Omega, \mathbf{F}\}$ if and only if for every $A \in \mathbf{F}$, we have $P(A) = 0$ implies that $Q(A) = 0$. If Q is absolutely continuous with respect to P and P is absolutely continuous with respect to Q, then the two probability measures are called equivalent.

The next theorem asserts that the transformation $Q(A) = \int_A \rho dP$ with a nonnegative random variable ρ is the only way of getting an absolutely continuous Q from P.

Theorem 9.2 (Radon-Nikodym) *If Q is absolutely continuous with respect to P, then there is a nonnegative random variable ρ such that for any $A \in \mathbf{F}$*

$$Q(A) = \int_A \rho dP$$

The random variable ρ is unique with P-probability one.

Definition 9.3 The unique random variable ρ in the preceding theorem is called the density of the probability measure Q with respect to the probability measure P, or the Radon Nikodym derivative of Q with respect to P, and is denoted

$$\rho = \frac{dQ}{dP}$$

Definition 9.4 Let $\{\Omega, \mathbf{F}, P, \{\mathbf{F}_t\}\}$ be a filtered probability space and let Q be a probability measure on $\{\Omega, \mathbf{F}\}$ that is absolutely continuous with respect to P. Then the likelihood ratio process is

$$z_t = E_P\left(\left.\frac{dQ}{dP}\right| \mathbf{F}_t\right)$$

When the probability measures P and Q are equivalent, the likelihood ratio process is a positive martingale. The next theorem relates the likelihood ratio process to conditional expectations with respect to the probability measures P and Q.

Theorem 9.3 *Suppose that the probability measures P and Q are equivalent. Then for any adapted process $\{x_t\}$ and any $0 \le s \le t \le T$*

$$\frac{E_P(z_t x_t | \mathbf{F}_s)}{E_P(z_t | \mathbf{F}_s)} = E_Q(x_t | \mathbf{F}_s)$$

Corollary 9.1 *An adapted process $\{x_t\}$ is a Q-martingale if and only if the process $\{z_t x_t\}$ is a P-martingale.*

Girsanov's Theorem

In this subsection we consider a version of Girsanov's theorem for the Wiener process $\{W_t\}$. In comparison with the discrete version of Girsanov's theorem in Chapter 5, the present version involves a stronger assumption and a stronger conclusion.

Theorem 9.4 (Girsanov) *Let $\{W_t\}$ be a Wiener process on the Wiener probability space $\{\Omega, \mathbf{F}, P\}$, let $\{x_t\}$ be a measurable process adapted to the natural filtration of the Wiener process, $\{\mathbf{F}_t^W\}$, such that*

$$E_P\left[\exp\left(\lambda \int_0^T x_s^2 ds\right)\right] < \infty \text{ for some } \lambda > 1$$

and let Q be a probability measure on $\{\Omega, \mathbf{F}\}$ such that

$$\frac{dQ}{dP} = \mathcal{E}_t(x \bullet W)$$

Denote by $\{z_t\}$ the likelihood ratio process

$$z_t = E_P\left(\frac{dQ}{dP}\,\middle|\,\mathbf{F}_t^W\right)$$

Then

$$W_t - \int_0^t \frac{d\langle W, z\rangle_s}{z_s}$$

is a Wiener process on the filtered probability space $\{\Omega, \mathbf{F}, Q, \{\mathbf{F}_t^W\}\}$.

Notice that the condition

$$E_P\left[\exp\left(\lambda \int_0^T x_s^2 ds\right)\right] < \infty \text{ for some } \lambda > 1$$

is stronger than $E_P\left(\int_0^T x_s^2 ds\right) < \infty$. This stronger condition guarantees that $E_P\left[\mathcal{E}_t(x \bullet W)\right] = 1$ for all $0 \leq t \leq T$.

Equilibrium Price Measures

This subsection presents the definition of equilibrium price measures in the Black-Scholes model and delivers the result that the equilibrium price measure in the Black-Scholes model is unique.

Definition 9.5 An equilibrium price measure in the Black-Scholes model is a probability measure Q on the space $\{\Omega, \mathbf{F}\}$ such that:

1. The probability measures Q and P are equivalent.

2. The Radon-Nikodym derivative satisfies $\dfrac{dQ}{dP} \in \mathcal{L}^2(\Omega, \mathbf{F}, P)$.

3. The price ratio $\left\{ \dfrac{p_{2t}}{p_{1t}} \right\}$ is a Q-martingale.

Comparing this definition with the definition of an equilibrium price measure in the discrete multiperiod model, the reader can see that condition 1 replaces the requirement that $Q(\omega) > 0$ for all $\omega \in \Omega$, condition 2 is new, and condition 3 is a representation of the discounted price of security 2 as a Q-martingale. The new requirement 2 is used later to prove the uniqueness of Q and the continuity of the price functional. It was satisfied automatically in the discrete model and, therefore, was not stated there explicitly.

The next theorem asserts the existence and uniqueness of the equilibrium price measure in the Black-Scholes model. Notice the resemblance between the representation of the Radon-Nikodym derivative here and the representation of the likelihood ratio in the simple option pricing model in Chapter 6.

Theorem 9.5 *For the Black-Scholes prices the equilibrium price measure Q exists and is unique. This equilibrium price measure is such that*

$$\frac{dQ}{dP} = \mathcal{E}_T \left(-\frac{\mu - r}{\sigma} \bullet W \right)$$

Proof. Recall that

$$\mathcal{E}_T \left(-\frac{\mu - r}{\sigma} \bullet W \right) = \exp \left[-\frac{\mu - r}{\sigma} W_T - \frac{1}{2} \left(\frac{\mu - r}{\sigma} \right)^2 T \right]$$

and suppose that Q is as specified in the theorem. The equivalence of Q and P follows immediately from the fact that $\dfrac{dQ}{dP}$ is an exponential function and, therefore, strictly positive. The second requirement for an equilibrium price measure is that

$$E_P\left[\left(\frac{dQ}{dP}\right)^2\right] < \infty$$

This is established by a calculation similar to the computation at the end of Example 8.4. The final requirement for an equilibrium price measure Q is that the price ratio $\left\{\frac{p_{2t}}{p_{1t}}\right\}$ be a Q-martingale. To prove this, use Itô's formula to write the representation of $\left\{\frac{p_{2t}}{p_{1t}}\right\}$ as an Itô process

$$d\left(\frac{p_{2t}}{p_{1t}}\right) = (\mu - r)\frac{p_{2t}}{p_{1t}}dt + \sigma\frac{p_{2t}}{p_{1t}}dW_t \qquad (9.1)$$

By definition, the stochastic exponential $z_t = \mathcal{E}_t(w)$ is the unique solution of the equation

$$z_t = 1 + \int_0^t z_s dw_s$$

Therefore, the present likelihood ratio process

$$z_t = E_P\left(\frac{dQ}{dP}\bigg|\mathbf{F}_t^W\right) - \mathcal{E}_t\left(-\frac{\mu - r}{\sigma} \bullet W\right)$$

is an Itô process with the representation

$$dz_t = -\frac{\mu - r}{\sigma}z_t dW_t$$

Using Theorem 8.3, the predictable quadratic covariation of the Wiener process W and the present likelihood ratio process z is, therefore

$$d\langle W, z\rangle_t = -\frac{\mu - r}{\sigma}z_t dt$$

Finally, from Girsanov's theorem, the process

$$V_t = W_t - \int_0^t \frac{d\langle W, z\rangle_s}{z_s} = W_t + \frac{\mu - r}{\sigma}t$$

is a Wiener process on the probability space $\{\Omega, \mathbf{F}, Q\}$. Writing $dW_t = dV_t - \frac{\mu - r}{\sigma}dt$ and substituting into Equation 9.1 yields the representation of the process $\left\{\frac{p_{2t}}{p_{1t}}\right\}$ as an Itô integral with respect to the Wiener process V

$$d\left(\frac{p_{2t}}{p_{1t}}\right) = \sigma\frac{p_{2t}}{p_{1t}}dV_t$$

Using integral notation

$$\frac{p_{2t}}{p_{1t}} = p_{20} + \sigma\int_0^t \frac{p_{2s}}{p_{1s}}dV_s$$

and because, as can be verified with a direct calculation

$$E_Q\left[\int_0^T \left(\frac{p_{2s}}{p_{1s}}\right)^2 ds\right] < \infty$$

the process $\left\{\frac{p_{2t}}{p_{1t}}\right\}$ is the stochastic exponential

$$\frac{p_{2t}}{p_{1t}} = p_{20}\mathcal{E}_t(\sigma \bullet V)$$

and a martingale on the filtration $\{\mathbf{F}_t^V\}$. The final step in the existence proof is the observation that $\mathbf{F}_t^V = \mathbf{F}_t^W$ and, therefore, $\left\{\frac{p_{2t}}{p_{1t}}\right\}$ is a martingale on $\{\mathbf{F}_t^W\}$, as required. This equality of the two filtrations is an immediate implication of the fact that $\{V_t\}$ is a nontrivial, linear and, therefore, invertible and measurable function of $\{W_t\}$.

To prove uniqueness suppose that Q is an equilibrium price measure and denote $\frac{dQ}{dP} = \rho$. Because Q and P are equivalent, the Radon-Nikodym derivative ρ is positive with probability one, and because Q is an equilibrium price measure, we have $\rho \in \mathcal{L}^2(\Omega, \mathbf{F}, P)$. Consider the likelihood ratio process

$$z_t = E_P\left(\rho\,|\mathbf{F}_t^W\right)$$

The process $\{z_t\}$ is a positive square integrable martingale. Indeed, by Jensen's inequality, for any continuous convex function f, a random variable y such that both y and $f(y)$ are integrable, and a σ-field $\mathbf{G} \subset \mathbf{F}$

$$f[E_P(y|\mathbf{G})] \leq E_P[f(y)|\mathbf{G}]$$

Therefore

$$E_P\left(\rho^2\,|\mathbf{F}_t^W\right) \geq \left[E_P\left(\rho\,|\mathbf{F}_t^W\right)\right]^2 = z_t^2$$

and taking expectations

$$\sup_{0 \le t \le T} E_P \left(z_t^2 \right) \le E_P \left(\rho^2 \right) < \infty$$

From the theorem of Kunita and Watanabe, there is an adapted measurable process $\{\alpha_t\}$ such that $E_P \left(\int_0^T \alpha_s^2 ds \right) < \infty$ and

$$z_t = 1 + \int_0^t \alpha_s dW_s$$

or, in shorthand notation

$$dz_t = \alpha_t dW_t$$

The price ratio process $\left\{ \dfrac{p_{2t}}{p_{1t}} \right\}$ is a Q-martingale if and only if the process $\left\{ z_t \dfrac{p_{2t}}{p_{1t}} \right\}$ is a P-martingale. Together, the representation of the price ratio process in Equation 9.1

$$d \left(\frac{p_{2t}}{p_{1t}} \right) = (\mu - r) \frac{p_{2t}}{p_{1t}} dt + \sigma \frac{p_{2t}}{p_{1t}} dW_t$$

the representation of the likelihood ratio process, and the formula for integration by parts

$$d \left(z_t \frac{p_{2t}}{p_{1t}} \right) = z_t d \left(\frac{p_{2t}}{p_{1t}} \right) + \left(\frac{p_{2t}}{p_{1t}} \right) dz_t + d \left[z, \frac{p_2}{p_1} \right]_t$$

imply the representation

$$d \left(z_t \frac{p_{2t}}{p_{1t}} \right) = [(\mu - r)z_t + \sigma \alpha_t] \frac{p_{2t}}{p_{1t}} dt + (\sigma z_t + \alpha_t) \frac{p_{2t}}{p_{1t}} dW_t$$

In integral notation the preceding equation takes the form

$$z_t \frac{p_{2t}}{p_{1t}} = p_{20} + \int_0^t [(\mu - r)z_s + \sigma \alpha_s] \frac{p_{2s}}{p_{1s}} ds + \int_0^t (\sigma z_s + \alpha_s) \frac{p_{2s}}{p_{1s}} dW_s$$

and because both $\left\{ z_t \dfrac{p_{2t}}{p_{1t}} \right\}$ and

$$\left\{ \int_0^t (\sigma z_s + \alpha_s) \frac{p_{2s}}{p_{1s}} dW_s \right\}$$

are P-martingales, the time integral

$$\left\{ \int_0^t [(\mu - r)z_s + \sigma\alpha_s] \frac{p_{2s}}{p_{1s}} ds \right\}$$

is a P-martingale. Next, notice that we also have

$$\int_0^t |(\mu - r)z_s + \sigma\alpha_s| \frac{p_{2s}}{p_{1s}} ds < \infty$$

Example 7.4 indicates then that the continuous P-martingale

$$\left\{ \int_0^t [(\mu - r)z_s + \sigma\alpha_s] \frac{p_{2s}}{p_{1s}} ds \right\}$$

has finite variation on compact intervals. It is shown in Chapter 10 that a continuous martingale of finite variation on compact intervals is constant and, therefore

$$\alpha_t = -\frac{\mu - r}{\sigma} z_t$$

so that

$$\frac{dQ}{dP} = \mathcal{E}_T \left(-\frac{\mu - r}{\sigma} \bullet W \right)$$

and the equilibrium price measure is unique. ∎

Because the process $\left\{ z_t \frac{p_{2t}}{p_{1t}} \right\}$ is a P-martingale, we have that the likelihood ratio process $\{z_t\}$ is the unique risk adjustment process in the Black-Scholes model.

Now come the definitions of a budget set and an equilibrium in the Black-Scholes model. To simplify notation we will use the price vector

$$p_t = \begin{pmatrix} p_{1t} \\ p_{2t} \end{pmatrix}$$

and a similar terminal payout vector d.

Definition 9.6 Given an endowment process $e^i = \{e_0^i, e_T^i\}$ and the Black-Scholes prices $\{p_t\}$, the budget set $B(e^i)$ is the subset of the consumption set X such that a consumption process $c = \{c_0, c_T\}$ belongs to $B(e^i)$ if and only if there exist adapted measurable stochastic processes

$$\theta_t = \begin{pmatrix} \theta_{1t} \\ \theta_{2t} \end{pmatrix}$$

such that:

1. The expectation $E_Q \left[\int_0^T (\theta_{2t} p_{2t})^2 dt \right] < \infty$.

2. The initial consumption $c_0 = e_0^i - \theta_0' p_0$.

3. For all $0 \le t \le T$ we have $\theta_t' p_t = \theta_0' p_0 + \int_0^t \theta_s' dp_s$.

4. The terminal consumption $c_T = e_T^i + \theta_T' d$.

The vector process $\{\theta_t\}$ is called a self-financing trading strategy that attains the consumption process c.

The preceding definition says that the budget set of trader i consists of all the consumption processes that trader i can attain by using self-financing trading strategies that are adapted, measurable, and satisfy the condition

$$E_Q \left[\int_0^T (\theta_{2t} p_{2t})^2 dt \right] < \infty$$

The interpretation of the four items in this definition is as follows. Notice that item 3 includes a sum of two integrals

$$\int_0^t \theta_t' dp_t = \int_0^t \theta_{1t} dp_{1t} + \int_0^t \theta_{2t} dp_{2t}$$

Item 1 guarantees the existence of the integrals in item 3 and excludes arbitrage strategies. The first of these two integrals is a Lebesgue-Stieltjes integral and its existence follows from the fact that θ_1 is adapted and measurable. The second integral is a stochastic integral with respect to the Itô process $\{p_{2t}\}$, and its existence follows from item 1. Indeed, item 1 implies that $Q \left\{ \int_0^T (\theta_{2t} p_{2t})^2 dt < \infty \right\} = 1$ and, because the probability measures P and Q are equivalent, it follows that $P \left\{ \int_0^T (\theta_{2t} p_{2t})^2 dt < \infty \right\} = 1$. Item 1 and Hölder's inequality also imply that

$$P \left\{ \int_0^T |\theta_{2t}| p_{2t} dt < \infty \right\} = Q \left\{ \int_0^T |\theta_{2t}| p_{2t} dt < \infty \right\} = 1$$

Together, the last two restrictions on the trading strategy θ imply the existence of the integral $\int_0^t \theta_{2t} dp_{2t}$. Moreover, it will be shown in the course of the proof of Theorem 9.6 that item 1 implies that the discounted value process $\dfrac{\theta'_t p_t}{p_{1t}}$ is a square integrable Q-martingale. As shown in Corollary 9.2, this property of the discounted value process eliminates arbitrage strategies. In addition, this property of the discounted value process means that, after adjustment for risk, the expected rate of return of any trading strategy is the riskless rate of interest r. Also, because a square integrable martingale is a uniformly integrable martingale, a stopping strategy does not change the risk-adjusted expected rate of return. This is explained in detail in Chapters 10 through 12. It will also be shown in Example 9.1 that the weaker restriction, $Q\left\{\displaystyle\int_0^T (\theta_{2t} p_{2t})^2 \, dt < \infty\right\} = 1$, although sufficient for the existence of the integral in 3, does not eliminate arbitrage strategies and, therefore, invalidates the Black-Scholes prices as equilibrium prices.

Item 3 is a suitably modified characterization of a self-financing trading strategy given in Theorem 3.6. Items 2 and 4 describe $\theta'_0 p_0$ as the postconsumption value process at time 0, and $\theta'_T p_T$ as the preconsumption value process at time T. The next definition says when the Black-Scholes prices are equilibrium prices.

Definition 9.7 We say that the Black-Scholes prices are equilibrium prices for a given population of traders if and only if there exist self-financing trading strategies $\{\theta_t^i\}$ that optimize preferences over the budget sets $B^i(e^i)$ and the market clears, $\displaystyle\sum_{i=1}^{I} \theta_{nt}^i = 0$, with probability one, for all $0 \le t \le T$ and $n = 1, 2$.

Arbitrage trading strategies in the Black-Scholes model are defined exactly as in the discrete model. As before, arbitrage strategies do not exist in equilibrium.

Definition 9.8 A self-financing trading strategy $\{\theta_t\}$ is an arbitrage strategy if and only if either:

1. At the initial time $\theta'_0 p_0 \le 0$.

2. At the terminal time $P\{\theta'_T p_T \ge 0\} = 1$.

3. At the terminal time $P\{\theta'_T p_T > 0\} > 0$.

or:

1. At the initial time $\theta'_0 p_0 < 0$.

2. At the terminal time $P\{\theta'_T p_T \ge 0\} = 1$.

To summarize, the elements of the Black-Scholes model are:

- A time interval $[0, T]$.

- The Wiener probability space $\{\Omega, \mathbf{F}, P\}$ with the filtration $\{\mathbf{F}_t^W\}$.

- A single, perishable, consumption good.

- Two endogenous securities whose terminal payouts are

$$d_1 = e^{rT}$$
$$d_2 = p_{20}\mathcal{E}_T(x)$$

where $x_t = \mu t + \sigma W_t$ is the return process for security 2 and r, μ, σ are positive constants.

- A finite number I of traders. The information structure of traders is $\{\mathbf{F}_t^W\}$.

- The initial endowment of trader i is $e_0^i \in \mathcal{R}$ and his terminal endowment is a random variable $e_T^i \in \mathcal{L}^2\left(\Omega, \mathbf{F}_T^W, P\right)$. Traders do not receive intermediate endowments.

- The initial consumption of trader i is $c_0^i \in \mathcal{R}$ and his terminal consumption is a random variable $c_T^i \in \mathcal{L}^2\left(\Omega, \mathbf{F}_T^W, P\right)$. Traders do not consume at intermediate times. The consumption set is

$$X = \mathcal{R} \times \mathcal{L}^2\left(\Omega, \mathbf{F}_T^W, P\right)$$

- On the consumption set X traders have complete preference orderings that are continuous, increasing, and convex.

- For any $0 \le t \le T$ the prices of securities 1 and 2 are

$$p_{1t} = e^{rt}$$
$$p_{2t} = p_{20}\mathcal{E}_t(x)$$

9.2   Completeness

The main result of this section is a characterization of attainable terminal consumptions and their conditional expectations as Itô integrals. This in turn implies a representation of the price functional and the absence of arbitrage trading strategies in this model. Finally, the results of this section demonstrate that the Black-Scholes model, as defined in this chapter, is approximately complete. Later, we will see that the Black-Scholes model can be made complete by redefining the consumption set to be $\mathcal{R} \times \mathcal{L}^2(\Omega, \mathbf{F}_T^V, Q)$.

The next definition extends in an obvious way the notion of an attainable consumption process to the Black-Scholes model.

Definition 9.9 A consumption process $c = \{c_0, c_T\} \in X$ is attainable at Black-Scholes prices if and only if there is an endowment process $e = \{e_0, e_T\}$ such that $e_T = 0$ and $c \in B(e)$. The set of consumption processes that are attainable at Black-Scholes prices is denoted by M.

The next theorem characterizes attainable consumption processes. Let Q be the equilibrium price measure in the Black-Scholes model, that is

$$\frac{dQ}{dP} = \mathcal{E}_T \left(-\frac{\mu - r}{\sigma} \bullet W \right)$$

let $\{z_t\}$ be the corresponding risk adjustment process, and let

$$V_t = W_t - \int_0^t \frac{d\langle W, z \rangle_s}{z_s} = W_t + \frac{\mu - r}{\sigma} t$$

be the Girsanov transformation of the Wiener process $\{W_t\}$. To simplify notation we use the single symbol $\{\mathbf{F}_t\}$ for the equivalent filtrations

$$\mathbf{F}_t = \mathbf{F}_t^{p_1, p_2} = \mathbf{F}_t^{p_2} = \mathbf{F}_t^W = \mathbf{F}_t^V$$

Theorem 9.6 *Suppose that $c = \{c_0, c_T\}$ is a consumption process satisfying $c_T \in \mathcal{L}^1(\Omega, \mathbf{F}_T, Q)$. Then $c \in M$ if and only if there exists an adapted measurable process $\{h_t\}$ such that $E_Q \left(\int_0^T h_t^2 dt \right) < \infty$ and for every $0 \leq t \leq T$*

$$E_Q \left(\frac{c_T}{p_{1T}} \middle| \mathbf{F}_t \right) = E_Q \left(\frac{c_T}{p_{1T}} \right) + \int_0^t h_s dV_s$$

Proof. To prove the direct part of the theorem suppose first that the consumption process $c = \{c_0, c_T\}$ is attainable. Then, there is an endowment process $e = \{e_0, e_T\}$ and an adapted, measurable, trading strategy $\theta_t' = (\theta_{1t}, \theta_{2t})$ such that $e_T = 0$ and:

1. $E_Q \left[\int_0^T (\theta_{2t} p_{2t})^2 dt \right] < \infty.$

2. $c_0 = e_0 - \theta_0' p_0.$

3. For all $0 \leq t \leq T$ we have $\theta_t' p_t = \theta_0' p_0 + \int_0^t \theta_s' dp_s.$

4. $c_T = \theta_T' dT.$

Using shorthand notation, item 3 is written

$$d\left(\theta_t' p_t\right) = \theta_t' dp_t = \left(r\theta_{1t} p_{1t} + \mu\theta_{2t} p_{2t}\right) dt + \sigma\theta_{2t} p_{2t} dW_t$$

We apply Itô's formula to the function $f(t, \theta_t' p_t) = \dfrac{\theta_t' p_t}{p_{1t}} = e^{-rt}\theta_t' p_t$. The result is

$$
\begin{aligned}
d\frac{\theta_t' p_t}{p_{1t}} &= \frac{\partial f}{\partial t} dt + \frac{\partial f}{\partial(\theta_t' p_t)} d(\theta_t' p_t) \\
&= (\mu - r)\theta_{2t}\frac{p_{2t}}{p_{1t}} dt + \sigma\theta_{2t}\frac{p_{2t}}{p_{1t}} dW_t \\
&= \sigma\theta_{2t}\frac{p_{2t}}{p_{1t}} dV_t
\end{aligned}
$$

Using integral notation and item 4, the preceding equation implies that

$$\frac{c_T}{p_{1T}} = \theta_0' p_0 + \sigma \int_0^T \theta_{2t}\frac{p_{2t}}{p_{1t}} dV_t$$

Taking conditional expectations and using the martingale property of the Itô integral yields

$$E_Q\left(\frac{c_T}{p_{1T}}\,\Big|\,\mathbf{F}_t\right) = \theta_0' p_0 + \sigma \int_0^t \theta_{2s}\frac{p_{2s}}{p_{1s}} dV_s$$

Finally, setting $h_t = \sigma\theta_{2t}\dfrac{p_{2t}}{p_{1t}}$ and substituting in the preceding equation $t = 0$ to obtain $E_Q\left(\dfrac{c_T}{p_{1T}}\right) = \theta_0' p_0$ ends the direct part of the proof.

Conversely, suppose that there exists a process $\{h_t\}$ such that

$$E_Q\left(\int_0^T h_t^2\,dt\right) < \infty$$

and for every $0 \leq t \leq T$

$$E_Q\left(\frac{c_T}{p_{1T}}\,\Big|\,\mathbf{F}_t\right) = E_Q\left(\frac{c_T}{p_{1T}}\right) + \int_0^t h_s\,dV_s \qquad (9.2)$$

Define the trading strategy

$$
\begin{aligned}
\theta_{2t} &= \sigma^{-1} h_t \frac{p_{1t}}{p_{2t}} \\
\theta_{1t} &= E_Q\left(\frac{c_T}{p_{1T}}\right) + \int_0^t h_s\,dV_s - \theta_{2t}\frac{p_{2t}}{p_{1t}} \qquad (9.3)
\end{aligned}
$$

In Equation 9.3 substitute $t = 0$ to get

$$\theta_0' p_0 = E_Q \left(\frac{c_T}{p_{1T}} \right) \tag{9.4}$$

and substitute this and

$$h_s = \sigma \theta_{2s} \frac{p_{2t}}{p_{1t}} \tag{9.5}$$

back into Equation 9.3 to obtain

$$\frac{\theta_t' p_t}{p_{1t}} = \theta_0' p_0 + \sigma \int_0^t \theta_{2s} \frac{p_{2s}}{p_{1s}} dV_s \tag{9.6}$$

Substitute $t = T$ in Equation 9.2, which together with Equations 9.4 and 9.5 implies that

$$\frac{c_T}{p_{1T}} = \theta_0' p_0 + \sigma \int_0^T \theta_{2t} \frac{p_{2t}}{p_{1t}} dV_t \tag{9.7}$$

Substituting $V_t = W_t + \frac{\mu - r}{\sigma} t$ in Equations 9.6 and 9.7 establishes $\{\theta_t\}$ as a self-financing trading strategy that attains the consumption process c. ∎

Corollary 9.2 *For any self-financing trading strategy* $\{\theta_t\}$

$$\theta_0' p_0 = e^{-rT} E_Q \left(\theta_T' p_T \right)$$

Corollary 9.3 *Black-Scholes prices do not permit arbitrage strategies.*

Proof. Because the probability measures P and Q are equivalent, the statements

$$P \{\theta_T' p_T \geq 0\} = 1 \quad \text{and} \quad Q \{\theta_T' p_T \geq 0\} = 1$$

are equivalent. Similarly, the statements

$$P \{\theta_T' p_T > 0\} > 0 \quad \text{and} \quad Q \{\theta_T' p_T > 0\} > 0$$

are also equivalent. This, and Corollary 9.2, imply that if $P \{\theta_T' p_T \geq 0\} = 1$, then $\theta_0' p_0 \geq 0$ and if, in addition, $P \{\theta_T' p_T > 0\} > 0$, then $\theta_0' p_0 > 0$. ∎

The following example demonstrates the importance of the requirement that the trading strategies satisfy $E_Q \left[\int_0^T \left(\theta_{2t} p_{2t} \right)^2 dt \right] < \infty$.

Example 9.1 Let $c_T \in \mathcal{L}^2(\Omega, \mathbf{F}_T, Q)$ be such that $Q\{c_T \geq 0\} = 1$ and $Q\{c_T > 0\} > 0$. It follows from a theorem of R.M. Dudley that there is an adapted measurable process $\{h_t\}$ such that $Q\left\{\int_0^T h_t^2 dt < \infty\right\} = 1$ and

$$\frac{c_T}{p_{1T}} = \int_0^T h_t dV_t$$

The reader should note the difference between the preceding representation and the theorem of Kunita and Watanabe. The present result refers to the representation of random variables that are measurable on the terminal σ-field $\mathbf{F}_T$, whereas the theorem of Kunita and Watanabe delivers the representation of square integrable martingales on the filtration $\{\mathbf{F}_t\}$. In addition, the integrand in the integral representation of a square integrable martingale satisfies a stronger condition than the integrand in the integral representation of a random variable. Because $c_T \in \mathcal{L}^2(\Omega, \mathbf{F}_T, Q)$, the process $\left\{E_Q\left(\frac{c_T}{p_{1T}} \middle| \mathbf{F}_t\right)\right\}$ is a square integrable martingale and, therefore, the discounted terminal consumption $\frac{c_T}{p_{1T}}$ also has the representation

$$\frac{c_T}{p_{1T}} = E_Q\left(\frac{c_T}{p_{1T}}\right) + \int_0^T g_t dV_t$$

where the integrand g satisfies $E_Q\left(\int_0^T g_t^2 dt\right) < \infty$. For the purpose of this example, we intentionally choose the first representation. Consider the trading strategy

$$\theta_{2t} = \sigma^{-1} h_t \frac{p_{1t}}{p_{2t}}$$

$$\theta_{1t} = \int_0^t h_s dV_s - \theta_{2t} \frac{p_{2t}}{p_{1t}}$$

Then $\{\theta_t\}$ is a self-financing trading strategy that attains c_T with the initial cost

$$\theta_0' p_0 = \int_0^0 h_s dV_s = 0$$

The trading strategy $\{\theta_t\}$ is an arbitrage strategy because the probability measures P and Q are equivalent so that $P\{c_T \geq 0\} = 1$, $P\{c_T > 0\} > 0$, and c_T is attainable at zero cost. This is possible because the trading strategy $\{\theta_t\}$ does not satisfy $E_Q\left[\int_0^T (\theta_{2t}p_{2t})^2\, dt\right] < \infty$. If we require that the trading strategy $\{\theta_t\}$ satisfies the preceding condition, then from Theorem 8.4 we have $E_Q(c_T) = 0$. That in turn makes it impossible for c_T to satisfy $Q\{c_T \geq 0\} = 1$ and $Q\{c_T > 0\} > 0$ and the arbitrage trade disappears.

Theorem 9.7 *In the Black-Scholes model*

$$M = \mathcal{R} \times \left[\mathcal{L}^2\left(\Omega, \mathbf{F}_T, P\right) \cap \mathcal{L}^2\left(\Omega, \mathbf{F}_T, Q\right)\right]$$

Proof. Theorem 9.7 follows readily from Theorem 9.6 and the representation theorem of Kunita and Watanabe. Let $c = \{c_0, c_T\} \in X$ and

$$c_T \in \mathcal{L}^2\left(\Omega, \mathbf{F}_T, Q\right)$$

Consider the martingale

$$x_t = E_Q\left(\frac{c_T}{p_{1T}}\,\bigg|\, \mathbf{F}_t\right)$$

The process $\{x_t\}$ is a square integrable martingale. Indeed, choose $0 \leq u \leq t \leq T$ and apply Jensen's inequality to the random variable x_t, the function $f(y) = y^2$, and the σ-field $\mathbf{F}_u$ producing

$$x_u^2 \leq E_Q\left(x_t^2\,\big|\, \mathbf{F}_u\right)$$

Taking expectations

$$E_Q\left(x_u^2\right) \leq E_Q\left(x_t^2\right)$$

and in particular

$$\sup_{0 \leq u \leq T} E_Q\left(x_u^2\right) \leq E_Q\left(x_T^2\right) = E_Q\left(c_T^2\right) < \infty$$

which proves that $\{x_t\}$ is a square integrable martingale. From the representation theorem of Kunita and Watanabe there exists an adapted measurable process $\{h_t\}$ such that $E_Q\left(\int_0^T h_t^2\, dt\right) < \infty$ and

$$x_t = x_0 + \int_0^t h_t\, dV_t$$

Taking expectations yields $x_0 = E_Q\left(\dfrac{c_T}{p_{1T}}\right)$ and the attainability of c follows immediately from Theorem 9.6.

Conversely, if $c = \{c_0, c_T\} \in X$ is attainable, then there exists an adapted process $\{h_t\}$ such that $E_Q \left(\int_0^T h_t^2 dt \right) < \infty$ and

$$E_Q \left(\frac{c_T}{p_{1T}} \bigg| \mathbf{F}_t \right) = E_Q \left(\frac{c_T}{p_{1T}} \right) + \int_0^t h_s dV_s$$

In particular

$$\frac{c_T}{p_{1T}} = E_Q \left(\frac{c_T}{p_{1T}} \right) + \int_0^T h_t dV_t$$

which, together with Theorem 8.4, implies that

$$E_Q \left[\left(\frac{c_T}{p_{1T}} \right)^2 \right] = E_Q \left[\left(\int_0^T h_t dV_t \right)^2 \right] = E_Q \left(\int_0^T h_t^2 dt \right) < \infty$$

This completes the proof. ∎

Theorem 9.6 is sharp in the sense that $\mathcal{L}^2(\Omega, \mathbf{F}_T, P)$ is not a subset of $\mathcal{L}^2(\Omega, \mathbf{F}_T, Q)$ and, therefore, the attainable set M is not equal to the consumption set X. The following example identifies a terminal consumption c_T that belongs to $\mathcal{L}^2(\Omega, \mathbf{F}_T, P)$ but does not belong to $\mathcal{L}^2(\Omega, \mathbf{F}_T, Q)$.

Example 9.2 Denote $\alpha = \dfrac{\mu - r}{\sigma} > 0$ and let $0 < \beta < 2\alpha$. The terminal consumption

$$c_T = \exp \left[\frac{1}{4} \left(\frac{W_T^2}{T} - \beta |W_T| \right) \right]$$

is measurable on $\mathbf{F}_T$, and because $\zeta = \dfrac{W_T}{\sqrt{T}}$ has standard normal distribution

$$E_P \left(c_T^2 \right) = \frac{1}{\sqrt{2\pi}} \int_{-\infty}^{\infty} \exp \left[\frac{1}{2} \left(\zeta^2 - \beta \sqrt{T} |\zeta| \right) - \frac{1}{2} \zeta^2 \right] d\zeta$$

$$= \frac{1}{\sqrt{2\pi}} \int_{-\infty}^{\infty} \exp \left(-\frac{1}{2} \beta \sqrt{T} |\zeta| \right) d\zeta < \infty$$

However

$$E_Q \left(c_T^2 \right) = \frac{1}{\sqrt{2\pi}} \int_{-\infty}^{\infty} \exp \left[\frac{1}{2} \left(\zeta^2 - \beta \sqrt{T} |\zeta| \right) - \frac{1}{2} \zeta^2 - \frac{1}{2} \alpha^2 T - \alpha \sqrt{T} \zeta \right] d\zeta$$

$$= \frac{\exp \left(-\frac{1}{2} \alpha^2 T \right)}{\sqrt{2\pi}} \int_{-\infty}^{\infty} \exp \left[-\frac{1}{2} \left(\beta \sqrt{T} |\zeta| + \alpha \sqrt{T} \zeta \right) \right] d\zeta = \infty$$

Although the preceding example demonstrates that the attainable set M is a proper subset of the consumption set X, the negative impact of this conclusion is mitigated by Corollary 9.4. First, a definition.

Definition 9.10 A subset S of the space $\mathcal{L}^2(\Omega, \mathbf{F}_T, P)$ is called dense in

$$\mathcal{L}^2(\Omega, \mathbf{F}_T, P)$$

if and only if for every $c_T \in \mathcal{L}^2(\Omega, \mathbf{F}_T, P)$ there is a sequence $c_{mT} \in S$ such that

$$\lim_{m \to \infty} E_P\left[(c_{mT} - c_T)^2\right] = 0$$

The definition says that S is dense in $\mathcal{L}^2(\Omega, \mathbf{F}_T, P)$ if and only if each terminal consumption can be approximated arbitrarily closely by a terminal consumption in S.

Theorem 9.8 $\mathcal{L}^\infty(\Omega, \mathbf{F}_T, P)$ *is dense in* $\mathcal{L}^2(\Omega, \mathbf{F}_T, P)$.

Corollary 9.4 *The Black-Scholes model is approximately complete, that is, M is dense in X.*

Proof. Because the probability measures P and Q are equivalent

$$\mathcal{L}^\infty(\Omega, \mathbf{F}_T, P) = \mathcal{L}^\infty(\Omega, \mathbf{F}_T, Q)$$

so that

$$\mathcal{L}^\infty(\Omega, \mathbf{F}_T, P) \subset \mathcal{L}^2(\Omega, \mathbf{F}_T, P) \cap \mathcal{L}^2(\Omega, \mathbf{F}_T, Q)$$

Because $\mathcal{L}^\infty(\Omega, \mathbf{F}_T, P)$ is dense in $\mathcal{L}^2(\Omega, \mathbf{F}_T, P)$, so is

$$\mathcal{L}^2(\Omega, \mathbf{F}_T, P) \cap \mathcal{L}^2(\Omega, \mathbf{F}_T, Q)$$

This ends the proof. ∎

Corollary 9.4 describes the approximate completeness of the Black-Scholes model. Although not every consumption process in the consumption set X is attainable, a consumption process in X that is not attainable can be approximated arbitrarily closely by an attainable consumption process.

The specification of the consumption set in this model, although intuitively appealing, fails to deliver completeness despite the fact that the equilibrium price measure is unique. It is easy to see that an alternative specification of the consumption set

$$X = \mathcal{R} \times \mathcal{L}^2(\Omega, \mathbf{F}_T, Q)$$

makes the model complete. The difference between the two specifications of the consumption set is that $X = \mathcal{R} \times \mathcal{L}^2(\Omega, \mathbf{F}, P)$ has the easy interpretation that each terminal consumption has finite mean and variance with respect to the given probability measure P. By contrast, the alternative specification, $X = \mathcal{R} \times \mathcal{L}^2(\Omega, \mathbf{F}, Q)$, in general eliminates some terminal consumptions with finite means and variances with respect to P, and introduces some terminal consumptions with either infinite means or infinite variances with respect to the probability measure P.

The Price Functional

The equilibrium price measure produces the familiar representation of the price functional. As in the discrete model, the price functional is defined as the initial cost of an attainable consumption process.

Definition 9.11 The price functional $\phi : M \to \mathcal{R}$ is such that for every $c = \{c_0, c_T\} \in M$

$$\phi(c) = c_0 + \theta_0' p_0$$

for any self-financing trading strategy $\{\theta_t\}$ that satisfies

$$c_T = \theta_T' p_T$$

As in the discrete model, the price functional in the Black-Scholes model is linear. It also has the usual representation in terms of the equilibrium price measure Q.

Theorem 9.9 *For any $c \in M$*

$$\phi(c) = c_0 + e^{-rT} E_Q(c_T)$$

Proof. Follows immediately from Corollary 9.2. ∎

As an obvious extension of the discrete concept, the price functional is called positive if and only if for every $c \in M$, $P\{c \geq 0\} = 1$ implies $\phi(c) \geq 0$, and both $P\{c \geq 0\} = 1$ and $P\{c > 0\} > 0$ imply that $\phi(c) > 0$. The price functional is called continuous if and only if it is continuous in the norm of $\mathcal{L}^2(\Omega, \mathbf{F}_T, P)$. That is, for every sequence of attainable consumption processes $c_m = \{c_{m0}, c_{mT}\}$ and an attainable consumption process $c = \{c_0, c_T\}$ the convergence $\lim_{m \to \infty} c_{m0} = c_0$ and $\lim_{m \to \infty} E_P\left[(c_{mT} - c_T)^2\right] = 0$ implies $\lim_{m \to \infty} \phi(c_m) = \phi(c)$. With this concept of continuity, two terminal consumptions that are close in terms of mean and variance have similar initial prices.

Corollary 9.5 *The price functional is positive and continuous.*

Proof. Theorem 9.9 implies that ϕ is positive. To show that ϕ is continuous on M consider a sequence of attainable consumption processes $c_m = \{c_{m0}, c_{mT}\}$ and an attainable consumption process $c = \{c_0, c_T\}$ such that $\lim_{m \to \infty} c_{m0} = c_0$ and $\lim_{m \to \infty} E_P\left[(c_{mT} - c_T)^2\right] = 0$. Because

$$[E_Q(|c_{mT} - c_T|)]^2 \le E_P\left[(c_{mT} - c_T)^2\right] E_P\left[\left(\frac{dQ}{dP}\right)^2\right]$$

and $E_P\left[\left(\frac{dQ}{dP}\right)^2\right] < \infty$, we get that $\lim_{m \to \infty} \phi(c_m) = \phi(c)$. ∎

The price functional $\phi : M \to \mathcal{R}$ can be uniquely extended to a functional $\psi : X \to \mathcal{R}$ that is positive and continuous. This extension is obtained through the obvious device of defining for all $c \in X$

$$\psi(c) = c_0 + e^{-rT} E_Q(c_T)$$

Theorem 9.10 *There is a population of traders with continuous, increasing, and convex preferences for whom the Black-Scholes prices are equilibrium prices.*

Proof. On the consumption set X consider traders whose preferences are given by the following rule. Each trader prefers c'' to c' if and only if $\psi(c'') \ge \psi(c')$. Because of the properties of the price functional, these preferences are continuous, strictly increasing, and convex. The allocation $c^i = e^i$ is an equilibrium allocation because each trader prefers c^i to any other c that is affordable, that is, such that $\psi(c) \le \psi(c^i)$. There is no trade in this equilibrium. ∎

The Black-Scholes Formula

As an application of this model consider a terminal consumption $c_T = g(p_{2T})$, where g is a Borel measurable function such that

$$g(p_{2T}) \in \mathcal{L}^2\left(\Omega, \mathbf{F}_T, P\right) \cap \mathcal{L}^2\left(\Omega, \mathbf{F}_T, Q\right)$$

The initial cost of such a terminal consumption is

$$\phi(\{0, g(p_{2T})\}) = e^{-rT} E_Q[g(p_{2T})]$$

and is equal to

$$\frac{e^{-rT}}{\sqrt{2\pi T}} \int_{-\infty}^{\infty} g\left\{p_{20}\exp\left[\left(r-\frac{1}{2}\sigma^2\right)T+\sigma\zeta\right]\right\}\exp\left(-\frac{\zeta^2}{2T}\right)d\zeta$$

In particular, for a call option on security 2, the terminal consumption is an attainable $g(p_{2T}) = \max(0, p_{2T} - a)$. Denote the normal distribution function $N(z) = \frac{1}{\sqrt{2\pi}} \int_{-\infty}^{z} \exp\left(-\frac{\zeta^2}{2T}\right)d\zeta$. Then

$$\begin{aligned}
p_{30} &= \frac{e^{-rT}}{\sqrt{2\pi T}} \int_{-\gamma}^{\infty} p_{20}\exp\left[\left(r-\frac{1}{2}\sigma^2\right)T+\sigma\zeta\right]\exp\left(-\frac{\zeta^2}{2T}\right)d\zeta \\
&\quad - \frac{ae^{-rT}}{\sqrt{2\pi T}} \int_{-\gamma}^{\infty} \exp\left(-\frac{\zeta^2}{2T}\right)d\zeta
\end{aligned}$$

where

$$\gamma = -\frac{\log\frac{p_{20}}{a} + \left(r-\frac{1}{2}\sigma^2\right)T}{\sigma}$$

A direct computation yields

$$p_{30} = p_{20}N\left[\frac{\log\frac{p_{20}}{a}+\left(r+\frac{1}{2}\sigma^2\right)T}{\sigma\sqrt{T}}\right] - ae^{-rT}N\left[\frac{\log\frac{p_{20}}{a}+\left(r-\frac{1}{2}\sigma^2\right)T}{\sigma\sqrt{T}}\right]$$

This is the Black-Scholes formula for the price of a call option.

9.3   An Explicit Trading Strategy

Consider again the terminal consumption $c_T = g(p_{2T})$ where g is a Borel measurable function such that

$$g(p_{2T}) \in \mathcal{L}^2\left(\Omega, \mathbf{F}_T, P\right) \cap \mathcal{L}^2\left(\Omega, \mathbf{F}_T, Q\right)$$

Let $\{\theta_t\}$ be a self-financing trading strategy that attains this c_T. Denote the value of the portfolio that is generated by this trading strategy

$$v_t = \theta_t' p_t$$

The process $\{v_t\}$ is adapted to $\mathbf{F}_t^{p_2}$ and, therefore, there is a measurable function $v : [0, T] \times \mathcal{R}^+ \to \mathcal{R}^+$ such that

$$v_t(\omega) = v[t, p_{2t}(\omega)]$$

Proceeding formally, apply Itô's formula to the function $v(t, p_{2t})$. The formalism in this computation will be resolved later when the function $v(t, p_{2t})$ is computed and shown to be continuously differentiable with respect to t and twice continuously differentiable with respect to p. Right now, the representation of v is

$$dv = \left(\frac{\partial v}{\partial t} + \mu p_{2t} \frac{\partial v}{\partial p_{2t}} + \frac{1}{2} \sigma^2 p_{2t}^2 \frac{\partial^2 v}{\partial p_{2t}^2} \right) dt + \sigma p_{2t} \frac{\partial v}{\partial p_{2t}} dW_t$$

and because $\{\theta_t\}$ is self-financing

$$dv = (\theta_{1t} r p_{1t} + \theta_{2t} \mu p_{2t}) dt + \theta_{2t} \sigma p_{2t} dW_t$$

Choose $\theta_{2t} = \dfrac{\partial v}{\partial p_{2t}}$ and equate the right sides of the two preceding equations. Because of the choice of θ_{2t}, the coefficients of dW_t are identical and, therefore, we can equate the coefficients of dt in both equations. Remembering that $\theta_{1t} p_{1t} + \theta_{2t} p_{2t} = v(t, p_{2t})$, we get

$$\frac{1}{2} \sigma^2 p_{2t}^2 \frac{\partial^2 v}{\partial p_{2t}^2} + r p_{2t} \frac{\partial v}{\partial p_{2t}} - rv + \frac{\partial v}{\partial t} = 0$$

and, by assumption

$$v(T, p_{2T}) = g(p_{2T})$$

If it exists, then the solution v of the preceding linear partial differential equation and terminal condition determines the trading strategy $\{\theta_t\}$ that attains $c_T = g(p_{2T})$

$$\theta_{1t} = e^{-rt} \left(v_t - p_{2t} \frac{\partial v}{\partial p_{2t}} \right)$$

$$\theta_{2t} = \frac{\partial v}{\partial p_{2t}}$$

In particular, for a call option on security 2

$$g(p_{2T}) = \max(0, p_{2T} - a)$$

the value at time t of the attaining portfolio, $v(t, p_{2t})$, is equal to the equilibrium price of the option with remaining maturity $T - t$

$$p_{2t} N \left[\frac{\log \dfrac{p_{2t}}{a} + \left(r + \frac{1}{2} \sigma^2 \right) (T - t)}{\sigma \sqrt{T - t}} \right]$$

$$- a e^{-r(T-t)} N \left[\frac{\log \dfrac{p_{2t}}{a} + \left(r - \frac{1}{2} \sigma^2 \right) (T - t)}{\sigma \sqrt{T - t}} \right]$$

The function $v(t, p_{2t})$ is continuously differentiable as required, justifying, in this instance, the earlier use of Itô's formula. Using the formulas for the trading strategy delivers the explicit strategy

$$\theta_1(t, p_{2t}) = -ae^{-r(T-t)} N \left[\frac{\log \frac{p_{2t}}{a} + \left(r - \frac{1}{2}\sigma^2\right)(T-t)}{\sigma\sqrt{T-t}} \right]$$

$$\theta_2(t, p_{2t}) = N \left[\frac{\log \frac{p_{2t}}{a} + \left(r + \frac{1}{2}\sigma^2\right)(T-t)}{\sigma\sqrt{T-t}} \right]$$

At first glance, the preceding formulas appear to be incorrect because the calculation of $\theta_2(t, p_{2t})$ as the partial $\dfrac{\partial v}{\partial p_{2t}}$ seems to ignore the fact that p_{2t} appears inside the normal distribution function. A number of terms in the calculation cancel, however, and the above formulas are correct. It is easy to verify that

$$E_Q \left\{ \int_0^T [\theta_2(t, p_{2t})p_{2t}]^2 dt \right\} < \infty$$

and therefore, this trading strategy in securities 1 and 2 satisfies the requirements of Definition 9.6. This trading strategy is also self-financing and produces at time T the payout $\max(0, p_{2T} - a)$. Notice that $\theta_{1t} < 0$ and $\theta_{2t} > 0$, that is, the trading strategy involves buying the stock on a variable margin.

Compared with Section 9.2 the discussion in this section offers a second, and simpler, procedure for the computation of initial equilibrium prices of certain attainable securities. Suppose that the terminal payout, $d_n(p_{2T})$, of security n ($n \geq 3$) depends on the terminal price of security 2, p_{2T}, and does not depend on the earlier history of the process $\{p_{2t}\}$. Then the initial equilibrium price of security n emerges as the value at time 0 of the function $v(t, p_{2t})$ that solves the linear partial differential equation above with the terminal condition $v(T, p_{2T}) = d_n(p_{2T})$. By contrast, the procedure in Section 9.2 is much more complicated. Yet, the method of this section can not substitute for the deeper analysis in Section 9.2. We need the methods of Section 9.2 for three reasons: they apply to attainable securities whose terminal payouts depend on the whole history of the price of $\{p_{2t}\}$, they can be extended to more general models, and, most importantly, the methods of Section 9.2 identify restrictions on trading strategies and prove that the Black-Scholes prices do not permit arbitrage strategies. Without this knowledge, the solution of the partial differential equation in this section has no economic meaning.

Problems

1. Show directly that $\mathcal{L}^2(\Omega, F, P) \subset \mathcal{L}^1(\Omega, F, P)$.

2. Show that if $\dfrac{dQ}{dP} > 0$, then P and Q are equivalent.

3. Show that if both $\dfrac{dQ}{dP}$ and $\dfrac{dQ}{dP}^{-1}$ are bounded, then

$$\mathcal{L}^2(\Omega, \mathbf{F}, P) = \mathcal{L}^2(\Omega, \mathbf{F}, Q)$$

4. Prove that if x is a right continuous martingale on $[0, T]$ and $E_P(x_T^2) < \infty$, then x is a square integrable martingale.

5. Consider the Black-Scholes model on the time interval $[0, T]$.

   (a) Compute the initial equilibrium price of a loan that is collateralized with one unit of security 2, that is, a security that has the terminal payout $\min(p_{2T}, a)$.

   (b) Compute the initial equilibrium price of a convertible bond, that is, a security whose terminal payout is $\max(p_{1T}, p_{2T})$.

   (c) The terminal consumption

   $$c_T = \max(0, p_{2T} - 5) + \max(0, p_{2T} - 15) - 2\max(0, p_{2T} - 10)$$

   is called a "butterfly spread." Is it attainable? At what initial cost?

   (d) Let m be a positive integer. Is the terminal consumption $c_T = p_{2T}^m$ attainable? At what initial cost?

   (e) Is the terminal consumption $c_T = \exp(p_{2T})$ attainable? At what initial cost?

6. Consider a self-financing "suicide" trading strategy θ such that $\theta_0' p_0 = 1$ and $\theta_T' d = 0$. Is it an arbitrage strategy? Is it an admissible strategy in the Black-Scholes model?

7. In the Black-Scholes model security 3 has the terminal payout

$$d_3 = \mathcal{E}_T(\gamma \bullet W)$$

where γ is a constant. Find the initial equilibrium price of security 3.

8. In the Black-Scholes model replace the assumptions about the information structure and the return process of security 2 with the following. The return process of security 2 is

$$x_t = \int_0^t \mu_s ds + \sigma W_t$$

where $\{\mu_t\}$ is an adapted measurable process such that $\int_0^T |\mu_s| ds < \infty$, σ is a constant, and the information structure of traders is the filtration $\{\mathbf{F}_t^{p_2}\}$ generated by the price process of security 2. Show that the equilibrium price measure exists and is unique. Find the equilibrium price measure, the attainable set, and the representation of the price functional.

Notes

The model presented here is a formalization of [7]. This formal version of the Black-Scholes model is based on the martingale representation theorem of [55], the use of which was pioneered by [39]. The first use of a Wiener process to model the behavior of security prices appears in [6]. The assumed exponential Wiener character of the price of the stock in the Black-Scholes model is consistent with [45], who demonstrates that if the information structure is generated by a Wiener process, then the equilibrium prices of securities are Itô processes. In this regard the reader should also note the result of [40], who proved that if there are no arbitrage strategies and prices have continuous sample paths, then they have infinite variation.

Theorem 9.3 on the relationship between conditional expectations with respect to two equivalent probability measures is a special case of Theorem 11.32, which is proved in Chapter 11. The statement of Girsanov's theorem in Theorem 9.4 is proved in [86]. Theorem 9.5 is due to [39]. Theorem 9.6 is a special case of a corresponding theorem in [41]. Example 9.1 uses a result of [27].

The Black-Scholes formula at the end of Section 9.2 and the partial differential equation in Section 9.3 appeared first in [7]. Stochastic representation of solutions of partial differential equations is presented in [36]. The economic intuition behind this stochastic representation of solutions is examined in [16].

The Black-Scholes model is a special case of [39], who examined the questions of this chapter for securities with prices that are general Itô processes. The study of other aspects of security pricing and the related problem of optimal portfolio choice in such a market can be found in [60], [62], [59], [68], [8], [11], [15], [14], [12], [26], [13], [66], [46], and [31].

Chapter 10

Local Martingales and Semimartingales

10.1 Introduction

This chapter describes the stochastic processes that serve as integrators and integrands in stochastic integrals. The concepts in this chapter include stopping times, uniformly integrable processes, localization, maximal spaces of martingales, orthogonal martingales, predictable processes, semimartingales, projections, the Doob Meyer decomposition, quadratic variation processes, and special semimartingales.

The theory in this chapter is used in Chapter 11 to define general stochastic integrals. Together, Chapters 10 and 11 deliver the required mathematical preparation for the general continuous model in Chapter 12.

Initial Definitions and Theorems

The time interval of stochastic processes in this chapter is the open or closed half-line $(0, \infty)$. We consider a given filtered probability space that, by assumption, satisfies the following "usual conditions."

Definition 10.1 A filtered probability space

$$\{\Omega, \mathbf{F}, P, \{\mathbf{F}_t\}\}$$

satisfies the "usual conditions" if and only if:

1. The σ-field $\mathbf{F}$ is P-complete, that is, if $A \in \mathbf{F}$, $P(A) = 0$, and $B \subset A$, then $B \in \mathbf{F}$.

2. The σ-field $\mathbf{F}_0$ contains all the P-null sets of $\mathbf{F}$, that is, if $A \in \mathbf{F}$ and $P(A) = 0$, then $A \in \mathbf{F}_0$.

3. The filtration $\{\mathbf{F}_t\}$ is right continuous, that is, for all $t \geq 0$

$$\mathbf{F}_t = \bigcap_{u > t} \mathbf{F}_u$$

Most of the time, we consider stochastic processes whose sample paths satisfy certain regularity conditions.

Definition 10.2 A function $f : (0, \infty) \to \mathcal{R}$ is called regular if and only if it has left and right limits at every point.

Definition 10.3 A stochastic process $\{x_t\}$ is called regular right continuous if and only if it is adapted and for every $w \in \Omega$:

1. For every $t \in [0, \infty)$ the sample path is right continuous

$$\lim_{u > t, \ u \to t} x(u, w) = x(t, w)$$

2. For every $t \in (0, \infty)$ the left limit $x(t-, w) = \lim_{s < t, \ s \to t} x(s, w)$ exists.

The set of processes that are regular right continuous is denoted $\mathcal{D}$. If $x \in \mathcal{D}$ and, by convention, $x_{0-} = 0$, then the jump of x at time $t \geq 0$ is

$$\Delta x_t = x_t - x_{t-}$$

A stochastic process $\{x_t\}$ is regular left continuous if and only if it is adapted and for every $w \in \Omega$:

1. For every $t \in (0, \infty)$ the sample path is left continuous

$$\lim_{s < t, \ s \to t} x(s, w) = x(t, w)$$

2. For every $t \in [0, \infty)$ the right limit $x(t+, w) = \lim_{u > t, \ u \to t} x(u, w)$ exists.

The set of adapted processes that are regular left continuous is denoted $\mathcal{G}$.

Figure 10.1 illustrates regular right continuous and left continuous sample paths. Theorem 10.1 implies that the sample paths of regular processes have at most a countable number of jumps.

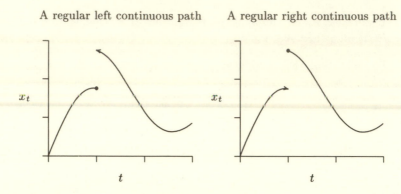

Figure 10.1: Regular left continuous and right continuous processes.

Theorem 10.1 *Suppose that $f : (0, \infty) \to \mathcal{R}$ is regular. Then the set of points of discontinuity of f is at most countable.*

The following special processes are very important.

Definition 10.4 An adapted process $\{x_t\}$ is called a submartingale (supermartingale) if and only if:

1. For each $t \geq 0$ we have $E_P(|x_t|) < \infty$.

2. For each $t \geq u \geq 0$, with probability one

$$E_P(x_t | \mathbf{F}_u) \geq x_u \ \left(E_P(x_t | \mathbf{F}_u) \leq x_u \right)$$

An adapted process is called a martingale if and only if it is both a submartingale and a supermartingale.

The preceding definition is consistent with the notions of a submartingale and a martingale that were introduced in earlier chapters. If the filtered probability space satisfies the "usual conditions," then we can assume that every submartingale (supermartingale) is right continuous with left limits, as the following definition and theorem demonstrate.

Definition 10.5 The stochastic process $\{y_t\}$ is called a modification, or a version, of the stochastic process $\{x_t\}$ if and only if for every $t \geq 0$

$$P\{y_t = x_t\} = 1$$

Theorem 10.2 *Every submartingale (supermartingale) has a regular right continuous modification.*

The next definition adapts the concept of a stopping time from the discrete to the continuous framework. In a discrete setup, a stopping time was defined in Chapter 5, Problem 16, as a random variable $\tau : \Omega \to \{0, \ldots, T\}$ such that for each $0 \leq t \leq T$ the event $\{\tau = t\}$ is either empty or is a union of sets of the partition $\mathbf{f}_t$. This definition says that for any $0 \leq t \leq T$ the event $\{\tau = t\}$ is decidable at time t.

To adapt this definition to the present framework recall that the set $\mathcal{F}_t$ of all the unions of sets of the partition $\mathbf{f}_t$ is a field that represents the same information as the partition $\mathbf{f}_t$. Therefore, the random variable τ is a stopping time if and only if for every $0 \leq t \leq T$ we have $\{\tau = t\} \in \mathcal{F}_t$. Now, for each $0 \leq s \leq t$ the field $\mathcal{F}_s$ generated by the partition $\mathbf{f}_s$ is a subset of the field $\mathcal{F}_t$. Consequently, for each $0 \leq s \leq t$, we have $\{\tau = s\} \in \mathcal{F}_t$ or, equivalently, for every $0 \leq t \leq T$ the event $\{\tau \leq t\}$ belongs to $\mathcal{F}_t$. Hence, the following definition.

Definition 10.6 A stopping time on a filtered probability space is a random variable $\tau : \Omega \to [0, \infty]$ such that for all $t > 0$ we have $\{\tau \leq t\} \in \mathbf{F}_t$.

Notice that a stopping time may assume the value $\tau = \infty$. The next definition extends the concept of a measurable stochastic process in Definition 8.2. This extension is necessary to guarantee that a debut, as defined in Theorem 10.5, is a stopping time.

Definition 10.7 A stochastic process $\{x_t\}$ is progressive if and only if for every $t > 0$ the function

$$x : [0, t] \times \Omega \to \mathcal{R}$$

is measurable on the product σ-field $\mathbf{B}([0, t]) \otimes \mathbf{F}_t$.

The following are important examples of progressive processes.

Theorem 10.3 *An adapted right continuous (left continuous) process is progressive.*

Theorem 10.4 *An adapted, measurable, process has a progressive modification.*

Theorem 10.5 *Let $\{x_t\}$ be a progressive stochastic process and B a Borel set in $\mathcal{R}$. Then the debut*

$$\tau = \inf\{t \geq 0 \mid x_t \in B\}$$

is a stopping time.

The next definition introduces the concept of the stopping-time σ-field $\mathbf{F}_\tau$. In a discrete framework, the natural definition of the partition $\mathbf{f}_\tau$ is that it consists of all the sets A such that for some $0 \leq t \leq T$ the event A is a set of the partition $\mathbf{f}_t$ and a subset of the event $\{\tau = t\}$, that is, $A \cap \{\tau = t\} \in \mathbf{f}_t$.

Example 10.1 Suppose that $\Omega = \{\omega_1, \omega_2, \omega_3, \omega_4, \omega_5, \omega_6, \omega_7, \omega_8\}$, $T = 3$, and the information structure is

$$\mathbf{f}_1 = \{\{\omega_1, \omega_2, \omega_3, \omega_4, \omega_5, \omega_6\}, \{\omega_7, \omega_8\}\}$$
$$\mathbf{f}_2 = \{\{\omega_1, \omega_2\}, \{\omega_3, \omega_4\}, \{\omega_5, \omega_6\}, \{\omega_7, \omega_8\}\}$$

Let τ be

$$\tau(\omega_1) = \tau(\omega_2) = \tau(\omega_5) = \tau(\omega_6) = 2$$
$$\tau(\omega_3) = \tau(\omega_4) = \tau(\omega_7) = \tau(\omega_8) = 3$$

Then

$$\{\tau = 0\} = \emptyset, \ \{\tau = 1\} = \emptyset$$

$$\{\tau = 2\} = \{\omega_1, \omega_2, \omega_5, \omega_6\}, \ \{\tau = 3\} = \{\omega_3, \omega_4, \omega_7, \omega_8\}$$

and

$$\mathbf{f}_\tau = \{\{\omega_1, \omega_2\}, \{\omega_5, \omega_6\}, \{\omega_3\}, \{\omega_4\}, \{\omega_7\}, \{\omega_8\}\}$$

This is the information available at time τ. If the prevailing state is $\{\omega\}$, then the partition set known at time $\tau(\omega)$ is $\mathbf{f}_\tau(\omega)$. For instance, if the prevailing state is ω_5, then the information at time $\tau(\omega_5) = 2$ is $\{\omega_5, \omega_6\}$. Similarly, if the prevailing state is $\{\omega_8\}$, then the information at time $\tau(\omega_8) = 3$ is $\{\omega_8\}$.

The intuition derived from the discrete framework, and the relationship between a partition and the field it generates, motivate the following definition.

Definition 10.8 For a filtered probability space and a stopping time τ the stopping-time σ-field $\mathbf{F}_\tau$ is such that

$$A \in \mathbf{F}_\tau \text{ if and only if } A \cap \{\tau \leq t\} \in \mathbf{F}_t \text{ for all } t \geq 0$$

The following theorem offers an alternative characterization of the σ-field $\mathbf{F}_\tau$.

Theorem 10.6 *The stopping-time σ-field $\mathbf{F}_\tau$ is the σ-field generated by the random variables $\{x_\tau \mid x \in \mathcal{D}\}$.*

Let x be a martingale and suppose that σ and τ are stopping times with $\sigma \leq \tau$. Is it then true that $E_P(x_\tau|\mathbf{F}_\sigma) = x_\sigma$? In general, the answer is negative. If the martingale x has a certain additional property, however, then the answer is affirmative. This leads to the concept of a uniformly integrable martingale.

Uniformly Integrable Processes

We start with the definition of a uniformly integrable set of random variables. For a random variable x and a real number $h \geq 0$ denote

$$x_h = x\chi_{\{|x|\geq h\}}$$

Definition 10.9 A set $\Gamma \subset \mathcal{L}^1(\Omega, \mathbf{F}, P)$ is uniformly integrable if and only if $\lim\limits_{h\to\infty} \sup\limits_{x\in\Gamma} \|x_h\|_1 = 0$.

It is easy to see that in the preceding definition

$$\|x_h\|_1 = \int_{\{|x|\geq h\}} |x| dP$$

Moreover, the convergence of $\sup\limits_{x\in\Gamma} \|x_h\|_1$ is equivalent to the uniform convergence of $\|x_h\|_1$ in $x \in \Gamma$. Thus, an equivalent statement of uniform integrability is as follows. A set $\Gamma \subset \mathcal{L}^1(\Omega, \mathbf{F}, P)$ is uniformly integrable if and only if for every $\epsilon > 0$ there is a $K \geq 0$ such that $h \geq K$ implies $\int_{\{|x|\geq h\}} |x| dP < \epsilon$ for all $x \in \Gamma$. The following theorem offers an alternative characterization of uniform integrability.

Theorem 10.7 *A set $\Gamma \subset \mathcal{L}^1(\Omega, \mathbf{F}, P)$ is uniformly integrable if and only if:*

1. *The set Γ is bounded in $\mathcal{L}^1(\Omega, \mathbf{F}, P)$, that is*

$$\sup_{x\in\Gamma} E_P(|x|) < \infty$$

2. *For every $\epsilon > 0$ there is a $\delta > 0$ such that for every $A \in \mathbf{F}$ and every $x \in \Gamma$*

$$P(A) < \delta \text{ implies that } \int_A |x| dP < \epsilon$$

Proof. First, notice that for every $x \in \mathcal{L}^1(\Omega, \mathbf{F}, P)$ and every $h \geq 0$

$$\int_A |x| dP \leq hP(A) + E_P(|x_h|)$$

Suppose that Γ is uniformly integrable and let $\epsilon > 0$. Then there is an $h \geq 0$ such that $E_P(|x_h|) < \dfrac{\epsilon}{2}$ for all $x \in \Gamma$. It follows that $E_P(|x|) \leq h + \dfrac{\epsilon}{2}$ for all $x \in \Gamma$. This establishes item 1. In addition, choosing $\delta = \dfrac{\epsilon}{2h}$ establishes item 2.

Conversely, suppose that items 1 and 2 are satisfied. Choose $\epsilon > 0$ and let $\delta > 0$ be such that item 2 is satisfied. If

$$K = \frac{\sup\limits_{x \in \Gamma} E_P(|x|)}{\delta}$$

then Chebyshev's inequality implies for any $h \geq K$

$$P\{|x| \geq h\} \leq \frac{E_P(|x|)}{h} \leq \delta$$

and item 2 implies that Γ is uniformly integrable. ∎

The next two theorems offer sufficient conditions for uniform integrability.

Theorem 10.8 *If there is a $y \in \mathcal{L}^1(\Omega, \mathbf{F}, P)$ such that $|x| \leq y$ for all $x \in \Gamma$, then Γ is uniformly integrable.*

Theorem 10.9 *Let $\Gamma \in \mathcal{L}^1(\Omega, \mathbf{F}, P)$ and suppose that there is a positive increasing function $f : [0, \infty) \to \mathcal{R}$ such that:*

1. $\lim\limits_{t \to \infty} \dfrac{f(t)}{t} = \infty.$

2. $\sup\limits_{x \in \Gamma} E_P[f(x)] < \infty.$

Then the set Γ is uniformly integrable.

A uniformly integrable stochastic process is defined as follows.

Definition 10.10 Suppose that a stochastic process $\{x_t\}$ is such that

$$x_t \in \mathcal{L}^1(\Omega, \mathbf{F}, P)$$

for each $t \geq 0$. We say that the process $\{x_t\}$ is uniformly integrable if and only if the set $\{x_t \mid t \geq 0\}$ is uniformly integrable.

Theorem 10.10 *Let $y \in \mathcal{L}^1(\Omega, \mathbf{F}, P)$. Then the martingale $x_t = E_P(y|\mathbf{F}_t)$ is uniformly integrable.*

Proof. For any $t \geq 0$ and positive real numbers h and k denote

$$H = \{\omega \mid |x_t(\omega)| \geq h\}$$
$$K = \{\omega \mid |y(\omega)| \geq k\}$$

Because x_t is measurable on $\mathbf{F}_t$, we have that $H \in \mathbf{F}_t$. Because $E_P(y|\mathbf{F}_t) = x_t$ we get that $E_P(y\chi_H|\mathbf{F}_t) = x_t\chi_H$. This, and Jensen's inequality, imply that

$$\int_H |x_t|dP \leq \int_H |y|dP$$

Next, using Chebyshev's inequality and Jensen's inequality

$$
\begin{aligned}
\int_H |y|dP &= \int_{H \cap K} |y|dP + \int_{H \cap (\Omega - K)} |y|dP \\
&\leq \int_K |y|dP + kP(H) \\
&\leq \int_K |y|dP + \frac{k}{h}E_P(|x_t|) \\
&\leq \int_K |y|dP + \frac{k}{h}E_P(|y|)
\end{aligned}
$$

It follows that

$$\lim_{h \to \infty} \sup_{t \geq 0} \int_H |x_t|dP \leq \int_K |y|dP$$

and because k is an arbitrary positive number, we get that

$$\lim_{h \to \infty} \sup_{t \geq 0} \int_H |x_t|dP = 0$$

This completes the proof. ∎

We denote by $\mathcal{M}$ the set of uniformly integrable, regular, right continuous martingales. Uniformly integrable martingales have the following property.

Theorem 10.11 (Optional Stopping) *Let $x \in \mathcal{M}$ and suppose that σ and τ are stopping times with $\sigma \leq \tau$. Then*

$$E_P(x_\tau|\mathbf{F}_\sigma) = x_\sigma$$

The next definition introduces processes of class **D**.

Definition 10.11 A stochastic process $\{x_t\}$ is of class **D** if and only if the set

$$\Gamma = \{x_\tau \mid \tau \text{ is a finite stopping time of the filtration } \{\mathbf{F}_t\}\}$$

is uniformly integrable.

Theorem 10.12 *Every uniformly integrable martingale is of class* **D**.

Proof. For every stopping time τ we have

$$x_\tau = E_P(x_\infty | \mathbf{F}_\tau)$$

where $x_\infty \in \mathcal{L}^1(\Omega, \mathbf{F}, P)$. The proof is identical to the proof of Theorem 10.10. ∎

Localization

To motivate the definition of localization we begin with two examples.

Example 10.2 In the first example, suppose that Ω is an infinite set and let $\{\Omega, \mathcal{F}, P\}$ be a given probability space. Suppose that $\{\mathcal{F}_t\}$, $t = 0, 1, 2, \ldots$ is a sequence of σ-fields such that $\mathcal{F}_0 \subset \mathcal{F}_1 \subset \ldots \subset \mathcal{F}$. An adapted sequence of random variables $\{x_t\}$, $t = 0, 1, 2, \ldots$ is a martingale if and only if for all $t \geq 0$:

1. $E_P(|x_t|) < \infty$.

2. $E_P(x_{t+1} | \mathcal{F}_t) = x_t$.

Item 1 guarantees that the conditional expectation in item 2 exists. The conditional expectation in item 2, however, may exist for all $t \geq 0$ even when item 1 is not satisfied. If item 2 is satisfied, then the sequence $\{x_t\}$, $t = 0, 1, 2, \ldots$ is called a local martingale. It turns out that we have the following characterization of local martingales.

A sequence $\{x_t\}$, $t = 0, 1, 2, \ldots$ is a local martingale if and only if there exists a sequence $\{\tau_m\}$, $m = 1, 2, \ldots$ of stopping times such that $\tau_m \leq \tau_{m+1}$ for all $m \geq 1$, $\lim_{m \to \infty} \tau_m = \infty$, and for every $m \geq 1$ the sequence $\{x_{t \wedge \tau_m}\}$ is a martingale.

Example 10.3 The second example involves the Itô integral from Chapter 8. Let $\{\alpha_t\}$ be a measurable process adapted to the natural filtration of a Wiener process such that the integral $\int_0^\infty \alpha_s^2 ds$ is finite with probability one and $E_P \left(\int_0^\infty \alpha_s^2 ds \right) = \infty$. Then the Itô integral $\int_0^t \alpha_s dW_s$ need not be a martingale. Define the sequence of stopping times

$$\tau_m = m \wedge \inf \left\{ t \ \middle| \ \int_0^t \alpha_s^2 ds \geq m \right\}$$

Because the sample paths of $\int_0^t \alpha_s^2 ds$ are increasing, the sequence $\{\tau_m\}$ is increasing, and because the sample paths of $\int_0^t \alpha_s^2 ds$ are continuous, the sequence $\{\tau_m\}$ tends to infinity. In addition, for every $m \geq 1$, we have

$$\int_0^\infty \alpha_s^2 \chi_{\{s \leq \tau_m\}} ds \leq m$$

Thus, $E_P \left(\int_0^\infty \alpha_s^2 \chi_{\{s \leq \tau_m\}} ds \right) < \infty$ for each $m \geq 1$, and consequently the Itô integral $\int_0^t \alpha_s \chi_{\{s \leq \tau_m\}} dW_s$ is a square integrable martingale. Because

$$\int_0^{t \wedge \tau_m} \alpha_s dW_s = \int_0^t \alpha_s \chi_{\{s \leq \tau_m\}} dW_s$$

the integral $\{(\alpha \bullet W)_{t \wedge \tau_m}\}$ is a uniformly integrable martingale.

Now, let $\mathcal{N}$ be a set of stochastic processes. Depending on the situation, the definition of the set $\mathcal{N}_{loc}$ is in terms of processes either stopped or killed at a sequence of stopping times increasing to infinity.

Definition 10.12 Stopped and killed processes are defined as follows:

1. Suppose that $\{x_t\}$ is a stochastic process and τ is a stopping time. Then the process $\{x_t\}$ stopped at τ is the process $\{x_{t \wedge \tau_m}\}$.

2. Suppose that $\{\alpha_t\}$ is a stochastic process and τ is a stopping time. Then the process $\{\alpha_t\}$ killed at τ is the process $\{\alpha_t \chi_{\{t \leq \tau\}}\}$.

The preceding definition is such that each sample path of a process $\{x_t\}$ stopped at τ has the constant value $x_{\tau_m(\omega)}(\omega)$ for all $t > \tau_m(\omega)$. By contrast, each sample path of a process $\{\alpha_t\}$ killed at τ has zero value for all $t > \tau_m(\omega)$.

It is interesting to note that the debut of a stopped process is a stopping time. This follows immediately from the following theorem.

Theorem 10.13 *If $\{x_t\}$ is a progressive process and τ is a stopping time, then the random variable x_τ is measurable on the stopping time σ-field $\mathbf{F}_\tau$, and the process stopped at τ, $\{x_{t \wedge \tau}\}$, is progressive.*

Depending on the circumstances, we apply to the set $\mathcal{N}$ one of the following two concepts of localization.

Definition 10.13 The first item below is the definition of localization in the usual sense, and the second item is the definition of localization for integrands:

1. Suppose that $\mathcal{N}$ is a set of stochastic processes. Then a process x belongs to $\mathcal{N}_{loc}$ if and only if there is a sequence $\{\tau_m\}$ of stopping times, increasing to infinity, such that for each $m \geq 1$ the process x stopped at τ_m belongs to $\mathcal{N}$.

2. Suppose that $\mathcal{N}$ is a set of stochastic processes. Then a process α belongs to $\mathcal{N}_{loc}$ if and only if there is a sequence $\{\tau_m\}$ of stopping times, increasing to infinity, such that for each $m \geq 1$ the process α killed at τ_m belongs to $\mathcal{N}$.

The choice of the right concept of localization depends on the context. In most cases we apply the usual concept of localization. While dealing with stochastic integrals we apply the usual concept of localization to integrators and the concept of localization for integrands to integrands.

10.2   Local Martingales

Localization in the usual sense of the set $\mathcal{M}$ of uniformly integrable martingales produces the set $\mathcal{M}_{loc}$ of local martingales. When $\int_0^\infty \alpha_s^2 ds$ is finite with probability one, then the Itô integral $\int_0^t \alpha_s dW_s$ is an example of a local martingale that is not necessarily a martingale. This is explained in Example 10.3.

Local martingales are the primary integrators in stochastic integrals. In this section we present three theorems about local martingales.

Theorem 10.14

$$\mathcal{M} \subset \mathcal{M}_{loc}$$

Proof. Choose $m \geq 1$ and $t \geq 0$. Then

$$E_P(x_m | \mathbf{F}_t) = \begin{cases} x_t & \text{if } t \leq m \\ x_m & \text{if } t > m \end{cases}$$

It follows that $x_{t \wedge m} = E_P(x_m|\mathbf{F}_t)$ and, therefore, $\{x_{t \wedge m}\}$ is a uniformly integrable martingale. ∎

The proofs of the next two theorems rely on a partial convergence result known as Fatou's lemma. For a sequence $\{\xi_m\}$ of random variables denote $\xi_m^- = -\min(\xi_m, 0)$ and $\xi_m^+ = \max(\xi_m, 0)$.

Theorem 10.15 (Fatou's lemma) *If $\{\xi_m\}$ is a sequence of random variables and $\mathbf{G}$ is a sub-σ-field of $\mathbf{F}$, then:*

1. *If the sequence $\{\xi_m^-\}$ is uniformly integrable, then*

$$E_P\left(\liminf_{m \to \infty} \xi_m \,\middle|\, \mathbf{G}\right) \leq \liminf_{m \to \infty} E_P(\xi_m|\mathbf{G})$$

2. *If the sequence $\{\xi_m^+\}$ is uniformly integrable, then*

$$\limsup_{m \to \infty} E_P(\xi_m|\mathbf{G}) \leq E_P\left(\limsup_{m \to \infty} \xi_m \,\middle|\, \mathbf{G}\right)$$

Fatou's lemma and Theorem 10.8 imply the following corollary.

Corollary 10.1 *If $\{\xi_m\}$ is a sequence of random variables and $\mathbf{G}$ is a sub-σ-field of $\mathbf{F}$, then:*

1. *If there is an integrable random variable η such that $\xi_m \geq \eta$ for all $m \geq 1$, then*

$$E_P\left(\liminf_{m \to \infty} \xi_m \,\middle|\, \mathbf{G}\right) \leq \liminf_{m \to \infty} E_P(\xi_m|\mathbf{G})$$

2. *If there is an integrable random variable η such that $\xi_m \leq \eta$ for all $m \geq 1$, then*

$$\limsup_{m \to \infty} E_P(\xi_m|\mathbf{G}) \leq E_P\left(\limsup_{m \to \infty} \xi_m \,\middle|\, \mathbf{G}\right)$$

Proof. The corollary follows immediately from the inequalities

$$\xi_m \geq \eta \Rightarrow \xi_m^- \leq \eta^- \text{ and } \xi_m \leq \eta \Rightarrow \xi_m^+ \leq \eta^+$$

The details are left to the reader. ∎

Fatou's lemma implies the following theorem.

Theorem 10.16 *A nonnegative local martingale is a supermartingale.*

Proof. Let $\{x_t\}$ be a nonnegative local martingale. Then there is a sequence $\{\tau_m\}$ of stopping times, increasing to infinity, such that for every $0 \le s \le t \le T$ and every $m \ge 1$

$$E_P\left(x_{t \wedge \tau_m} \mid \mathbf{F}_s\right) = x_{s \wedge \tau_m}$$

First, notice that for any $0 \le u \le T$

$$\lim_{m \to \infty} x_{u \wedge \tau_m} = x_u$$

Second, apply Fatou's lemma to the sequence of non-negative random variables $\{x_{t \wedge \tau_m}\}$. We have

$$E_P\left(\liminf_{m \to \infty} x_{t \wedge \tau_m} \,\middle|\, \mathbf{F}_s\right) \le \liminf_{m \to \infty} E_P\left(x_{t \wedge \tau_m} \mid \mathbf{F}_s\right) = \liminf_{m \to \infty} x_{s \wedge \tau_m}$$

It follows that

$$E_P\left(x_t \mid \mathbf{F}_s\right) \le x_s$$

This ends the proof. ∎

The next theorem states that local martingales of class **D** are uniformly integrable martingales.

Theorem 10.17 *Suppose that $x \in \mathcal{M}_{loc}$. Then $x \in \mathcal{M}$ if and only if x is of class* **D**.

Proof. The direct part of the proof follows from Theorem 10.12. Conversely, suppose that $x \in \mathcal{M}_{loc}$ is of class **D** and let $\{\tau_m\}$ be a sequence of stopping times increasing to infinity such that each $\{x_{t \wedge \tau_m}\}$ is a uniformly integrable martingale. Thus, for all $0 \le s \le t$ and $m \ge 1$

$$x_{s \wedge \tau_m} = E_P(x_{t \wedge \tau_m} \mid \mathbf{F}_s)$$

The sequences $\{x_{s \wedge \tau_m}\}$ and $\{x_{t \wedge \tau_m}\}$ converge to x_s and x_t, respectively. The uniform integrability of the process $\{x_{t \wedge \tau_m}\}$ is the same as the uniform integrability of the sequence $\{|x_{t \wedge \tau_m}|\}$ and Fatou's lemma implies that

$$\lim_{m \to \infty} E_P(x_{t \wedge \tau_m} \mid \mathbf{F}_s) = E_P(x_t \mid \mathbf{F}_s)$$

This completes the proof. ∎

10.3   Maximal and Quadratic Spaces

This section deals with certain special spaces of martingales. First, we need a theorem on the convergence of right continuous submartingales. Denote $x_t^+ = \max(x_t, 0)$.

Theorem 10.18 *Suppose that $\{x_t\}$ is a right continuous submartingale such that $\sup_{t \geq 0} E_P\left(x_t^+\right) < \infty$. Then the limit $x_\infty = \lim_{t \to \infty} x_t$ is an integrable random variable.*

Corollary 10.2 *If $x \in \mathcal{M}$, then x_∞ is an integrable random variable and for each $0 \leq t \leq \infty$ we have $x_t = E_P\left(x_\infty | \mathbf{F}_t\right)$.*

Both sample paths are regular right continuous

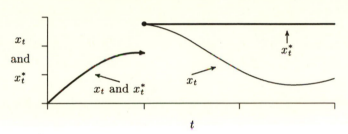

Figure 10.2: Sample paths of x_t and $x_t^* = \sup_{0 \leq s \leq t} |x_s|$.

For a stochastic process $\{x_t\}$ we denote

$$x_t^* = \sup_{0 \leq s \leq t} |x_s|$$

Notice that if $\{x_t\}$ is a right continuous adapted process, then the process $\{x_t^*\}$ is a right continuous submartingale. Figure 10.2 illustrates a sample path of the process $\{x_t^*\}$. Let $x \in \mathcal{M}_{loc}$ be such that

$$\sup_{t \geq 0} E_P\left(x_t^*\right) < \infty$$

Then $x_\infty^* \in \mathcal{L}^1(\Omega, \mathbf{F}_\infty, P)$. We now introduce the following definition.

Definition 10.14 Let $1 \leq k < \infty$. We define the k-maximal space of local martingales, denoted $\mathcal{H}^k$, as the set of local martingales $\{x_t\}$ such that $\sup_{t \geq 0} E_P\left(x_t^*\right) < \infty$ and $E_P\left[\left(x_\infty^*\right)^k\right] < \infty$. Denoting

$$\|x\|_k^* = \left\{E_P\left[\left(x_\infty^*\right)^k\right]\right\}^{\frac{1}{k}}$$

we can restate the definition of the k-maximal space of local martingales as

$$\mathcal{H}^k = \{x \in \mathcal{M}_{loc} \mid \|x\|_k^* < \infty\}$$

In addition, we denote by $\mathcal{H}^\infty$ the space of local martingales whose sample paths are bounded with probability one, and set

$$\|x\|_\infty^* = \operatorname*{ess\,sup}_{\omega \in \Omega} x_\infty^*(\omega)$$

In general, when Q is a probability measure on $\{\Omega, \mathbf{F}\}$, we denote by $\mathbf{F}^Q$ the σ-field generated by $\mathbf{F}$ and the subsets of Q-null sets in $\mathbf{F}$. In addition, we denote by $\mathbf{F}_t^Q$ the smallest σ-field generated by the σ-field $\mathbf{F}_t$ and the Q-null sets of the σ-field $\mathbf{F}^Q$. Notice that for all $t \geq 0$ we have $\mathbf{F}_t^P = \mathbf{F}_t$ because the filtration $\{\mathbf{F}_t\}$ satisfies the "usual conditions." Furthermore, if a probability measure Q_1 is equivalent to a probability measure Q_2, then for all $t \geq 0$, we have $\mathbf{F}_t^{Q_1} = \mathbf{F}_t^{Q_2}$.

We denote by $\mathcal{H}^{k,Q}$ the k-maximal space of Q-local martingales on the filtration $\left\{\mathbf{F}_t^Q\right\}$ that satisfy $E_Q\left[(x_\infty^*)^k\right] < \infty$. When the context involves both the probability measure P and another probability measure Q, we use the notation $\mathcal{H}^{k,P}$ and $\mathcal{H}^{k,Q}$ to distinguish between the two spaces.

If $\sup_{t \geq 0} E_P(x_t^*) < \infty$, then the random variable x_∞^* is integrable, and for all $t \geq 0$ we have $|x_t| \leq x_\infty^*$, Theorem 10.8 immediately implies that $\{x_t\}$ is a uniformly integrable martingale. Thus, we have the following theorem.

Theorem 10.19 *Suppose that* $1 \leq k \leq \infty$. *Then*

$$\mathcal{H}^k \subset \mathcal{M}$$

The following theorem and its corollary help characterize the spaces $\mathcal{H}^k$.

Theorem 10.20 (Doob's inequality) *Suppose that* $x \in \mathcal{M}$ *and* $1 < k < \infty$. *Then*

$$\|\sup_{t \geq 0} |x_t|\|_k \leq \frac{k}{k-1} \sup_{t \geq 0} \|x_t\|_k$$

Corollary 10.3 *If* $1 < k < \infty$ *and* $x \in \mathcal{H}^k$, *then*

$$\|x_\infty\|_k \leq \|x_\infty\|_k^* \leq \frac{k}{k-1}\|x_\infty\|_k$$

In addition

$$\|x_\infty\|_\infty^* = \|x_\infty^*\|_\infty$$

Proof. If $x \in \mathcal{H}^k$, then x is a uniformly integrable martingale. Therefore, Corollary 10.2 implies that x_∞ is an integrable random variable. In addition, from Jensen's inequality, the process $\{|x_t|^k\}$ is a submartingale on $[0, \infty]$ and, therefore

$$E_P\left(|x_t|^k\right) \le E_P\left(|x_\infty|^k\right) \le E_P\left(|x_\infty^*|^k\right)$$

Together, the preceding inequality and Doob's inequality imply the corollary. ∎

Identifying each uniformly integrable martingale $\{x_t\}$ in $\mathcal{H}^k$ with its value at infinity, x_∞, establishes an equivalence of the spaces $\mathcal{H}^k$ and $\mathcal{L}^k(\Omega, \mathbf{F}_\infty, P)$.

Corollary 10.4 *If $1 < k < \infty$, then the spaces $\mathcal{H}^k$ and $\mathcal{L}^k(\Omega, \mathbf{F}_\infty, P)$ are equivalent. The spaces $\mathcal{H}^k$ are complete.*

The spaces $\mathcal{H}^1$ and $\mathcal{L}^1(\Omega, \mathbf{F}_\infty, P)$ are not equivalent. We have that

$$x \in \mathcal{H}^1 \text{ implies that } x_\infty \in \mathcal{L}^1(\Omega, \mathbf{F}_\infty, P)$$

but the converse is not always true. Notice that Doob's inequality, Theorem 10.20, does not hold for $k = 1$. Theorem 10.10 indicates that the space $\mathcal{L}^1(\Omega, \mathbf{F}_\infty, P)$ is equivalent to the space $\mathcal{M}$ of uniformly integrable martingales, and it is easy to see that $\mathcal{H}^1$ is a proper subset of $\mathcal{M}$. We have, however, the following additional characterization of $\mathcal{H}^1$.

Theorem 10.21 *The space $\mathcal{H}^\infty$ is dense in $\mathcal{H}^1$.*

Paralleling Theorem 9.1 we have the following inclusion between spaces of different order.

Theorem 10.22 *If $1 \le k' \le k'' \le \infty$, then $\mathcal{H}^{k''} \subset \mathcal{H}^{k'}$.*

For $1 < k < \infty$ the space $\mathcal{H}^k$ coincides with the space of martingales x such that $\sup_{t \ge 0} E_P\left(|x_t|^k\right) < \infty$. Indeed, if $x \in \mathcal{H}^k$, then the obvious inequality $|x_t|^k \le |x_\infty^*|^k$ for all $t \ge 0$ implies that $\sup_{t \ge 0} E_P\left(|x_t|^k\right) < \infty$. Conversely, if x is a martingale and $\sup_{t \ge 0} E_P\left(|x_t|^k\right) < \infty$, then, by Theorem 10.8, the process x is uniformly integrable, and Doob's inequality implies that $x \in \mathcal{H}^k$. In particular, the space $\mathcal{H}^2$ coincides with the set of square integrable martingales.

We now introduce k-quadratic spaces of local martingales.

Definition 10.15 Let $1 < k < \infty$. We define the k-quadratic space of local martingales, denoted $\mathcal{H}_2^k$, as the following set of local martingales

$$\mathcal{H}_2^k = \left\{ x \in \mathcal{M}_{loc} \mid \left\| [x,x]_\infty^{\frac{1}{2}} \right\|_k < \infty \right\}$$

The following theorem establishes the identity of the k-maximal and k-quadratic spaces.

Theorem 10.23 (Burkholder-Davis-Gundy) *Suppose that* $1 \le k < \infty$ *and* $x \in \mathcal{M}_{loc}$. *Then*

$$\frac{1}{4k} \|x_\infty^*\|_k \le \left\| [x,x]_\infty^{\frac{1}{2}} \right\|_k \le 6k \|x_\infty^*\|_k$$

Corollary 10.5 *For all* $1 \le k < \infty$ *we have* $\mathcal{H}_2^k = \mathcal{H}^k$.

When $k = 2$ the space $\mathcal{H}^2$ is a Hilbert space with the scalar product $(x,y) = E_P(x_\infty y_\infty)$. Using this concept of scalar product we call two elements $x, y \in \mathcal{H}^2$ weakly orthogonal if and only if $E_P(x_\infty y_\infty) = 0$. The next section introduces the stronger and more general concept of orthogonal local martingales.

10.4　Orthogonal Local Martingales

The definition of orthogonal local martingales parallels the development in discrete stochastic calculus. We denote by $\mathcal{M}_{0,loc}$ the set of local martingales that are null at zero, and by $c\mathcal{M}_{0,loc}$ the set of continuous local martingales that are null at zero.

Definition 10.16 Suppose that $x, y \in \mathcal{M}_{loc}$. We say that the local martingales x and y are orthogonal, and write $x \perp y$, if and only if $xy \in \mathcal{M}_{0,loc}$. If $x \in \mathcal{M}_{loc}$ and $M \subset \mathcal{M}_{loc}$, then we say that x is orthogonal to M, and write $x \perp M$, if and only if $x \perp y$ for all $y \in M$.

Notice that the preceding definition is equivalent to the following two conditions:

1. At the initial time $x_0 y_0 = 0$.

2. There is a sequence $\{\tau_m\}$ of stopping times increasing to infinity such that for all $0 \le s \le t$

$$E_P\left(x_{t \wedge \tau_m} y_{t \wedge \tau_m} \mid \mathbf{F}_s \right) = E_P\left(x_{t \wedge \tau_m} \mid \mathbf{F}_s \right) E_P\left(y_{t \wedge \tau_m} \mid \mathbf{F}_s \right)$$

In the space $\mathcal{H}^2$ orthogonality implies weak orthogonality. This follows immediately from the following property of orthogonal martingales

$$E_P(x_\infty y_\infty) = E_P(x_\infty)E_P(y_\infty) = x_0 y_0 = 0$$

The preceding remark is a special case of the following theorem.

Theorem 10.24 *Suppose that* $x, y \in \mathcal{H}^2$ *and* $x \perp y$. *Then for every stopping time* $\tau \in \mathcal{T}$ *we have* $E_P(x_\tau y_\tau) = 0$. *Conversely, if* $x_0 y_0 = 0$ *and for every* $\tau \in \mathcal{T}$ *we have* $E_P(x_\tau y_\tau) = 0$, *then* $x \perp y$.

The next definition introduces purely discontinuous local martingales.

Definition 10.17 A local martingale $x \in \mathcal{M}$ is called purely discontinuous if and only if it is orthogonal to every local martingale in $c\mathcal{M}_{0,loc}$. The set of purely discontinuous local martingales is denoted $d\mathcal{M}_{loc}$.

The next two theorems characterize purely discontinuous local martingales.

Theorem 10.25

$$\mathcal{M}_{loc} \cap f\mathcal{V} \subset d\mathcal{M}_{loc}$$

Theorem 10.26 *If* $x, y \in d\mathcal{M}_{loc}$ *are such that* $\Delta x_t = \Delta y_t$ *for all* $t \geq 0$, *then* $x_t = y_t$ *for all* $t \geq 0$.

The following theorem defines the continuous and purely discontinuous parts of a local martingale.

Theorem 10.27 *Every* $x \in \mathcal{M}_{loc}$ *has a unique decomposition*

$$x = x^c + x^d$$

such that $x^c \in c\mathcal{M}_{0,loc}$ *and* $x^d \in d\mathcal{M}_{loc}$.

Definition 10.18 In the notation of Theorem 10.27 the continuous local martingale x^c is called the continuous part of the local martingale x and the purely discontinuous process x^d is called the purely discontinuous part of the local martingale x.

We end this section with a theorem that asserts that if a continuous local martingale has finite variation on compacts, then it is constant.

Theorem 10.28 *If* $x \in c\mathcal{M}_{0,loc} \cap f\mathcal{V}$, *then* $x = 0$.

Proof. Theorem 10.25 implies that $x \in c\mathcal{M}_{0,loc} \cap d\mathcal{M}_{loc}$. Therefore, x has the orthogonal decompositions

$$x = x + 0 = 0 + x$$

Because the orthogonal decomposition is unique, $x = 0$. ∎

10.5   Predictable Processes

Predictable processes are important because they are the most general integrands in stochastic integrals. To interpret the formal definition of a predictable process we introduce the concepts of predictable and accessible stopping times, the σ-field of events strictly before a stopping time, and accessible and optional stochastic processes.

Definition 10.19 Define the predictable σ-field, a predictable stochastic process, and a predictable stopping time as follows:

1. The predictable σ-field $\mathbf{\Pi}$ on $(0, \infty) \times \Omega$ is the σ-field generated by the set $\mathcal{G}$.

2. A stochastic process $\alpha : (0, \infty) \times \Omega \to \mathcal{R}$ is called predictable if and only if it is measurable on the predictable σ-field $\mathbf{\Pi}$.

3. A stopping time τ is called predictable if and only if

$$\{(t, \omega) \mid \tau(\omega) \leq t < \infty\} \in \mathbf{\Pi}$$

The set of predictable processes is denoted $\mathcal{P}$.

The next theorem characterizes predictable stopping times.

Theorem 10.29 *A stopping time τ is predictable if and only if there is an increasing sequence $\{\tau_m\}$ of stopping times such that:*

1. *The limit $\lim_{m \to \infty} \tau_m = \tau$.*

2. *The stopping times satisfy $\tau_m \chi_{\{\tau > 0\}} < \tau \chi_{\{\tau > 0\}}$ for all $m \geq 1$.*

Example 10.4 The following are examples of predictable stopping times:

1. Let τ be a stopping time and k a positive real number. Then the sequence of stopping times

$$\tau_m = \tau + \left(1 - \frac{1}{m}\right) k$$

converges to $\tau + k$, and therefore the latter is a predictable stopping time.

2. It can be shown that every positive stopping time on the natural filtration of the Wiener process is predictable.

To offer a characterization of predictable processes we introduce the concept of a simple predictable process.

Definition 10.20 A stochastic process $\{\alpha_t\}$ on a filtered probability space is simple predictable if and only if there exist stopping times $0 = \tau_0 < \tau_1 < \ldots < \tau_m < \infty$ and random variables $a_1, \ldots, a_m$ such that for all $1 \leq j \leq m$ the random variable a_j is finite and measurable on $\mathbf{F}_{\tau_{j-1}}$, and for all $t \in (0, \infty)$

$$\alpha_t = \sum_{j=1}^{m} a_j \chi_{(\tau_{j-1}, \tau_j]}(t)$$

with probability one. The set of simple predictable processes is denoted $s\mathcal{P}$.

Notice that $s\mathcal{P} \subset \mathcal{G}$ and that a simple predictable process is not defined at $t = 0$. Every bounded predictable process is obtained from simple predictable processes by taking repeated uniform and monotone limits. This is formalized in the next theorem.

Theorem 10.30 *Let $\mathcal{N}$ be a set of functions on $(0, \infty) \times \Omega$ such that:*

1. *We have $s\mathcal{P} \subset \mathcal{N}$.*

2. *If $\{x_m\}$ is a sequence of functions in $\mathcal{N}$ that converges uniformly on $(0, \infty) \times \Omega$ to a function x, then $x \in \mathcal{N}$.*

3. *If $\{x_m\}$ is a uniformly bounded, nonnegative, increasing sequence of functions in $\mathcal{N}$ that converges to a function x, then $x \in \mathcal{N}$.*

Then $\mathcal{N}$ contains all the bounded predictable processes on $(0, \infty)$.

In the discrete framework, a stochastic process $\{\alpha_t\}$ is predictable if and only if for each $t \geq 1$ the random variable α_t is measurable on the partition $\mathbf{f}_{t-1}$. For a similar, but weaker, characterization of predictable processes in continuous time we need several additional concepts. We start with the definitions of accessible and totally inaccessible stopping times.

Definition 10.21 We set:

1. A stopping time τ is called totally inaccessible if and only if for every predictable stopping time σ

$$P\{\tau = \sigma < \infty\} = 0$$

2. A stopping time τ is called accessible if and only if for every totally inaccessible stopping time σ

$$P\{\tau = \sigma < \infty\} = 0$$

We have the following alternative characterization of accessible stopping times.

Theorem 10.31 *A stopping time τ is accessible if and only if there is a sequence $\{\tau_m\}$ of stopping times such that for every $0 \le t \le \infty$ and $\omega \in \Omega$, if $\tau(\omega) = t$, then there is an $m \ge 1$ for which $\tau_m(\omega) = t$.*

The preceding theorem says that a stopping time is accessible if and only if its graph is contained in the union of graphs of a countable set of predictable stopping times. The following definition complements the definition of the predictable σ-field $\mathbf{\Pi}$.

Definition 10.22 The optional σ-field $\mathbf{O}$ on $[0, \infty) \times \Omega$ is the σ-field generated by the set $\mathcal{D}$.

The next theorem offers a different way of describing the predictable and optional σ-fields.

Theorem 10.32 *We have:*

1. *The predictable σ-field $\mathbf{\Pi}$ on $(0, \infty) \times \Omega$ is the σ-field generated by the null sets and sets of the form $\{(t, \omega) \mid \tau(\omega) \le t < \infty\}$, where τ is a predictable stopping time.*

2. *The optional σ-field $\mathbf{O}$ on $[0, \infty) \times \Omega$ is the σ-field generated by the null sets and sets of the form $\{(t, \omega) \mid \tau(\omega) \le t < \infty\}$, where τ is any stopping time.*

The next definition is patterned after the preceding theorem.

Definition 10.23 The accessible σ-field $\mathbf{A}$ on $[0, \infty) \times \Omega$ is the σ-field generated by the null sets and sets of the form $\{(t, \omega) \mid \tau(\omega) \le t < \infty\}$, where τ is an accessible stopping time.

For completeness, we record one more definition. The collection of subsets A of $[0, \infty) \times \Omega$ such that the characteristic process $\{\chi_A(t, \omega)\}$ is progressive is a σ-field, called the progressive σ-field. We denote the progressive σ-field by $\mathbf{\Gamma}$.

The predictable, accessible, optional, and progressive σ-fields are ordered by the inclusion

$$\mathbf{\Pi} \subset \mathbf{A} \subset \mathbf{O} \subset \mathbf{\Gamma}$$

We are now ready to define optional and accessible stochastic processes.

Definition 10.24 We set:

1. A stochastic process $\alpha : [0, \infty) \times \Omega \rightarrow \mathcal{R}$ is called optional if and only if it is measurable on the optional σ-field **O**.

2. A stochastic process $\alpha : [0, \infty) \times \Omega \rightarrow \mathcal{R}$ is called accessible if and only if it is measurable on the accessible σ-field **A**.

The inclusion relationship among the four special σ-fields above implies that every predictable process is accessible, every accessible process is optional, and every optional process is progressive.

Next, we define the prestopping-time σ-field $\mathbf{F}_{\tau-}$. To motivate this definition, consider first the discrete framework and the natural definition of the prestopping-time partition $\mathbf{f}_{\tau-}$. In Section 10.1 we defined the stopping-time partition $\mathbf{f}_\tau$ as the set of events A such that for some $0 \leq t \leq T$ we have $A \cap \{\tau = t\} \in \mathbf{f}_t$. This definition relies on the fact that the set $\{\tau = t\}$ is a union of events in $\mathbf{f}_t$. The set $\{\tau = t\}$, however, need not be a union of events in $\mathbf{f}_{t-1}$. We define the prestopping-time partition $\mathbf{f}_{\tau-}$ to be the set of events $A \cap \{\tau = t\}$ such that $A \in \mathbf{f}_{t-1}$.

Example 10.5 In Example 10.1 it is easy to verify that the prestopping-time partition is

$$\mathbf{f}_{\tau-} = \{\{\omega_1, \omega_2, \omega_5, \omega_6\}, \{\omega_3, \omega_4\}, \{\omega_7, \omega_8\}\}$$

The partition $\mathbf{f}_{\tau-}$ represents the information available one period before the time τ. For instance, if the prevailing state is ω_5, then the information at time $\tau(\omega_5) - 1 = 1$ is $\{\omega_1, \omega_2, \omega_5, \omega_6\}$, reflecting the additional knowledge that if $\tau = 2$, then the prevailing state is in the set $\{\omega_1, \omega_2, \omega_5, \omega_6\}$.

The above discussion, and the relationship between a partition and the field it generates, motivate the following definition.

Definition 10.25 The prestopping-time σ-field $\mathbf{F}_{\tau-}$ is the σ-field generated by $\mathbf{F}_0$ and sets of the form $A \cap \{\tau > t\}$, where $t \geq 0$ and $A \in \mathbf{F}_t$.

The following theorem describes the similarity between predictable processes in discrete time and in continuous time.

Theorem 10.33 *An accessible process $\{x_t\}$ is predictable if and only if for every predictable stopping time τ the random variable $x_\tau \chi_{\{\tau < \infty\}}$ is measurable on $\mathbf{F}_{\tau-}$.*

Because every predictable process in accessible, this theorem says that if the process $\{x_t\}$ is predictable, then for every predictable stopping time τ the random variable $x_\tau \chi_{\{\tau < \infty\}}$ is measurable on the prestopping-time

σ-field $\mathbf{F}_{\tau-}$. The converse is true, however, only when the process $\{x_t\}$ is accessible. In general, even if $x_\tau \chi_{\{\tau < \infty\}}$ is measurable on the prestopping-time σ-field $\mathbf{F}_{\tau-}$ for every predictable time τ, the process $\{x_t\}$ need not be predictable.

The final characterization of predictable processes involves their comparison with optional processes. Speaking loosely, optional processes and predictable processes differ only on small sets.

Theorem 10.34 *Suppose that x is an optional process. Then, there exists a predictable process y and a sequence $\{\tau_m\}$ of stopping times, such that the set $\{(t, \omega) \mid x_t(\omega) \neq y_t(\omega)\}$ is contained in the set $\bigcup_{m \geq 1} \{(t, \omega) \mid \tau_m(\omega) = t\}$.*

The preceding theorem says that an optional process coincides with a predictable process, except on a subset of the union of graphs of a countable set of stopping times.

10.6   Semimartingales

In this section we introduce several additional types of stochastic processes: increasing processes, integrable processes, processes of finite variation on compacts, processes of integrable variation, and semimartingales. Semimartingales are important because they are the most general integrators in stochastic integrals.

Processes of Finite and Integrable Variation

The purpose of this subsection is to introduce notation for several special types of adapted stochastic processes.

$\mathcal{C}$ – Set of adapted increasing processes such that for each $t \geq 0$ the random variable x_t is finite with probability one

$\mathcal{I}$ – Set of processes in $\mathcal{C}$ such that $E_P(x_\infty) < \infty$

$f\mathcal{V}$ – Set of adapted, regular, right continuous processes whose sample paths have, with probability one, finite variation on compacts

$i\mathcal{V}$ – Set of processes in $f\mathcal{V}$ such that $E_P \left(\int_0^\infty |dx_t| \right) < \infty$

The processes in $\mathcal{I}$ are called increasing integrable processes and the processes in $i\mathcal{V}$ are called processes of integrable variation.

Semimartingales

Definition 10.26 A stochastic process $x \in \mathcal{D}$ is a semimartingale if and only if it has a decomposition $x = m + a$ where $m \in \mathcal{M}_{0,loc}$ and $a \in f\mathcal{V}$. The set of semimartingales is denoted $\mathcal{S}$.

Example 10.6 The following are examples of semimartingales:

1. $\mathcal{M}_{loc} \subset \mathcal{S}$.

2. $f\mathcal{V} \subset \mathcal{S}$.

3. A supermartingale is a semimartingale.

4. A process $x \in \mathcal{D}$ with stationary independent increments is a semi-martingale.

The following are examples of processes that are not semimartingales:

1. Any process that is not right continuous with left limits.

2. The process $x_t = |W_t|^{\frac{1}{2}}$ is not a semimartingale. A partial proof of this assertion is as follows. It can be shown that the paths of a continuous semimartingale satisfy with probability one a Hölder condition of order k for any $0 < k < \frac{1}{2}$. We say that a function $f : X \to \mathcal{R}$ satisfies a Hölder condition of order $k > 0$ if and only if there is a constant $0 \leq \gamma < \infty$ such that

$$|f(x'') - f(x')| \leq \gamma |x'' - x'|^k$$

for all $x', x'' \in X$. We demonstrate that the function $f(t) = |W_t|^{\frac{1}{2}}$ fails, with probability one, to satisfy the Hölder condition of order $\frac{1}{4}$. It is enough to show that there is no constant $0 \leq \gamma < \infty$ such that $\dfrac{|W_t|}{\sqrt{t}} \leq \gamma$ for all $t \geq 0$. It is easy to see that the latter assertion follows immediately from the ensuing property of the Wiener process (called the law of the iterated logarithm)

$$\limsup_{t \to \infty} \frac{|W_t|}{\sqrt{2t \log \log t}} = 1$$

Indeed, the law of the iterated logarithm implies that for every $t' \geq 0$ there is a $t > t'$ such that

$$\frac{|W_t|}{\sqrt{t}} \frac{1}{\sqrt{\log \log t}} > 1$$

The contradiction completes the proof.

The reader should keep in mind that although a semimartingale is defined through a decomposition $x = m + a$, where $m \in \mathcal{M}_{0,loc}$ and $a \in f\mathcal{V}$, this decomposition need not be unique. For example, if $x \in \mathcal{M}_{0,loc} \cap f\mathcal{V}$, then x is a semimartingale and it has the two different decompositions $x = x + 0 = 0 + x$.

The following three theorems state some of the stability properties of semimartingales.

Theorem 10.35 *Let $\{\mathbf{G}_t\}$ be a filtration of $\{\Omega, \mathbf{F}\}$ such that $\mathbf{G}_t \subset \mathbf{F}_t$ for each $t \geq 0$. If the process $\{x_t\}$ is a semimartingale on $\{\mathbf{F}_t\}$, and is adapted to the filtration $\{\mathbf{G}_t\}$, then it is also a semimartingale on $\{\mathbf{G}_t\}$.*

Theorem 10.36

$$\mathcal{S}_{loc} = \mathcal{S}$$

The next concept is used to state Theorem 10.37.

Definition 10.27 *A linear lattice is an ordered linear space X such that for all $x, y \in X$ the supremum $x \vee y$ and the infimum $x \wedge y$ exist in X.*

Theorem 10.37 *We have the following stability properties of semimartingales:*

1. *The set $\mathcal{S}$ is a linear lattice.*

2. *If $x, y \in \mathcal{S}$, then $xy \in \mathcal{S}$.*

3. *If $f : \mathcal{R} \to \mathcal{R}$ is either convex or twice continuously differentiable, then $x \in \mathcal{S}$ implies $f(x) \in \mathcal{S}$.*

Summary of Notation

Following is a summary of the notation used for sets of special processes:

$\mathcal{D}$	—	Set of regular right continuous processes
$\mathcal{G}$	—	Set of regular left continuous processes
$\mathcal{M}$	—	Set of uniformly integrable, regular, right continuous martingales
$\mathcal{M}_{loc}$	—	Set of local martingales
$\mathcal{M}_{0,loc}$	—	Set of local martingales that are null at zero
$c\mathcal{M}_{loc}$	—	Set of continuous local martingales
$d\mathcal{M}_{loc}$	—	Set of purely discontinuous local martingales
$\mathcal{H}^k$	—	k-maximal space of martingales
$\mathcal{C}$	—	Set of finite increasing processes
$\mathcal{I}$	—	Set of increasing integrable processes
$f\mathcal{V}$	—	Set of processes with finite variation on compacts
$i\mathcal{V}$	—	Set of processes of integrable variation
$\mathcal{P}$	—	Set of predictable processes
$\mathcal{S}$	—	Set of semimartingales

10.7   Projections

This section introduces predictable projections and dual predictable projections of certain stochastic processes. In the framework of discrete stochastic calculus these projections were introduced in Chapter 5.

Predictable Projections

The following theorem is central to the definition of predictable projections.

Theorem 10.38 *Let x be a positive measurable process. Then there is a unique predictable process $\{(\pi x)_t\}$ such that for every predictable stopping time τ and every $\omega \in \Omega$ such that $\tau(\omega) < \infty$*

$$(\pi x)_\tau(\omega) = E_P\left(x_\tau | \mathbf{F}_{\tau-}\right)(\omega)$$

Theorem 10.38 defines the predictable projection of a positive measurable process. The following decomposition leads to the extension of the predictable projection to other measurable processes. The positive part of the stochastic process $\{x_t\}$ is $x_t^+ = \max(x_t, 0)$ and the negative part of $\{x_t\}$ is $x_t^- = -\min(x_t, 0)$. Notice that for any stochastic process $\{x_t\}$

$$x_t = x_t^+ - x_t^-$$

For every $t > 0$, the predictable projection of a measurable process is defined on the complement of the set $\{\omega \mid (\pi x^+)_t(\omega) = (\pi x^-)_t(\omega) = \infty\}$ in terms of the above decomposition.

Definition 10.28 *Let x be a measurable process such that for every $t > 0$ either $(\pi x^+)_t < \infty$ or $(\pi x^-)_t < \infty$. Then the predictable projection of x is the process $(\pi x)_t = (\pi x^+)_t - (\pi x^-)_t$.*

The predictable projection of a local martingale is particularly simple.

Theorem 10.39 *If $x \in \mathcal{M}_{0,loc}$, then $\pi x = x_-$.*

Dual Predictable Projections

The definition of dual predictable projections rests on the following theorem.

Theorem 10.40 *If $x \in i\mathcal{V}_{loc}$, then there is a unique process $\pi^* x \in \mathcal{P} \cap i\mathcal{V}_{loc}$ such that $x - \pi^* x \in \mathcal{M}_{0,loc}$.*

Definition 10.29 *If $x \in i\mathcal{V}_{loc}$, then the process $\pi^* x$ is called the dual predictable projection of the process x.*

Theorem 10.41 explains the name dual predictable projection.

Theorem 10.41 *Let $y \in i\mathcal{V}_{loc}$. Then the process $(\pi^* x)_t$ is such that for every measurable process x that satisfies*

$$E_P \left[\int_0^\infty |(\pi x)_s| \, dy_s \right] < \infty$$

we have

$$E_P \left[\int_0^\infty (\pi x)_s dy_s \right] = E_P \left[\int_0^\infty x_s d(\pi^* y)_s \right]$$

10.8   The Doob-Meyer Decomposition

The Doob-Meyer decomposition generalizes the Doob decomposition in discrete stochastic calculus. The immediate context for the Doob-Meyer decomposition is set in Theorem 10.40, which delivers a decomposition of processes of locally integrable variation. We start with a definition.

Definition 10.30 A uniformly integrable submartingale x is consistent if and only if for every predictable stopping time τ

$$E_P(x_{\tau-}) = E_P(x_\tau)$$

Theorem 10.42 (Meyer) *Suppose that x is a submartingale of class* **D**. *Then there is a unique process $a \in \mathcal{P} \cap \mathcal{I}$ such that $x - a \in \mathcal{M}_0$. The process a is continuous if and only if the process x is consistent.*

Theorem 10.42 indicates that the process x has a unique decomposition in which the first term is a predictable, increasing, integrable process, and the second term is a uniformly integrable martingale. Using the terminology of Chapter 5, we call a the predictable part of x and $x - a$ the innovation part of x. In addition, matching the discrete framework, we denote the predictable part of x by $\pi^* x$. Notice that if the process x is both a submartingale of class **D** and a process of locally integrable variation, then the predictable part of x is also the dual predictable projection of x and, therefore, the notation $\pi^* x$ does not cause confusion.

To extend the Doob-Meyer decomposition by localization we make use of the fact that every submartingale is locally of class **D**. We get the following corollary.

Corollary 10.6 *Suppose that x is a local submartingale. Then there is a unique process $a \in \mathcal{P} \cap \mathcal{I}_{loc}$ such that $x - a \in \mathcal{M}_{0,loc}$.*

Again, we call the process a the predictable part of x and denote it by $\pi^* x$. If the process x is a local submartingale of locally integrable variation, then $\pi^* x$ is both the predictable part of x and the dual predictable projection of x.

Example 10.7 For the Wiener process $\{W_t\}$:

1. The process $\{W_t^2\}$ is a continuous submartingale. The Doob-Meyer decomposition of $\{W_t^2\}$ is

$$W_t^2 = t + \left(W_t^2 - t\right)$$

2. The process $\{W_t^4\}$ is a continuous submartingale. From Itô's formula

$$dW_t^4 = 6W_t^2 dt + 4W_t^3 dW_t$$

so that

$$\left(\pi^* W^4\right)_t = 6 \int_0^t W_s^2 ds$$

and we get the Doob-Meyer decomposition

$$W_t^4 = 6 \int_0^t W_s^2 ds + \left(W_t^4 - 6 \int_0^t W_s^2 ds\right)$$

10.9 Quadratic Variation Processes

To motivate the next definition recall that if x is a discrete time martingale, then the predictable quadratic variation $\langle x, x \rangle$ is the predictable part of x. Returning to continuous time suppose that $x \in \mathcal{H}^2$. Then

$$x_\tau^2 \le (x_\infty^*)^2$$

for every stopping time τ and $E_P\left[(x_\infty^*)^2\right] < \infty$. This, and Jensen's inequality, imply that x^2 is a submartingale of class $\mathbf{D}$. Applying the Doob-Meyer decomposition to the process x^2 we get that there is a unique process $\langle x, x \rangle \in \mathcal{P} \cap \mathcal{I}$ such that $x^2 - \langle x, x \rangle \in \mathcal{M}_0$. By localization, we have the following definition.

Definition 10.31 Suppose that $x \in \mathcal{H}_{loc}^2$. Then the predictable quadratic variation of x is the unique process $\langle x, x \rangle \in \mathcal{P} \cap \mathcal{I}_{loc}$ such that

$$x^2 - \langle x, x \rangle \in \mathcal{M}_{0,loc}$$

Example 10.8 The Wiener process $\{W_t\}$ is in $\mathcal{H}_{loc}^2$ (but not in $\mathcal{H}^2$). Because $W_t^2 - t$ is a martingale that is null at zero, we have

$$\langle W, W \rangle_t = t$$

The following two theorems provide a basis for the definition of an optional quadratic variation process.

Theorem 10.43

$$c\mathcal{M}_{loc} \subset \mathcal{H}_{loc}^2 \subset \mathcal{M}_{loc}$$

Proof. Let

$$\tau_m = \inf\{t \mid |x_t| \geq m\}$$

Then the sequence $\{\tau_m\}$ is increasing, $\lim_{m \to \infty} \tau_m = \infty$, and $|x_{t \wedge \tau_m}| \leq m$ for all $t \geq 0$. This proves the first part of the theorem and the second part is proved easily by localization. ∎

Theorem 10.44 leads to a definition of the continuous local martingale part of a semimartingale.

Theorem 10.44 *Suppose that $x \in \mathcal{S}$ and*

$$x = m' + a' = m'' + a''$$

are two decompositions of x such that $m', m'' \in \mathcal{M}_{0,loc}$ and $a', a'' \in \text{f}\mathcal{V}$. Then $(m')^c = (m'')^c$.

Proof. First, we have

$$m'' - m' = a' - a'' \in \mathcal{M}_{0,loc} \cap \text{f}\mathcal{V}$$

Second, Theorem 10.28 implies that $(m'' - m')^c = 0$. ∎

Definition 10.32 Let x be the semimartingale $x = m + a$, where $m \in \mathcal{M}_{0,loc}$ and $a \in \text{f}\mathcal{V}$. The continuous local martingale part of the semimartingale x, denoted x^c, is the continuous part of the local martingale m, that is, $x^c = m^c$.

For example, if $x \in \text{f}\mathcal{V}$, then $x^c = 0$. Indeed, x has a decomposition $x = 0 + x$ with $0 \in \mathcal{M}_{0,loc}$ and $x \in \text{f}\mathcal{V}$. Because the continuous local martingale part of x is the same for all decompositions, we have

$$x^c = 0^c = 0$$

From Theorem 10.43, if $x \in \mathcal{S}$, then $x^c \in \mathcal{H}_{loc}^2$ and, therefore, the predictable quadratic variation process $\langle x^c, x^c \rangle$ exists. This allows the following definition.

Definition 10.33 Suppose that $x \in \mathcal{S}$. Then the optional quadratic variation process of x is defined as

$$[x, x]_t = \langle x^c, x^c \rangle_t + \sum_{0 \le s \le t} (\Delta x_s)^2$$

Definition 10.33 implies that $[x, x]_0 = x_0^2$ and $\Delta[x, x]_t = (\Delta x_t)^2$ for all $t > 0$.

Theorem 10.45 *The optional quadratic variation process has the following properties:*

1. *Suppose that $x \in \mathcal{S}$. Then $[x, x] \in \mathcal{C}$.*

2. *Suppose that $x \in \mathcal{S}$. Then $[x, x] = 0$ if and only if $x \in f\mathcal{V}$, x is continuous, and $x_0 = 0$.*

3. *If $x \in \mathcal{M}_{loc}$ then $x^2 - [x, x] \in \mathcal{M}_{0,loc}$.*

4. *Suppose that $x \in \mathcal{M}_{loc}$. Then $[x, x] = 0$ if and only if $x = 0$.*

Proof. Item 1 is obvious. To prove item 2 notice that from $x \in f\mathcal{V}$ we have $x^c = 0$, which together with the continuity of x and $x_0 = 0$ implies that $[x, x] = 0$. Conversely, if $[x, x] = 0$, then x is continuous, $x_0 = 0$, and $\langle x^c, x^c \rangle = 0$. The definition of the predictable quadratic variation process then implies that $(x^c)^2 \in \mathcal{M}_{0,loc}$. Therefore, from Theorem 10.16, $(x^c)^2$ is a supermartingale, that is, for every $0 \le s \le t$

$$E_P\left[(x_t^c)^2 \, \middle| \, \mathbf{F}_s \right] \le (x_s^c)^2$$

In particular

$$E_P\left[(x_t^c)^2 \right] \le (x_0^c)^2 = 0$$

so that $x^c = 0$ and it follows that $x = 0$. Item 4 follows from item 2 and Theorem 10.28. ∎

Example 10.9 Because the Wiener process is a continuous semimartingale, we have

$$[W, W]_t = \langle W, W \rangle_t = t$$

If $x \in \mathcal{H}^2$, then the Burkholder-Davis-Gundy inequality implies that

$$[x, x] \in \mathcal{I}$$

By localization, if $x \in \mathcal{H}^2_{loc}$, then $[x, x] \in \mathcal{I}_{loc} \subset i\mathcal{V}_{loc}$. Thus, $x^2 - [x, x] \in \mathcal{M}_{0,loc}$ and $x^2 - \langle x, x \rangle \in \mathcal{M}_{0,loc}$, so that

$$[x, x] - \langle x, x \rangle \in \mathcal{M}_{0,loc}$$

It follows that if $x \in \mathcal{H}^2_{loc}$, then $\langle x, x \rangle = \pi^*[x, x]$. Therefore, the following definition generalizes the predictable quadratic variation process described in Definition 10.31.

Definition 10.34 If the semimartingale x is such that $[x, x] \in i\mathcal{V}_{loc}$, then we define the predictable quadratic variation process

$$\langle x, x \rangle = \pi^*[x, x]$$

Notice that Definition 10.29 of a dual predictable projection indicates that $\langle x, x \rangle$ is the unique process in $\mathcal{P} \cap i\mathcal{V}_{loc}$ such that $[x, x] - \langle x, x \rangle \in \mathcal{M}_{0,loc}$. We now introduce a Poisson process $\{N_t\}$ and compute the predictable and optional quadratic variation processes of $\{N_t\}$.

Definition 10.35 A Poisson process $\{N_t\}$ with parameter λ is such that:

1. $N_t = \sum_{m \geq 1} \chi_{\{t \geq \tau_m\}}$, where $\{\tau_m\}$ is a strictly increasing sequence of positive stopping times.

2. For any $0 < t_1 < \ldots < t_m$ and any Borel sets $B_1, \ldots, B_m$ the probability $P\{N_{t_1} \in B_1, \ldots, N_{t_m} \in B_m\}$ is equal to

$$\sum_{j_1 \in B_1} \cdots \sum_{j_m \in B_m} e^{-\lambda t_1} \frac{(\lambda t_1)^{j_1}}{j_1!} \cdots e^{-\lambda(t_m - t_{m-1})} \frac{[\lambda(t_m - t_{m-1})]^{j_m - j_{m-1}}}{(j_m - j_{m-1})!}$$

The definition implies that a Poisson process starts at zero, has increasing, regular, right continuous paths with unit jumps, independent increments, and every increment $N_t - N_s$ has a Poisson distribution with mean $\lambda(t - s)$ and variance $\lambda(t - s)$. Furthermore, the process $\{N_t - \lambda t\}$ is a martingale, called a Poisson martingale with parameter λ.

Example 10.10 Consider a Poisson process $\{N_t\}$ with parameter λ. The decomposition

$$N_t = (N_t - \lambda t) + \lambda t$$

shows that N is a semimartingale. It is easy to see that the continuous martingale part of N is zero. Therefore

$$[N, N]_t = \sum_{0 \leq s \leq t} (\Delta N_s)^2 = N_t$$

Furthermore, the Poisson process is locally integrable (but not integrable). Because $\{N_t - \lambda t\}$ is a martingale that is null at zero, we have

$$\langle N, N \rangle_t = (\pi^* N)_t = \lambda t$$

Theorem 10.46 *The predictable quadratic variation process has the following properties:*

1. *If $x \in S$ is such that $[x, x] \in i\mathcal{V}_{loc}$, then $\langle x, x \rangle \in \mathcal{P} \cap i\mathcal{V}_{loc}$.*

2. *If $x \in f\mathcal{V}$, x is continuous and $x_0 = 0$, then $\langle x, x \rangle = 0$.*

3. *Suppose that $x \in \mathcal{H}^2_{loc}$. Then $\langle x, x \rangle = 0$ if and only if $x = 0$.*

Proof. Item 1 follows from the definition of predictable quadratic variation. The proof of item 2 follows from Theorem 10.45. To prove item 3 notice that if $\langle x, x \rangle = 0$, then $x^2 \in \mathcal{M}_{0,loc}$. Therefore, x^2 is a supermartingale. Because $x_0^2 = 0$, we have that $E_P\left(x_t^2\right) \leq 0$ for all $t \geq 0$. Consequently, $x = 0$. ∎

Definition 10.36 We define the quadratic covariation processes by polarization:

1. Suppose that $x, y \in S$. Then

$$[x, y] = \frac{1}{2}\left([x + y, x + y] - [x, x] - [y, y]\right)$$

2. Suppose that $x, y \in S$ such that $[x, y] \in i\mathcal{V}_{loc}$. Then

$$\langle x, y \rangle = \pi^*[x, y]$$

Theorem 10.47 *Suppose that $x, y \in S$ is such that $[x, y] \in i\mathcal{V}_{loc}$. Then the predictable quadratic covariation process $\langle x, y \rangle$ is the unique predictable process of locally integrable variation such that $[x, y] - \langle x, y \rangle \in \mathcal{M}_{0,loc}$.*

Theorem 10.48 *Suppose that $x, y \in \mathcal{M}_{loc}$ such that $[x, y] \in i\mathcal{V}_{loc}$. Then $x \perp y$ if and only if $\langle x, y \rangle = 0$.*

Proof. Follows from the preceding theorem and the fact that $x \perp y$ if and only if $xy \in \mathcal{M}_{0,loc}$. ∎

Theorem 10.49 *The optional quadratic covariation process has the following properties:*

1. *Suppose that $x, y \in S$. Then $[x, y] \in f\mathcal{V}$.*

2. *Suppose that* $x, y \in \mathcal{M}_{loc}$. *Then* $xy - [x, y] \in \mathcal{M}_{0,loc}$.

3. *Suppose that* $x, y \in \mathcal{H}^2$. *Then* $[x, y] \in i\mathcal{V}$ *and* $xy - [x, y] \in \mathcal{H}^1$.

4. *Suppose that* $x \in \mathcal{M}_{0,loc}$ *and* $y \in \mathcal{P} \cap f\mathcal{V}$. *Then* $[x, y] \in \mathcal{M}_{0,loc}$.

Corollary 10.7 *Let* $x, y \in \mathcal{M}_{loc}$. *Then* $x \perp y$ *if and only if* $[x, y] \in \mathcal{M}_{0,loc}$.

Theorem 10.50 *If* $x \in f\mathcal{V}$ *is continuous and* $x_0 = 0$, *then* $[x, y] = 0$ *for any* $y \in \mathcal{S}$.

Proof. Because x is continuous and $x_0 = 0$, then

$$[x, y] = \langle x^c, y^c \rangle = \langle 0, y^c \rangle = 0$$

This ends the proof. ∎

Defining a suitable topology on the space $\mathcal{D}$ allows an intuitive characterization of the optional quadratic variation process of a semimartingale.

Definition 10.37 We say that a sequence $\{x_m\}$ of elements of $\mathcal{D}$ converges to x if and only if for every $\epsilon > 0$ and $t > 0$ the sequence

$$P \left\{ \sup_{0 \le s \le t} |x_{m,s} - x_s| \ge \epsilon \right\}$$

converges to zero. This topology is called the topology of uniform convergence on compacts in probability and the resulting topological space is denoted $\mathcal{D}_{ucp}$.

Definition 10.38 We call an increasing sequence of stopping times

$$\tau_0 \le \tau_1 \le \cdots$$

a random partition Π. Define the boundary of a random partition as

$$\tau(\Pi) = \sup_{j \ge 0} \tau_j$$

and its mesh as

$$\mu(\Pi) = \sup_{j \ge 1} (\tau_j - \tau_{j-1})$$

Next, consider a sequence of random partitions

$$\Pi_m = \{\tau_{m,0}, \tau_{m,1}, \ldots\}$$

We say that the sequence $\{\Pi_m\}$ tends to the identity if and only if

1. For all $m \geq 1$ we have $\tau(\Pi_m) < \infty$, and $\lim_{m \to \infty} \tau(\Pi_m) = \infty$ with probability one.

2. $\lim_{m \to \infty} \mu(\Pi_m) = 0$ with probability one.

Theorem 10.51 *Suppose that $x \in S$. Then if the sequence of random partitions*

$$\Pi_m = \{\tau_{m,0}, \tau_{m,1}, \ldots\}$$

tends to the identity, then, in $\mathcal{D}_{ucp}$, for every $t \geq 0$

$$\lim_{m \to \infty} \left[x_0^2 + \sum_{j \geq 1} \left(x_{t \wedge \tau_{m,j}} - x_{t \wedge \tau_{m,j-1}} \right)^2 \right] = [x, x]_t$$

Paralleling Theorem 10.51 we have the following intuitive characterization of the optional quadratic covariation of two semimartingales.

Theorem 10.52 *Suppose that $x, y \in S$. Then if the sequence of random partitions*

$$\Pi_m = \{\tau_{m,0}, \tau_{m,1}, \ldots\}$$

tends to the identity, then, in $\mathcal{D}_{ucp}$, for every $t \geq 0$

$$\lim_{m \to \infty} \left[x_0 y_0 + \sum_{j \geq 1} \left(x_{t \wedge \tau_{m,j}} - x_{t \wedge \tau_{m,j-1}} \right) \left(y_{t \wedge \tau_{m,j}} - y_{t \wedge \tau_{m,j-1}} \right) \right] = [x, y]_t$$

If x and y are semimartingales, then the optional covariation process $[x, y]$ has finite variation on compacts. Consequently, for a predictable process α, the integral $\int_0^t \alpha_s d[x, x]_s$ is a pathwise Stieltjes integral with the right intuitive interpretation.

Theorem 10.53 *If the sequence of random partitions*

$$\Pi_m = \{\tau_{m,0}, \tau_{m,1}, \ldots\}$$

tends to the identity, then, in $\mathcal{D}_{ucp}$, for every $t \geq 0$

$$\lim_{m \to \infty} \sum_{j \geq 1} \alpha_{\tau_{m,j-1}} \left(x_{t \wedge \tau_{m,j}} - x_{t \wedge \tau_{m,j-1}} \right) \left(y_{t \wedge \tau_{m,j}} - y_{t \wedge \tau_{m,j-1}} \right)$$

is equal to

$$\int_0^t \alpha_s d[x, y]_s$$

The last concept in this chapter is a special semimartingale. In general, a semimartingale is a sum of a local martingale and a process of infinite variation. We distinguish semimartingales that decompose into a local martingale and a process of locally integrable variation.

Definition 10.39 A stochastic process $x \in \mathcal{D}$ is a special semimartingale if and only if it has a decomposition $x = m + a$ where $m \in \mathcal{M}_{0,loc}$ and $a \in i\mathcal{V}_{loc}$.

Because $i\mathcal{V} \subset f\mathcal{V}$ and $f\mathcal{V}_{loc} = f\mathcal{V}$, it follows that $i\mathcal{V}_{loc} \subset f\mathcal{V}$ and, therefore, a special semimartingale is a semimartingale. We have the following alternative characterization of special semimartingales.

Theorem 10.54 *The following statements are equivalent:*

1. *The process x is a special semimartingale.*

2. *The process x has a decomposition $x = m + a$ such that $m \in \mathcal{M}_{0,loc}$ and $a \in \mathcal{P} \cap i\mathcal{V}_{loc}$, and this decomposition is unique.*

3. *In every decomposition $x = m + a$ such that $m \in \mathcal{M}_{0,loc}$ and $a \in f\mathcal{V}$, the process a is such that $a \in i\mathcal{V}_{loc}$.*

4. *The process $\sup\limits_{0 \le s \le t} |x_s|$ is locally integrable.*

5. *The process x is a difference of two local submartingales.*

The decomposition of a special martingale in item 2 is called the canonic decomposition. The equivalence between items 2 and 5 is an extension of the Doob-Meyer decomposition in Corollary 10.6. Indeed, if the process x is a difference of two local submartingales, say $x = x' - x''$, then Corollary 10.6 implies that there are processes $a', a'' \in \mathcal{P} \cap \mathcal{I}_{loc}$ such that $x' - a', x'' - a'' \in \mathcal{M}_{0,loc}$. Therefore, $x - (a' - a'') \in \mathcal{M}_{0,loc}$, where $a' - a'' \in i\mathcal{V}_{loc}$.

In the canonic decomposition of a special semimartingale, $x = m + a$, we call the local martingale, m, the innovation part of x, and the predictable process of locally integrable variation, a, the predictable part of x. We also extend the notation $\pi^* x$ to designate the predictable part of the special semimartingale x.

Problems

1. Denote by $\bigvee\limits_{0 \le s < t} \mathbf{F}_s$ the smallest σ-field that contains the union of σ-fields $\bigcup\limits_{0 \le s < t} \mathbf{F}_s$. Prove that if the stopping time τ is constant, $\tau = t$, then

$$\mathbf{F}_{\tau-} = \overline{\mathbf{F}}_{t-} = \bigvee_{0 \le s < t} \mathbf{F}_s$$

that is, $\mathbf{F}_{\tau-}$ is the σ-field generated by the σ-fields $\mathbf{F}_s$, $0 \le s < t$.

2. Prove that if $\{N_t\}$ is a Poisson process with parameter λ, then the process $\{(N_t - \lambda t)^2 - \lambda t\}$ is a martingale.

3. Is the Wiener process a uniformly integrable martingale on $[0, \infty)$?

4. Prove that the stopping time $\tau = \infty$ is both predictable and totally inaccessible.

5. Find the Doob-Meyer decomposition of a Poisson process N_t with parameter λ.

6. Find the Doob-Meyer decomposition of the process $\{N_t^2 + (\lambda t)^2\}$.

7. Let $J_t = \sum_{m \ge 1} a_m \chi_{\{t \ge \tau_m\}}$, where $\{\tau_m\}$ is a strictly increasing sequence of positive stopping times and each a_m is a finite random variable measurable on $\mathbf{F}_{\tau_m}$. Calculate the optional quadratic variation $[J_t, J_t]$.

8. Find the Doob-Meyer decomposition of the process $\{W_t^{2m}\}$, where $m \ge 1$.

9. Prove that if $x, y \in \mathcal{S}$, then $[x, y]$ is the unique process $a \in f\mathcal{V}$ such that $xy - a \in \mathcal{M}_{0,loc}$ and $\Delta a = \Delta x \Delta y$.

10. Prove that for the Wiener process $\{W_t\}$ and a Poisson process $\{N_t\}$ with parameter λ, the optional quadratic covariation $[N, W]_t = 0$ for all $t \ge 0$.

11. For the Wiener process $\{W_t\}$ and a Poisson process $\{N_t\}$ with parameter λ compute $[W + N, W + N]_t$.

12. For the Wiener process $\{W_t\}$ and a Poisson process $\{N_t\}$ with parameter λ compute the process $\langle W + N, W + N \rangle_t$.

13. Prove Theorem 10.43.

Notes

The general references to this chapter include [75], [69], [35], [63], [48], [20], [21], [64], [67], and [54]. The presentation here follows mostly [35], [48], [69], and [21].

Chapter 11

General Stochastic Calculus

11.1 Lebesgue-Stieltjes Integrals

The first concept in this chapter is an integral of a Borel measurable function with respect to a function that has finite variation on compacts. This is the standard Lebesgue-Stieltjes integral, first defined as a Lebesgue integral with respect to a measure generated by an increasing function, and then extended to integrators that have finite variation on compacts. We then extend this integral by localization to predictable, locally bounded, integrands. We begin with a theorem of Carathèodory on the extension of measures from a field to a σ-field.

Theorem 11.1 (Carathèodory) *Let Ω be a nonempty set, μ a measure on a field $\mathcal{F}$ of subsets of Ω, and suppose that μ satisfies the following condition: there is a sequence of sets $A_m \in \mathcal{F}$ such that $\Omega = \bigcup_{m \geq 1} A_m$ and $\mu(A_m) < \infty$ for all $m \geq 1$. Then the measure μ has a unique extension to a measure on the σ-field $\mathbf{F}$ generated by $\mathcal{F}$.*

Set $\Omega = (0, \infty)$ and let $\mathcal{F}$ be the set of finite unions of disjoint left-open and right-closed intervals $(a, b]$ with $a < b$. It is easy to verify that $\mathcal{F}$ is a field. Next, let $x : [0, \infty) \to \mathcal{R}$ be an increasing right continuous function and set

$$\mu_x((a, b]) = x(b) - x(a)$$

Then μ_x is a measure on the field $\mathcal{F}$ that satisfies

$$\mu_x(A_m) = x(m) - x(m-1) < \infty$$

for the sequence of intervals $A_m = (m-1, m]$. By Carathèodory's theorem, the measure μ_x has a unique extension to a measure on the Borel σ-field $\mathcal{B}\Big((0, \infty)\Big)$. These comments set the stage for the following definition of a Lebesgue-Stieltjes integral.

Definition 11.1 Suppose that x is an increasing right continuous function and α is a Borel measurable function. Then the Lebesgue integral

$$\int_{(0,t)} \alpha \, d\mu_x$$

is called the Lebesgue-Stieltjes integral of α with respect to x and is denoted $\int_0^t \alpha \, dx$.

We can extend the previous definition to integrators x that have finite variation on compacts. If x is a right continuous function of finite variation on the interval $[0, t]$, consider the increasing right continuous functions

$$x'(t) = \frac{1}{2} \left[\int_0^t |dx_s| - x(t) \right]$$

$$x''(t) = \frac{1}{2} \left[\int_0^t |dx_s| + x(t) \right]$$

Then $x = x'' - x'$, and for any Borel measurable, bounded, function α the integrals $\int_0^t \alpha \, dx'$ and $\int_0^t \alpha \, dx''$ are finite, and the natural definition is

$$\int_0^t \alpha \, dx = \int_0^t \alpha \, dx'' - \int_0^t \alpha \, dx'$$

It is easy to show that the right side of the preceding equation does not depend on the choice of functions x' and x'' such that $x = x'' - x'$. In particular, for a stochastic process $x \in \mathfrak{f}\mathcal{V}$ and a stochastic process α that is measurable and bounded, we define the stochastic integral $\alpha \bullet x$ as the pathwise Lebesgue-Stieltjes integral $\int_0^t \alpha_s(\omega) dx_s(\omega)$. To extend this definition further, consider the concept of a locally bounded process.

Definition 11.2 A process x is locally bounded if and only if there is a sequence $\{\tau_m\}$ of stopping times increasing to infinity and a sequence of positive real numbers $\{K_m\}$ such that $x_{\tau_m}^* \leq K_m$ for all $m \geq 1$.

The following theorem offers an example of predictable, locally bounded, processes.

Theorem 11.2 *We have:*

    1. *If $\alpha \in \mathcal{G}$, then α is predictable and locally bounded.*

    2. *If $\alpha \in \mathcal{D}$, then α_- is predictable and locally bounded.*

    3. *If $\alpha \in \mathcal{D} \cap \mathcal{P}$, then α is locally bounded.*

Proof. To prove item 1 define for $m \geq 1$

$$\tau_m = \inf\{t \mid |\alpha_t| \geq m\}$$

Items 2 and 3 follow from item 1. ∎

    We can extend the definition of the Lebesgue-Stieltjes integral to locally bounded integrands. Suppose that $x \in f\mathcal{V}$ and that α is predictable and locally bounded. Then, first, α is measurable, and second, there is a sequence $\{\tau_m\}$ of stopping times increasing to infinity, such that the process $\{\alpha_t \chi\{t \leq \tau_m\}\}$ is bounded for all $m \geq 1$. The integral $\int_0^t \alpha_s dx_s$ is then defined by localization

$$\int_0^{t \wedge \tau_m} \alpha_s dx_s = \int_0^t \alpha_s \chi\{s \leq \tau_m\} dx_s$$

The preceding definition does not depend on the choice of the localizing sequence $\{\tau_m\}$. Indeed, suppose that $\{\sigma_m\}$ is another localizing sequence. Then

$$\int_0^{t \wedge \sigma_m} \alpha_s \chi\{s \leq \tau_m\} dx_s = \int_0^{t \wedge \tau_m} \alpha_s \chi\{s \leq \sigma_m\} dx_s$$

    The Lebesgue-Stieltjes integral is associative with respect to the optional quadratic covariation process and preserves local martingales.

Theorem 11.3 *We have:*

    1. *If $x \in f\mathcal{V}$ and α is predictable and locally bounded, then for any $y \in \mathcal{S}$*

$$[\alpha \bullet x, y] = \alpha \bullet [x, y]$$

    2. *If $x \in \mathcal{M}_{0,loc} \cap f\mathcal{V}$ and α is predictable and locally bounded, then the integral $\alpha \bullet x \in \mathcal{M}_{0,loc} \cap f\mathcal{V}$.*

Proof. We prove item 1. From Theorem 10.44, if $x \in f\mathcal{V}$, then $x^c = 0$. Therefore, for any $y \in \mathcal{S}$

$$[x, y]_t = \sum_{0 \leq s \leq t} \Delta x_s \Delta y_s$$

If α is Borel measurable and bounded, $|\alpha| \leq K$, then for any s and t

$$|(\alpha \bullet x)_t - (\alpha \bullet x)_s| \leq K|x_t - x_s|$$

and consequently

$$\int_0^t |d(\alpha \bullet x)_s| \leq K \int_0^t |dx_s|$$

Therefore, $\alpha \bullet x \in f\mathcal{V}$. It follows that for every $y \in \mathcal{S}$

$$\begin{aligned}
[\alpha \bullet x, y]_t &= \sum_{0 \leq s \leq t} \Delta(\alpha \bullet x)_s \Delta y_s \\
&= \sum_{0 \leq s \leq t} \alpha_s \Delta x_s \Delta y_s \\
&= (\alpha \bullet [x, y])_t
\end{aligned}$$

The proof for locally bounded α follows by localization. ∎

The definition of the Itô integral in Chapter 8 suggests that the extension of the definition of a stochastic integral to integrators that do not have finite variation on compacts is not trivial. The next section describes this extension.

11.2 Stochastic Integrals

We introduce the concept of a stochastic integral in five stages. First, we consider the special case a stochastic integral with respect to a local martingale. This first stage is an extension of the Itô integral martingale in Chapter 8. Second, we expand the set of integrands but restrict the integrators to be continuous local martingales. Third, we consider the general case of integrals with respect to local martingales. Fourth, we define the integral of a locally bounded predictable process with respect to a semimartingale. Fifth, in integrals with respect to semimartingales, we expand the set of integrands from locally bounded predictable processes to a larger class of predictable processes. Initially, we consider the following sets of integrands.

Definition 11.3 Let $x \in \mathcal{M}_{loc}$ and $1 \le k < \infty$. Denote

$$\Lambda^k(x) = \left\{ \alpha \in \mathcal{P} \mid \left\| (\alpha^2 \bullet [x,x])_\infty^{\frac{1}{2}} \right\|_k < \infty \right\}$$

For any local martingale x, if $k'' > k' \ge 1$, then $\Lambda^{k''}(x) \subset \Lambda^{k'}(x)$. Also, notice that the definition of the spaces $\Lambda^k(x)$ depends on the probability measure P. When the context involves both the probability measure P and another probability measure Q, and if the process $\{x_t\}$ is also a Q-local martingale on the filtration $\{\mathbf{F}_t^Q\}$, we use the notation $\Lambda^{k,P}(x)$ and $\Lambda^{k,Q}(x)$ to distinguish between the two spaces.

In the next subsection we use the second inequality in the following theorem, called the inequality of Kunita and Watanabe.

Theorem 11.4 *Suppose that* $x, y \in \mathcal{H}^2$, $\alpha \in \Lambda^2(x)$, *and* $\beta \in \Lambda^2(y)$. *Then for all* $t \ge 0$:

1. $[(\alpha\beta) \bullet [x,y]]_t^2 \le (\alpha^2 \bullet [x,x])_t \, (\beta^2 \bullet [y,y])_t$.

2. $E_P \{[(\alpha\beta) \bullet [x,y]]_t\} \le \left\{ E_P \left[(\alpha^2 \bullet [x,x])_t \right] \right\}^{\frac{1}{2}} \left\{ E_P \left[(\beta^2 \bullet [y,y])_t \right] \right\}^{\frac{1}{2}}$.

Finally, the following general version of Theorem 2.9 is used to establish the existence of the stochastic integral in this subsection.

Theorem 11.5 (F. Riesz) *If* X *is a Hilbert space and* f *is a continuous linear functional on* X, *then there is a unique element* $z \in X$ *such that for every* $y \in X$ *we have the representation* $f(y) = (y, z)$.

Integrals with Respect to Local Martingales: A Special Case

In this subsection we assume that $x \in \mathcal{M}_{loc}$ and define the stochastic integral for $\alpha \in \Lambda^2(x)$. By definition, if $\alpha \in \Lambda^2(x)$, then

$$E_P \left[(\alpha^2 \bullet [x,x])_\infty \right] < \infty$$

Consider the linear functional $f : \mathcal{H}^2 \to \mathcal{R}$ such that for every $y \in \mathcal{H}^2$

$$f(y) = E_P \left[(\alpha \bullet [x,y])_\infty \right]$$

From Burkholder's inequality $E_P ([x,x]_\infty) < \infty$, and from the inequality of Kunita and Watanabe

$$E_P [(\alpha \bullet [x,y])_\infty] \le \left\{ E_P \left[(\alpha^2 \bullet [x,x])_\infty \right] \right\}^{\frac{1}{2}} [E_P ([y,y]_\infty)]^{\frac{1}{2}}$$

It follows that f is bounded and, therefore, continuous, and from the Riesz representation theorem, Theorem 11.5, there is a unique element $z \in \mathcal{H}^2$ such that

$$E_P\left(y_\infty z_\infty\right) = E_P\left[(\alpha \bullet [x, y])_\infty\right]$$

This property of the square integrable martingale z has a counterpart in the theory if Itô integrals in Chapter 8 with $z_t = \int_0^t \alpha_s dW_s$. First, choose $x = W$, the Wiener process. From the representation theorem of Kunita and Watanabe, Theorem 8.6, every square integrable martingale y on the Wiener filtration is of the form $y_t = \int_0^t \eta_s dW_s$ with $E_P\left(\int_0^\infty \eta_t^2 dt\right) < \infty$.

Second, the following property of the Itô integral follows immediately from Theorem 8.4. For any adapted, measurable, processes $\{\alpha_t\}$ and $\{\eta_t\}$ if

$$E_P\left(\int_0^\infty \alpha_t^2 dt\right) < \infty \quad \text{and} \quad E_P\left(\int_0^\infty \eta_t^2 dt\right) < \infty$$

then

$$E_P\left(\int_0^\infty \alpha_t dW_t \int_0^\infty \eta_t dW_t\right) = E_P\left(\int_0^\infty \alpha_t \eta_t dt\right)$$

Thus we have the following extension of the Itô integral.

Definition 11.4 Suppose that $x \in \mathcal{M}_{loc}$ and $\alpha \in \Lambda^2(x)$. The stochastic integral $\alpha \bullet x$ is the unique element of $\mathcal{H}^2$ such that

$$E_P\left[(\alpha \bullet x)_\infty y_\infty\right] = E_P\left[(\alpha \bullet [x, y])_\infty\right]$$

for all $y \in \mathcal{H}^2$.

Theorem 11.6 *Suppose that $x \in \mathcal{M}_{loc}$ and $\alpha \in \Lambda^2(x)$. Then:*

1. *The integral $\alpha \bullet x$ is a continuous square integrable martingale.*

2. *The integral $\alpha \bullet x$ is the unique square integrable martingale such that*

$$[\alpha \bullet x, y] = \alpha \bullet [x, y]$$

   for every square integrable martingale y.

3. *For every stopping time τ*

$$(\alpha \bullet x)_{t \wedge \tau} = \int_0^t \alpha_s dx_{s \wedge \tau} = \int_0^t \alpha_s \chi\{s \leq \tau\} dx_s$$

Integrals with Respect to Continuous Local Martingales

First, define the set $\Lambda_{loc}^k(x)$ by using the concept of localization for integrands, that is, α is in $\Lambda_{loc}^k(x)$ if and only if the killed process satisfies

$$\left\{\alpha_t \chi_{\{t \le \tau_m\}}\right\} \in \Lambda^k(x)$$

Second, in this subsection assume that $x \in c\mathcal{M}_{loc}$. With this restriction of integrators, item 3 in Theorem 11.6 is the basis for an extension of the stochastic integral to integrands $\alpha \in \Lambda_{loc}^1(x)$. First, because x is a continuous local martingale, $\Lambda_{loc}^k(x) = \Lambda_{loc}^1(x)$ for all $1 < k < \infty$. Therefore, if $\alpha \in \Lambda_{loc}^1(x)$, then $\alpha \in \Lambda_{loc}^2(x)$. Let $\{\tau_m\}$ be a sequence of stopping times, increasing to infinity, such that $\alpha_t \chi_{\{t \le \tau_m\}} \in \Lambda^2(x)$. Then the integral $\int_0^t \alpha_s \chi_{\{s \le \tau_m\}} dx_s$ is described in Definition 11.4 and the formula

$$(\alpha \bullet x)_{t \wedge \tau_m} = \int_0^t \alpha_s \chi_{\{s \le \tau_m\}} dx_s$$

defines a local martingale $\alpha \bullet x \in \mathcal{H}_{loc}^2$. This definition does not depend on the localizing sequence $\{\tau_m\}$.

Definition 11.5 Suppose that $x \in c\mathcal{M}_{loc}$ and $\alpha \in \Lambda_{loc}^1(x)$. The stochastic integral $\alpha \bullet x \subset \mathcal{H}_{loc}^2$ is defined by the formula

$$(\alpha \bullet x)_{t \wedge \tau_m} = \int_0^t \alpha_s \chi_{\{s \le \tau_m\}} dx_s$$

We have a characterization analogous to Theorem 11.6.

Theorem 11.7 Suppose that $x \in c\mathcal{M}_{loc}$ and $\alpha \in \Lambda_{loc}^1(x)$. Then:

1. The integral $\alpha \bullet x$ is a continuous process and $\alpha \bullet x \in \mathcal{H}_{loc}^2$.

2. The integral $\alpha \bullet x$ is the unique process in $\mathcal{H}_{loc}^2$ such that

$$[\alpha \bullet x, y] = \alpha \bullet [x, y]$$

for every $y \in \mathcal{H}_{loc}^2$.

3. For every stopping time τ

$$(\alpha \bullet x)_{t \wedge \tau} = \int_0^t \alpha_s dx_{s \wedge \tau} = \int_0^t \alpha_s \chi_{\{s \le \tau\}} dx_s$$

Integrals with Respect to Local Martingales: The General Case

The extension of stochastic integration from integrals with respect to continuous local martingales to integrals with respect to local martingales is accomplished through the following theorem.

Theorem 11.8 *Suppose that $x \in \mathcal{M}_{loc}$ and $\alpha \in \Lambda^1_{loc}(x)$. Then there is a unique $y \in \mathcal{M}_{loc}$ such that:*

  1. *The continuous part of y is the integral of α with respect to the continuous part of x, that is, $y^c_t = (\alpha \bullet x^c)_t$ for all $t \geq 0$.*

  2. *For all $t \geq 0$ the jumps of y are $\Delta y_t = \alpha_t \Delta x_t$.*

Definition 11.6 In the notation of Theorem 11.8

$$\alpha \bullet x = y$$

The preceding definition indicates that this stochastic integral preserves local martingales. The following associativity of the integral in this subsection with respect to optional quadratic covariation processes parallels item 2 in Theorem 11.6.

Theorem 11.9 *Suppose that $x \in \mathcal{M}_{loc}$ and $\alpha \in \Lambda^1_{loc}(x)$. Then the integral $\alpha \bullet x$ is the unique local martingale such that*

$$[\alpha \bullet x, y]_t = (\alpha \bullet [x, y])_t$$

for every local martingale y and every $t \geq 0$.

The next theorem establishes the k-maximal properties of the stochastic integral.

Theorem 11.10 *Let $x \in \mathcal{M}_{loc}$ and $\alpha \in \Lambda^1(x)$. Then:*

  1. *The integral satisfies $\alpha \bullet x \in \mathcal{H}^k$ if and only if the integrand satisfies $\alpha \in \Lambda^k(x)$.*

  2. *The integral satisfies $\alpha \bullet x \in \mathcal{H}^k_{loc}$ if and only if the integrand satisfies $\alpha \in \Lambda^k_{loc}(x)$.*

The preceding theorem has the corollary that the set $\Lambda^1_{loc}(x)$ is the largest set of predictable integrands for which the stochastic integral is a local martingale.

Corollary 11.1 *Suppose that $x \in \mathcal{M}_{loc}$. Then*

$$\alpha \bullet x \in \mathcal{M}_{loc} \Leftrightarrow \alpha \in \Lambda^1_{loc}(x)$$

Proof. Follows immediately from the preceding theorem and the fact that $\mathcal{H}^1_{loc} = \mathcal{M}_{loc}$. ∎

The last theorem in this subsection establishes the dominated convergence of stochastic integrals.

Theorem 11.11 *Suppose that $x \in \mathcal{M}_{loc}$, $1 \leq k < \infty$, and $\{\alpha_m\}$ is a sequence of predictable processes converging to a limit α. If there exists a process $\beta \in \Lambda^k(x)$ such that $|\alpha_m| \leq \beta$ for all $m \geq 1$, then $\alpha_m \in \Lambda^k(x)$ for all $m \geq 1$, the limit satisfies $\alpha \in \Lambda^k(x)$, and in the topology of $\mathcal{H}^k$*

$$\lim_{m \to \infty} \alpha_m \bullet x = \alpha \bullet x$$

Integrals with Respect to Semimartingales

Stochastic integrals with respect to semimartingales are defined in two stages. First, we use the definition of an integral with respect to a local martingale to define an integral of a locally bounded predictable process with respect to a semimartingale. Second, we extend the latter integral to a larger set of predictable integrands. Suppose that $x \in \mathcal{S}$. Then there are processes $m \in \mathcal{M}_{0,loc}$ and $a \in f\mathcal{V}$ such that $x = m + a$. If α is locally bounded, then $\alpha \in \Lambda^1_{loc}(m)$ and the integral $\alpha \bullet m$ is defined. Furthermore, the Lebesgue-Stieltjes integral $\alpha \bullet a$ is also defined. If the semimartingale x has two decompositions

$$x = m' + a' = m'' + a''$$

such that $m', m'' \in \mathcal{M}_{0,loc}$ and $a', a'' \in f\mathcal{V}$, then $m'' - m' = a' - a'' \in f\mathcal{V}$. Therefore, we get the equality of the Lebesgue-Stieltjes integrals

$$\alpha \bullet (m'' - m') = \alpha \bullet (a' - a'')$$

and consequently, the equality of the integrals

$$\alpha \bullet m' + \alpha \bullet a' = \alpha \bullet m'' + \alpha \bullet a''$$

The preceding discussion justifies the following definition of the integral $\alpha \bullet x$.

Definition 11.7 Suppose that $x \in \mathcal{S}$ has the decomposition $x = m + a$ where $m \in \mathcal{M}_{0,loc}$ and $a \in f\mathcal{V}$, and let α be a predictable, locally bounded, process. Then

$$\alpha \bullet x = \alpha \bullet m + \alpha \bullet a$$

Theorem 11.2 establishes the associativity of this stochastic integral with respect to quadratic covariation processes.

Theorem 11.12 *Suppose that x and y are semimartingales and α is a predictable, locally bounded, process. Then:*

1. *We have*

$$[\alpha \bullet x, y] = \alpha \bullet [x, y]$$

2. *If, in addition, x and y are such that $[x, y] \in iV_{loc}$, then the integral $\alpha \bullet [x, y] \in iV_{loc}$ and*

$$\langle \alpha \bullet x, y \rangle = \alpha \bullet \langle x, y \rangle$$

Proof. First, we prove that

$$[\alpha \bullet x, y] = \alpha \bullet [x, y]$$

Let $x = m + a$ and $y = n + b$ be such that m and n are local martingales and a and b have finite variation on compacts. Then, from Theorems 11.9 and 11.3 and the formula

$$[\alpha \bullet m, b]_t = \sum_{0 \leq s \leq t} \alpha_s \Delta m_s \Delta b_s = (\alpha \bullet [m, b])_t$$

we get

$$
\begin{aligned}
[\alpha \bullet x, y] &= [\alpha \bullet m, n] + [\alpha \bullet m, b] + [\alpha \bullet a, n] + [\alpha \bullet a, b] \\
&= \alpha \bullet [m, n] + \alpha \bullet [m, b] + \alpha \bullet [a, n] + \alpha \bullet [a, b] \\
&= \alpha \bullet [x, y]
\end{aligned}
$$

Second

$$[x, y] - \langle x, y \rangle \in \mathcal{M}_{0,loc}$$

and

$$\alpha \bullet ([x, y] - \langle x, y \rangle) \in \mathcal{M}_{0,loc}$$

Therefore

$$\alpha \bullet [x, y] - \alpha \bullet \langle x, y \rangle \in \mathcal{M}_{0,loc}$$

and

$$[\alpha \bullet x, y] - \alpha \bullet \langle x, y \rangle \in \mathcal{M}_{0,loc}$$

Consequently

$$\langle \alpha \bullet x, y \rangle - \pi^*([\alpha \bullet x, y]) = \alpha \bullet \langle x, y \rangle$$

which proves the theorem. ∎

For $x \in \mathcal{S}$ we now describe the largest set of integrands $\alpha \in \Lambda(x)$ for which the stochastic integral $\alpha \bullet x$ can be defined.

Definition 11.8 Suppose that $x \in \mathcal{S}$. Then $\alpha \in \Lambda(x)$ if and only if $\alpha \in \mathcal{P}$ and there is a decomposition $x = m + a$ such that:

1. The first component satisfies $m \in \mathcal{M}_{0,loc}$.

2. The second component satisfies $a \in f\mathcal{V}$.

3. The predictable process satisfies $\alpha \in \Lambda^1_{loc}(m)$.

4. The Lebesgue-Stieltjes integral satisfies $\alpha \bullet a \in f\mathcal{V}$.

By the definition of the semimartingale x, there always exists a decomposition of x that satisfies items 1 and 2. The preceding definition restricts the elements of $\Lambda(x)$ to those predictable processes for which there is a decomposition of x that also satisfies items 3 and 4. Moreover, the definition of the space $\Lambda(x)$ depends on the probability measure P. When the context involves both the probability measure P and another probability measure Q, we use the notation $\Lambda^P(x)$ and $\Lambda^Q(x)$ to distinguish the two spaces.

Theorem 11.13 *If $x \in \mathcal{S}$ and $x = m' + a' = m'' + a''$ are two decompositions of x that satisfy conditions 1 to 4 in Definition 11.8, then*

$$\alpha \bullet m' + \alpha \bullet a' = \alpha \bullet m'' + \alpha \bullet a''$$

Therefore, we have the following definition.

Definition 11.9 Suppose that $x \in \mathcal{S}$ and $\alpha \in \Lambda(x)$. Let $x = m + a$ be a decomposition of x that satisfies conditions 1 to 4 in Definition 11.8. Then we define the stochastic integral $\alpha \bullet x$ with the formula

$$\alpha \bullet x = \alpha \bullet m + \alpha \bullet a$$

Theorem 11.14 *If $x \in \mathcal{S}$ and $\alpha \in \Lambda(x)$, then*

1. $(\alpha \bullet x)^c = \alpha \bullet x^c$.

2. $\Delta(\alpha \bullet x) = \alpha \bullet \Delta x$.

The stochastic integral is associative with respect to optional quadratic processes.

Theorem 11.15 *If $x \in \mathcal{S}$, $\alpha \in \Lambda(x)$, and $y \in \mathcal{S}$, then $[\alpha \bullet x, y] = \alpha \bullet [x, y]$.*

The next theorem states that Definition 11.9 of the stochastic integral generalizes Definitions 11.6 and 11.7. To formulate this theorem we need a strong concept of identity of two stochastic processes. Definition 10.5 of a modification, or a version, of a stochastic process describes one concept of identity of stochastic processes. A stronger definition of identity of two processes is as follows.

Definition 11.10 The stochastic process y is called indistinguishable from the stochastic process x if and only if

$$P\{y_t = x_t \text{ for all } t \geq 0\} = 1$$

Notice that when the process $\{y_t\}$ is a modification of the process $\{x_t\}$, then the set of probability zero outside which $x_t = y_t$ depends on time t, whereas when $\{y_t\}$ is indistinguishable from $\{x_t\}$, then there is only one set of probability zero outside which $y_t = x_t$ for all $t > 0$. The next theorem compares the several definitions of a stochastic integral in this chapter.

Theorem 11.16 *The stochastic integral has the following properties:*

1. *If $x \in \mathcal{S}$ and α is a locally bounded, predictable process, then $\alpha \in \Lambda(x)$ and the stochastic integrals in Definitions 11.7 and 11.9 are indistinguishable.*

2. *If $x \in \mathcal{M}_{loc}$, then $\Lambda^1_{loc}(x) \subset \Lambda(x)$ and the stochastic integrals in Definitions 11.6 and 11.9 are indistinguishable.*

3. *If $x \in f\mathcal{V}$ and α is a predictable process such that the Lebesgue-Stieltjes integral satisfies $\displaystyle\int_0^t \alpha_s dx_s \in f\mathcal{V}$, then $\alpha \in \Lambda(x)$ and the Lebesgue-Stieltjes integral is indistinguishable from the stochastic integral $\alpha \bullet x$ in Definition 11.9.*

The next theorem establishes the associativity of stochastic integrals.

Theorem 11.17 *If $x \in \mathcal{S}$, $\beta \in \Lambda(x)$, and $\alpha \in \Lambda(\beta \bullet x)$, then $\alpha\beta \in \Lambda(x)$ and*

$$\alpha \bullet (\beta \bullet x) = (\alpha\beta) \bullet x$$

Theorem 11.18 establishes the dominated convergence of stochastic integrals.

Theorem 11.18 *Suppose that $x \in S$ and $\{\alpha_m\}$ is a sequence of predictable processes converging to a limit α. If there exists a process $\beta \in \Lambda(x)$ such that $|\alpha_m| \leq \beta$ for all $m \geq 1$, then $\alpha_m \in \Lambda(x)$ for all $m > 1$, the limit satisfies $\alpha \in \Lambda(x)$, and in the topology of uniform convergence on compacts in probability*

$$\lim_{m \to \infty} \alpha_m \bullet x = \alpha \bullet x$$

Corollary 11.2 provides an intuitive characterization of the stochastic integral.

Corollary 11.2 *Let $x \in S$ and $\alpha \in \Lambda(x)$. If the sequence of random partitions*

$$\Pi_m = \{\tau_{m,0}, \tau_{m,1}, \ldots\}$$

tends to the identity, then, in the topology of uniform convergence on compacts in probability, for every $t \geq 0$

$$\lim_{m \to \infty} \sum_{j \geq 1} \alpha_{\tau_{m,j-1}} \left(x_{t \wedge \tau_{m,j}} - x_{t \wedge \tau_{m,j-1}} \right) = \int_0^t \alpha_s dx_s$$

A simple example of a stochastic integral is an integral with respect to the Poisson process $\{N_t\}$. In fact, the integral $\int_0^t \alpha_s dN_s$ is a Lebesgue-Stieltjes integral.

Example 11.1 Suppose that $\{N_t\}$ is a Poisson process with parameter λ and let $\alpha \in \Lambda(N)$. Because the Poisson process $\{N_t\}$ is increasing, it has finite variation on compacts, and by Theorem 11.16 the integral $\int_0^t \alpha_s dN_s$ is a Lebesgue-Stieltjes integral calculated path by path. Because the Poisson process has at most a finite number of discontinuities in a finite interval $[0, t]$, the integral in question is the sum

$$\int_0^t \alpha_s dN_s = \sum_{0 \leq s \leq t} \alpha_s \Delta N_s$$

As a special case of this integral choose $\alpha_t = N_{t-}$. At any jump time s, the value of the integrand $\{N_{s-}\}$ is $N_{s-} = N_s - 1$. Therefore

$$\int_0^t N_{s-}dN_s = \sum_{0 \le s \le t} (N_s - 1)\Delta N_s$$

$$= 1 + 2 + \ldots + (N_t - 1)$$

$$= \frac{1}{2}(N_t - 1)N_t$$

Another example of a stochastic integral is analogous to Theorem 5.8 in discrete stochastic calculus. Suppose that $x \in \mathcal{S}$, then $x_- \in \mathcal{G}$ so that $x_- \in \Lambda(x)$ and we have

$$\int_0^t x_{s-}dx_s = \frac{1}{2}(x_t^2 - [x,x]_t)$$

The previous integral is a special case of the formula for integration by parts. A more complicated example of stochastic integration is given in Section 11.4.

Theorem 11.19 *Let $x, y \in \mathcal{S}$. Then*

$$\int_0^t x_{s-}dy_s = x_t y_t - \int_0^t y_{s-}dx_s - [x,y]_t$$

11.3   Itô's Formula

This section deals with Itô's formula for the change of variables in a stochastic integral. The reader should compare the first part of this formula with Theorem 8.10 and the second part of this formula with Theorem 5.10.

Theorem 11.20 *Let $x \in \mathcal{S}$ and let $f : \mathcal{R} \to \mathcal{R}$ be twice continuously differentiable. Then $\{f(x_t)\} \in \mathcal{S}$ and*

$$f(x_t) = f(x_0) + \int_0^t f'(x_{s-})dx_s + \frac{1}{2}\int_0^t f''(x_{s-})d\langle x^c, x^c \rangle_s$$

$$+ \sum_{0 \le s \le t} [f(x_s) - f(x_{s-}) - f'(x_{s-})\Delta x_s]$$

The next theorem describes the multidimensional version of Itô's formula.

Theorem 11.21 *Let $x_1, \ldots, x_m \in \mathcal{S}$, $x = (x_1, \ldots, x_m)$, and let $f : [0, \infty) \times \mathcal{R}^m \to \mathcal{R}$ be continuously differentiable in the first argument and twice*

continuously differentiable in the remaining arguments. Then $\{f(t, x_t)\} \in \mathcal{S}$
and

$$f(t, x_t) = f(0, x_0) + \int_0^t \frac{\partial f}{\partial s}(s, x_{s-})ds + \sum_{j=1}^m \int_0^t \frac{\partial f}{\partial x_j}(s, x_{s-})dx_{js}$$

$$+ \frac{1}{2}\sum_{k=1}^m \sum_{j=1}^m \int_0^t \frac{\partial^2 f}{\partial x_j \partial x_k}(s, x_{s-})\, d\langle x_j^c, x_k^c\rangle_s$$

$$+ \sum_{0 \le s \le t} \left[f(s, x_s) - f(s, x_{s-}) - \sum_{j=1}^m \frac{\partial f}{\partial x_j}(s, x_{s-})\Delta x_{js} \right]$$

The next subsection describes an application of Itô's formula to the solution of a certain stochastic differential equation.

11.4   Stochastic Exponentials

Paralleling the definition of stochastic exponentials in discrete stochastic calculus and Itô calculus, the stochastic exponential of a semimartingale is defined as the unique solution of the stochastic differential equation

$$dx_t = x_{t-}dw_t$$

Theorem 11.22 *Let $w \in \mathcal{S}$. Then the semimartingale*

$$x_t = \exp\left(w_t - \frac{1}{2}[w, w]_t\right) \prod_{0 \le s \le t} (1 + \Delta w_s) \exp\left[-\Delta w_s + \frac{1}{2}(\Delta w_s)^2\right]$$

is the unique solution of the equation

$$x_t = 1 + \int_0^t x_{s-}dw_s$$

Proof. First, notice that the formula for x is equivalent to

$$x_t = \exp\left(w_t - \frac{1}{2}\langle w^c, w^c\rangle_t\right) \prod_{0 \le s \le t} (1 + \Delta w_s) \exp\left(-\Delta w_s\right)$$

It is easy to see that

$$\exp\left(w_t - \frac{1}{2}\langle w^c, w^c\rangle_t\right)$$

is a semimartingale, and that

$$\prod_{0 \leq s \leq t} (1 + \Delta w_s) \exp(-\Delta w_s)$$

is regular right continuous and has finite variation on compacts. We have to show that $\{x_t\}$ is a solution. Denote

$$
\begin{aligned}
u_t &= \left(w_t - \frac{1}{2} \langle w^c, w^c \rangle_t \right) \\
&= \prod_{0 \leq s \leq t} (1 + \Delta w_s) \exp(-\Delta w_s)
\end{aligned}
$$

and let $f(u_t, v_t) = e^{u_t} v_t$. From Itô's formula

$$
\begin{aligned}
x_t &= 1 + \int_0^t x_{s-} du_s + \int_0^t e^{u_{s-}} dv_s + \frac{1}{2} \int_0^t x_{s-} d\langle w^c, w^c \rangle_s \\
&\quad + \sum_{0 \leq s \leq t} (x_s - x_{s-} - x_{s-} \Delta u_s - e^{u_{s-}} \Delta v_s) \\
&= 1 + \int_0^t x_{s-} dw_s + \int_0^t e^{u_{s-}} dv_s \\
&\quad + \sum_{0 \leq s \leq t} (x_s - x_{s-} - x_{s-} \Delta u_s - e^{u_{s-}} \Delta v_s) \tag{11.1}
\end{aligned}
$$

Because $\{v_t\}$ is a pure jump process, we have

$$\int_0^t e^{u_{s-}} dv_s = \sum_{0 \leq s \leq t} e^{u_{s-}} \Delta v_s \tag{11.2}$$

In addition

$$x_s = x_{s-}(1 + \Delta w_s) \text{ and } x_{s-} \Delta u_s = x_{s-} \Delta w_s \tag{11.3}$$

The substitution of Equations 11.2 and 11.3 into the right side of Equation 11.1 yields

$$x_t = 1 + \int_0^t x_{s-} dw_s$$

This completes the proof. ∎

By analogy with discrete and Itô calculus we have the following definition.

Definition 11.11 Let $\{w_t\}$ be a semimartingale. The unique semimartingale $\{x_t\}$ such that

$$x_t = 1 + \int_0^t x_{s-} dw_s$$

is called the stochastic exponential of the semimartingale $\{w_t\}$ and is denoted

$$x_t = \mathcal{E}_t(w)$$

Example 11.2 Consider the following examples:

1. For a continuous semimartingale, null at zero, w, we have

$$\mathcal{E}_t(w) = \exp\left(w_t - \frac{1}{2}[w,w]_t\right)$$

   In particular, for the Wiener process $\{W_t\}$

$$\mathcal{E}_t(W) = \exp\left(W_t - \frac{1}{2}t\right)$$

2. For the Poisson process $\{N_t\}$ notice that

$$N_t = \sum_{0 \leq s \leq t} \Delta N_s$$

   and, therefore

$$\mathcal{E}_t(N) = 2^{N_t}$$

Theorem 11.23 *Suppose that $w \in \mathcal{S}$. Then:*

1. *If w is a special semimartingale, then $\mathcal{E}(w)$ is a special semimartingale.*

2. *If $w \in \mathcal{M}_{loc}$, then $\mathcal{E}(w) \in \mathcal{M}_{loc}$.*

3. *If $w \in \mathfrak{f}\mathcal{V}$, then $\mathcal{E}(w) \in \mathfrak{f}\mathcal{V}$.*

4. *If $w \in \mathcal{P} \cap \mathfrak{f}\mathcal{V}$, then $\mathcal{E}(w) \in \mathcal{P} \cap \mathfrak{f}\mathcal{V}$.*

This section ends with a multiplication formula for stochastic exponentials.

Theorem 11.24 *Let $x, y \in \mathcal{S}$. Then*

$$\mathcal{E}_t(x)\mathcal{E}_t(y) = \mathcal{E}_t\left(x + y + [x,y]\right)$$

11.5   Stable Spaces of Martingales

This section deals with linear subspaces of the space $\mathcal{H}^k$ that are generated by stochastic integrals.

Definition 11.12 Let $1 \leq k < \infty$. A closed linear subspace H of $\mathcal{H}^k$ is called stable if and only if for every $x \in H$ and $\alpha \in \Lambda^k(x)$ we have $\alpha \bullet x \in H$.

Definition 11.13 Let $1 \leq k < \infty$ and $M \subset \mathcal{M}_{loc}$. The stable subspace of $\mathcal{H}^k$ generated by M is the smallest stable subspace H of $\mathcal{H}^k$ such that if $x \in M$ and $\alpha \in \Lambda^k(x)$, then $\alpha \bullet x \in H$. The stable subspace of $\mathcal{H}^k$ generated by M is denoted $\mathcal{Z}^k(M)$.

When Q is a probability measure on $\{\Omega, \mathbf{F}\}$, we denote by $\mathcal{Z}^{k,Q}(M)$ the stable subspace of $\mathcal{H}^{k,Q}$ generated by M. When the context involves both the probability measure P and another probability measure Q, we use the notation $\mathcal{Z}^{k,P}(M)$ and $\mathcal{Z}^{k,Q}(M)$ to distinguish between the two spaces.

The stable subspace of $\mathcal{H}^k$ generated by a single local martingale x is a set of stochastic integrals with integrator x.

Theorem 11.25 *If* $x_1, \ldots, x_m \in \mathcal{M}_{loc}$, *then*

$$\mathcal{Z}^k(x_1, \ldots, x_m) = \left\{ \sum_{h=1}^{m} \alpha_h \bullet x_h \;\middle|\; \alpha_h \in \Lambda^k(x_h) \text{ for } 1 \leq h \leq m \right\}$$

The stable subspace of $\mathcal{H}^k$ generated by a set M of local martingales can be described as follows.

Theorem 11.26 *If* $M \subset \mathcal{M}_{loc}$, *then* $\mathcal{Z}^k(M)$ *is the smallest closed linear subspace of* $\mathcal{H}^k$ *that contains the union* $\bigcup_{x \in M} \mathcal{Z}^k(x)$.

The following theorem describes a condition for a set M of local martingales to generate the space $\mathcal{H}^k$ in the sense that $\mathcal{Z}^k(M) = \mathcal{H}^k$.

Theorem 11.27 *Suppose that* $M \subset \mathcal{M}_{loc}$, $1 \leq k < \infty$, *and* $1 < l \leq \infty$ *such that* $\dfrac{1}{k} + \dfrac{1}{l} = 1$. *Then:*

1. *If* $\mathcal{Z}^k(M) = \mathcal{H}^k$, *then every* $y \in \mathcal{H}^l$ *orthogonal to* M *is null.*

2. *If* $M \subset \mathcal{H}^k_{loc}$, *then* $\mathcal{Z}^k(M) = \mathcal{H}^k$ *if and only if every* $y \in \mathcal{H}^l$ *orthogonal to* M *is null.*

We end this section with the definition of a basis in a stable space of martingales. Notice that the elements of a basis are local martingales, and that they need not be pairwise orthogonal.

Definition 11.14 Let $1 \leq k < \infty$ and suppose that H is a stable subspace of $\mathcal{H}^k$. Then:

1. A subset M of H_{loc} such that $\mathcal{Z}^k(M) = H$ is called a k-generator of H.

2. Suppose that M is a k-generator of H such that there is no other k-generator of H that has less elements than M. Then the number of elements in M is called the k-dimension of H.

3. A k-generator of H whose number of elements equals the k-dimension of H is called a k-basis of H.

Square Integrable Martingales

When $x \in \mathcal{H}^2_{loc}$, the spaces $\Lambda^2(x)$ and $\Lambda^2_{loc}(x)$ can be defined in terms of the predictable rather than the optional quadratic variation process of x. Indeed, $[x, x] \in i\mathcal{V}_{loc}$ and $\langle x, x \rangle = \pi^*[x, x]$ exists. Furthermore, for any predictable process α, Theorem 10.41 implies that

$$E_P \left(\int_0^\infty \alpha_s^2 d[x, x]_s \right) = E_P \left(\int_0^\infty \alpha_s^2 d\langle x, x \rangle_s \right)$$

Thus, we have that $\alpha^2 \bullet [x, x] \in \mathcal{I}$ if and only if $\alpha^2 \bullet \langle x, x \rangle \in \mathcal{I}$. Therefore, for $x \in \mathcal{H}^2_{loc}$

$$\Lambda^2(x) = \left\{ \alpha \in \mathcal{P} \mid \alpha^2 \bullet \langle x, x \rangle \in \mathcal{I} \right\}$$

and

$$\Lambda^2_{loc}(x) = \left\{ \alpha \in \mathcal{P} \mid \alpha^2 \bullet \langle x, x \rangle \in \mathcal{I}_{loc} \right\}$$

In addition, the integral $\alpha \bullet x$ is the unique process in $\mathcal{H}^2_{loc}$ such that for every $y \in \mathcal{H}^2_{loc}$

$$\langle \alpha \bullet x, y \rangle = \alpha \bullet \langle x, y \rangle$$

The following theorem offers a characterization of stable subspaces of $\mathcal{H}^2$.

Theorem 11.28 *Let H be a closed linear subspace of $\mathcal{H}^2$. Then H is stable if and only if each $x \in \mathcal{H}^2$ that is weakly orthogonal to H is orthogonal to H.*

The next theorem establishes a result similar to the projection theorem in Hilbert spaces.

Theorem 11.29 *Let $x, y \in \mathcal{H}^2$. Then there exist processes $\alpha \in \Lambda^2(x)$ and $z \in \mathcal{H}^2$ such that $z \perp x$ and*

$$y = \alpha \bullet x + z$$

The process α is the derivative of the predictable quadratic covariation process $\langle x, y \rangle$ with respect to the predictable quadratic variation process $\langle x, x \rangle$, that is, the unique process $\alpha \in \Lambda^2(x)$ that satisfies

$$\langle x, y \rangle = \alpha \bullet \langle x, x \rangle$$

The following theorem is a simple application of the Gram-Schmidt orthogonalization procedure.

Theorem 11.30 *Suppose that M is a finite or countable subset of $\mathcal{H}^2_{loc}$. Then the stable space $\mathcal{Z}^2(M)$ has a two-generator of pairwise orthogonal square integrable martingales.*

If information is generated by a countable set of events, then $\mathcal{H}^2$ has a countable two-generator of pairwise orthogonal square integrable martingales.

Definition 11.15 A σ-field is called separable if and only if it is generated by a countable family of subsets of Ω.

Theorem 11.31 *Suppose that the σ-field $\mathbf{F}_\infty$ is separable. Then there is a sequence $\{x_m\}$ of pairwise orthogonal square integrable martingales such that $\mathcal{Z}^2(x_1, x_2, \ldots) = \mathcal{H}^2$.*

11.6   Girsanov's Theorem

This section delivers suitably modified concepts and results concerning the likelihood ratio process and Girsanov's theorem. The elementary results in discrete stochastic calculus appear in Section 5.4.

Suppose that P and Q are equivalent probability measures on the σ-field $\mathbf{F}$. Because the probability space $\{\Omega, \mathbf{F}, P, \{\mathbf{F}_t\}\}$ satisfies the "usual conditions," then also the probability space $\{\Omega, \mathbf{F}, Q, \{\mathbf{F}_t\}\}$ satisfies the "usual conditions," and both spaces have the same predictable σ-field. The definition of the likelihood ratio process parallels Definition 5.8 in the discrete framework.

Definition 11.16 The likelihood ratio process is

$$z_t = E_P\left(\frac{dQ}{dP}\,\middle|\,\mathbf{F}_t\right)$$

Relative to the probability measure P, the likelihood ratio process is a uniformly integrable positive martingale. Theorem 11.32 relates this process to conditional expectations relative to the probability measures P and Q.

Theorem 11.32 *For any adapted process $\{x_t\}$ and any $0 \le s \le t$*

$$\frac{E_P(z_t x_t | \mathbf{F}_s)}{E_P(z_t | \mathbf{F}_s)} = E_Q(x_t | \mathbf{F}_s)$$

Proof. The proof is based on the following fact. If $t \ge 0$, $A \in \mathbf{F}_t$, and the random variable y is measurable on $\mathbf{F}_t$, then

$$\int_A y \, dQ = \int_A y z_t \, dP$$

Indeed

$$
\begin{aligned}
\int_A y z_t \, dP &= \int_A y E_P \left(\frac{dQ}{dP} \bigg| \mathbf{F}_t \right) dP \\
&= \int_A E_P \left(y \frac{dQ}{dP} \bigg| \mathbf{F}_t \right) dP \\
&= \int_A y \frac{dQ}{dP} \, dP \\
&= \int_A y \, dQ
\end{aligned}
$$

Now, for any $0 \le s \le t$ and $A \in \mathbf{F}_s \subset \mathbf{F}_t$

$$\int_A x_t z_t \, dP = \int_A x_t \, dQ = \int_A E_Q(x_t | \mathbf{F}_s) \, dQ$$

which is equal to

$$\int_A z_s E_Q(x_t | \mathbf{F}_s) \, dP = \int_A E_Q(z_s x_t | \mathbf{F}_s) \, dP$$

and because $E_Q(z_s x_t | \mathbf{F}_s)$ is measurable on $\mathbf{F}_s$, we get the theorem. ∎

Corollary 11.3 *A process $\{x_t\}$ is a Q-(local) martingale if and only if the process $\{z_t x_t\}$ is a P-(local) martingale.*

Theorem 11.33 *If the probability measures P and Q are equivalent, then every P-semimartingale is a Q-semimartingale.*

Proof. Suppose that x is a P-semimartingale, then $x = m + a$ where $m \in \mathcal{M}_{0,loc}^P$ and $a \in f\mathcal{V}$. Because z is a P-martingale, then the product xz is a P-semimartingale and, therefore, $xz = m' + a'$ where $m' \subset \mathcal{M}_{0,loc}^P$ and $a' \in f\mathcal{V}$. Because z is positive we can write

$$x = \frac{m'}{z} + \frac{a'}{z}$$

where $\dfrac{m'}{z} \in \mathcal{M}_{0,loc}^Q$ and $\dfrac{a'}{z}$ is a product of the process a' of finite variation on compacts and the Q-martingale $\dfrac{1}{z}$, so that $\dfrac{a'}{z}$ is a Q-semimartingale. This proves that x is a Q-semimartingale. The same proof also demonstrates that every Q-semimartingale is a P-semimartingale. $\blacksquare$

Theorem 11.34 *Suppose that the probability measure Q is absolutely continuous with respect to the probability measure P, $x \in \mathcal{S}$ and $\alpha \in \Lambda^P(x)$. Then $\alpha \in \Lambda^Q(x)$ and the stochastic integral $\alpha \bullet x$, computed under the probability measure Q, is a modification of the stochastic integral $\alpha \bullet x$ computed under the probability measure P.*

Theorem 11.35 *Let Q be any probability measure and suppose that x is a semimartingale relative to both P and Q, and that α is a predictable, locally bounded process. Then there exists a process $\alpha \bullet x$ that is a version of both $(\alpha \bullet x)_P$ and $(\alpha \bullet x)_Q$.*

Next, we prove two auxiliary results.

Theorem 11.36 *Suppose that $a \in \mathcal{P} \cap f\mathcal{V}$ is null at zero. Then the integral $za - z_- \bullet a \in \mathcal{M}_{0,loc}$.*

Proof. Indeed, from the formula for integration by parts

$$za - z_- \bullet a = a_- \bullet z + [z, a]$$

Because $z \in \mathcal{M}_{loc}$ and a is locally bounded, the integral on the right side satisfies $a_- \bullet z \in \mathcal{M}_{0,loc}$. From Theorem 10.49, the optional quadratic covariation process satisfies $[z, a] \in \mathcal{M}_{0,loc}$. This completes the proof that $za - z_- \bullet a \in \mathcal{M}_{0,loc}$. $\blacksquare$

Theorem 11.37 *Suppose that $x \in \mathcal{M}_{0,loc}$ and that $a \in \mathcal{P} \cap f\mathcal{V}$ is null at zero. Then $zx - za \in \mathcal{M}_{0,loc}$ if and only if $\langle z, x \rangle - z_- \bullet a \in \mathcal{M}_{0,loc}$.*

The next theorem is a generalization of Theorems 5.14 and 9.4, and is frequently called Girsanov's theorem.

Theorem 11.38 *Suppose that x is a P-local martingale that is null at zero. Then:*

1. *The process*

$$x_t - \int_0^t \frac{d[x, z]_s}{z_s}$$

   is a Q-local martingale.

2. *If the predictable quadratic covariation process $\langle x, z \rangle$ exists with respect to P, then x is a Q-special semimartingale and its canonic decomposition is*

$$x_t = \left(x_t - \int_0^t \frac{d\langle x, z \rangle_s}{z_{s-}} \right) + \int_0^t \frac{d\langle x, z \rangle_s}{z_{s-}}$$

   where the first term is a Q-local martingale and the second term is a predictable process of locally integrable variation.

Proof. Apply Theorems 11.36 and 11.37 to the P-local martingale x and the process

$$a = \frac{1}{z_-} \bullet \langle z, x \rangle$$

Then, by the associativity of the stochastic integral

$$z_- \bullet a = z_- \bullet \left[\frac{1}{z_-} \bullet \langle z, x \rangle \right] = \frac{z_-}{z_-} \bullet \langle z, x \rangle = \langle z, x \rangle$$

and consequently $z(x - a)$ is a P-local martingale and $z - a$ is a Q-local martingale. ∎

Corollary 11.4 *Suppose that w is a semimartingale, null at zero, such that the stochastic exponential*

$$z_t = \mathcal{E}_t(w)$$

is a uniformly integrable positive martingale. Define the probability measure Q by setting

$$\frac{dQ}{dP} = z_\infty$$

Then, if x is a P-local martingale, null at zero, and the process $\langle x, w \rangle$ exists with respect to P, then x is a Q-special semimartingale with the canonic decomposition

$$x = (x - \langle x, w \rangle) + \langle x, w \rangle$$

Proof. First, the associativity of the stochastic integral implies that

$$w_t = \int_0^t \frac{dz_s}{z_{s-}}$$

Second, from Theorem 11.12

$$\frac{1}{z_-} \bullet \langle z, x \rangle = \left\langle \frac{1}{z_-} \bullet z, x \right\rangle = \langle w, x \rangle$$

This completes the proof. ∎

This section ends with the following theorem on predictable quadratic covariation processes relative to the probability measure Q.

Theorem 11.39 *Suppose that w is a semimartingale, null at zero, such that the stochastic exponential*

$$z_t = \mathcal{E}_t(w)$$

is a uniformly integrable positive martingale. Define the probability measure Q by setting

$$\frac{dQ}{dP} = z_\infty$$

Furthermore, suppose that $x_1, \ldots, x_m \in c\mathcal{M}^P_{loc}$ and for all $1 \leq h \leq m$

$$x'_h = x_h - \langle x_h, w \rangle$$

Then, for all $1 \leq h \leq m$ and $1 \leq k \leq m$

$$\langle x'_h, x'_k \rangle^Q = \langle x_h, x_k \rangle^P$$

Problems

1. For a Poisson process $\{N_t\}$ with parameter λ compute the integral

$$\int_0^t N_{s-} d(N_t - \lambda t)$$

2. Prove that if $x, y \in \mathcal{S}$ and α and β are predictable, locally bounded processes, then

$$[\alpha \bullet x, \beta \bullet y] = (\alpha\beta) \bullet [x, y]$$

3. Prove that if $x, y \in \mathcal{H}^2$, $\alpha \in \Lambda(x)$, and $\beta \in \Lambda(y)$, then

$$E_P[(\alpha \bullet x)(\beta \bullet y)] = E_P[(\alpha\beta) \bullet [x, y]]$$

4. Use Itô's formula to compute dN_t^2 and dx_t where $\{N_t\}$ is a Poisson process with parameter λ, $\{W_t\}$ is the Wiener process, and

$$x_t = 2^{N_t} \exp\left(W_t - \frac{1}{2}t \right)$$

5. Prove that

$$\int_0^t 2^{N_{s^-}} dN_s = 2^{N_t} - 1$$

6. Prove that if $\{w_t\}$ is a semimartingale, then the process

$$u_t = \exp\left(w_t - \frac{1}{2}\langle w^c, w^c \rangle_t \right)$$

is also a semimartingale, and that the process

$$v_t = \prod_{0 \le s \le t} (1 + \Delta w_s) \exp(-\Delta w_s)$$

is a regular right continuous process with finite variation on compacts.

7. For the Wiener process $\{W_t\}$ and $\alpha \in \Lambda(W)$ compute the stochastic exponential $\mathcal{E}_t(\alpha \bullet W)$.

8. Prove that the reciprocal of the likelihood ratio process, $\left\{ \dfrac{1}{z_t} \right\}$, is a Q-uniformly integrable martingale.

Notes

The general references to this chapter include [69], [35], [63], [48], [21], [64], [67], and [54]. The definition of the stochastic integral in Section 11.2 and the discussion of stable spaces in Section 11.5 follow [48]. The generalization of Itô's formula in Section 11.3, the exponential formula in Section 11.4, and the generalization of Girsanov's theorem in Section 11.6 follow [35].

Chapter 12

A Continuous Multiperiod Model

12.1 Introduction

This chapter uses the probability theory in Chapters 10 and 11 to design a general continuous multiperiod model. The initial presentation of this model assumes intermediate trading but no intermediate endowment or consumption. Section 12.8 shows how the model is extended to permit intermediate endowment and consumption.

Following the definition of equilibrium price measures, the listing of the elements of the model, and the definition of trading strategies, we describe restrictions on trading strategies that are sufficient for the absence of arbitrage trading strategies. The main result in this regard is that if a self-financing trading strategy is such that the negative part of every value process is uniformly integrable with respect to an equilibrium price measure, then there are no arbitrage trading strategies. The preceding uniform integrability condition can be interpreted as a restriction on short sales. In particular, if the restriction is such that the value processes are nonnegative, then the negative part is zero, and there are no arbitrage strategies.

Section 12.5 offers a characterization of complete price systems that resembles the results in the discrete theory of Chapter 6. Next, in the section on risk and return, we prove a version of Girsanov's theorem that we use to characterize the likelihood ratio process as the single risk factor in the general continuous multiperiod model. We also use this version of Girsanov's theorem to obtain a representation result for the equilibrium price measure generated by a complete price system. This representation result permits the calculation of equilibrium prices of derivative securities in the general framework of this chapter.

293

The definitions and theorems in Chapters 10 and 11 are for stochastic processes on the open or closed half-line 0 to ∞ and the model in this chapter has a finite horizon T. Therefore, we formally extend the definition of any stochastic process $\{x_t\}$ in the continuous multiperiod model beyond time T by setting $x_t = x_T$ for all $t > T$. Then the stopped extended process $\{x_t\}$ satisfies $x_{t \wedge T} = x_t$ and $x_\infty = x_T$. Similarly, we extend the definition of the filtration $\{\mathbf{F}_t\}$ by setting $\mathbf{F}_t = \mathbf{F}_T$ for all $t > T$. Then the σ-field $\mathbf{F}_\infty$, generated by the union of all the σ-fields $\mathbf{F}_t$ for $t \geq 0$, coincides with the σ-field $\bigvee_{0 \leq t \leq T} \mathbf{F}_t$ generated by the σ-fields $\mathbf{F}_t$ for $0 \leq t \leq T$.

12.2   Equilibrium Price Measures

The time period of the continuous multiperiod model is a finite time interval $[0, T]$. Uncertainty is represented by a filtered probability space

$$\{\Omega, \mathbf{F}, P, \{\mathbf{F}_t\}\}$$

that satisfies the "usual conditions." There is a single, perishable, consumption good and a finite number N of endogenous securities with the terminal payouts $d_1, \ldots, d_N$. The random variables $d_1, \ldots, d_N$ are measurable on the terminal σ-field $\mathbf{F}_T$. The prices $p_t = (p_{1t}, \ldots, p_{Nt})$ of securities $1, \ldots, N$ are semimartingales. At the terminal time $p_{nT} = d_n$ for each $1 \leq n \leq N$. We need the semimartingale property of prices for the existence of the gain from trade integrals in Section 12.4.

In addition, we assume that security 1 is a locally riskless bond in the sense that the price $\{p_{1t}\}$ is a positive continuous process with finite variation on compacts and $p_{10} = 1$. This specification of the bond corresponds to an accumulation account which pays a random positive of interest.

The next definition describes equilibrium price measures in the continuous multiperiod model.

Definition 12.1 Given a price system p, an equilibrium price measure is a probability measure Q on $\{\Omega, \mathbf{F}\}$ such that:

1. The probability measures P and Q are equivalent.

2. For each $1 \leq n \leq N$ the discounted price $\left\{\dfrac{p_{nt}}{p_{1t}}\right\}$ is a Q-uniformly integrable martingale.

The set of equilibrium price measures is denoted $\mathcal{Q}_p$.

We assume that the set $\mathcal{Q}_p$ is not empty and choose a particular $Q \in \mathcal{Q}_p$. The continuous multiperiod model is relative to this equilibrium price measure Q, and choosing different measures Q in general results in different models. Most of the results in this chapter do not depend on the choice of the particular equilibrium price measure Q. In addition, unless explicitly stated to the contrary, we do not assume that the chosen equilibrium price measure Q is unique.

We define the consumption set in the continuous multiperiod model to be

$$X = \mathcal{R} \times \mathcal{L}^1(\Omega, \mathbf{F}_T, Q)$$

The definition of equilibrium price measures and the specification of the consumption set above differ from the definitions of the corresponding concepts in the Black-Scholes model. First, in the Black-Scholes model we require that the Radon-Nikodym derivative be square integrable

$$\frac{dQ}{dP} \in \mathcal{L}^2(\Omega, \mathbf{F}, P)$$

Second, in the Black-Scholes model, the consumption set is

$$X = \mathcal{R} \times \mathcal{L}^2(\Omega, \mathbf{F}_T, P)$$

There are two reasons for these differences. In the Black-Scholes model we rely on the representation theorem of Kunita and Watanabe, and therefore, require that terminal consumptions and the Radon-Nikodym derivative be square integrable. For the general theory of this chapter it is enough to require that terminal consumptions be integrable rather than square integrable. Furthermore, instead of requiring that the Radon-Nikodym derivative be square integrable and discounted prices be martingales with respect to the equilibrium price measure, we require that discounted prices be uniformly integrable martingales with respect to every equilibrium price measure. In this regard, the conditions in the Black-Scholes model are stronger than in the general continuous model. The requirement that the Radon-Nikodym derivative in the Black-Scholes model be square integrable implies that discounted prices are square integrable, and therefore, uniformly integrable Q-martingales, as required in Definition 12.1.

Next, the specification of the consumption set in the Black-Scholes model is intuitively attractive, but fails to deliver completeness of the given price system. Even though the equilibrium price measure is unique, the attainable set M in the Black-Scholes model is a proper dense subset of the consumption set X, making the Black-Scholes model only approximately complete. We pointed out in Chapter 9 that an alternative specification of the consumption set, $X = \mathcal{R} \times \mathcal{L}^2(\Omega, \mathbf{F}, Q)$, makes the model complete.

Using the representation theory in this chapter and assuming that the consumption set is $X = \mathcal{R} \times \mathcal{L}^1(\Omega, \mathbf{F}_T, Q)$ allows us to prove that a price system is complete if and only if every Q-uniformly integrable martingale has a representation as a sum of stochastic integrals with respect to discounted prices, and that a price system is complete if and only if the equilibrium price measure is unique.

If the equilibrium price measure Q is such that $\dfrac{dQ}{dP} \in \mathcal{L}^2(\Omega, \mathbf{F}, P)$, then the standard argument with Hölder's inequality implies that

$$\mathcal{L}^2(\Omega, \mathbf{F}_T, P) \subset \mathcal{L}^1(\Omega, \mathbf{F}_T, Q)$$

so that

$$\mathcal{R} \times \mathcal{L}^2(\Omega, \mathbf{F}_T, P) \subset X$$

In particular, if the equilibrium price measure Q is such that there are constants $0 < K_1 < K_2$ for which

$$K_1 \le \frac{dQ}{dP} \le K_2$$

then

$$\mathcal{L}^1(\Omega, \mathbf{F}_T, Q) = \mathcal{L}^1(\Omega, \mathbf{F}_T, P)$$

and therefore

$$X = \mathcal{R} \times \mathcal{L}^1(\Omega, \mathbf{F}_T, P)$$

12.3   Elements of the Model

A complete listing of the elements of the continuous multiperiod model is as follows:

- A finite time interval $[0, T]$.

- A filtered probability space $\{\Omega, \mathbf{F}, P, \{\mathbf{F}_t\}\}$ that satisfies the "usual conditions." In addition, we assume that $A \in \mathbf{F}_0$ if and only if $P(A) = 0$ or $P(A) = 1$, and that $\bigvee_{0 \le t \le T} \mathbf{F}_t = \mathbf{F}_T = \mathbf{F}$.

- A single perishable consumption good.

- A finite number N of endogenous securities with the terminal payouts $d_1, \ldots, d_N$. The random variables $d_1, \ldots, d_N$ are measurable on the terminal σ-field $\mathbf{F}_T$. The securities are infinitely divisible, and there are no taxes or trading costs.

- The prices $p_t = (p_{1t}, \ldots, p_{Nt})$ of securities $1, \ldots, N$ are semimartingales. At the terminal time $p_{nT} = d_n$ for each $1 \leq n \leq N$. In addition, we assume that security 1 is a locally riskless bond in the sense that the price $\{p_{1t}\}$ is a positive continuous increasing process with finite variation on compacts and $p_{10} = 1$.

- A nonempty set $\mathcal{Q}_p$ of equilibrium price measures and a particular equilibrium price measure $Q \in \mathcal{Q}_p$.

- A finite number I of traders. At time t the information of traders is $\mathbf{F}_t$.

- The initial endowment of trader i, e_0^i, is measurable on $\mathbf{F}_0$, and his or her terminal endowment is a random variable $e_T^i \in \mathcal{L}^1(\Omega, \mathbf{F}_T, Q)$. Traders do not receive intermediate endowments.

- The initial consumption of trader i, c_0^i, is measurable on $\mathbf{F}_0$, and his or her terminal consumption is a random variable $c_T^i \in \mathcal{L}^1(\Omega, \mathbf{F}_T, Q)$. Traders do not consume at intermediate times. The consumption set is

$$X = \mathcal{R} \times \mathcal{L}^1(\Omega, \mathbf{F}_T, Q)$$

- On the consumption set X traders have complete preference orderings that are continuous, increasing, and convex.

In the next section we turn to the discussion of trading strategies in the continuous multiperiod model.

12.4   Trading Strategies

Intuitively, a trading strategy $\theta = (\theta_1, \ldots, \theta_N)$ must be such that the integrals $\theta_n \bullet p_n$ are defined for all $1 \leq n \leq N$. Then the sum of these integrals

$$(\theta' \bullet p)_t = \sum_{n=1}^{N} (\theta_n \bullet p_n)_t$$

represents the gain from trade during the time interval $[0, t]$. We adopt a temporary definition of a trading strategy as a vector of stochastic processes $\theta = (\theta_1, \ldots, \theta_N)$ such that the integral $\theta_n \bullet p_n$ exists for every $1 \leq n \leq N$. In other words, a trading strategy is a vector of stochastic processes such that $\theta_n \in \Lambda^P(p_n)$, or equivalently, $\theta_n \in \Lambda^Q(p_n)$ for every $1 \leq n \leq N$. We use this temporary concept of a trading strategy to introduce additional concepts and to demonstrate results that motivate the final description of a trading strategy in Definition 12.4.

The definition of self-financing trading strategies parallels the corresponding definitions in the discrete model and the Black-Scholes model.

Definition 12.2 A trading strategy θ is self-financing if and only if for all $0 \leq t \leq T$

$$\theta'_t p_t = \theta'_0 p_0 + (\theta' \bullet p)_t$$

The following theorem matches a characterization of self-financing trading strategies in the discrete theory and in the Black-Scholes model.

Theorem 12.1 *A trading strategy θ is self-financing if and only if for all $0 \leq t \leq T$ we have*

$$\frac{\theta'_t p_t}{p_{1t}} = \theta'_0 p_0 + \left(\theta' \bullet \frac{p}{p_1} \right)_t$$

Proof. Suppose that the trading strategy θ is self-financing, then

$$d(\theta'_t p_t) = \theta'_t dp_t$$

Applying Itô's formula to the discounted value process $f\left(\theta'_t p_t, p_{1t}\right) = \dfrac{\theta'_t p_t}{p_{1t}}$ we have

$$\frac{\theta'_t p_t}{p_{1t}} = \theta'_0 p_0 + \int_0^t \frac{\theta'_s dp_s}{p_{1s}} - \int_0^t \frac{\theta'_{s-} p_{s-}}{p_{1s}} \frac{dp_{1s}}{p_{1s}}$$

Similarly, for any $1 \leq n \leq N$

$$\frac{p_{nt}}{p_{1t}} = p_{n0} + \int_0^t \frac{dp_{ns}}{p_{1s}} - \int_0^t \frac{p_{n,s-}}{p_{1s}} \frac{dp_{1s}}{p_{1s}}$$

Together with the associativity of the stochastic integral, the two preceding equations imply that

$$\int_0^t \theta'_s d \left(\frac{p_s}{p_{1s}} \right) = \int_0^t \frac{\theta'_s dp_s}{p_{1s}} - \int_0^t \frac{\theta'_s p_{s-}}{p_{1s}} \frac{dp_{1s}}{p_{1s}}$$

and finally, because the process $\{p_{1t}\}$ is continuous, we have

$$\int_0^t \frac{(\theta'_s - \theta'_{s-}) p_{s-}}{p_{1s}} \frac{dp_{1s}}{p_{1s}} = 0$$

The proof of the converse assertion is similar. ∎

We have the following corollary.

Corollary 12.1 *Suppose that θ is a self-financing trading strategy such that $\theta_n \in \Lambda_{loc}^{Q,1}\left(\dfrac{p_n}{p_1}\right)$ for each $1 \le n \le N$. Then the discounted value process $\left\{\dfrac{\theta_t' p_t}{p_{1t}}\right\}$ is a Q-local martingale.*

Proof. Because $\theta_n \in \Lambda_{loc}^{Q,1}\left(\dfrac{p_n}{p_1}\right)$ and each $\dfrac{p_n}{p_1}$ is a Q-martingale, Theorem 11.1 implies that the integrals $\theta_n' \bullet \left(\dfrac{p_n}{p_1}\right)$ are Q-local martingales. Because

$$\Lambda_{loc}^{Q,1}\left(\frac{p_n}{p_1}\right) \subset \Lambda^Q\left(\frac{p_n}{p_1}\right)$$

for each $1 \le n \le N$, the corollary follows from the preceding theorem. ∎

Arbitrage trading strategies in the continuous multiperiod model are defined exactly as in the discrete model and the Black-Scholes model.

Definition 12.3 A self-financing trading strategy θ is an arbitrage strategy if and only if either:

1. At the initial time $\theta_0' p_0 \le 0$.

2. At the terminal time $P\{\theta_T' p_T \ge 0\} = 1$.

3. At the terminal time $P\{\theta_T' p_T > 0\} > 0$.

   or:

1. At the initial time $\theta_0' p_0 < 0$.

2. At the terminal time $P\{\theta_T' p_T \ge 0\} = 1$.

The next several theorems describe sufficient conditions for the absence of arbitrage strategies. In particular, we show that imposing restrictions on short sales such that every value process dominates some random variable that is integrable with respect to the equilibrium price measure Q excludes arbitrage strategies.

Theorem 12.2 *Suppose that for each self-financing trading strategy θ the discounted value process $\left\{\dfrac{\theta_t' p_t}{p_{1t}}\right\}$ is a Q-supermartingale. Then there are no arbitrage strategies.*

Proof. Because the probability measures P and Q are equivalent, the statements

$$P\left\{\theta_T' p_T \geq 0\right\} = 1 \quad \text{and} \quad Q\left\{\theta_T' p_T \geq 0\right\} = 1$$

are equivalent. Similarly, the statements

$$P\left\{\theta_T' p_T > 0\right\} > 0 \quad \text{and} \quad Q\left\{\theta_T' p_T > 0\right\} > 0$$

are also equivalent. Because the discounted value process

$$\left\{\frac{\theta_t' p_t}{p_{1t}}\right\}$$

is a Q-supermartingale, we have

$$\theta_0' p_0 \geq E_Q\left(\frac{\theta_T' p_T}{p_{1T}}\right)$$

Finally, we have $P\{p_{1T} > 0\} = 1$. Together, these observations imply that if $P\left\{\theta_T' p_T \geq 0\right\} = 1$, then $\theta_0' p_0 \geq 0$ and if, in addition, $P\left\{\theta_T' p_T > 0\right\} > 0$, then $\theta_0' p_0 > 0$. ∎

Theorem 12.3 describes sufficient conditions for the discounted value process to be a Q-supermartingale.

Theorem 12.3 *Suppose that the self-financing trading strategy θ is such that $\theta_n \in \Lambda_{loc}^{Q,1}\left(\dfrac{p_n}{p_1}\right)$ for every $1 \leq n \leq N$, and the value process $\{\theta_t' p_t\}$ is nonnegative. Then the discounted value process*

$$\left\{\frac{\theta_t' p_t}{p_{1t}}\right\}$$

is a Q-supermartingale.

Proof. From Corollary 12.1 the discounted value process is a Q-local martingale. Theorem 10.16 then says that the discounted value process is a Q-supermartingale. ∎

Theorems 12.2 and 12.3 imply that if we require that the trading strategies satisfy $\theta_n \in \Lambda_{loc}^{Q,1}\left(\dfrac{p_n}{p_1}\right)$ for every $1 \leq n \leq N$, and exclude trading strategies that allow the value process to become negative, then we exclude all arbitrage trading strategies.

Corollary 12.2 *Suppose that every self-financing trading strategy θ is such that $\theta_n \in \Lambda_{loc}^{Q,1}\left(\frac{p_n}{p_1}\right)$ for every $1 \leq n \leq N$, and the value process $\{\theta_t' p_t\}$ is nonnegative. Then there are no arbitrage strategies.*

The preceding results are a special case of the following, more general, theorem. Recall the definition of the positive and negative parts of a stochastic process, $x^+ = \max(x, 0)$ and $x^- = -\min(x, 0)$, respectively.

Theorem 12.4 *Suppose that the self-financing trading strategy θ is such that $\theta_n \in \Lambda_{loc}^{Q,1}\left(\frac{p_n}{p_1}\right)$ for every $1 \leq n \leq N$, and the negative part of the value process $\{\theta_t' p_t\}$ is uniformly integrable with respect to Q. Then the discounted value process $\left\{\frac{\theta_t' p_t}{p_{1t}}\right\}$ is a Q-supermartingale.*

Proof. Follows immediately from Fatou's lemma, Theorem 10.15. ∎

Theorem 12.4 indicates that if we require that the trading strategies satisfy $\theta_n \in \Lambda_{loc}^{Q,1}\left(\frac{p_n}{p_1}\right)$ for every $1 \leq n \leq N$ and the process $\min(\theta_t' p_t, 0)$ is uniformly integrable with respect to the equilibrium price measure Q, then there are no arbitrage strategies. In particular, if there is a random variable η that is Q-integrable, and such that $\theta_t' p_t \geq \eta$ for all $0 \leq t \leq T$, then the process $\min(\theta_t' p_t, 0)$ is uniformly integrable, and there are no arbitrage strategies.

We have established that if we restrict the trading strategies in such a way that every discounted value process is a Q-supermartingale, then there are no arbitrage strategies. In addition, the following reasoning shows that we need to restrict the trading strategies to make every discounted value process a Q-uniformly integrable martingale.

First, paralleling the discrete model and the Black-Scholes model, the risk-adjusted expected rate of return of any trading strategy should be consistent with the rate of return of the locally riskless bond. In addition, we would like this property to hold both between any pair of fixed dates and any pair of stopping times. In other words, we want the optional stopping theorem, Theorem 10.11, to apply. Consequently, we require that the discounted value process be not just a Q-martingale, but a Q-uniformly integrable martingale.

Second, if we want a characterization of attainable consumption processes that parallels Theorems 6.1 and 9.6 in the discrete model and the Black-Scholes model, then we need to restrict the trading strategies to make every discounted value process a Q-uniformly integrable martingale.

Indeed, suppose that $\{c_0, c_T\} \in \mathcal{R} \times \mathcal{L}^1(\Omega, \mathbf{F}_T, Q)$ is a consumption process for which there is a self-financing trading strategy θ satisfying $c_T =$

$\theta'_T d$. If we have an analog of Theorems 6.1 and 9.6, then the trading strategy θ satisfies for every $0 \le t \le T$

$$E_Q \left(\frac{c_T}{p_{1T}} \,\middle|\, \mathbf{F}_t \right) = E_Q \left(\frac{c_T}{p_{1T}} \right) + \int_0^t \theta'_s d \left(\frac{p_s}{p_{1s}} \right)$$

Because the trading strategy θ is self-financing, the preceding equation and Theorem 12.1 imply that

$$\frac{\theta'_t p_t}{p_{1t}} = \theta'_0 p_0 + E_Q \left(\frac{c_T}{p_{1T}} \,\middle|\, \mathbf{F}_t \right) - E_Q \left(\frac{c_T}{p_{1T}} \right)$$

and the discounted value process is a Q-uniformly integrable martingale. The requirement that every trading strategy be such that the discounted value process is a Q-uniformly integrable martingale is satisfied when the trading strategies satisfy the following condition.

Theorem 12.5 *Suppose that the trading strategy θ is such that for every $1 \le n \le N$*

$$\theta_n \in \Lambda_{loc}^{Q,1} \left(\frac{p_n}{p_1} \right)$$

and the positive and negative parts of the value process $\{\theta'_t p_t\}$ are uniformly integrable with respect to Q. Then the discounted value process $\left\{ \dfrac{\theta'_t p_t}{p_{1t}} \right\}$ is a Q-uniformly integrable martingale.

Proof. Follows immediately from Fatou's lemma, Theorem 10.15. ∎

In particular, if for every trading strategy θ there are Q-integrable random variables η_1 and η_2 such that

$$\eta_1 \le \frac{\theta'_t p_t}{p_{1t}} \le \eta_2$$

for all $0 \le t \le T$, then the positive and negative parts of $\left\{ \dfrac{\theta'_t p_t}{p_{1t}} \right\}$ are Q-uniformly integrable processes and $\left\{ \dfrac{\theta'_t p_t}{p_{1t}} \right\}$ is a Q-uniformly integrable martingale. The random variables η_1 and η_2 can be negative. Thus, a restriction on purchases and short sales that prevents the discounted value processes from becoming too large in absolute value makes the discounted value processes Q-uniformly integrable martingales. This then guarantees that, after adjustment for risk, the expected rate of return of any trading strategy is consistent with the rate of return of the locally riskless bond.

To exclude arbitrage strategies and to obtain an analog of Theorems 6.1 and 9.6 we adopt the following formal definition of budget sets and trading strategies.

Definition 12.4 For an endowment process $e = \{e_0, e_T\}$ and a price system p, the budget set $B(e,p)$ is the set of consumption processes $c = \{c_0, c_T\}$ such that $c \in X$ and there exists a vector of stochastic processes

$$\theta = (\theta_1, \dots, \theta_N)$$

that satisfies:

1. For each $1 \leq n \leq N$ we have $\theta_n \in \Lambda^P(p_n)$.

2. For every $0 \leq t \leq T$ we have $\theta_t' p_t = \theta_0' p_0 + (\theta' \bullet p)_t$.

3. The discounted value process $\left\{ \dfrac{\theta_t' p_t}{p_{1t}} \right\}$ is a Q-uniformly integrable martingale.

4. At the initial time $c_0 = e_0 - \theta_0' p_0$.

5. At the terminal time $c_T = e_T + \theta_T' d$.

We call a vector process θ that satisfies the preceding conditions a trading strategy, and denote the set of trading strategies by Θ. Notice that Theorem 11.34 implies that $\theta_n \in \Lambda^Q(p_n)$ for every n and that $\theta' \bullet p$, computed with respect to Q, is a version of $\theta' \bullet p$ computed with respect to P.

The desired analog of Theorems 6.1 and 9.6 is Theorem 12.7 in Section 12.5. We continue this section with the definition of an equilibrium and a description of the price functional.

Definition 12.5 We say that prices p are equilibrium prices for a given population of traders with endowment processes e^i if and only if there exist trading strategies θ^i that optimize preferences over the budget sets $B(e^i, p)$, and the market clears, $\sum_{i=1}^{I} \theta_t^i = 0$, with probability one, for all $0 \leq t \leq T$.

The next two definitions extend in an obvious way the notion of an attainable consumption process and a complete price system to the continuous multiperiod model.

Definition 12.6 A consumption process $c = \{c_0, c_T\} \in X$ is attainable if and only if there is an endowment process $e = \{e_0, e_T\}$ such that $e_T = 0$ and $c \in B(e, p)$. The set of consumption processes that are attainable at prices p is denoted $M(p)$.

Definition 12.7 A price system p is complete relative to the equilibrium price measure Q if and only if $M(p) = \mathcal{R} \times \mathcal{L}^1(\Omega, \mathbf{F}_T, Q)$.

In the next subsection we examine the price functional in the continuous multiperiod model.

The Price Functional

As before, we define the price functional as the initial cost of an attainable consumption process. The existence of the price functional is due to the fact that our definition of the set Θ of trading strategies excludes arbitrage strategies.

Definition 12.8 The price functional $\phi : M(p) \to \mathcal{R}$ is such that for every $c = \{c_0, c_T\} \in M(p)$

$$\phi(c) = c_0 + \theta_0' p_0$$

for any trading strategy $\theta \in \Theta$ such that

$$c_T = \theta_T' d$$

The requirement that every discounted value process be a Q-martingale implies that for every consumption process $\{c_0, c_T\} \in M(p)$

$$\phi(\{c_0, c_T\}) = c_0 + E_Q \left(\frac{c_T}{p_{1T}} \right)$$

Theorem 12.6 *The price functional is positive. In addition, if there is a positive real number a such that $P\{p_{1T} \geq a\} = 1$, then the price functional is continuous in the topology of the product norm on the consumption set X.*

Proof. Both properties follow from the representation

$$\phi(\{c_0, c_T\}) = c_0 + E_Q \left(\frac{c_T}{p_{1T}} \right)$$

In particular, to prove that ϕ is continuous, notice that a linear functional is continuous if and only if it is bounded. Because $Q\{p_{1T} \geq a\} = 1$, we have

$$\left| E_Q \left(\frac{c_T}{p_{1T}} \right) \right| \leq \frac{E_Q \left(|c_T| \right)}{a}$$

and therefore

$$|\phi(\{c_0, c_T\})| \leq |c_0| + \frac{|E_Q(|c_T|)|}{a} \leq \sqrt{2} \max \left(1, \frac{1}{a} \right) \left\{ c_0^2 + [E_Q \left(|c_T| \right)]^2 \right\}^{\frac{1}{2}}$$

so that the price functional is bounded, and therefore, continuous. ∎

The preceding theorem says that if two consumption processes have similar initial components, and the mean, after adjustment for risk, of the

absolute value of the difference of their terminal components is small, then
the initial costs of these two consumption processes are close.

If the equilibrium price measure Q is such that $\dfrac{dQ}{dP} \in \mathcal{L}^2(\Omega, \mathbf{F}, P)$, then

$$\mathcal{R} \times \mathcal{L}^2(\Omega, \mathbf{F}_T, P) \subset X$$

In this case, the restriction of the price functional to the set

$$M(p) \cap \left[\mathcal{R} \times \mathcal{L}^2(\Omega, \mathbf{F}_T, P) \right]$$

is continuous in the topology of the product norm on $\mathcal{R} \times \mathcal{L}^2(\Omega, \mathbf{F}_T, P)$. This
means that if two consumption processes have similar initial components
and, with respect to the probability measure P, the mean and the variance
of their difference are small, then the initial costs of these two consumption
processes are close.

Furthermore, if the equilibrium price measure Q is such that there are
constants $0 < K_1 < K_2$ for which

$$K_1 \leq \frac{dQ}{dP} \leq K_2$$

then

$$X = \mathcal{R} \times \mathcal{L}^1(\Omega, \mathbf{F}_T, P)$$

and the restriction of the price functional to the set

$$M(p) \cap \left[\mathcal{R} \times \mathcal{L}^1(\Omega, \mathbf{F}_T, P) \right]$$

is continuous in the topology of the product norm on $\mathcal{R} \times \mathcal{L}^1(\Omega, \mathbf{F}_T, P)$.
This describes risk-neutral pricing in the sense that if the absolute value of
the difference of two terminal consumptions has a small mean with respect
to the probability measure P, then the initial costs of these two terminal
consumptions are close.

The next section characterizes complete price systems.

12.5   Completeness

The following characterization of attainable consumption processes parallels
Theorem 6.1 in the discrete model and Theorem 9.6 in the Black-Scholes
model.

Theorem 12.7 *A consumption process $\{c_0, c_T\} \in X$ is attainable if and
only if there is a vector of processes $\alpha = \{\alpha_1, \dots, \alpha_N\}$ such that for every
$1 \leq n \leq N$ we have $\alpha_n \in \Lambda_{loc}^{Q,1}\left(\frac{p_n}{p_1}\right)$ and for every $0 \leq t \leq T$*

$$E_Q\left(\frac{c_T}{p_{1T}}\,\middle|\,\mathbf{F}_t\right) = E_Q\left(\frac{c_T}{p_{1T}}\right) + \int_0^t \alpha_s' d\left(\frac{p_s}{p_{1s}}\right)$$

Proof. Let $\{c_0, c_T\} \in X$ be attainable. Then there is a trading strategy that satisfies $\theta_n \in \Lambda^P(p_n)$ for every $1 \leq n \leq N$, and such that for all $0 \leq t \leq T$

$$\frac{\theta_t' p_t}{p_{1t}} = \theta_0' p_0 + \int_0^t \theta_s' d\left(\frac{p_s}{p_{1s}}\right)$$

and the discounted value process $\left\{\dfrac{\theta_t' p_t}{p_{1t}}\right\}$ is a Q-martingale. Therefore, the integral $\displaystyle\int_0^t \theta_s' d\left(\frac{p_s}{p_{1s}}\right)$ is a Q-martingale. Applying the terminal condition $c_T = \theta_T' p_T$ and taking conditional expectations

$$E_Q\left(\frac{c_T}{p_{1T}}\,\middle|\,\mathbf{F}_t\right) = \theta_0' p_0 + E_Q\left[\int_0^T \theta_s' d\left(\frac{p_s}{p_{1s}}\right)\,\middle|\,\mathbf{F}_t\right]$$

$$= \theta_0' p_0 + \int_0^t \theta_s' d\left(\frac{p_s}{p_{1s}}\right)$$

Finally, taking expectations

$$E_Q\left(\frac{c_T}{p_{1T}}\right) = \theta_0' p_0$$

and the direct assertion follows. Conversely, suppose that there is a vector of processes $\alpha_n \in \Lambda_{loc}^{Q,1}\left(\dfrac{p_n}{p_1}\right)$ such that for every $0 \leq t \leq T$

$$E_Q\left(\frac{c_T}{p_{1T}}\,\middle|\,\mathbf{F}_t\right) = E_Q\left(\frac{c_T}{p_{1T}}\right) + \int_0^t \alpha_s' d\left(\frac{p_s}{p_{1s}}\right) \qquad (12.1)$$

For $2 \leq n \leq N$ and $0 \leq t \leq T$ define

$$\theta_{nt} = \alpha_{nt}$$

and for $n = 1$ define

$$\theta_{1t} = E_Q\left(\frac{c_T}{p_{1T}}\right) + \int_0^t \alpha_s' d\left(\frac{p_s}{p_{1s}}\right) - \sum_{n=2}^N \theta_{nt}\frac{p_{nt}}{p_{1t}}$$

Then

$$\frac{\theta'_t p_t}{p_{1t}} = E_Q \left(\frac{c_T}{p_{1T}} \right) + \int_0^t \alpha'_s d \left(\frac{p_s}{p_{1s}} \right)$$

and Equation 12.1 implies that

$$\frac{\theta'_t p_t}{p_{1t}} = E_Q \left(\frac{c_T}{p_{1T}} \middle| \mathbf{F}_t \right)$$

so that the discounted value process is a uniformly integrable Q-martingale. Next, because $\dfrac{p_{1t}}{p_{1t}} = 1$ for all $0 \le t \le T$, we have

$$\int_0^t \alpha'_s d \left(\frac{p_s}{p_{1s}} \right) = \sum_{n=2}^N \int_0^t \alpha_{ns} d \left(\frac{p_{ns}}{p_{1s}} \right)$$

$$= \sum_{n=2}^N \int_0^t \theta_{ns} d \left(\frac{p_{ns}}{p_{1s}} \right)$$

$$= \int_0^t \theta'_s d \left(\frac{p_s}{p_{1s}} \right)$$

Thus

$$\frac{\theta'_t p_t}{p_{1t}} = E_Q \left(\frac{c_T}{p_{1T}} \right) + \int_0^t \theta'_s d \left(\frac{p_s}{p_{1s}} \right)$$

and, in particular, for $t = 0$, we have $\theta'_0 p_0 = E_Q \left(\dfrac{c_T}{p_{1T}} \right)$ and Theorem 12.1 implies that θ is self-financing. Next, for $t = T$

$$\frac{\theta'_T p_T}{p_{1T}} = E_Q \left(\frac{c_T}{p_{1T}} \right) + \int_0^T \theta'_s d \left(\frac{p_s}{p_{1s}} \right)$$

and from Equation 12.1

$$\frac{c_T}{p_{1T}} = E_Q \left(\frac{c_T}{p_{1T}} \right) + \int_0^T \theta'_s d \left(\frac{p_s}{p_{1s}} \right)$$

Therefore, $c_T = \theta'_T d$ and the consumption process $\{c_0, c_T\}$ is attainable. ∎

Local Martingale Measures

Suppose that $\{x_t\}$ is a regular right continuous process and Q_1 and Q_2 are two probability measures on $\{\Omega, \mathbf{F}\}$ such that $\{x_t\}$ is both a Q_1-(uniformly integrable) martingale on the filtration $\left\{\mathbf{F}_t^{Q_1}\right\}$ and a Q_2-(uniformly integrable) martingale on the filtration $\left\{\mathbf{F}_t^{Q_2}\right\}$. Let $0 \leq \lambda \leq 1$ and define $Q = \lambda Q_1 + (1 - \lambda) Q_2$. Then $\{x_t\}$ is a Q-(uniformly integrable) martingale on the filtration $\left\{\mathbf{F}_t^Q\right\}$. This assertion follows from the following theorem.

Theorem 12.8 *Consider two probability measures Q_1, Q_2, a real number $0 \leq \lambda \leq 1$, and the probability measure $Q = \lambda Q_1 + (1 - \lambda) Q_2$. Then Q_1 and Q_2 are absolutely continuous with respect to Q*

$$\lambda \frac{dQ_1}{dQ} + (1 - \lambda) \frac{dQ_2}{dQ} = 1$$

and for any random variable x and any sub-σ-field $\mathbf{G}$ of $\mathbf{F}$

$$E_Q(x|\mathbf{G}) = \lambda E_Q\left(\frac{dQ_1}{dQ}\bigg|\mathbf{G}\right) E_{Q_1}(x|\mathbf{G}) + (1 - \lambda) E_Q\left(\frac{dQ_2}{dQ}\bigg|\mathbf{G}\right) E_{Q_2}(x|\mathbf{G})$$

Proof. Indeed, the definition of conditional expectation implies that for any $A \in \mathbf{G}$

$$\int_A E_Q\left(\frac{dQ_1}{dQ}\bigg|\mathbf{G}\right) E_{Q_1}(x|\mathbf{G}) dQ = \int_A E_Q\left[\frac{dQ_1}{dQ} E_{Q_1}(x|\mathbf{G})\bigg|\mathbf{G}\right]$$

$$= \int_A \frac{dQ_1}{dQ} E_{Q_1}(x|\mathbf{G}) dQ$$

$$= \int_A E_{Q_1}(x|\mathbf{G}) dQ_1$$

$$= \int_A x dQ_1$$

and

$$\int_A E_Q\left(\frac{dQ_2}{dQ}\bigg|\mathbf{G}\right) E_{Q_2}(x|\mathbf{G}) dQ = \int_A E_Q\left[\frac{dQ_2}{dQ} E_{Q_2}(x|\mathbf{G})\bigg|\mathbf{G}\right]$$

$$= \int_A \frac{dQ_2}{dQ} E_{Q_2}(x|\mathbf{G}) dQ$$

$$= \int_A E_{Q_2}(x|\mathbf{G})dQ_2$$

$$= \int_A x dQ_2$$

and therefore

$$\int_A \left[\lambda E_Q \left(\left. \frac{dQ_1}{dQ} \right| \mathbf{G} \right) E_{Q_1}(x|\mathbf{G}) + (1-\lambda)E_Q \left(\left. \frac{dQ_2}{dQ} \right| \mathbf{G} \right) E_{Q_2}(x|\mathbf{G}) \right] dQ$$

$$= \int_A x dQ$$

The integrand on the left side of the preceding equation is measurable on **G**. Consequently, the preceding equation is a definition of the conditional expectation $E_Q(x|\mathbf{G})$ and the theorem follows. Notice that, in particular

$$E_Q(x) = \lambda E_{Q_1}(x) + (1-\lambda)E_{Q_2}(x)$$

This completes the proof. ∎

Therefore, if a process $\{x\}$ is both a Q_1-martingale and a Q_2-martingale, then it is a Q-martingale. It follows that the set of probability measures that make the regular right continuous process $\{x_t\}$ a martingale is convex. On the other hand, if a process $\{x\}$ is both a Q_1-local martingale and a Q_2-local martingale it need not be a Q-local martingale. Even though there is a sequence $\{\tau'_m\}$ of stopping times increasing to infinity with Q_1-probability one such that $\{x_{t\wedge\tau'_m}\}$ is a Q_1-martingale, and a sequence $\{\tau''_m\}$ of stopping times increasing to infinity with Q_2-probability one such that $\{x_{t\wedge\tau''_m}\}$ is a Q_2-martingale, the sequence of stopping times $\{\tau'_m \wedge \tau''_m\}$ need not increase to infinity with Q-probability one. Thus, the set of local martingale measures in the following definition need not be convex.

Definition 12.9 Suppose that $M \subset \mathcal{D}$ is a set of regular right continuous processes. A local martingale measure for the set M is any probability measure Q on $\{\Omega, \mathbf{F}\}$ such that each element of M is a Q-local martingale on the filtration $\{\mathbf{F}_t^Q\}$.

The following theorem provides a sufficient condition for the set of local martingale measures to be convex.

Theorem 12.9 *Let M be a set of optional processes. If for each $x \in M$ the processes $\{x_{t\wedge\tau_m}\}$, where $\tau_m = \inf\{t \mid x_t^* \geq m\}$, are bounded, then the set of local martingale measures for M is convex.*

Whether the set of local martingale measures is convex or not, we can define extremal local martingale measures.

Definition 12.10 An extremal local martingale measure for a set M of regular right continuous processes is any local martingale measure Q for which there are no distinct local martingale measures Q_1 and Q_2 and a real number $0 < \lambda < 1$ such that $Q = \lambda Q_1 + (1 - \lambda)Q_2$.

The following two theorems characterize extremal local martingale measures.

Theorem 12.10 *Suppose that M is a set of regular right continuous processes and Q is a local martingale measure for M. Then Q is extremal if and only if $\mathcal{H}_0^{1,Q} = \mathcal{Z}^{1,Q}(M)$ and $\mathbf{F}_0^Q = \mathbf{F}_0$.*

Theorem 12.11 *Suppose that M is a finite set of regular right continuous processes and Q is a local martingale measure for M. Then Q is extremal if and only if there is no other local martingale measure for M that is equivalent to Q.*

We use the following corollaries of the preceding theorems.

Corollary 12.3 *Suppose that M is a set of regular right continuous processes and Q is a local martingale measure for M. Then Q is extremal if and only if*

$$\mathcal{M}_0^Q = \mathcal{Z}^{1,Q}(M)$$

and $\mathbf{F}_0^Q = \mathbf{F}_0$.

Proof. The corollary follows from the observation that

$$\mathcal{H}_{loc}^1 = \mathcal{M}_{loc}$$

and, by localization, from Theorem 12.10. ∎

Corollary 12.4 *Suppose that for the equilibrium price measure Q*

$$\mathcal{M}_0^Q = \mathcal{Z}^{1,Q}\left(\frac{p_2}{p_1}, \dots, \frac{p_N}{p_1}\right)$$

Then the equilibrium price measure Q is unique.

Proof. If Q is an equilibrium price measure then it is a local martingale measure for the set $\left\{\dfrac{p_2}{p_1}, \dots, \dfrac{p_N}{p_1}\right\}$. Corollary 12.3 implies that Q is extremal, and Theorem 12.11 implies that there is no other local martingale measure that is equivalent to Q. Because every equilibrium price measure is a local martingale measure, Q is unique. ∎

The next theorem and its corollary establish the converse result.

Theorem 12.12 *If the equilibrium price measure Q is unique, then Q is an extremal local martingale measure for the set $\left\{ \dfrac{p_2}{p_1}, \ldots, \dfrac{p_N}{p_1} \right\}$ of discounted prices.*

Proof. Suppose that Q is not extremal. Then there exist two distinct probability measures Q_1 and Q_2 and a real number $0 < \lambda < 1$ such that each discounted price $\dfrac{p_n}{p_1}$ is both a Q_1-local martingale and a Q_2-local martingale and $Q = \lambda Q_1 + (1 - \lambda)Q_2$. We show that each discounted price is both a Q_1-uniformly integrable martingale and a Q_2-uniformly integrable martingale.

It is enough to show that each discounted price is of class **D** relative to the probability measures Q_1 and Q_2. We know that each discounted price is a Q-uniformly integrable martingale. Therefore, each discounted price is of class **D** relative to the probability measure Q. Now, the filtrations $\{\mathbf{F}_t\}$, $\left\{ \mathbf{F}_t^{Q_1} \right\}$, and $\left\{ \mathbf{F}_t^{Q_2} \right\}$ have the same finite stopping times and the probability measures Q_1 and Q_2 satisfy

$$ Q_1 \le \frac{Q}{\lambda} \quad \text{and} \quad Q_2 \le \frac{Q}{1 - \lambda} $$

Choose $2 \le n \le N$ and denote $x_t = \dfrac{p_{nt}}{p_{1t}}$. Then for any $h \ge 0$

$$ E_{Q_1}\left(|x_{\tau h}| \right) \le \frac{E_Q\left(|x_{\tau h}| \right)}{\lambda}, \quad E_{Q_2}\left(|x_{\tau h}| \right) \le \frac{E_Q\left(|x_{\tau h}| \right)}{1 - \lambda} $$

and

$$ \lim_{h \to \infty} \sup_\tau E_Q\left(|x_{\tau h}| \right) = 0 $$

Therefore

$$ \lim_{h \to \infty} \sup_\tau E_{Q_1}\left(|x_{\tau h}| \right) = 0 \quad \text{and} \quad \lim_{h \to \infty} \sup_\tau E_{Q_2}\left(|x_{\tau h}| \right) = 0 $$

which implies that each discounted price is of class **D** relative to the probability measures Q_1 and Q_2.

Choose $0 < \nu < 1$ such that $\nu \ne \lambda$. Then the probability measures Q and $\nu Q_1 + (1 - \nu)Q_2$ are distinct, equivalent, and make all discounted price processes uniformly integrable martingales. This contradicts the assumption that the equilibrium price measure Q is unique. ∎

Corollary 12.5 *If the equilibrium price measure Q is unique, then*

$$ \mathcal{M}_0^Q = \mathcal{Z}^{1,Q}\left(\frac{p_2}{p_1}, \ldots, \frac{p_N}{p_1} \right) $$

Together, Corollaries 12.4 and 12.5 say that the equilibrium price measure Q is unique if and only if

$$\mathcal{M}_0^Q = \mathcal{Z}^{1,Q}\left(\frac{p_2}{p_1}, \ldots, \frac{p_N}{p_1}\right)$$

This result and Theorem 12.7 imply a characterization of complete price systems that is analogous to Theorem 6.2 in the discrete multiperiod model.

Theorem 12.13 *Let Q be an equilibrium price measure. Then the following statements are equivalent:*

1. *The price system p is complete relative to the measure Q.*

2. *The equilibrium price measure is unique.*

3. $\mathcal{M}_0^Q = \mathcal{Z}^{1,Q}\left(\dfrac{p_2}{p_1}, \ldots, \dfrac{p_N}{p_1}\right).$

Proof. We have already demonstrated the equivalence of items 2 and 3. The equivalence of items 1 and 3 follows from Theorem 12.7. Indeed, suppose that item 1 is true and let $x \in \mathcal{M}^Q$. Then $x_T \in \mathcal{L}^1(\Omega, \mathbf{F}_T, Q)$ and the consumption process $\{0, x_T p_{1T}\}$ is attainable. Therefore, there is a vector of processes $\alpha = \{\alpha_1, \ldots, \alpha_N\}$ such that $\alpha_n \in \Lambda_{loc}^{1,Q}\left(\dfrac{p_n}{p_1}\right)$ for every $1 < n \leq N$, and the Q-martingale

$$x_t = E_Q\left(\frac{c_T}{p_{1T}} \,\middle|\, \mathbf{F}_t\right)$$

has the representation

$$x_t = x_0 + \int_0^t \alpha_s' d\left(\frac{p_s}{p_{1s}}\right)$$

so that

$$x \in \mathcal{Z}^{1,Q}\left(\frac{p_2}{p_1}, \ldots, \frac{p_N}{p_1}\right)$$

Conversely, suppose that item 3 is true and let

$$\{c_0, c_T\} \in \mathcal{R} \times \mathcal{L}^1(\Omega, \mathbf{F}_T, Q)$$

By Theorem 10.10, the process

$$x_t = E_Q\left(\frac{c_T}{p_{1T}} \,\middle|\, \mathbf{F}_t\right)$$

is a Q-uniformly integrable martingale. Then item 3 implies that there is a vector of processes $\alpha = \{\alpha_2, \ldots, \alpha_N\}$ such that $\alpha_n \in \Lambda_{loc}^{1,Q}\left(\dfrac{p_n}{p_1}\right)$ for every $2 \leq n \leq N$ and Theorem 12.7 implies that the consumption process $\{c_0, c_T\}$ is attainable. ∎

We can now see that the concept of a complete price system, originally defined in this chapter relative to a particular equilibrium price measure Q, can be defined in absolute terms. From the preceding theorem, the price system is complete relative to Q if and only if Q is unique. Therefore, completeness relative to a particular equilibrium price measure implies completeness relative to every equilibrium price measure.

The only one-dimensional martingales x that have stationary, independent, increments and have the property that every uniformly integrable martingale has a representation as a stochastic integral with respect to x, are the Wiener process and the Poisson martingale. In several dimensions, such representation theorems exist for certain diffusion processes, for "diffusion processes with jumps," and for certain processes with independent increments. The references on such representation theorems are listed in the Notes section at the end of this chapter.

12.6   Risk and Return

In this section we do not assume that the given price system p is complete. Let

$$z_t = E_P\left(\dfrac{dQ}{dP}\,\Big|\,\mathbf{F}_t\right)$$

be the likelihood ratio process of the equilibrium price measure Q with respect to the probability measure P. Then Theorem 11.32 implies that the processes $\left\{z_t\,\dfrac{p_{nt}}{p_{1t}}\right\}$ are P-martingales and therefore every likelihood ratio process is a risk adjustment process in the general continuous multiperiod model. In addition, Theorem 11.32 implies that

$$E_Q\left(\dfrac{dP}{dQ}\,\Big|\,\mathbf{F}_t\right) = \dfrac{E_P\left(\dfrac{dQ}{dP}\dfrac{dP}{dQ}\,\Big|\,\mathbf{F}_t\right)}{z_t} = \dfrac{1}{z_t}$$

and consequently the Q-uniformly integrable martingale $\left\{\dfrac{1}{z_t}\right\}$ is the likelihood ratio process of the probability measure P with respect to the equilibrium price measure Q.

Our present task is to prove an analog of Theorem 6.3 on the relationship between the predictable and innovation parts of discounted prices. We show that this relationship is an alternative version of Girsanov's theorem. To set the background, we repeat here the original statement of Girsanov's theorem in Chapter 11, reversing the roles of the probability measures P and Q.

Theorem 12.14 *Suppose that x is a Q-local martingale that is null at zero, and that the predictable quadratic covariation process $\left\langle x, \frac{1}{z} \right\rangle^Q$ exists. Then x is a P-special semimartingale and its canonic decomposition is*

$$x = \left(x - z_- \bullet \left\langle x, \frac{1}{z} \right\rangle^Q \right) + z_- \bullet \left\langle x, \frac{1}{z} \right\rangle^Q$$

where the first term is a P-local martingale, null at zero, and the second term is a predictable process of P-locally integrable variation.

We now prove the following alternative version of the preceding theorem.

Theorem 12.15 *Suppose that x is a Q-local martingale that is null at zero, and that the predictable quadratic covariation processes*

$$\left\langle x, \frac{1}{z} \right\rangle^Q \quad \text{and} \quad \langle x, z \rangle^P$$

exist. Then x is a P-special semimartingale and its canonic decomposition is

$$x = \left(x + \frac{1}{z_-} \bullet \langle x, z \rangle^P \right) - \frac{1}{z_-} \bullet \langle x, z \rangle^P$$

where the first term is a P-local martingale, null at zero, and the second term is a predictable process of P-locally integrable variation.

Proof. From the definition of the predictable quadratic covariation process $\langle x, z \rangle^P$ we have

$$[x, z] - \langle x, z \rangle^P \in \mathcal{M}^P_{0,loc}$$

and therefore

$$\frac{1}{z}[x, z] - \frac{1}{z}\langle x, z \rangle^P \in \mathcal{M}^Q_{0,loc}$$

By virtue of Theorem 11.36, if $a \in \mathcal{P} \cap f\mathcal{V}$, then

$$\frac{a}{z} - \frac{1}{z_-} \bullet a \in \mathcal{M}^Q_{loc}$$

Therefore

$$\frac{1}{z}\langle x, z \rangle^P - \frac{1}{z_-} \bullet \langle x, z \rangle^P \in \mathcal{M}^Q_{0,loc}$$

and adding the two preceding equations implies that

$$\frac{1}{z}[x, z] - \frac{1}{z_-} \bullet \langle x, z \rangle^P \in \mathcal{M}^Q_{0,loc} \qquad (12.2)$$

Next, from the definition of the predictable quadratic covariation process $\left\langle x, \frac{1}{z} \right\rangle^Q$

$$\left[x, \frac{1}{z} \right] - \left\langle x, \frac{1}{z} \right\rangle^P \in \mathcal{M}^Q_{0,loc}$$

and, because the process z_- is predictable and locally bounded, we have

$$z_- \bullet \left[x, \frac{1}{z} \right] - z_- \bullet \left\langle x, \frac{1}{z} \right\rangle^Q \in \mathcal{M}^Q_{0,loc} \qquad (12.3)$$

Using the representation of the Lebesgue-Stieltjes integral and the optional quadratic covariation process as limits of sums in the topology of uniform convergence on compacts in probability, it is easy to prove that

$$\frac{1}{z}[x, z] + z_- \bullet \left[x, \frac{1}{z} \right] = [x, z]_- \bullet \frac{1}{z}$$

Consequently

$$\frac{1}{z}[x, z] + z_- \bullet \left[x, \frac{1}{z} \right] \in \mathcal{M}^Q_{0,loc} \qquad (12.4)$$

and, together, Equations 12.2, 12.3, and 12.4 imply that

$$z_- \bullet \left\langle x, \frac{1}{z} \right\rangle^Q + \frac{1}{z_-} \bullet \langle x, z \rangle^P \in \mathcal{M}^Q_{0,loc}$$

Because the process $\frac{1}{z_-}$ is predictable and locally bounded, we have

$$\left\langle x, \frac{1}{z} \right\rangle^Q + \frac{1}{z_-^2} \bullet \langle x, z \rangle^P \in \mathcal{M}^Q_{0,loc}$$

To complete the proof, we apply Theorem 11.37 reversing the roles of the probability measures P and Q, that is, for $a \in \mathcal{P} \cap f\mathcal{V}$, we have $x - a \in \mathcal{M}^P_{loc}$

if and only if $\left\langle x, \dfrac{1}{z} \right\rangle^{Q} - \dfrac{1}{z_{-}} \bullet a \in \mathcal{M}_{loc}^{Q}$. Setting $a = -\dfrac{1}{z_{-}} \bullet \langle x, z \rangle^{P}$ implies that

$$x + \frac{1}{z_{-}} \bullet \langle x, z \rangle^{P} \in \mathcal{M}_{0,loc}^{P}$$

This ends the proof. ∎

Now, suppose that for every $1 \le n \le N$ the predictable quadratic covariation processes $\left\langle \dfrac{p_n}{p_1}, z \right\rangle^{P}$ and $\left\langle \dfrac{p_n}{p_1}, \dfrac{1}{z} \right\rangle^{Q}$ exist. Because every discounted price $\dfrac{p_n}{p_1}$ is a Q-uniformly integrable martingale, the preceding theorem implies that every process $\dfrac{p_n}{p_1} - p_{n0}$ is a P-special semimartingale with the canonic decomposition

$$\frac{p_n}{p_1} - p_{n0} = \left(\frac{p_n}{p_1} - p_{n0} + \frac{1}{z_{-}} \bullet \left\langle \frac{p_n}{p_1}, z \right\rangle^{P} \right) - \frac{1}{z_{-}} \bullet \left\langle \frac{p_n}{p_1}, z \right\rangle^{P}$$

Thus, we have the following analog of Theorem 6.3.

Theorem 12.16 *If the predictable quadratic covariation processes*

$$\left\langle \frac{p_n}{p_1}, z \right\rangle^{P} \quad and \quad \left\langle \frac{p_n}{p_1}, \frac{1}{z} \right\rangle^{Q}$$

exist, then for every $1 \le n \le N$ the predictable part of the price ratio $\dfrac{p_n}{p_1}$ has the representation

$$\left[\pi^{*} \left(\frac{p_n}{p_1} \right) \right]^{P} = -\frac{1}{z_{-}} \bullet \left\langle \frac{p_n}{p_1}, z \right\rangle^{P}$$

In the preceding theorem, we interpret the predictable part of the price ratio process $\dfrac{p_n}{p_1}$ as a generalized cumulative conditional expected change of the price ratio process, and the predictable quadratic covariation process as a generalized cumulative conditional covariance of the price ratio $\dfrac{p_n}{p_1}$ with the risk adjustment process z. Thus, the preceding theorem establishes that the risk adjustment process z is a single risk factor in the general multiperiod model.

Because the predictable part of the price ratio process has an integral representation, we can restate the relationship between risk and return in shorthand notation

$$d\left[\pi^*\left(\frac{p_n}{p_1}\right)\right]_t^{\Gamma} = -\frac{\left\langle \frac{p_n}{p_1}, z \right\rangle_t^P}{z_{t-}}$$

Next, we establish the analog of Theorem 6.4 on the relationship between risk and return for rate of return processes.

Definition 12.11 Suppose that the price system is such that $\dfrac{1}{p_n} \in \mathcal{D}$ for all $1 \leq n \leq N$. Then the rate of return process of security $1 \leq n \leq N$ is

$$r_n = \frac{1}{p_{n,-}} \bullet p_n$$

The rate of return process represents the cumulative rate of return. This is easy to see from the discrete time analog of the preceding definition

$$r_{nt} = \sum_{s=1}^{t} \frac{p_{ns} - p_{n,s-1}}{p_{n,s-1}}$$

Next, the associativity of the stochastic integral implies the following representation

$$p_{nt} = p_{n0} + (p_{n,-} \bullet r_n)_t$$

and because the price of the bond is continuous and has finite variation on compacts, Itô's formula implies that

$$\frac{p_{nt}}{p_{1t}} = p_{n0} + \left(\frac{1}{p_1} \bullet p_n\right)_t - \left(\frac{p_{n,-}}{p_1^2} \bullet p_1\right)_t$$

From the definition of the rate of return and the associativity of the stochastic integral

$$\frac{p_{n,-}}{p_1} \bullet r_1 = \frac{p_{n,-}}{p_1^2} \bullet p_1$$

and

$$\frac{p_{n,-}}{p_1} \bullet r_n = \frac{1}{p_1} \bullet p_n$$

Thus

$$\frac{p_{nt}}{p_{1t}} = p_{n0} + \left[\frac{p_{n,-}}{p_1} \bullet (r_n - r_1)\right]_t \tag{12.5}$$

Theorem 12.17 helps us express the predictable part of the price ratio process in terms of the predictable part of the rate of return process.

Theorem 12.17 *Suppose that the process x is a P-special semimartingale and $\alpha \in \Lambda^P(x)$. Then the integral $\alpha \bullet x$ is a P-special semimartingale and*

$$\pi^*(\alpha \bullet x) = \alpha \bullet (\pi^* x)$$

From Theorem 12.17 and Equation 12.5 we get that

$$\left[\pi^*\left(\frac{p_n}{p_1}\right)\right]^P = \frac{p_{n,-}}{p_1} \bullet \pi^*(r_n - r_1)$$

and from the associativity of the stochastic integral and Equation 12.5 we have

$$\left\langle \frac{p_n}{p_1}, z \right\rangle^P = \frac{p_{n,-}}{p_1} \bullet \langle r_n, z \rangle$$

Thus, we have proved the following corollary.

Corollary 12.6 *Suppose that the price system is such that $\frac{1}{p_n} \in \mathcal{D}$ for all $1 \leq n \leq N$. Then, for every $1 \leq n \leq N$*

$$[\pi^*(r_n - r_1)]_t^P = -\frac{\langle r_n, z \rangle_t^P}{z_{t-}}$$

12.7   Representation of Risk Adjustment Processes

In this section we assume that the price system p is complete and that the predictable quadratic covariation processes $\left\langle \frac{p_n}{p_1}, z \right\rangle^P$ and $\left\langle \frac{p_n}{p_1}, \frac{1}{z} \right\rangle^Q$ exist for every $1 \leq n \leq N$. From Theorem 12.16, the predictable part of the price ratio process $\frac{p_n}{p_1}$ is

$$\left[\pi^*\left(\frac{p_n}{p_1}\right)\right]^P = -\frac{1}{z_-} \bullet \left\langle \frac{p_n}{p_1}, z \right\rangle^P = -\left\langle \frac{p_n}{p_1}, \frac{1}{z_-} \bullet z \right\rangle^P$$

The associativity of the stochastic integral indicates that

$$z = 1 + z_- \bullet \left(\frac{1}{z_-} \bullet z\right)$$

so that, by definition

$$z = \mathcal{E}\left(\frac{1}{z_-} \bullet z\right)$$

Denote

$$y = \frac{1}{z_-} \bullet z$$

Then the risk adjustment process z has the representation

$$z = \mathcal{E}(y)$$

and the P-local martingale y satisfies for every $1 \leq n \leq N$

$$\left[\pi^* \left(\frac{p_n}{p_1} \right) \right]^P = - \left\langle \frac{p_n}{p_1}, y \right\rangle^P$$

The process y is a P-local martingale, and Girsanov's theorem implies that the process $y - \frac{1}{z_-} \bullet \langle y, z \rangle^P$ is a Q-local martingale, null at zero. Because the price system p is complete, we have

$$\mathcal{M}_0^Q = \mathcal{Z}^{1,Q} \left(\frac{p_2}{p_1}, \ldots, \frac{p_n}{p_1} \right)$$

Therefore, there is a vector of processes $\alpha = \{ \alpha_1, \ldots, \alpha_N \}$ such that

$$\alpha_n \in \Lambda_{loc}^{1,Q} \left(\frac{p_n}{p_1} \right)$$

and

$$y = \frac{1}{z_-} \bullet \langle y, z \rangle^P + \alpha' \bullet \left(\frac{p}{p_1} \right)$$

We have the following representation of the risk adjustment process.

Theorem 12.18 *The unique risk adjustment process z has the representation*

$$z_t = \mathcal{E}_t \left(\alpha' \bullet \left\{ \frac{p}{p_1} - \left[\pi^* \left(\frac{p}{p_1} \right) \right]^P \right\} \right)$$

where the processes $\alpha_2, \ldots, \alpha_N$ are such that for every $2 \leq n \leq N$ we have $\alpha_n \in \Lambda_{loc}^{1,Q} \left(\frac{p_n}{p_1} \right)$ and

$$\sum_{m=2}^{N} \alpha_m \bullet \left\langle \frac{p_m}{p_1} - \left[\pi^* \left(\frac{p_m}{p_1} \right) \right]^P, \frac{p_n}{p_1} \right\rangle^P = - \left[\pi^* \left(\frac{p_n}{p_1} \right) \right]^P$$

Proof. Together, Theorem 12.17 and the fact that $\dfrac{1}{z_-} \bullet \langle y, z \rangle^P \in i\mathcal{V}_{loc}^P$ imply that

$$(\pi^* y)^P = \frac{1}{z_-} \bullet \langle y, z \rangle^P + \alpha' \bullet \left[\pi^* \left(\frac{p}{p_1} \right) \right]^P$$

Next, because y is a P-local martingale, $(\pi^* y)^P = 0$, so that

$$\frac{1}{z_-} \bullet \langle y, z \rangle^P + \alpha' \bullet \left[\pi^* \left(\frac{p}{p_1} \right) \right]^P = 0$$

Therefore

$$y = \frac{1}{z_-} \bullet \langle y, z \rangle^P + \alpha' \bullet \left(\frac{p}{p_1} \right) + \alpha' \bullet \left[\pi^* \left(\frac{p}{p_1} \right) \right]^P - \alpha' \bullet \left[\pi^* \left(\frac{p}{p_1} \right) \right]^P$$

$$= \alpha' \bullet \left\{ \frac{p}{p_1} - \left[\pi^* \left(\frac{p}{p_1} \right) \right]^P \right\}$$

Notice that $\dfrac{p_1}{p_1} = 1$ is constant, and therefore

$$y = \sum_{m=2}^{N} \alpha_m \bullet \left\{ \frac{p_m}{p_1} - \left[\pi^* \left(\frac{p_m}{p_1} \right) \right]^P \right\}$$

so that the process α_1 does not matter. To show that the processes

$$\alpha_2, \ldots, \alpha_N$$

satisfy the system of equations identified in the theorem, substitute the preceding representation of y into the equations

$$\left[\pi^* \left(\frac{p_n}{p_1} \right) \right]^P = - \left\langle \frac{p_n}{p_1}, y \right\rangle^P$$

for $2 \leq n \leq N$, and use the associativity of the stochastic integral with respect to the predictable quadratic covariation process. ∎

It helps to interpret the preceding theorem in the discrete framework. In that case, the predictable part of a process is its dual predictable projection, and we have the representation

$$y_t = \sum_{m=2}^{N} \alpha_{mt} \left[\frac{p_{mt}}{p_{1t}} - p_{n0} - \sum_{s=1}^{t} E_P \left(\frac{p_{ms}}{p_{1s}} - \frac{p_{m,s-1}}{p_{1,s-1}} \bigg| \mathbf{f}_{s-1} \right) \right]$$

In differential form, the system of equations for the predictable processes $\alpha_2, \ldots, \alpha_N$ is that for every $1 \le t \le T$ the sum

$$\sum_{m=2}^{N} \alpha_{mt} \left\{ E_P \left[\left(\frac{p_{mt}}{p_{1t}} - \frac{p_{m,t-1}}{p_{1,t-1}} \right) \left(\frac{p_{nt}}{p_{1t}} - \frac{p_{n,t-1}}{p_{1,t-1}} \right) \middle| \mathbf{f}_{t-1} \right] \right.$$

$$\left. - E_P \left(\frac{p_{mt}}{p_{1t}} - \frac{p_{m,t-1}}{p_{1,t-1}} \middle| \mathbf{f}_{t-1} \right) E_P \left(\frac{p_{nt}}{p_{1t}} - \frac{p_{n,t-1}}{p_{1,t-1}} \middle| \mathbf{f}_{t-1} \right) \right\}$$

is equal to the conditional expectation

$$-E_P \left(\frac{p_{nt}}{p_{1t}} - \frac{p_{n,t-1}}{p_{1,t-1}} \middle| \mathbf{f}_{t-1} \right)$$

or equivalently, this system of equations is

$$\sum_{m=2}^{N} \alpha_{mt} \text{covar}_P \left[d \left(\frac{p_{mt}}{p_{1t}} \right), \; d \left(\frac{p_{nt}}{p_{1t}} \right) \middle| \mathbf{f}_{t-1} \right] = -E_P \left[d \left(\frac{p_{nt}}{p_{1t}} \right) \middle| \mathbf{f}_{t-1} \right]$$

which is another way of writing the corresponding equations in Chapter 6.

Theorem 12.18 delivers a formula for the equilibrium price measure Q generated by a complete price system p and the attendant representation of the price functional

$$Q(A) = \int_A z_T dP$$

$$\phi(\{c_0, c_T\}) = c_0 + E_P \left(\frac{c_T z_T}{p_{1T}} \right)$$

where $A \in \mathbf{F}$ and $\{c_0, c_T\} \in X$.

Example 12.1 Suppose that W_1 and W_2 are two independent Wiener processes and there are $N = 3$ securities with the prices

$$p_{1t} = \exp \left(\int_0^t r_{1s} ds \right), \quad p_{2t} = \mathcal{E}_t(r_2), \quad \text{and} \quad p_{3t} = \mathcal{E}_t(r_3)$$

where, for $1 \le n \le 3$

$$r_{nt} = \int_0^t \mu_{ns} ds + \int_0^t \sigma_{n1s} dW_{1s} + \int_0^t \sigma_{n2s} dW_{2s}$$

The processes $\{r_{2t}\}$ and $\{r_{3t}\}$ are the rates of return for securities 2 and 3, and $\{r_{1t}\}$ is the interest rate process. The terminal payouts of the securities are $d_n = p_{nT}$ and the information of traders is the filtration generated by the prices of securities 1, 2, and 3

$$\mathbf{F}_t = \mathbf{F}_t^{p_1, p_2, p_3}$$

It follows from a theorem of Fujisaki, Kallianpur, and Kunita, that every square integrable martingale x with respect to the filtration $\{\mathbf{F}_t\}$ has an integral representation

$$x_t = x_0 + (\alpha' \bullet W)_t$$

where the vector of processes $\alpha = \{\alpha_1, \ldots, \alpha_N\}$ is such that $\alpha_n \in \Lambda^2(x)$ for every $1 \leq n \leq N$. Therefore, in this example, the equilibrium price measure Q is unique and $M(p) = \mathcal{R} \times \mathcal{L}^2(\Omega, \mathbf{F}_T, Q)$. Our task is to determine the likelihood ratio process of the equilibrium price measure Q with respect to the probability measure P. We use the matrix notation

$$W = \begin{pmatrix} W_1 \\ W_2 \end{pmatrix}, \ \mu = \begin{pmatrix} \mu_1 \\ \mu_2 \end{pmatrix}$$

and

$$\sigma = \begin{pmatrix} \sigma_{21} & \sigma_{22} \\ \sigma_{31} & \sigma_{32} \end{pmatrix}$$

Using shorthand notation, the system of equations for the processes α_2 and α_3 identified in Theorem 12.18 is

$$\alpha_2 \sigma_2^2 \left(\frac{p_2}{p_1}\right)^2 dt + \alpha_3 \sigma_{23} \frac{p_2}{p_1} \frac{p_3}{p_1} dt = -(\mu_2 - r)\frac{p_2}{p_1} dt$$

$$\alpha_2 \sigma_{23} \frac{p_2}{p_1} \frac{p_3}{p_1} dt + \alpha_3 \sigma_3^2 \left(\frac{p_3}{p_1}\right)^2 dt = -(\mu_3 - r)\frac{p_3}{p_1} dt$$

Denoting $\beta_2 = \alpha_2 \frac{p_2}{p_1}$, $\beta_3 = \alpha_3 \frac{p_3}{p_1}$, $\beta = \begin{pmatrix} \beta_2 \\ \beta_3 \end{pmatrix}$, and $1 = \begin{pmatrix} 1 \\ 1 \end{pmatrix}$ the preceding system of equations can be written

$$(\sigma \sigma')\beta = -(\mu - r1)$$

and the risk adjustment process has the representation

$$z = \mathcal{E}\left[\beta' \bullet (\sigma \bullet W)\right]$$

Solving for the vector β we get

$$\beta = -\left(\sigma\sigma'\right)^{-1}\left(\mu - r1\right)$$

and

$$z = \mathcal{E}\left\{-\left[\left(\sigma\sigma'\right)^{-1}\left(\mu - r1\right)\right]' \bullet \left(\sigma \bullet W\right)\right\}$$

The preceding equation extends the formula for the Black-Scholes model in Theorem 9.5.

$$z = \mathcal{E}\left(-\frac{\mu - r}{\sigma} \bullet W\right) = \mathcal{E}\left[-\frac{\mu - r}{\sigma^2} \bullet \left(\sigma \bullet W\right)\right]$$

Notice that the vector process $\left(\sigma\sigma'\right)^{-1}\left(\mu - r1\right)$ extends the concept of risk premium per unit of variance, and the vector process $x = \sigma \bullet W$ represents the innovation parts of the rates of return of securities 2 and 3.

Example 12.2 Suppose that $\{N_t\}$ is a Poisson process with parameter λ, the information of traders is the natural filtration $\{\mathbf{F}_t^N\}$, and there are $N = 2$ securities with the prices

$$
\begin{aligned}
p_{1t} &= e^{rt}\\
p_{2t} &= e^{(\mu+\lambda\sigma)t}2^{-\sigma N_t}
\end{aligned}
$$

where r, μ, and σ are positive constants. Security 1 is a bond and the price of security 2 increases exponentially between the jumps of the Poisson process $\{N_t\}$. A sample path of p_2 is shown in Figure 12.1. When the Poisson process jumps, the rate of return of security 2 is $2^{-\sigma} - 1$. It is easy to verify that this price system is complete.

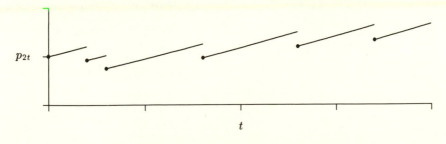

Figure 12.1: Price path of security 2 in Example 12.2.

Security 2 has a constant mean rate of return μ. Indeed, if $\{N_t^*\}$ is the Poisson martingale $N_t^* = N_t - \lambda t$, then

$$\mathcal{E}_t(kN_t^*) = e^{-k\lambda t} 2^{kN_t}$$

The price of security 2 can be written $p_{2t} = e^{\mu t}\mathcal{E}_t(-\sigma N^*)$, so that for $0 \leq s \leq t$

$$E_P\left(p_{2t}\,\middle|\,\mathbf{F}_s^N\right) = e^{\mu(t-s)}$$

The representation $p_{2t} = e^{\mu t}\mathcal{E}_t(-\sigma N^*)$ and Itô's formula imply that

$$dp_{2t} = \mu p_{2t-}dt - \sigma p_{2t-}dN_t^*$$

and similarly, for the discounted price $\left\{\dfrac{p_2}{p_1}\right\}$

$$d\left(\frac{p_{2t}}{p_{1t}}\right) = (\mu - r)\frac{p_{2t-}}{p_{1t}}dt - \sigma\frac{p_{2t-}}{p_{1t}}dN_t^*$$

Consequently, the predictable part of the discounted price of security 2 is

$$\left[\pi^*\left(\frac{p_2}{p_1}\right)\right]_t^P = (\mu - r)\int_0^t \frac{p_{2s-}}{p_{1s}}ds$$

and, in shorthand notation, the process α_2 in Theorem 12.18 satisfies

$$\alpha_{2t}\sigma^2\left(\frac{p_{2t-}}{p_{1t}}\right)^2 \lambda dt = -(\mu - r)\frac{p_{2t-}}{p_{1t}}dt$$

Denoting $\beta_2 = \alpha_2\dfrac{p_2}{p_1}$ we have

$$\beta_2 = -\frac{\mu - r}{\lambda\sigma^2}$$

and, therefore, the risk adjustment process is

$$z_t = \mathcal{E}_t\left(\frac{\mu - r}{\lambda\sigma}\bullet N^*\right) = \exp\left(-\frac{\mu - r}{\lambda\sigma}t\right)2^{\frac{\mu - r}{\lambda\sigma}N_t}$$

In particular, this representation of $\{z_t\}$ delivers the unique equilibrium price measure Q and a formula for the price functional.

The rest of this section deals with the representation of the Q-uniformly integrable martingale $\dfrac{1}{z}$. From Theorem 12.13, we have

$$\frac{1}{z} - 1 \in \mathcal{Z}^{1,Q}\left(\frac{p_2}{p_1},\dots,\frac{p_N}{p_1}\right)$$

Let $\beta = \{\beta_1,\dots,\beta_N\}$ be such that $\beta_n \in \Lambda_{loc}^{1,Q}\left(\dfrac{p_n}{p_1}\right)$ for every $1 \leq n \leq N$ and

$$\frac{1}{z} = 1 + \beta' \bullet \left(\frac{p}{p_1} \right)$$

Next, denote

$$\eta = z_- \bullet \frac{1}{z} = z_- \beta' \bullet \left(\frac{p}{p_1} \right)$$

The associativity of the stochastic integral implies that

$$\frac{1}{z_-} \bullet \eta = \beta' \bullet \left(\frac{p}{p_1} \right) = \frac{1}{z} - 1$$

and, denoting $\gamma_n = z_- \beta_n$, we have

$$\frac{1}{z_t} = \mathcal{E}_t(\eta) = \mathcal{E}_t \left(\gamma' \bullet \frac{p}{p_1} \right)$$

Suppose that the predictable quadratic covariation processes

$$\left\langle \frac{p_m}{p_1}, \frac{p_n}{p_1} \right\rangle^Q$$

exist for all $1 \leq m, n \leq N$. The associativity of the stochastic integral with respect to the predictable quadratic covariation process implies that for every $1 \leq m \leq N$

$$\left\langle \frac{p_n}{p_1}, \frac{1}{z} \right\rangle^Q = \sum_{m=2}^{N} \beta_m \bullet \left\langle \frac{p_m}{p_1}, \frac{p_n}{p_1} \right\rangle^Q$$

Next, using the associativity of the Lebesgue-Stieltjes integral

$$z_- \bullet \left\langle \frac{p_n}{p_1}, \frac{1}{z} \right\rangle^Q = \sum_{m=2}^{N} \gamma_m \bullet \left\langle \frac{p_m}{p_1}, \frac{p_n}{p_1} \right\rangle^Q$$

and because the predictable part of the price ratio process can be written

$$\left[\pi^* \left(\frac{p_n}{p_1} \right) \right]^P = z_- \bullet \left\langle \frac{p_n}{p_1}, \frac{1}{z} \right\rangle^Q$$

we have a system of equations for the processes $\gamma_2, \ldots, \gamma_N$

$$\sum_{m=2}^{N} \gamma_m \bullet \left\langle \frac{p_m}{p_1}, \frac{p_n}{p_1} \right\rangle^Q = \left[\pi^* \left(\frac{p_n}{p_1} \right) \right]^P$$

for $2 \leq n \leq N$.

Example 12.3 In the Black-Scholes model we have

$$\gamma_2 \left\langle \frac{p_2}{p_1}, \frac{p_2}{p_1} \right\rangle^Q = (\mu - r) \int_0^t \frac{p_{2s}}{p_{1s}} ds$$

and

$$d \left(\frac{p_2}{p_1} \right) = \sigma \frac{p_2}{p_1} dV$$

where

$$V_t = W_t + \frac{\mu - r}{\sigma} t$$

is a Wiener process with respect to the equilibrium price measure Q. Therefore

$$d \left\langle \frac{p_2}{p_1}, \frac{p_2}{p_1} \right\rangle^Q = \sigma^2 \left(\frac{p_2}{p_1} \right)^2 dt$$

and

$$\gamma_2 = \frac{\mu - r}{\sigma^2} \frac{p_1}{p_2}$$

Consequently

$$\gamma_2 \bullet \frac{p_2}{p_1} = \frac{\mu - r}{\sigma} \bullet V$$

and $\dfrac{1}{z}$ has the representation

$$\frac{1}{z_t} = \mathcal{E}_t \left(\frac{\mu - r}{\sigma} \bullet V \right)$$

12.8   Intermediate Consumption

The general continuous model in this chapter can be extended to include intermediate consumption. To this end, we define cumulative consumption processes, cumulative endowment processes, and their discounted forms as follows.

A cumulative endowment process is a triple $\left\{ e_0, \{e_t^*\}, e_T \right\}$, where e_0 is endowment at time 0, for $0 < t < T$ the process $\{e_t^*\}$ is cumulative intermediate endowment process, that is, e_t^* is cumulative endowment in the open interval $(0, t)$, and e_T is terminal endowment.

A cumulative consumption process is a triple $\left\{c_0, \{c_t^*\}, c_T\right\}$, where c_0 is consumption at time 0, for $0 < t < T$ the process $\{c_t^*\}$ is cumulative intermediate consumption process, that is, c_t^* is cumulative consumption in the open interval $(0, t)$, and c_T is terminal consumption.

The discounted cumulative endowment process is

$$\left\{e_0, \left\{\left(\frac{1}{p_1} \bullet e^*\right)_t\right\}, \frac{e_T}{p_{1T}}\right\}$$

and the discounted cumulative consumption process is

$$\left\{c_0, \left\{\left(\frac{1}{p_1} \bullet c^*\right)_t\right\}, \frac{c_T}{p_{1T}}\right\}$$

The process $\{\theta_t' p_t\}$ is interpreted as the preconsumption value process. Given a cumulative endowment process

$$e = \left\{e_0, \{e_t^*\}, e_T\right\}$$

the budget set $B(e, p)$ is defined as the set of cumulative consumption processes

$$c = \left\{c_0, \{c_t^*\}, c_T\right\}$$

such that:

1. We have $c_0 \in \mathcal{R}$, $c^* \in i\mathcal{V}^Q$, and $c_T \in \mathcal{L}^1(\Omega, \mathbf{F}_T, Q)$.

2. At the initial time $c_0 = e_0 - \theta_0' p_0$.

3. At every intermediate time $0 < t < T$ we have

$$c_t^* + \theta_t' p_t = e_t^* + (\theta' \bullet p)_t$$

4. At the terminal time $c_T = e_T + \theta_T' + \theta_T' p_T$.

A cumulative consumption process $c = \left\{c_0, \{c_t^*\}, c_T\right\}$ is attainable if and only if there is a cumulative endowment process $e = \left\{e_0, \{e_t^*\}, e_T\right\}$ such that $e_t^* = 0$ for all $0 < t < T$ and $e_T = 0$, and that satisfies $c \in B(e, p)$. The characterization of attainable cumulative consumption processes is then based on the following extension of Theorem 12.7.

Theorem 12.19 *A cumulative consumption process* $\left\{c_0, \{c_t^*\}, c_T\right\} \in X$ *is attainable if and only if there is a vector of processes* $\alpha = \{\alpha_1, \dots, \alpha_N\}$ *such that* $\alpha_n \in \Lambda_{loc}^{Q,1}\left(\dfrac{p_n}{p_1}\right)$ *for every* $1 \le n \le N$, *and for every* $0 \le t \le T$

$$E_Q\left[\left(\frac{1}{p_1} \bullet c^*\right)_T + \frac{c_T}{p_{1T}}\,\middle|\, \mathbf{F}_t\right] = E_Q\left[\left(\frac{1}{p_1} \bullet c^*\right)_T + \frac{c_T}{p_{1T}}\right] + \int_0^t \alpha_s' d\left(\frac{p_s}{p_{1s}}\right)$$

Theorem 12.19 allows us to extend the results of Sections 12.6, 12.7, and 12.8 to a model with intermediate consumption.

Problems

1. Suppose that $W_t = (W_{1t}, \dots, W_{Kt})$ is a K-dimensional vector of independent Wiener processes, the information of traders is $\{\mathbf{F}_t^W\}$, and there are N securities with the prices

$$p_{1t} = \exp\left(\int_0^t r_{1s}ds\right)$$

and

$$p_{nt} = f_t(r_n)$$

for $2 \le n \le N$. For $1 \le n \le N$ the rate of return of security n is

$$r_{nt} = \int_0^t \mu_{ns}ds + \sum_{k=1}^{K}\int_0^t \sigma_{nks}dW_{ks}$$

where the processes $\{\mu_{nt}\}$ and $\{\sigma_{nkt}\}$ are adapted, measurable, and satisfy

$$\int_0^T |\mu_{nt}|dt < \infty \quad \text{and} \quad \int_0^T \sigma_{nkt}^2 dt < \infty$$

(a) Does an equilibrium price measure exist for this market?

(b) What restrictions on the trading strategies exclude arbitrage?

(c) Find a necessary and sufficient condition for this price system to be complete.

(d) When the price system is not complete, characterize the set of equilibrium price measures.

(e) Find the attainable set when the price system is not complete.

(f) Compute the price functional. Is it continuous?

(g) Find a representation of risk adjustment processes in this market.

2. Suppose that $\{W_t\}$ is a Wiener process, $\{N_t\}$ is a Poisson process with parameter λ, and the two processes are independent. The information of traders is the filtration $\{\mathbf{F}_t^{W,N}\}$, and there are $N = 3$ securities with the prices

$$p_{1t} = \exp\left(\int_0^t r_{1s}ds\right)$$

and

$$p_{nt} = \mathcal{E}_t(r_n)$$

for $n = 2, 3$. For $1 \le n \le 3$ the rate of return of security n is

$$r_{nt} = \int_0^t \mu_{ns}ds + \int_0^t \sigma_{ns}dW_s - \int_0^t \eta_{ns}dN_s^*$$

where $\{N_t^*\}$ is the Poisson martingale, and the processes $\{\mu_{nt}\}$, $\{\sigma_{nt}\}$, and $\{\eta_{nt}\}$ are adapted, measurable, and satisfy

$$\int_0^T |\mu_{nt}|dt < \infty \quad \text{and} \quad \int_0^T \sigma_{nt}^2 dt < \infty$$

(a) Does an equilibrium price measure exist for this market?

(b) What restrictions on the trading strategies exclude arbitrage?

(c) Find a necessary and sufficient condition for this price system to be complete.

(d) When the price system is not complete, characterize the set of equilibrium price measures.

(e) Find the attainable set when the price system is not complete.

(f) Compute the price functional. Is it continuous?

(g) Find a representation of risk adjustment processes in this market.

Notes

Theorem 12.3 is a generalization of [33]. Theorems 12.4 and 12.5 present further new results on wealth constraints. The characterization of attainable consumption processes in Theorem 12.7 has been obtained by [41]. The discussion of local martingale measures in Section 12.5 follows [48]. The characterization of complete price systems in Corollary 12.4, Theorem 12.12, Corollary 12.5, and Theorem 12.13 is due to [41] and [42]. The assertion that the Wiener process and the Poisson martingale are the only one-dimensional processes with independent, stationary, increments that have the predictable representation property is proved in [76]. A discussion of general theorems of representation for martingales appears in [49].

Section 12.6 on risk and return is new. Further results along these lines appear in [25]. The relationship between risk and return in the general multiperiod model is also examined in [10], subject to the assumption that the marginal utility of the representative agent is a measurable function of a (one-dimensional) Wiener process. Section 12.7 on the representation of equilibrium price measures is new. Example 12.1 uses a result of [37].

The relationship between an equilibrium in a one-period model with an infinite number of states and the corresponding continuous multiperiod model is examined in [30]. Using additional restrictions on endowments and preferences [28] establishes the existence of a complete equilibrium price system in the general multiperiod model.

Bibliography

[1] L. Arnold. *Stochastic Differential Equations: Theory and Applications.* Wiley, New York, 1974.

[2] K. Arrow and G. Debreu. Existence of an equilibrium for a competitive economy. *Econometrica*, 22:265–290, 1954.

[3] K. J. Arrow. An extension of the basic theorems of classical welfare economics. In *Proceedings of the Second Berkeley Symposium on Mathematical Statistics and Probability*, pages 507–532, University of California Press, Berkeley, 1951.

[4] K. J. Arrow. The role of securities in the optimal allocation of risk-bearing. *Review of Economic Studies*, 31:91–96, 1964. Translation of: Le rôle des valeurs boursières pour la répartition la meilleure des risques. *Econometrie*, pages 41–48, Centre National de la Recherche Scientifique, Paris, 1953.

[5] R. B. Ash. *Measure, Integration, and Functional Analysis.* Academic Press, New York, 1972.

[6] L. Bachelier. Theory of speculation. In P. Cootner, editor, *The Random Character of Stock Market Prices*, pages 17–78, MIT Press, Cambridge, 1964. Translation of: Théorie de la speculation. *Annales Scientifiques de l'Ecole Normale Supérieure*, 17:21–88, 1900.

[7] F. Black and M. Scholes. The pricing of options and corporate liabilities. *Journal of Political Economy*, 3:637–654, 1973.

[8] D. Breeden. An intertemporal asset pricing model with stochastic consumption and investment opportunities. *Journal of Financial Economics*, 265–296, 1979.

[9] D. Cass. *Competitive Equilibria in Incomplete Financial Markets.* Technical Report, University of Pennsylvania, April 1984.

[10] G. Chamberlain. Asset pricing in multiperiod securities markets. *Econometrica*, 56:1283–1300, 1988.

[11] G. M. Constantinides. Capital market equilibrium with personal tax. *Econometrica*, 51:611–636, 1983.

[12] G. M. Constantinides. Capital market equilibrium with transactions costs. *Journal of Political Economy*, 94:842–862, 1986.

[13] J. C. Cox and C. Huang. *Optimal Comsumption and Portfolio Policies when Asset Prices Follow a Diffusion Process*. Technical Report, Massachusetts Institute of Technology, May 1986.

[14] J. C. Cox and C. Huang. *A Variational Problem Arising in Financial Economics*. Technical Report, MIT, December 1985.

[15] J. C. Cox, J. E. Ingersoll, and S. A. Ross. An intertemporal general equilibrium model of asset prices. *Econometrica*, 53:363–384, 1985.

[16] J. C. Cox and S. A. Ross. The valuation of options for alternative stochastic processes. *Journal of Financial Economics*, 3:145–166, 1976.

[17] J. C. Cox, S. A. Ross, and M. Rubinstein. Option pricing: a simplified approach. *Journal of Financial Economics*, 7:229–263, 1979.

[18] G. Debreu. The coefficient of resource utilization. *Econometrica*, 19:273–292, 1951.

[19] G. Debreu. *Une économie de l'incertain*. Technical Report, Electricité de France, 1953.

[20] C. Dellacherie and P. Meyer. *Probabilities and Potential*. North-Holland, New York, 1978. Translation of: *Probabilités et potentiel*. Hermann, Paris, 1975.

[21] C. Dellacherie and P. Meyer. *Probabilities and Potential B: Theory of Martingales*. North-Holland, New York, 1982. Translation of: *Probabilités et potentiel: théorie des martingales*. Hermann, Paris, 1980.

[22] J. L. Doob. *Stochastic Processes*. Wiley, New York, 1953.

[23] M. U. Dothan. *Budget Operators and Portfolio Choice*. Technical Report, University of Minnesota, December 1989.

[24] M. U. Dothan. A random volatility correction for the Black-Scholes option pricing formula. In F. J. Fabozzi, editor, *Advances in Futures and Options Research*, pages 97–115, JAI Press, Greenwich, 1987.

[25] M. U. Dothan. *Risk and Return in Multiperiod Financial Markets.* Technical Report, University of Minnesota, September 1989.

[26] M. U. Dothan and D. Feldman. Equilibrium, interest rates, and multiperiod bonds in a partially observable economy. *Journal of Finance,* 41:369–382, 1986.

[27] R. M. Dudley. Wiener functionals as Itô integrals. *The Annals of Probability,* 5:140–141, 1977.

[28] D. Duffie. Stochastic equilibria: existence, spanning number, and the 'No Expected Gain From Trade' hypothesis. *Econometrica,* 54:1161–1184, 1986.

[29] D. Duffie. Stochastic equilibria with incomplete financial markets. *Journal of Economic Theory,* 41:405–416, 1987.

[30] D. Duffie and C. Huang. Implementing Arrow-Debreu equilibria by continuous trading of few long-lived securities. *Econometrica,* 53:1337–1356, 1985.

[31] D. Duffie and W. Zame. *The Consumption-Based Capital Asset Pricing Model.* Technical Report, Stanford University, March 1987.

[32] J. Dutta and H. Polemarchakis. *Asset Pricing and Observability.* Technical Report, Columbia University, September 1989.

[33] P. H. Dybvig and C. Huang. Nonnegative wealth, absence of arbitrage, and feasible consumption plans. *Review of Financial Studies,* 1:377–401, 1988.

[34] P. H. Dybvig and J. E. Ingersoll. Mean-variance theory in complete markets. *Journal of Business,* 55:233–251, 1982.

[35] R. J. Elliott. *Stochastic Calculus and Applications.* Springer, New York, 1982.

[36] A. Friedman. *Stochastic Differential Equations and Applications I.* Academic Press, New York, 1975.

[37] M. Fujisaki, G. Kallianpur, and H. Kunita. Stochastic differential equations for the nonlinear filtering problem. *Osaka Journal of Mathematics,* 1:19–40, 1972.

[38] I. I. Gihman and V. Skorohod. *Stochastic Differential Equations.* Springer, New York, 1972. Translation of: *Stokasticheskie differentsialnie uravneniya.* Naukova Dumka, Kiev, 1968.

[39] J. M. Harrison and D. M. Kreps. Martingales and arbitrage in multiperiod securities markets. *Journal of Economic Theory*, 20:381–408, 1979.

[40] J. M. Harrison, R. Pitbladdo, and S. M. Schaefer. Continuous price processes in frictionless markets have infinite variation. *Journal of Business*, 57:353–365, 1984.

[41] J. M. Harrison and S. Pliska. Martingales and stochastic integrals in the theory of continuous trading. *Stochastic Processes and their Applications*, 11:215–260, 1981.

[42] J. M. Harrison and S. Pliska. A stochastic calculus model of continuous trading: complete markets. *Stochastic Processes and their Applications*, 15:313–316, 1983.

[43] O. Hart. The optimality of equilibrium when markets are incomplete. *Journal of Economic Theory*, 11:418–443, 1975.

[44] H. He and N. D. Pearson. *Consumption and Portfolio Policies with Incomplete Markets and Short-Sale Constraints: The Finite Dimensional Case*. Technical Report, Massachusetts Institute of Technology, November 1988.

[45] C. Huang. Information structure and equilibrium asset prices. *Journal of Economic Theory*, 35:33–71, 1985.

[46] C. Huang. An intertemporal general equilibrium asset pricing model: the case of diffusion information. *Econometrica*, 55:117–142, 1987.

[47] K. Itô and H. P. McKean, Jr. *Diffusion Processes and their Sample Paths*. Springer, New York, 1974.

[48] J. Jacod. *Calcul Stochastique et Problèmes de Martingales*. Springer, New York, 1979.

[49] J. Jacod. A general theorem of representation for martingales. *Proceedings of Symposia in Pure Mathematics*, 31:37–53, 1977.

[50] G. Kallianpur. *Stochastic Filtering Theory*. Springer, New York, 1980.

[51] I. Karatzas and S. E. Shreve. *Brownian Motion and Stochastic Calculus*. Springer, New York, 1988.

[52] S. Karlin and H. M. Taylor. *A First Course in Stochastic Processes*. Academic Press, New York, 1975.

[53] D. M. Kreps. Multiperiod securities and the efficient allocation of risk: a comment on the Black-Scholes option pricing model. In J. McCall, editor, *The Economics of Uncertainty and Information*, pages 203–232, University of Chicago Press, Chicago, 1982.

[54] V. Krishnan. *Nonlinear Filtering and Smoothing*. Wiley, New York, 1984.

[55] H. Kunita and S. Watanabe. On square integrable martingales. *Nagoya Mathematics Journal*, 30:209–245, 1967.

[56] J. Lintner. The valuation of risk assets and the selection of risky investments in stock portfolios and capital budgets. *Review of Economics and Statistics*, 47:13–37, 1965.

[57] R. S. Liptser and A. N. Shiryayev. *Statistics of Random Processes I: General Theory*. Springer, New York, 1977. Translation of: *Statistika sluchaĭnyk protsessov*. Nauka, Moscow, 1974.

[58] H. P. McKean, Jr. *Stochastic Integrals*. Academic Press, New York, 1969.

[59] R. C. Merton. An intertemporal capital asset pricing model. *Econometrica*, 41:867–887, 1973.

[60] R. C. Merton. Lifetime portfolio selection under uncertainty: the continuous time case. *Review of Economics and Statistics*, 51:247–257, 1969.

[61] R. C. Merton. On the pricing of contingent claims and the Modigliani-Miller theorem. *Journal of Financial Economics*, 5:241–249, 1977.

[62] R. C. Merton. Optimum consumption and portfolio rules in a continuous time model. *Journal of Economic Theory*, 3:373–413, 1971.

[63] M. Métivier. *Semimartingales: A Course on Stochastic Proceses*. Walter de Gruyter, New York, 1982.

[64] P. Meyer. Un cours sur les intégrales stochastiques. In *Séminaire de Probabilités X*, pages 245–400, Springer, New York, 1976.

[65] B. Øksendal. *Stochastic Differential Equations*. Springer, New York, 1985.

[66] S. Pliska. A stochastic calculus model of continuous time trading: optimal portfolios. *Mathematics of Operations Research*, 11:371–382, 1986.

[67] P. Protter. *Semimartingales and Stochastic Differential Equations.* Technical Report, Purdue University, September 1985.

[68] S. F. Richard. Optimal consumption, portfolio, and life insurance rules for an uncertain lived individual in a continuous time model. *Journal of Financial Economics*, 2:185–203, 1975.

[69] C. Rogers and D. Williams. *Diffusions, Markov Processes, and Martingales: Itô Calculus.* Wiley, New York, 1987.

[70] Z. Schuss. *Theory and Applications of Stochastic Differential Equations.* Wiley, New York, 1980.

[71] W. Sharpe. Capital asset prices: a theory of capital market equilibrium under conditions of risk. *Journal of Finance*, 19:425–442, 1964.

[72] W. Sharpe. *Investments.* Prentice-Hall, Englewood Cliffs, third edition, 1985.

[73] L. Walras. *Elements of Pure Economics.* Irwin, Chicago, 1954. Translation of: *Eléments d'économie politique pure.* Corbaz, Lausanne, 1874-7.

[74] J. Werner. Equilibrium in economies with incomplete financial markets. *Journal of Economic Theory*, 36:110–119, 1985.

[75] D. Williams. *Diffusions, Markov Processes, and Martingales: Foundations.* Wiley, New York, 1979.

[76] M. Yor and J. de Sam Lazaro. Sous-espaces denses dans $\mathcal{L}^1$ ou $\mathcal{H}^1$ et représentation des martingales, Appendice. In *Séminaire de Probabilités XII*, pages 302–306, Springer, New York, 1978.

Index